Thorns & Arabesques

Thorns & Arabesques

Contexts for Conrad's Fiction

WILLIAM W. BONNEY

THE JOHNS HOPKINS UNIVERSITY PRESS
Baltimore & London

This book has been brought to publication with the generous
assistance of the Andrew W. Mellon Foundation.

The Johns Hopkins University Press, Baltimore, Maryland 21218
The Johns Hopkins Press Ltd., London

Library of Congress Cataloging in Publication Data

Bonney, William Wesley, 1942–
   Thorns and arabesques, contexts for Conrad's
fiction.

   Includes bibliographical references and index.
   1. Conrad, Joseph, 1857–1924—Criticism and
interpretation.   I. Title
PR6005.04Z5637   823'.912   80–13308
ISBN 0–8018–2345–5

FOR MY MOTHER

Contents

Preface

Fifteen years ago, when I set out to write a doctoral dissertation on Conrad, I was advised by several members of the graduate faculty at the University of Pennsylvania to cease this particular pursuit and choose another writer upon whom to focus my efforts, since, according to these men, it was no longer feasible to contribute significantly to the already extant body of Conrad scholarship. Nevertheless, I undertook, against much sage advice, to write the dissertation. It was completed, perhaps fittingly, late one autumn in a tent in the snow, some miles north of Fairbanks, Alaska. I was very much alone, quite chilly, and deeply uncertain as to the appropriateness and significance of my intellectual effort. During subsequent years my uncertainty has largely been dispelled, I am happy to say; but a general attitude persists that Conrad criticism is "at the end of the tether" and that Conrad is "a writer about whom very little new remains to be said,"[1] even though the decade that has just closed has seen both the publication of a good many lucid studies of Conrad's art and the gathering of important American and European critics at several international conferences devoted to this author's work.

As the existence of the present volume attests, I do not agree that it is futile for critics rigorously to scrutinize Conrad's fiction any further. I do feel, however, that the techniques of such scrutiny must be altered. There is indeed little need for additional critical studies that, chapter by abrupt and repetitious chapter, offer expeditious readings of the major novels. The vitality of Conrad studies now and in the near future will, in my opinion, be defined and maintained by versatile scholars who are well acquainted with contemporary theoretical criticism and who can engender through application of these critical methods a more thorough comprehension of (1) the phenomenology of Conrad's philosophical outlook, (2) Conrad's conscious manipulation of traditional generic and characterological models, and (3) the substantial portion of Conrad's work that has heretofore been neglected.

It would be less than honest for me not to admit that these are some of the goals I set for myself in the present book, although the title, *Thorns and Arabesques,* is meant to suggest the extent to which I acknowledge at once the contestability of my selected areas of inquiry and of my radically varying analytical methodology, and the fundamental incompleteness of whatever insights I offer. The phrase "Thorns and Arabesques" appears in Conrad's admirable short story "The Return." It constitutes the title of a rival's book of verses, which the despairing husband, Alvan Hervey, discovers lying about his house; and it helps Hervey confirm a dark "new creed" in reponse to his wife's duplicity, a creed that he articulates in capitulation to the ultimate inability of words to render a barbed and tangled enigma painlessly linear: "You haven't the gift" (*TU*, 179).

This book is conceived, gift or no gift, as a series of essays that proceeds in a circular manner, from a speculative inquiry into the philosophical derivations of Conrad's *"le neant"* to a rigorous technical description of some of the ways in which Conrad vandalizes linguistic surfaces in order to make possible evanescent revelations of the definitive nothingness that perpetually haunts his texts. The space that figuratively appears within the boundary of this rather bleak circle is comparable to existence itself, to the glittering illusions of substance and significance in terms of which all of us, "forlorn magicians that we are" (*LJ*, 315), forge the fatuous narratives of our lives. This space can best be understood in generic terms. Conrad conceives of all perceptual events as being analogous to a deluded quest for "a promised land, all flowers and blessings," where "animated flowers smile at bewitched knights." This quest consists of a constant "cultivation of a . . . crop of lies in the sweat of one's brow, to sustain life, to make it supportable, to make it fair" (*TU*, 134, 152). In other words, human existence for Conrad involves primarily the constant improvisation of a solipsistic romance.

Appropriately, the only character in all of Conrad's works who ever attains a final happiness and fulfills Conrad's own oft-cited aesthetic ideal, "to make you *see*" (*NN*, x), appears in a piece entitled *Romance*. At the end of this novel the protagonist, Jack Kemp, melodramatically saves himself from death by "narrat[ing] the story of [his] life" to an English jury. The unique teleological permissiveness of *Romance* allows him thereby to constitute and confirm his own romance and to fulfill the dictates of Conradian aesthetics, for, as Kemp affirms, "I had made them see" (*Rom*, 532, 534). Accordingly, in the central part of this book I attempt initially to suggest some of the more important characteristics of the romance genre as Conrad inherited it in a dysteleological form late in the nineteenth century; I then proceed to analyze at length Conrad's innovative and subversive use of situations and characters that are derived from traditional romance narratives as he demolishes the illusory stabilities of self and semiotics in his fiction.

Cary Nelson recently occasioned a good bit of controversy by making some points publicly the validity of which it seems to me all candid scholars must acknowledge at least in private: "Critics must attempt to re-create themselves and their readers in the otherness of a text they cannot claim as their own. To do so, they have to pretend to be engaged but disinterested. That requires a language of meticulous duplicity. . . ." Because "criticism works very hard to depersonalize its insights, to mask its fears and wishes in a language of secure authority," in order to be effective readers, Nelson affirms, we must seek to "come face to face with the conflict behind the mask" and confront the critic's "special way of projecting individual experience through the medium of pre-existent texts."[2]

My book on Conrad was indeed engendered by a great deal of conflict, most of which was not immediately relevant to literary criticism at all. I will spare my readers the tedium of specific details. Suffice it to say that during the summer of 1974, when I worked as a park ranger in the Juneau area, and during subsequent years I contemplated in despair the corporate desecration of much of the Alaskan wilderness—a territory I dearly love—as the construction of the Trans-Alaska Pipeline was accomplished. An introverted reaction to this depression consisted of a renewal of my study of Conrad, and I found that I seemed to understand with a sudden increase in acuity the bleak perspectives from which Conrad so masterfully anatomizes the destructive psychology of those who, to use Conrad's terms, manufacture steamships and use them as a means whereby to shell and mine the forests and mountains. I trust my discussions of Conrad's fiction quite transcend the attitudes of those unhappy years, although readers who, perhaps correctly, decide that there is altogether too much dissolution, death, and darkness in this study now have a context in which to place their judgments.

Parts of this book in somewhat different form previously appeared in the *Journal of Narrative Technique, ELH, Conradiana, College Literature,* and *Nineteenth Century Fiction.* I thank the publishers of these journals for permission to reprint.

My deepest gratitude is due to Robert D. Bamberg, who long ago introduced me to the delights of reading prose fiction; to Morse Peckham, who always insisted upon the most productive sort of iconoclasm among his students; to Richard Hinman, the most brilliant teacher I have ever encountered; to Avrom Fleishman, who provided advice and encouragement during the years this book was taking shape; and to Cam La Bossiere, Paul Bruss, Dick Betts, Steve Spector, Richard Unger, Juliet McLauchlan, and John Crompton, whose conversation and correspondence helped me repeatedly. My enormous debts to other scholars who have published criticism of Conrad's fiction are inadequately suggested by the footnotes; most specifically, the influence of J. Hillis Miller will be apparent to anyone familiar with his distinguished work. Associate Dean Charles Lowery has on a number of occasions extended financial assistance that aided in the completion of the manuscript. My occasional wife, Brenda Bridges, helped immeasurably by smiling a great deal and by typing swiftly and accurately for me; without her most generous efforts the book could not have been finished. Finally, I wish to acknowledge the abiding influence of my dear friends and former colleagues at the University of Alaska, none of whom, I regret to say, is in the academic profession any longer: Hilton Wolfe, Dudley Hascall, Frank Reuter, Susan Kalen, Ned Haines, and Bill Lentsch. Had I not enjoyed the rare privilege of their friendship, the book never would have been begun.

ONTOLOGICAL CONTEXTS
Affirming Discontinuity

But salvation lies in being illogical. —Conrad to Cunninghame Graham, 14 January 1898

. . . for verily there is a devil at the end of every
road. Let us pray to the pot bellied gods, to gods with more
legs than a centipede and more arms than a dozen windmills,
let us pray to them to guard us from the mischance of arriving
somewhere. —Conrad to Cunninghame Graham, 26 August 1898

"Eastern logic under my Western eyes": Conrad, Schopenhauer, and the Orient

It is very difficult to determine the extent to which Conrad uncritically appropriates Schopenhauer's philosophy and the Oriental concepts that form the basis of *The World as Will and Idea*.[1] Ultimately, an inquiry into this matter may be only suggestive. No ideological system exists in Conrad's works that is validated implicitly through sustained coherences, although critics have persistently concocted a sequence of systemic definitions of Conradian values.[2] Only Edward W. Said seems willing to try to cope directly with Conrad's protean authorial absences: the sole consistency in Conrad's works may well be the "willful inaccuracy" of his dramatizations of his own relationships with these works.[3] Personal origins of Conrad's ideas cannot be located, nor did Conrad ever intend for his writings to be investigated in these terms. He emphatically asserts his right to inconsistency: "My attitude to subjects and expressions, the angles of vision . . . will, within limits, be always changing—not because I am unstable or unprincipled but because I am free."[4] Consequently, one can at best only seek to recognize the demarcations of those "limits" within which Conrad suggests his transformations will probably occur. Speculations about Conrad's relationship with Schopenhauer's philosophy and Oriental concepts lend themselves to such a project. A criticism limited to the technology of language, inasmuch as it acknowledges its linguistic nature, cannot but call into doubt its instrumental validity as it struggles to comprehend that which remains, say, of Schopenhauer or Conrad: namely, the words that they wrote and the words written about the words that they wrote. Indeed, there is a troublesome indeterminacy in efforts to treat as an object of knowledge the very linguistic matrices that make possible the formulation of the inquiry in the first place. In view of this acknowledgment, the methodology of the early parts of this essay is limited to enlightened juxtaposition and concomitant discussion, as opposed to any efforts at discovering dynastic conceptual sequences.[5]

A necessarily isolated and therefore convenient text to consider initially is Conrad's letter to Edward Sanderson, composed late in 1899, in which Conrad protests concerning the act of writing, "One's will becomes the slave of hallucinations, responds only to shadowy impulses. . . . And one goes through with it [writing] with an exaltation as false as all the rest of it. One goes through with it,—and there's nothing to show at the end. Nothing!

Nothing! Nothing!"[6] Marked signs of Conrad's radical skepticism are present: the denial of any justification whatsoever for the manipulation of words, and in turn for the activity whereby Conrad sporadically seeks to authenticate his existence; the insistence that an essential psychic discontinuity deprives one of any chance at self-comprehension or self-control, forcing rather only compulsive, repetitive verbal symptoms of the primal rupture when any effort at communication is made; the abolition of emotive response as a possible source of reification that can supersede a bewildered intellect; the abandonment of any sense of purpose or potential for accomplishment. Yet Conrad makes any number of statements that contrast directly with remarks made in the letter to Sanderson and that can be alluded to as examples of affirmations of significance and value: the manipulation of words seems to be a satisfying means of authentication after all, since "a good book is a good action," "a man is worth neither more nor less than the work he accomplishes . . . ," and "what is life worth if one cannot jabber to one [sic] heart's content?" Moreover, emotive reactions deserve trust because "fidelity to passing emotions . . . is perhaps a nearer approach to truth than any other philosophy of life."[7]

Such radical semantic and conceptual discontinuity within Conrad's personal writings is one reason for the varied critical specifications of his supposed orderly perception of virtue and vice. Depending upon one's own bias, one can discover in Conrad a predilection for "reducing the complex to the simple," a rendition of human experience according to traditional moral criteria such as "whether or not [a character] is faithful to the community." [8] Or, like J. Hillis Miller, one can find a nihilistic outlook so complicated that only the language of paradox can approach competent description: "Action is authentic only insofar as it is recognized that no action is authentic. True action must be based on that which denies it[;] . . . its meaning [is] its meaninglessness. . . . There is nothing true about any action or judgment except their relation to the darkness, and the darkness makes any positive action impossible." [9]

The rhetoric of paradox that Miller adopts in order to discuss Conrad's metaphysics seems inappropriate to the portrayal of a consistent ontic darkness, since one might logically expect such consistency to be accessible to more conventional prose and more sharply defined categorization. The fact is, of course, such negation is not consistently present. Miller rightly tries to circumscribe the most bleak of Conrad's attitudes the only way he can, by indicating the extremities of the darkness through the flash that engenders it as antitheses coincide. But in the process Miller makes Conrad seem more consistent than he is.

Actually, Conrad eludes even Miller's specifications by using Miller's own conceptual trick: Conrad perpetually generates inconsistencies by means of statements that are mutually exclusive if evaluated according to Aristotelian logic, and he thereby reveals the absence of meaning that is central to his ontology the only way he can. If Conrad is always encysted within a given perspective at a given moment in time, he can nevertheless reverse his perspectives at will and thereby undo two crucial Occidental myths, the concept of a knowable, logically consistent self and the idea that the Law of the Excluded Middle embodies an absolutely valid perceptual principle. Conrad knows without embarrassment that "extremes touch," that the facade of a stable humanity is in fact "the intimate alliance of contradictions" (*PR*, 160, 36), that "it's very likely that [his] impressions set down truthfully are altogether untrue" (*LE*, 52). Statements Conrad makes in even his personal writings are conceived in the light of a violent inconsistency, which he seems to regard as definitive of existence itself. Thus, Conrad can alter even autobiographical facts to suit his mood. R. L. Megroz recalls a conversation between Conrad and his wife: "On one of his naughty days he said that *The Black Mate* was his first work, and when [Jessie] said 'No, *Almayer's Folly* was the first thing you ever did,' he burst out: 'If I like to say *The Black Mate* was my first work, I shall say so.'"[10] Indeed, in *A Personal Record* Conrad does not even give his true Polish name.

Such factual irregularity is related to the way Conrad conceives of his life as a sequence of unique perceptual coagulations, which may refer to each other but which need not be consistent with one another. Consequently, the

'time-shift' technique is basic to Conrad's self-analysis, just as it is basic to the analysis of many of his fictional characters. . . . The reminiscences cluster about certain stable points. Key scenes, from which the account digresses and to which it periodically returns, offer coherence to the whole. . . . The flow of memory falls into a series of currents, each having its own narrative centre. . . . Conrad does not critically explore his . . . decisions in life so much as envelop them in a romantic historical and biographical haze, and then attribute them to inexplicable impulse.[11]

Conrad feels no responsibility to remain systematic in a universe that itself may conceal a primal discontinuity: "two universes may exist in the same place and in the same time—and not only two universes but an infinity of different universes. . . ."[12] His attitude even toward the medium of his art is fundamentally discordant. On one hand, "half the words we use have no meaning whatever and of the other half man understands each word after the fashion of his own folly and conceit," and, on the other hand, "words, groups of words, words standing alone . . . have the power in their sound or their aspect to present the very thing you wish to hold up before the mental vision of your readers. The things 'as they are' exist in words. . . ." [13]

In this manner Conrad appeals to both the relativistic Marlows and pre-Kantian MacWhirrs practicing modern literary criticism, with the result that the history of efforts to define Conradian ontology is largely the history of a collision of one form of discourse with another, since "Conrad's own statements on the kind of general meanings he attempted in his fiction do not compose a clear and systematic critical theory; what is most systematic about them, indeed, is their refusal to submit to the conceptual mode of discourse." [14] Thus, on the one hand, there exist the perceptions of sophisticated intellects, like the aforementioned rhetoric of paradox wielded by J. Hillis Miller or the pointed acquiescence in confusion expressed by E. M. Forster:

> What is so elusive about [Conrad] is that he is always promising to make some general philosophic statement about the universe, and then refraining with a gruff disclaimer [which] suggest[s] that he is misty in the middle as well as at the edges, that the secret casket of his genius contains a vapour rather than a jewel; and that we need not try to write him down philosophically, because there is . . . nothing to write. [15]

And on the other hand, there exist the perceptions of simplifiers like Thomas Moser, who concludes comfortingly that Conrad regards "loyalty and service as the central virtues of his world" and that Conrad's supreme moral test is to determine "whether or not [a character] is faithful to the community." [16] Like the credulous narrators of *The Shadow-Line* and *The Nigger of the "Narcissus,"* such critics remain securely insulated from Conrad's relativistic skepticism, which does not shrink from dramatizing the absurdity of having "steered with care" (*NN*, 89) during days of dead calm or while a ship is swamped and on its side.

The disjunctions in Conrad's linguistic world are precisely the loci of *"le neant"* (*NLL*, 94), which is the ground of Conrad's phenomenal world, the "inconceivable tenuity through which the various vibrations of waves . . . are propagated, thus giving birth to our sensations—then emotions—then thought." [17] The "limits" that Conrad suggests are operating somehow to contain his acknowledged conceptual reversals are those implied by the degree of intellectual violence necessary in order to allow any disjunction to become visible as such. By scrupulously avoiding this twilight zone of radical inconsistency in their efforts to interpret Conrad's works definitively, critics, with rare exceptions, simply confirm the troublesome presence of these alinguistic points of disorder. Conrad's entire literary career involves an impertinent flirtation with confusion through the purposeful creation of opposing verbal constructs, for he is "a Janiform writer—vividly two-faced." [18] The untrustworthy nature of both his Author's Notes and his private comments about his works, and the fictive essence of his autobiographical narratives, *A Personal Record* and *The Mirror of the Sea,* have been recognized for years. [19] But even in his personal social interaction Conrad "was smiling, inscrutable, and, no matter in what company, living behind his mask. . . ." [20] And as Arthur Mizener concludes, this mask of "elaborate politeness makes Conrad's expressed opinions contradictory and unreliable. . . ." [21]

Since it is not possible to determine "whether the sanity of our outlook on the world consists in secret revolt against its facts but in the final acceptance of the whole, or in the conformity with all the multiple forms and the mental rejection of life's inscrutable purpose" (*LE*, 92), Conrad's intellectual strategy is to insist upon the interpenetration and interdependence of opposites. Although ever circumscribed by a specific perspective like all human beings, Conrad nevertheless finds it possible deliberately to invert any given perspective and thereby subvert both sides of the opposition. The concept of unified opposites is, of course, nothing new. For hundreds of years oxymoron served as a figure whereby the presence of Divinity could be intimated linguistically. Thus, Richard Crashaw can invoke the Orient tropologically as the veritable epitome of fulfillment of Occidental teleology as he praises Jesus as "thou Day of night! thou East of West! / Lo, we at last have found the way / To Thee, the world's great universal East."[22] Moreover, the cultural climate of the nineteenth century was fraught with a multitude of self-conscious secular quests for transcendence, most of which found surcease amidst some sort of visionary experience that bypassed Aristotle's Law of the Excluded Middle and thereby logic, language, and earthbound ideation itself. Wordsworth's narrator, standing at the bottom of a chasm at high altitude while entertaining perceptions of "woods decaying, never to be decayed" and "stationary blasts of waterfalls" (*The Prelude*, VI, 625–26) is only one of many possible examples. As Western thought in the nineteenth century evolves, Wordsworth's insistence that the poet's vatic power is coextensive with ". . . the motions of the viewless winds, / Embodied in the mystery of words: / There, darkness makes abode . . ." (*The Prelude*, V, 595–97) collides with Schopenhauer's appropriation of Oriental thought in order to recommend the abolition of all fundamental form so that one might discover "before us there is certainly only nothingness" (*WWI*, I, 531).[23] And at the point of this collision there lurks the prototype of Conradian ontic vacancy.

Wordsworth's animated "darkness" is ultimately transfigured: "There . . . all the host / Of shadowy things work endless changes,—there, / . . . Even forms and substances are circumfused / . . . with light divine" (*The Prelude*, V, 597–601). Moreover, it is responsive in a positive manner to words, which, "through the turnings intricate of verse," can reveal the "forms and substances" as ". . . objects recognised / In flashes, and with a glory not their own" (*The Prelude*, V, 603, 600, 604–5). To Wordsworth, language is a medium of knowledge that seems to transcend its human host to reveal the existence of a divine plenum, a veritable "Uncreated," with which a duet is possible at the frontiers of conceptualization: Wordsworth relates that his narrator peered "toward the Uncreated with a countenance / Of adoration, with an eye of love. / One song they sang . . ." (*The Prelude*, II, 412–14). Schopenhauer, in marked contrast, seeks to divest his "nothing" of all the flatulent moralistic and mythic connotations whereby a direct contemplation of annihilatory authenticity has been evaded in the past:

> . . . We must banish the dark impression of that nothingness which we discern behind all virtue and holiness as their final goal, and which we fear as children fear the dark; we must not even evade it like the Indians, through myths and meaningless words, such as reabsorption in Brahma or the Nirvana of the Buddhists. Rather do we freely acknowledge that what remains after the entire abolition of will is for all those who are still full of will certainly nothing; but conversely, to those in whom the will has turned and denied itself, this our world, which is so real, with all its suns and milky ways—is nothing.   (*WWI*, I, 532)

Such a concept as this is probably the systole of Conrad's heart of darkness.

For twenty years a critical debate has continued concerning the significance of what have been termed "the Buddha tableaux" in *Heart of Darkness*. It is instructive to consider briefly several of these arguments in order to demonstrate the ways in which Conrad's use of Oriental concepts and icons has been understood. It is, of course, not clear why the narrator in *Heart of Darkness* compares Marlow to the Buddha (see *HD*, 50, 114, 162). William Bysshe Stein feels that the narrator is ignorantly mocking Marlow, that the Buddha tableaux are "blind impeachments." But these assertions cannot be sustained or denied by reference to the text; Conrad simply does not provide enough information. Stein also insists that the narrator's allusions to the Buddha are weighty interpretational aids that "instruct the reader how to interpret Marlow's descent into the underworld," since Conrad "understood" and "believed in" the metaphysics figured forth in "the stylized postures and gestures of Indian art."[24] Such uncritical enthusiasm is embarrassing, and serves only to encourage even more shrill efforts at demonstrating, by reference to Far Eastern dogma, Conrad's supposed Oriental ideological affiliation, the most extreme examples of which are Stein's own "*The Heart of Darkness: A Bodhisattva Scenario,*" H. C. Brashers's "Conrad, Marlow, and Gautama Buddha," and Francois Lombard's "Conrad and Buddhism."[25] The fact is that Conrad seems quite incapable of "believing in" any kind of thought-form, and his contempt is directed acidly toward a "humanity [that] doesn't know what it wants. But it will swallow everything. . . . It has swallowed Christianity, Buddhism, Mahomedanism and the Gospel of Mrs. Eddy." [26]

But the opposite of such credulous insistence upon Conrad's conscious emulation of Buddhist ritual is scarcely any more valid. For example, Robert O. Evans, reacting negatively to Stein's work, asserts, "It seems unlikely that Conrad knew a great deal about eastern religion," and "There are certainly no external reasons to assume that Conrad ever read deeply in the documents of eastern religion." Even more doggedly, he goes on to comment specifically upon the allusions to the Buddha in *Heart of Darkness*, which he feels are not references to "anything more than the commonplace image of Buddha . . .

[which] can be purchased anywhere in the Orient for a few shillings." [27] Although it cannot be demonstrated that Conrad studied, say, the Upanishads or the Bhagavadgita, he knew Schopenhauer's writings, as Galsworthy attests: "Of philosophy he had read a good deal. Schopenhauer used to bring him satisfaction. . . ."[28] Had Evans taken time to look through Schopenhauer's works he probably would not have published the reservations quoted above, for Schopenhauer discusses at length the philosophies of the Orient in *The World as Will and Idea*. From this source alone Conrad could derive a great deal of information concerning both the general outlines of Oriental thought and specific details of Oriental iconography. To Schopenhauer "the Vedas" are "the fruit of the highest human knowledge and wisdom, the kernel of which has at last reached us in the Upanishads as the greatest gift of this century" (*WWI*, I, 458). For the perceptions of the "Brahmans" and Buddhists his praise is extreme: "Never has a myth entered, and never will one enter, more closely into the philosophical truth which is attainable to so few than this primitive doctrine of the noblest and most ancient nation" (*WWI*, I, 460). And he anticipates a radical alteration in Occidental metaphysics as a result of the newly discovered Indian and Buddhist texts: "The ancient wisdom of the human race will not be displaced by what happened in Galilee. On the contrary, Indian philosophy streams back to Europe, and will produce a fundamental change in our knowledge and thought" (*WWI*, I, 460–61).

Although Schopenhauer is overly optimistic as to the impact the wisdom of the Far East will have in the West, there is no doubt that a number of important writers were deeply influenced by it, and one of these was Conrad. During the latter part of the nineteenth century there was a proliferation of books and articles dealing with travel in the Orient as well as with its philosophy. Conrad was well acquainted with these documentaries of travel and exploration. He used them to verify details presented in his fiction, and he refers to them in his own defense when his works are attacked for inaccuracy: "All the details about the little characteristic acts and customs which they hold up as proof [of factual errors] I have taken out (to be safe) from undoubted sources—dull wise books. In 'Karain' . . . there's not a single action of my man . . . that cannot be backed by a traveller's tale—I mean a serious traveller's."[29] As was pointed out, a familiarity with the primary sources of Oriental philosophy cannot be claimed with any certainty for Conrad, but he did read Schopenhauer, and Schopenhauer assimilated a great deal of this material in *The World as Will and Idea*.[30] Indeed, an understanding of this work is necessary for any comprehensive response to Conrad's fiction, and it is particularly important for an adequate response to the tales set in the Far East.

The Hindu concept of *Brahman*, the transcendent yet immanent Absolute, the ground of individuated phenomenal experience and accompanying limitations, antagonisms, polarities, and occasions for harmony, is embraced by Schopenhauer and becomes "the will." It

> lies outside the province of the principle of sufficient reason [ideation] in all its forms, and is consequently groundless. . . . Further, it is free from all *multiplicity*, although its manifestations in time and space are innumerable. It is itself one, for the unity of an object can only be known in opposition to a possible multiplicity; nor yet in the sense in which a concept is one, for the unity of a concept originates only in abstraction from a multiplicity; but it is one as that which lies outside time and space, the *principium individuationis, i.e.,* the possibility of multiplicity.
>
> (*WWI*, I, 146)

When seeking a collective term for the *principium individuationis,* the phenomenal world, Schopenhauer once again adopts a Hindu concept, the veil of *Maya,* and in this case appropriately even preserves the Sanskrit word: "The Vedas and Puranas have no better simile than a dream for the whole knowledge of the actual world, which they call the web of Maya" (*WWI*, I, 21). Moreover, for Schopenhauer the lifting of the veil of illusion is a prerequisite for an ability to act with compassion:

> For to him who does works of love the veil of Maya has become transparent, the illusion of the *principium individuationis* has left him. He recognizes himself, his will, in every being, and consequently also in the sufferer. He is now free from the perversity with which the will to live, not recognizing itself, here in one individual enjoys a fleeting and precarious pleasure, and there in another pays for it with suffering and starvation, and thus both inflicts and endures misery, not knowing that, like Thyestes, it eagerly devours its own flesh. . . .
>
> (*WWI*, I, 481–82) [31]

To rend the veil of Maya one must negate the "objectivity of will," which is the world and all its phenomena. This is accomplished through "free denial, the surrender of the will," whereupon is annulled

> that constant strain and effort without end and without rest at all the grades of objectivity, in which and through which the world consists; the multifarious forms succeeding each other in gradation; the whole manifestation of the will; and, finally, also the universal forms of this manifestation, time and space, and also its last fundamental form, subject and object; all are abolished. No will: no idea, no world. Before us there is certainly only nothingness.
>
> (*WWI*, I, 530–31)

Such is the cosmic absence, which alone confers authenticity. But neither Conrad nor Schopenhauer arrives at this awareness owing to a closet conversion to the religious forms of Hinduism or Buddhism. The "disappearance of god" is an inescapable dimension of contemporary thought for both men, and in Oriental philosophy they see an age-old collective tranquillity in the face of emptiness and a refreshing willingness on behalf of the individual to embrace annihilation. This intellectual posture generates one of Conrad's most characteristic thematic concerns: a dramatization of the ways in which the values and role models that traditionally sustain Western culture deconstruct when caressed by the void. This is precisely "the point where Eastern philosophy and religion begin to work for a deliverance from the fantasies of self-deception," but where "Western systems of metaphysics and morality lapse into baffled cynicism and despair or else shamelessly divorce themselves from the problems of living: they are not oriented to cross the frontiers of nothingness."[32] Indeed, the very nothingness that serves as a means of "demystification" within Conrad's aesthetic structures functions in a parallel fashion in the Orient, dissolving the Buddha himself: since "everything is 'void' . . . , the realm of *samsara* [the phenomenal world], and even the idea of the existence of nirvāna and of the Buddha, are all equally illusory."[33] It is into this intellectual context that the following resolvent suggestion, made by Bruce Johnson regarding the Buddha tableaux, must be placed:

> The terrible irony in Conrad's equipping his narrator with these vaguely Schopen-hauerian protections against Kurtz's egoism . . . is that the threat from Kurtz is not Will at all, not the egoism Conrad at times identifies so clearly. The emptiness, indeed nothingness, so often intimated, continually eludes the Buddha defense, which after all is equipped for nearly the opposite kind of threat.[34]

Sir Hugh Clifford observes that Conrad's use of Oriental material represents "the impression scored by Asiatics upon a sensitive, imaginative, European mind. Mr. Conrad has seen as white men do—from the outside." [35] According to C. G. Jung, Occidentals have no other choice. It is not possible to comprehend the East through direct imitation, for an Oriental "can always fall back on the authority of his whole civilization" when he starts on "the long way" to psychic liberation, while "the Westerner . . . has all authority against him—intellectual, moral, and religious."[36] Appropriately, there are no unadulterated practitioners of Oriental religions in Conrad's fiction, though there are many allusions to these religions made by Western characters who remain, however tenuously and inauthentically, within a Western context. In Conrad's early novels, particularly, an idea of economic destiny provides his protagonists with a way to impose value and direction on time. And when "the dissolution of the future which the protagonist had projected ahead of himself . . . occurs, a misuse of the past is exposed . . . , and the present is rendered meaningless[;] . . . the structure of existential time disintegrates and along with it the unity of personality." [37]

To the capitalistic and Christian West, founded upon a teleology of linear progress toward material acquisition and metaphysical redemption, nothingness has always been terrifying, what Coleridge calls, in a poem entitled "Limbo," ". . . not a Place, / Yet name it so," the "horror of blank Naught-at-all." The absence of purposeful activity is anathema. When Spenser's Phaedria persuades Cymochles to relax upon her isle, she is made to base her argument upon Matthew 6:28, a text that invites an abandonment of concern for the future: "Behold, O man, that toilsome pains dost take, / The flowers, the fields, and all that pleasant grows, / How they themselves do thine ensample make" (*Faerie Queene*, II, vi, 15). Of course, Spenser indicates that Phaedria is perverting the biblical passage by recommending natural phenomena to human beings as behavioral models, precisely the sort of disorderly sophistry that existed in Spenser's Orient until "Bacchus . . . with furious might / All th' East, before untamed, did overronne" (V, i, 2). Since Adam's fall, retreats into timeless repose are only legitimate if they continue to function within a greater temporal process as a pause midway between the cessation and subsequent continuation of meaningful labor. Relaxations of psychic tension such as that experienced by Willems in *An Outcast of the Islands* only make Occidental sense if perceived as something regressive and lethal, a fall "back into the darkness," whereupon "he gave up as a tired swimmer gives in" (*OI*, 81). A Christian epic would not have a place in Paradise for Conrad's Babalatchi, whose art is "in the nature of a recitative without any rhythm . . . and if Babalatchi considered it a song, then it was a song with a purpose and . . . for that reason, artistically defective" (*OI*, 138). Indeed, Babalatchi is one of the Oriental characters through whom Conrad expresses directly his serious reservations concerning Occidental teleology, which dictates "the even, regular advance of time and history (a delusion fostered by the evolutionary orientation of economic, scientific, and political theory during the nineteenth century)."[38] In marked contrast to colonial invaders, Conrad's Easterners

> ordinarily act in the present on the basis of the immemorial traditions of the past. . . . Fatalistic in regard to the future, they place little faith in temporal expectations . . . even though not wholly unaffected by the sudden upheavals of chance, they never . . . protest the injustice of the heavens. . . . Normally . . . Eastern man is content with his cultural sense of being. Beyond a kind of aimless materialism, he is not concerned with any of the forbidden fruit of becoming.[39]

The East has long posed a subversive threat. In *Paradise Lost*, on a throne like those found ". . . where the gorgeous East with richest hand / Show'rs on her Kings Barbaric Pearl and Gold, / Satan exalted sat" (II, 3–5). As Edward W. Said suggests, "It is Europe that articulates the Orient; this articulation is the prerogative . . . of a genuine creator, whose life-giving power represents, animates, constitutes the otherwise silent and dangerous space beyond familiar boundaries."[40] Thus, for example, James Thomson in *The Castle of Indolence* (1748) causes his Wizard of Indolence, who presides over a space beyond time, a "vernal year" (I, 18; references are to canto and stanza), paradoxically "atween June and May" (I, 2), to sing "beneath a spacious Palm" (I, 7) just beyond the walls of his stronghold, whose "soul-dissolving" (I, 39) enticements derive from "Turkey and Persia Land" (I, 33) and serve to outline the central abyss, the "perfect Silence" and "blank Area" of the court (I, 29), where Western understanding is completely frustrated. As might be expected, Thomson sees to it that the Incomprehensible is presented as a type of sinful deception, which conceals "a sleepy Horror" (I, 5), is supervised by an "Arch-image" adept at "feigning Virtue" (I, 46), and is vulnerable to a preposterous, sermonizing "Knight of Art and Industry" (II, 5). Although it is not certain, of course, that Conrad ever read *The Castle of Indolence*, the poem provides an excellent model of the characteristic Western pomposity, naive optimism, and intellectual arrogance against which Conrad typically strikes. When Willems perceives Aissa within a tropical bower of bliss "like an apparition behind a transparent veil" hovering where opposites join in "sunbeams and shadows" to form a transcendent "checkered light" (*OI*, 70), he ascends to an erotic empyrean which annuls his cultural heritage, and which precisely parallels the dangerous confines of the Castle of Indolence, where "embower-ing Trees" create an "Evening" at noon, "a Kind of checker'd Day and Night" (I, 7). Such locales are quite common in Conrad's Eastern world, although they do not bear the same sort of moral stigma that Thomson imposes upon his fascinating castle.

Depictions of isolated bowers of bliss, such as are rendered by poets from the Elizabethans through the Romantics, seem to provide Conrad with a pat-tern that he repeats whenever he wishes to provide an imagistic extension of characterological dissolution in a spasm of supernal love. Such delusions are especially tempting to Westerners because they offer, however briefly, a respite from the strain of sustaining a triadic conception of time, a sequence of past, present, and prospect, which must constantly be redeemed through optimistic amplification of futurity. This is the sort of respite offered to the despairing Frankenstein by the compassionate Clerval, a student of Oriental thought, wherein he has discovered a rejuvenating departure from Occidental obsessions: "When you read [Eastern] writings, life appears to consist in warm sun and a garden of roses. . . . How different from the manly and heroical poetry of Greece and Rome!"

Indeed, it is possible to erect a hierarchy of Conrad's characters based upon the respective concepts they use as substitutes for nothingness. Those of lesser awareness project their experiences of the void onto familiar ideas, like Clerval and his analogical "garden of roses" in *Frankenstein*, so that vacancy never becomes troublesome, because it never must be confronted directly. Women, for example, commonly serve in Conrad's works as analogues for the unknown, and loss of self in an experience of erotic transcendentalism serves to cloak in ordinary terms an irruption of the incomprehensible. And since the confusing reflectivity of an ultimately alien medium, woman, can be made to parallel analogically the capacity of the sea to tantalize the perceiver with floating simulations of himself, oceanic mirrors are also dangerous: "Like an unscrupulous woman, the sea . . . was glorious in its smiles, irresistible in its anger, capricious, enticing, illogical, irresponsible; a thing to love, a thing to fear" (OI, 12). Thus, the appropriateness of what seems to be an accidental conjunction in the life of M. George, who declares, "Woman and the sea revealed themselves to me together" (AG, 88). Such a revelation can be so dangerously disorienting as to excite a strange desperation devoid of comprehensible motive: Anthony "plunged" through the vortices of Flora's eyes "breathless and tense, deep, deep, like a mad sailor taking a desperate dive from the masthead into the blue unfathomable sea so many men have execrated and loved at the same time" (C, 332; echoes of Keats's "Ode on Melancholy" and Melville's crucial chapter "The Mast-head" in Moby Dick are quite significant).

Typically, such women are mirrors in which the once-stable self disintegrates because of a perception of its own enigmatic absence, an absence which initially becomes a problem when a character experiences the failure of one of Western man's illusory means of controlling time. Notice how Conrad's narrative voice analyzes Willems's escape from time in the presence of Aissa: "There are in our lives short periods which hold no place in memory but only as the recollection of a feeling. There is no remembrance of gesture, of action, of any outward manifestation of life" (OI, 72). To the Western mind such an experience is only analogous to death, though anticipatory terrors are avoided due to the immediacy of the moment. In the midst of this suspension it might indeed be "rich . . . / To cease upon the midnight with no pain," but Conrad's celestial lovers can never merge the illusion of timelessness with eternity: "Death in such a moment is the privilege of the fortunate, it is a high and rare favour, a supreme grace" (OI, 72). The ideal unity of this moment causes Willems to surrender "the unstained purity of his life, of his race, of his civilization" (OI, 80) as he is deracinated, ostensibly by a foreign woman but actually by the nothingness which she embodies. This experience is dangerously alien to Willems's cultural background and is consequent upon his growing realization that he is inadequate to compete in the arena imposed by capitalistic teleology. As a result, lying in Aissa's arms and dozing off Willems envisioned "a man going away from him and diminishing in a long perspective of fantastic trees. . . . He felt a desire to see him vanish, a hurried impatience of his disappearance, and he watched for it with a careful and irksome effort. There was something familiar about that figure. Why! Himself!" (OI, 145). Although Willems is consciously "indignant" over "that thing slinking off stealthily while he slept" (OI, 145), he cannot prevent the disintegration of his personality. Having experienced a pleasurable timelessness from the point of view of a socially defined self, it is only a short step to a concomitant abolition of this self.

It is of utmost importance to realize that Conrad does not disapprove of someone undergoing a startling recognition that the self is an illusion. Quite to the contrary, he emphatically holds that "before all one must divest oneself of every particle of respect for one's character,"[41] for only "when once the truth is grasped that one's own personality is only a ridiculous and aimless masquerade of something hopelessly unknown the attainment of serenity is not very far off."[42] The essential problem is that, unlike Far Eastern cultures, Western civilization does not enable its members to live with such a discovery, and this fact provides Conrad with no end of tragic amusement. In acknowledging "I would be a fool if I tried to become this thing rather than that; for I know well that I will never be anything,"[43] Conrad transcends the dualistic absurdities of the West, for he refuses to identify himself with an object of knowledge. He thereby avoids a rigid concept of self that can only make phenomenal processes unbearable due to the necessarily incomplete nature of serial experiences, which offer perpetually only a fantasy of fulfillment in futurity.

L. L. Whyte describes the formation of the Occidental myth of the self in the following way: "Some apparently permanent element is separated from the general process, treated as an entity, and endowed with active responsibility for a given occurrence. This procedure is so paradoxical that only long acquaintance with it conceals its absurdity."[44] Richard de Martino provides a more rigorous analysis of these inherent paradoxes: the ego's

> affirmation of itself includes both itself as affirmer and as affirmed. . . . The ego as subject-affirmer is not chronologically prior to itself as object-affirmed. Nor does its individuation precede its bifurcation. Immediately when there is ego-consciousness there is the ego, and immediately when there is the ego it is already object as well as subject, as much imparted to itself as it is the activator of itself. A living, active subject with freedom and responsibility, it is at the same time a passive, given object, destined, determined, and without responsibility.[45]

Few characters in Conrad's fiction approach a recognition of this dyad and survive. Much like Nostromo among the daughters Viola, Willems ends his life torn between two shrieking females, Aissa and Joanna, embodiments of his past involvement with the conflicting cultural alternatives that are competing for his future.

Preservation of the myth of self is often a function of the protagonists' abilities to elude such a reflective fragmentation. For example, though he ultimately resigns his command in retreat from the enticingly somnolent geographic domain of Alice Jacobus (who always is clothed in sleeping apparel), the narrator of "A Smile of Fortune" never entirely loses his unifying grip on his personality, for the mirror of the girl's glance is not sufficiently focused to inaugurate a rupture. Her eyes are "so empty of thought, and so absorbed in their own fixity that she seem[s] to be staring at her own lonely image, in some far-off mirror hidden from [his] sight amongst the trees" (*TLS*, 63). Consequently, though the narrator peers into a potentially seductive surface, his urgency does not rebound and he is not terminally disoriented by the subversive conflation of opposites lurking in the appearance of the "tragic and promising, pitiful and provoking" girl, who pierces to the metaphoric heart of the tale when she asserts, fittingly, "I love nothing" (*TLS*, 78). In like manner, M. George discovers Rita while standing upon a mirrorlike surface whose chromatic scheme suggests the inner fragmentation that the woman generates: "The floor inlaid in two kinds of wood in a bizarre pattern was highly waxed, reflecting objects like still water" (*AG*, 68). And later he rediscovers her amidst a whirl of varying sparks and reflexes, whose extreme nature echoes his own disorientation: "adrift in the big black-and-white hall as on a silent sea" (*AG*, 284), M. George decides to explore, and, finding an enticing "ebony door" unlocked, he penetrates the black surface only to be overwhelmed by a "room [that is] most unexpectedly dazzling to [his] eyes, as if illuminated," uncannily, for his arrival, "for a reception" (*AG*, 286). Amazed, he gapes at more reflections and chiaroscuro effects:

> I grabbed the back of the nearest piece of furniture and the splendour of marbles and mirrors, of cut crystals and carvings, swung before my eyes in the golden mist of walls and draperies round an extremely conspicuous pair of black stockings thrown over a music stool which remained motionless. The silence was profound. It was like being in an enchanted place.
>
> (*AG*, 286–87; cf. *LJ*, 348)

Rita, of course, is in this room. The threat to the coherence of M. George's personality that is indicated metaphorically in the above description can be grasped more directly when it is understood that he is in love with a woman who, much like Alice Jacobus, declares to him, "I don't exist" (*AG*, 224).

M. George can only protect himself against fragmentation in a reflexive and illogical simultaneity by vehemently asserting the absolute validity of the fictions of linearity and causality: "Love for Rita . . . if it was love, I asked myself desparingly, while I brushed my hair before a glass. It did not seem to have any sort of beginning as far as I could remember. A thing the origin of which you cannot trace cannot be seriously considered. It is an illusion" (*AG*, 163). In the same way Alvan Hervey, "beside himself with a despairing agitation" over his wife, gains a rudiment of defensive control by brushing his hair before a mirror and altering his identity with his changing appearance:

> He brushed with care, watching the effect of his smoothing; and another face, slightly pale and more tense than was perhaps desirable, peered back at him from the toilet glass. He laid the brushes down, and was not satisfied. He took them up again and brushed, brushed mechanically—forgot himself in that occupation. The tumult of his thoughts ended in a sluggish flow of *reflection*, such as, after the outburst of a volcano, the almost imperceptible progress of a stream of lava, creeping languidly over a convulsed land and pitilessly obliterating any landmark left by the shock of the earthquake. It is a destructive, but by comparison, it is a peaceful phenomenon.
>
> (*TU*, 136–37; italics mine)

As in the case of M. George, Alvan Hervey finds that once the ego has been entangled with a dangerously consuming surface (in these cases, woman), it cannot be disentangled intact. Though Hervey is "cooling," he discovers to his dismay that life now seems devoid of significant features: "His moral landmarks were going one by one" (*TU*, 137; cf. Marlow's experience "before a mahogany door," whence Kurtz "seemed to stare . . . out of the glassy panel," and Il Conde's confrontation in a "cafe . . . set all round with looking-glasses" [*HD*, 156; *SS*, 285]).

There is no alternative but to become a "skimmer" and avoid completely any mirroring alterities, as Hervey and his wife try to do: "They skimmed over the surface of life hand in hand, in a pure and frosty atmosphere—like two skilful skaters cutting figures on thick ice for the admiration of the beholders, and disdainfully ignoring the hidden stream, the stream restless and dark; the stream of life, profound and unfrozen" (*TU*, 123). Such a mentality can maintain the petrific integrity of the illusory self, but it culminates in a timid, compulsive pursuit of security, as in the case of Captain Hagberd, of the *Skimmer of the Seas*, in "To-morrow," whose longest voyage had "lasted a fortnight, of which the most part had been spent at anchor, sheltering from the weather" (*T*, 249). In marked contrast, Conrad himself has surrendered his personality to a female reflex that bears it away to the realm of shades where only the ruins of his society's fatuous structures remain: "My very being seems faded and thin like the ghost of a blonde and sentimental woman, haunting romantic ruins. . . ."[46] And if the personality itself is merely an illusion, abstracted by social influence from memories and feeding off fantasies of fulfillment in futurity through manipulation of physical matter, these media are finally no more substantial: "There is no space, time, matter, mind as vulgarly understood, there is only the eternal something that waves and an eternal force that causes the waves. . . ."[47]

Although the void lurks above, beneath, and beyond all experiences of all things, it cannot be displayed or articulated directly. Nevertheless, Conrad finds occasion to attract attention to the nothingness by making oblique references in his fiction to Far Eastern metaphysics. The language teacher in *Under Western Eyes* collides with the "inconceivable" during a talk with Nathalie Haldin (see *UWE*, 104–6). Ostensibly discussing a political trend, the narrator quickly discovers that Nathalie is able to inject what he feels is a logically inappropriate topic into the context of the discussion. She would speak of the "concord [that] is not so very far off," while he can only respond by challenging the suitability of the topic, suggesting that "these were strange times to talk of concord." To the narrator the idea of concord amounts to only "some sort of mystic expression." So far as he can see, "antagonistic ideas" can be reconciled only through "blood and violence," since any other possibility is, in the light of his "reasonable" position, "inconceivable." Nathalie replies, however, that "everything is inconceivable. . . . The whole world is inconceivable to the strict logic of ideas. And yet the world exists to our senses, and we exist in it. There must be a necessity superior to our conceptions" (*UWE*, 106). Nathalie's mind simply takes a different direction from that of the narrator. Whereas she attempts to emancipate her thought from dualistic, serial forms, the narrtor can only affirm the superior validity of physical substance, and then go on to react to Nathalie's qualification of logic by preserving as definitive a tension between the word and the flesh: "The most idealistic conceptions . . . must be clothed in flesh . . . before they can be made understandable" (*UWE*, 106).

Although to Conrad Russia does not connote "an empty void" (*NLL*, 100), the country does symbolize an incoherent limbo where two radically different cultures meet in fruitless negation: "She is a yawning chasm open between East and West" (*NLL*, 100). Conrad's remarks are offered in a spirit of condemnation. Yet they serve excellently to define the way Conrad reduces the teleology of the West to the level of a fatuous and destructive illusion; while witholding any positive recommendations, he hints at an alternative metaphysic (the Hindu-Buddhist tradition) that is not available to the West, its absurd and needful death throes notwithstanding. In marked contrast to the sort of wisdom that dwells with substance, assertion, and belief, and which is exemplified by Sophia's preposterous non sequitur at the end of *Under Western Eyes* (see *UWE*, 382), "True wisdom . . . is not certain of anything in this world of contradictions" (*SA*, 84).

Typically such wisdom is the exclusive possession of Conrad's narrative voices, which must express it in a negative manner by stating what characters do *not* know and implying thereby what these characters might be able to comprehend could they move outside Western dyads. The "high official" in *The Secret Agent* seems unaware of the mutual attraction exerted by opposites, but the narrative voice makes such awareness available in the abstract by suggesting that, if it were not for his "official kind" of "wisdom," "he might have reflected . . . that in the close-woven stuff of relations between conspirator and police there occur unexpected solutions of continuity, sudden holes in space and time" (*SA*, 85). And similarly, in *Victory*, amidst a furor of conflicting rumors and beliefs, Heyst tries to assemble an omnific name for his mistress by "combining detached letters and loose syllables" (*V*, 176), but the Logos has long since deconstructed and his efforts are futile. Only the narrative voice knows the magic word which can restore unity to such a babel, the "potent, creative, eternal syllables out of which the gods and the universe had proceeded."[48] And, again, its knowledge can only be expressed in a contrary-to-fact manner, by stating what Ricardo, that paragon of aggressive Occidental teleology, does *not* understand: "Cross-legged, his head drooping a little and perfectly still, he might have been meditating . . . upon the sacred syllable 'Om.' It was a striking illustration of the untruth of appearances" (*V*, 250; cf. Rita "sitting cross-legged . . . in the attitude of a very old idol or a very young child" [*AG*, 91]).[49]

A similar example can be found in *The Shadow-Line*, where the narrator, "under the *shadow* of the great gilt pagoda" in an "Oriental capital which had as yet suffered no white conqueror" (*SL*, 47; italics mine), obtusely reveres the "supreme authority" of "the Harbour-Master" (*SL*, 29) and seeks a simplistic "truth" (*SL*, 7, 27) in a world that he solipsistically populates with an absurd assortment of demonic Occidental phantoms; and just as he never transcends his crazy allegorizations, so he never gets his vessel under control. An even better instance is the excellent and deceptive story *Falk*, which ostensibly involves an "opposition . . . between ordered existence, exemplified in Hermann's *gemutlich* floating home, and Falk's total isolation on his tug and in his primitive experience on the drifting steamer."[50] But to see only this tension in the story is to see it through the Western eyes of its narrator, who frequently mentions the haunting "architectural mass of a Buddhist temple . . . projected . . . in dead black on the sky" (*T*, 158; see also 164, 166, 210), but who is incapable of comprehending the metaphysical alternative represented by the Buddhist monks, who "cherish the thoughts of . . . Annihilation'" (*T*, 210), as a perspective which might provide crucial insight into his and Falk's experiences. The narrator, telling his story years after the events occurred, is ritualistically reconfirming for himself the transcendent validity of the principle of life, as manifested by the marriage of Falk with Hermann's niece. The wedding suggests a triumph of eternal vitality, such as that embodied in the "Diana . . . of Ephesus" (*T*, 149),[51] over despair and cannibalism on one hand, and over the timid deceptions and moral superficiality of the petit bourgeois on the other. Indeed, so convinced is the narrator of the cosmic reliability of his perceptions that he endows the characters with mythic proportions. The virile Falk appears like a centaur, displays a Herculean torso, and embodies "the mighty truth of an unerring and eternal principle" (*T*, 235); while the girl resembles "a fortunate immortal" whose "olympian" beauty and form suggest so much "vigorous life" that "she could have stood for an allegoric statue of the Earth" (*T*, 152) and "seemed to illustrate the eternal truth of an unerring principle" (*T*, 236). That is, for the narrator Life has been vindicated, in the face of dire threat, through an archetypal union, which at the same time vindicates the values and social forms of his culture.

Yet, the story suggests that such naive optimism is unwarranted, regardless of the superficially satisfactory resolution of plot. Falk has had his opportunity to transcend the structures of his society, but he proved himself capable of responding to the opportunity only to the point of committing a physical act of cannibalism. Like his namesake the falcon, he is essentially an unthinking raptor. The metaphysical implications of his experience never occur to him, and he wants nothing more than to confess his transgression and then to marry, thereby rejoining the Western European middle class. The story includes a veritable personification of this social class in a character named Herman ("Mr. Man"), whose cleanliness is pathological, and whose ship, named after the goddess of chastity and painted "dazzling" white, is fitted out like a country cottage replete with flowerpots and white curtains, "world proof" in its "venerable innocence" (*T*, 157, 148, 156). It is to this character on this ship that Falk climactically states, "I have eaten man," to which remark Mr. Man replies, "Beast!" (*T*, 218). A radical polarization that could overthrow some of the most precious delusions of the West is approached but never achieved, thanks to Falk's dullness. Although he indeed drifted interminably on the *Borgmaster Dahl* in the company of "skeletons," toward the polar regions of the "South out of men's knowledge" (*T*, 230, 229), and, in a state of extreme need, devoured a shipmate, Falk's allegiance ultimately remains with the petit bourgeois world inhabited by burghers and run by dull burgomasters. He would exorcise his grisly act committed in a realm beyond men's knowledge rather than risk entering such a realm conceptually and abandoning the Occidental foundations of his identity, which coalesce adjectivally in his name, "Christian Falk" (*T*, 60).

However, presiding over the metaphysical conceit of the narrator, as he takes comfort in his vision of Olympian personae enacting a social ritual, is the enigmatic Buddhist pagoda, "rising lonely and massive with shining curves and pinnacles . . ." (*T*, 166). Its presence translates into the immediate surroundings of Falk's bourgeois comedy the emblematic territory "out of men's knowledge" of the South Pole, for the pagoda structure itself is "the very symbol of nirvāna," in which "the storeys and rings on top of the pagoda, represent the cosmic spheres, superimposed upon one another . . . [;] planes of cosmic existence [and] stages of consciousness . . . seen in the temporal sense, they are successive stages on the path to redemption leading ultimately beyond the limits of time and space."[52] Similarly, within "the frozen silence"[53] at either of the poles, the dubious grids and verbiage through which man has charted the elemental chaos of both the earth's geography and human experience must fail. Latitude and longitude are reduced to a single point, and all direction is the same; that is, at the South Pole all directions are north. Conrad uses the polar location at once to emphasize the characters' impercipience and to indicate that the act of eating a fellow burgher demolishes all social structures and figures forth the void underlying the struggling, copulating, bearing, and dying phenomena, the "vigorous life," which the narrator feels Falk and his lady so positively embody. As Schopenhauer puts it, "The will must live on itself, for there exists nothing beside it." Yet, even though "it alone is thing-in-itself," the will confers no supernal validation, since it generates only meaningless phenomena, "Life, the visible world . . . [which] accompanies the will as inseparably as the shadow accompanies the body" (*WWI*, I, 201, 200, 354).

Thus, it is not Falk, the "ruthless lover of the five senses" with "a clear perception of the thing itself" (*T*, 239, 161), who represents authenticity in this tale, nor is the narrator capable of perceiving the authentic as such. Only the pagoda, an edifice enclosing and indirectly intimating the nothingness, bears mute witness to the "Annihilation" (*T*, 210), which alone can take the measure of human experience, and which Buddhists treasure for that reason: "In the Buddhist reading of the nature of existence all is absolutely void and without a self; the forms of phenomenality ride like a mirage over nothing at all, conjured up by the force of ignorance, and the sole interest is in its dissolution." [54] In a parallel manner Conrad defines existence as "a life that is only a film of unsteady appearances stretched over regions deep indeed, but which have nothing to do with the half-truths, half-thoughts, and whole illusions of existence" (*NLL*, 22). And insofar as the narrator necessarily exists in "the domain of Art . . . where well-known voices quarrel noisily in a misty emptiness," far from the "path of toilsome silence," which alone leads to an encounter in the "depths" (*NLL*, 22), so he can do little but admire vitality incarnate in Falk—"He wanted to live. He had always wanted to live. So do we all" (*T*, 233)—as ignorance goes on generating and contemplating its own mirage. Fittingly, neither the narrator nor Falk is aware that the very name of the ill-fated ship on which Falk's act of cannibalism was committed suggests an Oriental spiritual and dietary alternative to the Occidental penchant for sustaining the self through consumption of meat: "The main source of protein in the daily Kṛṣṇa consciousness *yoga* diet is dahl, which is made from different types of dried beans." [55]

It should not be overlooked that most of Conrad's Far Eastern natives are Moslems, and that this religion shares with Christianity a dualistic morality and a linear conception of time that is organized into the familiar triad of past, present, and future. Like the ubiquitous Arab traders, Conrad's natives are as enmeshed as any Christian colonial in the Occidental teleology that dictates pursuit of temporal fulfillment. For example, although Hinduism and Buddhism dominated Indonesia from the second century A.D. until the thirteenth century A.D., when the area was subjected to Islamic invasion, these religious ideologies are not consciously contemplated or practiced by Conrad's Malaysians. To describe the contrast between the crew of the *Patna* and the Moslem pilgrims who are also sailing on board as definitive of the "opposition between Western and Eastern man"[56] is simply wrong. Probably none of the pious travelers bound for Mecca after having committed their fates to the *Patna* understands the preposterous irony stemming from the fact that the ship is named after one of the most famous Buddhist holy cities, Patna, historical capital of the greatest of Buddhist emperors, Ashoka, who came to power shortly after the departure from India of Alexander the Great.[57] The creation of this irony is one of Conrad's masterstrokes, directly illuminating the relativism that dominates *Lord Jim* and indirectly alluding to the darkness that constantly theatens to engulf its characters. The Islamic religion does not provide a metaphysical alternative to European Christianity. Conrad simply dramatizes by means of its adherents the sort of blind credulity in an absurdly specific unseen that is merely the obverse of London technologists' blind trust in the seen.

To Hindu-Buddhist understanding, the concept of transcendence offers reconciliation through the underlying identity of all differences, whereas Jehovah, Allah, or Westinghouse signifies merely one of the differences, albeit the ruling difference, and can offer merely conciliation. As Denis de Rougemont puts it,

> Eastern *askesis* is directed to negation of the Many and to absorption into the One; it looks to a *complete fusion* with a god, or, lacking a god (as in the case of Buddhism), with the universal One of Being. . . . By "West" I mean a religious attitude which actually reached us from the Near East, but has been supreme solely in the West. . . . This attitude accordingly does not look to any absorption or union in substance; but only to communion, the model of which is the *marriage* of the Church and her Lord.[58]

But beneath Christian and Islamic veneer lies the true Oriental perception, which is historically prior and metaphysically more acute. As "diffused through the Malayan Archipelago, Hindu-Buddhist wisdom colored the unconscious thinking of the natives,"[59] functioning as part of a subliminal awareness that figures forth the void with which both Conrad and these religions are so thoroughly preoccupied.

As a result, Conrad's Malaysians tend to be strange composites of West and East. Babalatchi participates in Islamic rites, bearing a "praying carpet" and pouring "the water of ablution" (*OI*, 104). He also falls prey to anxiety over personal fulfillment within serial time, to "suspense" because of "the thought of the future, the desire of success, the pain of waiting" (*OI*, 126). Thus, his judgment that a sense of "purpose" is something which illegitimately contaminates (*OI*, 138) conflicts with his Moslem heritage and suggests the Annihilation cherished by Buddhists, though uncomprehended by Babalatchi.

Karain also is afforded an opportunity to confront the ancient wisdom, and he likewise fails to understand, largely because he is a veritable incarnation of self-conscious phenomenality, pure surface: "He strutted, incomparably dignified, made important by the power he had to awaken an absurd expectation of something heroic going to take place" (*TU*, 6). A sufficiently devoted Moslem to excite temporary fears of "his puritanism" (*TU*, 49) among the narrator's crew, Karain is involved with the martial preservation of the Western illusion of self-determination in time as he prepares to counter a threat posed by Christians with their "moribund Spanish gunboats" (*TU*, 7). As might be expected, Karain's perceptions echo his dualistic metaphysics, and he simplistically organizes the world, in his "word-perfect way," according to two categories: " 'friends and enemies'—nothing else" (*TU*, 8). His life is rigorously ordered through ritual, and his fantasy of future war is becoming ever more tangibly reified through the accumulation of guns and powder. Yet, this robust, aggressive surface conceals a profound disorientation, which threatens to overwhelm Karain's identity in spite of all the physical props he might muster.

Karain is an expatriate. The son of an embarrassing union of his queenly mother and "a Korinchi man of no family" (*TU*, 14), and the murderer of his best friend, he is in psychophysical exile from his past, a situation the surrounding political confusion serves to figure forth: 'The historical disarray of the geographical region after the intrusion of white men serves as an inclusive metaphor for the chaotic regions of the mind on whose threshold the expatriate particularly finds himself."[60] As in the case with so many of Conrad's disoriented fugitives, Karain's fragmenting personality manifests itself in terms of competing female figures. There are five such figures in the tale: (1) Karain's mother; (2) Queen Victoria, whom Karain has never seen yet whom he calls "Great, Invincible, Pious, and Fortunate" (*TU*, 13); (3) Pata Matara's sister; (4) the phantom of Matara's sister; (5) "the image of the Great Queen," Victoria, on "a Jubilee sixpence" (*TU*, 49; the photograph of Hollis's girl is never seen by Karain).

Karain's quest is primarily for a means of validating his own outcast state, and it takes the form of a series of displacements. Initially, he focused upon the apparition of Matara's sister, a "beautiful" and "faithful" companion, who likewise had departed "from her land and her people" (*TU*, 34, 32). However, this phantom could not survive direct juxtaposition with the flesh-and-blood woman, who, after having been saved by Karain's treacherous murder of her brother, emphatically denied Karain's identity: "She looked at [him] with unflinching eyes, and said aloud, 'No! I never saw him before'" (*TU*, 39). He abandoned the real woman, and the phantom "came no more" (*TU*, 41).

To his dismay both females are displaced by the ghost of his dead friend, which in turn is eventually held at bay after Karain meets his supportive wizard. However, following the wizard's death, Karain finds himself once again haunted by his past, which he seeks to exorcise by completely exchanging one cultural heritage for another. Since the "memory of his mother . . . mingled somehow in his mind with the image he tried to form for himself of the far-off Queen, whom he called Great, Invincible, Pious, and Fortunate" (*TU*, 13), his desire to abandon Mindinao to become a subject of Queen Victoria is clearly regressive, an attempt to force the future into the mold of the past in order to recover lost innocence among a people "who despise the invisible voices" (*TU*, 24). Fortunately, he encounters the shrewd and understanding Hollis, who lays Matara's ghost once again by creating a mighty charm that combines the political magic of the queen's image, the economic power associated with money, the potency of Hollis's own trophies of erotic involvement (ribbon and glove), and the connotations of a Catholic talisman "like those Italian peasants wear" (*TU*, 50).

Thus, Karain eludes the "horrible void," restoring his "front," appropriately, by means of an image that is "gilt" and largely a matter of therapeutic verbiage (*TU*, 6, 49). Never having transcended his culture in spite of his agony, he reassumes the familiar role of warrior and continues to pursue still another Occidental amulet, guns, "the dark and polished tubes that can cure so many illusions" (*TU*, 54). And, of course, the last information given about Karain's territory, Mindinao, is that "they are fighting over there again. He's sure to be in it" (*TU*, 54).

Ironically, years before Karain uncomprehendingly confronted perhaps the most powerful emblem of all. A Moslem, he could not recognize the strange statue he encountered, fittingly, at the psychic nadir of his odyssey, the deepest penetration into the cultural palimpsest that is his historical and metaphysical heritage:[61]

> We lost ourselves . . . in the jungle; and one night, in a tangled forest, we came upon a place where crumbling old walls had fallen amongst the trees, and where strange stone idols—carved images of devils with many arms and legs, with snakes twined round their bodies, with twenty heads and holding a hundred swords—seemed to live and threaten in the light of our camp fire.
>
> (*TU*, 32)

Karain is unknowingly describing a statue of the "thousand-armed Kannon,"[62] an extremely common rendition of Buddha in a form particularly meant to connote the power of enlightenment to dissolve triumphantly the phenomenal world. A metaphysical alternative to all the bourgeois turmoil consequent upon a voyage beyond the pale to the South Pole was quietly suggested in *Falk* by the presence of the Buddhist temple. Similarly, in "Karain" the protagonists' efforts to maintain a sense of murderous purpose in time, while lost in an alien jungle and moving beyond time, are placed into the all-consuming context of the Buddhists' void by means of a mute and uncomprehended statue. Though Karain "ceased to count the number of nights, of moons, of years" (*TU*, 34), he never steps beyond the serial pursuit of a dream, and the figure in the jungle is left to decompose unperceived.

It is instructive to examine the story "Youth" from this perspective. Critics have frequently defined the central concern of this tale as an examination of the psychic maturation Marlow undergoes as a result of the sinking of his ship, the *Judea*.[63] A concensus has been reached: Marlow's conduct after the vessel dies is "responsible," indicating he has mastered a code of seamanship that Conrad approves.[64] A recent study even seeks to synthesize previous perceptions of the young Marlow's character by demonstrating that "such responsible conduct is firmly grounded in a *development of attitude*—and not in mere exigency."[65] Such a judgment can scarcely incorporate logically the fact that Marlow's journey to Java is ultimately an impetuous, irresponsible lark. In his egoistic quest for adventure, Marlow, at last in complete command of a vessel, refuses to obey orders to "keep together as much as possible," imposes the inane fiction of a race upon the serious task of achieving a safe landfall, and even ignores the sails of a deep-water ship because, as he says, "I was afraid she might be homeward bound, and I had no mind to turn back from the portals of the East" (*Y*, 36). Indeed, Conrad himself implicitly repudiates the young Marlow's conduct: "The mere love of adventure is no saving grace. It is no grace at all. It lays a man under no obligation of faithfulness to an idea and even to his own self" (*NLL*, 189). Latent in the dubitable critical responses summarized above is an approbation of Marlow's conduct because his arrival in Java triumphantly fulfills Western demands for success through physical action in time. By way of contrast, I would like to suggest that the central problem revealed in "Youth" is the very existence of the word "youth" itself, for by means of both the temporal compartmentalization and the value judgment implicit in this concept the potentially integrated continuum of human growth in time is hopelessly fragmented and polarized. Consequently, Marlow can only respond with static, maudlin, alcoholic cynicism after realizing that the values his conceptual categories isolate in his past are inexorably canceled by temporal flux.

At age forty-two Marlow is no longer young, but there is every indication that he wishes he were, for he must drink his way through his tale (see *Y*, 10, 12, 16, 21, 24, 42). Although he has mastered a rhetoric which insists upon the futility of human effort (see *Y*, 4) and tropes which ultimately define life as bitterness (see *Y*, 30), Marlow remains emotionally attached to an ideal of fulfillment through impetuous action. He can see in the demise of the *Judea* only a symbol of inevitable annihilation, but he resists and mourns this process. Thus, he fails to perceive a more profound level of metaphor: in the destruction of the *Judea*, a vessel that to Marlow seems like "the old village church at home" (*Y*, 18), whose motto is "Do or Die," whose captain is a feeble and incompetent Beard, steward an aged Abraham, and mate "Mann" himself, there is figured forth the demise of Judeo-Christian linear metaphysics. Far from glorifying human endurance, Conrad's broader vision seeks to "reveal the hopelessness of that endurance,"[66] and this is a vision Marlow cannot attain. As a young man he indeed gets to the East, but only by drawing upon the most rampant of Western illusions. The wisdom of the East ever remains hidden from him, for upon his arrival in Java, "a long coast . . . stretching . . . from west to east" (*TU*, 31), "the East spoke to me, but it was in a Western voice" (*Y*, 39). This "Western voice" significantly articulates a violent complaint that the warning light marking the end of a jetty has been permitted to go out. Such a concern with the maintenance of technical devices that allow physical motion to be accomplished with greater efficiency is definitive of the Occidental mind. That is, the "Western voice" is of more general import than merely as a source of specific practical complaint. It signifies the persistent presence of Western metaphysics which severely limits Marlow's comprehension.

Regardless of his age, Marlow maintains a single consistent analogue for whatever resists linear progress: hell, the traditional place of timeless confinement for those who do not revere the Judeo-Christian supernal goal (cf. the *Celestial*, whence the "Western voice" comes [*Y*, 39]). The gale that strikes the

Judea off the Lizards and forces an abandonment of its eastward course "seem[s] to last for months, for years, for all eternity, as though we [were] dead and [went] to a hell for sailors" (*Y*, 12). But the delay in Falmouth is even worse. Though the experience involves no hard labor, it does demand a simple ability to cope with the passage of time apart from sustaining illusions of linearity, an ability that Marlow lacks: "Morally it was worse than pumping for life. It seemed as though we had been forgotten by the world, belonged to nobody, would get nowhere" (*Y*, 16). In desperation he takes three months' pay and makes "a rush for London," where he spends all his money in a very few days as he seeks to exorcise the sensation "that, as if bewitched, we would have to live for ever and ever in that inner harbor" (*Y*, 16; cf. *HD*, 93). Thus, if the middle-aged Marlow's elegiac regret throughout "Youth" is due to the unvoidable fact of temporal process, he nevertheless reserves the idea of timelessness exclusively for the purposes of describing horrible ordeals, as the above examples reveal.

Clearly, he hates and fears time but he cannot bear the feeling that time is not passing. This is the logical impasse of the "Western voice" that continues to operate in the mind of the mature Marlow, causing him to perceive the stillness of the East, "not a light, not a stir, not a sound" (*Y*, 38), only as a deadly threat that parallels the stasis he encountered within the gale off the Lizards and at Falmouth harbor. To Marlow the East is "silent like death" (*Y*, 38). Its quietude conceals a "Nemesis" (*Y*, 41) that offers to negate the "knowledge" and "strength" of "the conquering race" (*Y*, 42). Fittingly, he can recall the sleep of his shipmates on the coast of Java only in lethal terms—the mariners lie "curled on bottomboards, in . . . attitudes of death" (*Y*, 41). Obviously, Marlow's "Western voice" continues to sustain itself by invalidly joining the concepts of death and inactivity, a prejudice he questions profoundly later in the Conrad canon: "Why is it that the stillness of a human being is often so impressive, so suggestive of evil—as if our proper fate were a ceaseless agitation" (*C*, 322).

Marlow's ability to articulate a final valuelessness—"youth, strength, genius, thoughts, achievements, simple hearts—all dies. . . . No matter" (*Y*, 7)—obviously does not prevent him from organizing his perceptions according to the dualistic metaphysics of the West. While spending a night in a lagoon that is "stagnant" yet covered with lovely "blossoms of the lotos," and embedded in the East, diurnal origin of "both light and darkness" (*TU*, 189, 188), the anonymous white man in "The Lagoon" suffers a similar plight. He can bleakly respond to Arsat's grief with the observation that "there is nothing" (*TU*, 203), but when at night he gazes upon the mysterious emptiness, feeling "as though there had been nothing left in the world" (*TU*, 193), he cannot help but perceive it according to the simplistic moral polarity of his heritage: he experiences a "suspicion of evil" that "flowed out into the stillness round him" (*TU*, 193). The difference between the white man and the Moslem polers, who conceive of their master by means of the same sort of inane allegory, seeing him as one "in league with the Father of evil" (*TU*, 190), is therefore not definitive, but only a matter of perspective. None of the men is capable of assimilating the forest's murmur, "the wisdom of . . . immense and lofty indifference" (*TU*, 194). And in a parallel fashion Marlow erects a preposterous hierarchy of "devils" in *Heart of Darkness* (see, e.g., *HD*, 65, 81, 97, 98, 104, 105, 114, 116), entangles himself in an absolutist value judgment concerning lies (which absolute he admits having violated when he lied to Kurtz's "Intended"), and cannot even regard his own compulsive tale-telling apart from participation in a moral dyad, asserting that "for good or evil mine is the speech that cannot be silenced" (*HD*, 97).

In *Lord Jim*, however, Marlow is indeed silenced as he perceives the futile and illusory nature of language itself. Unlike the narrator of *Falk* with his remote architectural reference to a pagoda housing thoughts of "Annihilation" (*T*, 210), Marlow is forced to confront "Annihilation" (*LJ*, 115) at arm's length when, during his conversation with Jewel concerning Jim's fidelity, he "los[es] all . . . words in the chaos of dark thoughts . . . contemplated . . . beyond the pale" and the "world . . . seem[s] to wear a vast and dismal aspect of disorder" (*LJ*, 313). In his urgency to communicate with the girl, Marlow finds that his conception of truth is inadequate—"the winged words of truth drop at your feet like lumps of lead" (*LJ*, 316)—and he is forced to wish for a more potent device. Significantly, he defines that device as a lie: when trying to nullify ambiguity, nothing will suffice but "an enchanted and poisoned shaft dipped in a lie too subtle to be found on earth" (*LJ*, 316). Absurdly, after having tried his best, short of such a lethal shaft, to articulate his truth, his efforts are rejected by Jewel with the accusation "You lie!" (*LJ*, 318). At the point Marlow realizes he needs a lie in order to sustain the truth, he intimates the inauthenticity of that same truth, and he "slip[s] away without another word" (*LJ*, 319). As a suspicion of the irrational and arbitrary nature of his culture threatens to displace his feeble truth, he even refuses to answer Jim's friendly call "You there, Marlow?" in his eagerness to elude the dark, alinguistic "disorder" conjured up by Jewel; and this refusal is appropriate, for Marlow has temporarily lost his identity and is not "there" or anywhere. On this particular unhallowed Sunday Marlow finds it very difficult to sustain his contact with "words . . . the sheltering conception of light and order which is our refuge" (*LJ*, 313), for shortly after his precipitous departure from Jewel he arrives at the grave of Jewel's mother, where language once again is negated along with all sense of community: "The very human speech itself, seemed to have passed away out of existence, living only for a while longer in my memory, as though I had been the last of mankind" (*LJ*, 323). Heretofore he understood in a factual sense that "Patusan had been used as a grave" (*LJ*, 219), but he must now realize the potential for ineffable metaphoric significance this fact bears. Alone, at night, by a burial plot in a murky jungle clearing, his "Western eye, so often concerned with mere surfaces" (*LJ*, 262), is forced to struggle with a sense of cosmic absence, "a great peace, as if the earth had been one grave" (*LJ*, 323; cf. *HD*, 58, 138). This palpable negation is achieved as Marlow contemplates the "lumps of white coral [that] shone round the dark mound like a chaplet of bleached skulls" where "all sound and all movements in the world seemed to come to an end" (*LJ*, 322).

It may seem as though Conrad is employing a hackneyed symbol in using a burial place as the site for such an experience, but this is not the case at all. The grave of Jewel's mother functions in *Lord Jim* in precisely the same manner as the Great Pagoda in *Falk* and the occult statue in "Karain." Conrad keenly appreciates that "straight vision is bad form" (*NLL*, 51), and Marlow's climactic intimation of the void suggests a metaphysical alternative to Occidental linear teleology, with its pathetically strenuous efforts to stand, move, and be "straight" (see *LJ*, 173, 3, 67; cf. 171, 285, 378, 385, 386) during a quest for a meaningful "end" that "exorcises from the house of life the haunting shadow of fate" (*LJ*, 176; cf. 158, 344, 385, 412, 416). Although there is no indication that Marlow understands the coincidence, his description of the grave repeats precisely one of the central icons of Tantric Buddhism which represents the cyclical, annihilatory principle personified under the name of Kāli, "feminine form of the word kāla, meaning 'Time',"[67] as a "black-bodied destructive goddess, garlanded with human heads,"[68] who "resides in the cremation ground, surrounded by corpses."[69] Conrad's acquaintance with this icon cannot be doubted, for Marlow's description echoes even Schopenhauer's citation of the definitive attribute, "the necklace of skulls" (*WWI*, I, 355), a fact that makes the "heads on stakes" (*HD*, 130) surrounding Kurtz's house take on an important new dimension.

But Kāli is a particularly threatening concept only for those who, like Marlow, are vulnerable to Occidental demands for humanly meaningful directions in time that assure the sacredness of the individual. To the traditional Oriental perspective, Kāli directs attention "in the most impressive manner away from the death of the mourned individual to the immortal life of nature" and for this reason displays a prominent phallic dimension also, "signifying that generation and death are essentially correlatives, which reciprocally neutralise and annul each other" (*WWI*, I, 355). Consequently, Kāli is commonly depicted, wearing her garland of skulls, in the midst of sexual intercourse,

> always . . . in inverted posture (i.e., herself on top) with the God Shiva who represents . . . the existential ground endowed with qualities or attributes. This couple rests upon the more remote ground of existence . . . the Brahman which is beyond qualities or attributes. . . . The Goddess, beautiful and terrible at once, straddles the body of one Shiva, who is shown as alive, moving, with the colours of the living. Beneath him lies another Shiva, shown as dead, inert, with the greenish tint of the corpse. He represents the Brahman without qualities. This

scene is usually shown taking place in the cremation ground . . . the place of the dissolution of the self. . . . For it is here that all apparent realities are destroyed— to be born once more.[70]

As Edward W. Said appropriately suggests, "Truth for Conrad was . . . the negation of intellectual differentiation."[71] But to Marlow the grave connotes only meaninglessness, as he valiantly tries to articulate the "visions of remote unattainable truth" he saw "dimly" while he was dispossessed of language, "the truth disclosed in a moment of illusion" (LJ, 323).

Yet, there is still another "grave" on Patusan: once each month the moon, which travels west to east among the stars, rises behind a cleft mountain at the center of the island and "float[s] away above the chasm between the hills like an ascending spirit out of a grave" (LJ, 245; cf. Faerie Queene, III, ii, 24). The night Marlow stumbles upon the grave of Jewel's mother happens to be the very night the moon "ascend[s] . . . like a leisurely rebound" from its burial place (LJ, 322). By juxtaposing the two graves, each with opposite connota- tions, Conrad transcends Marlow's myopic vision by offering a juncture of antitheses. Resurrection and death on a cosmic scale that cancels the individual along with serial time come together as the moonlight illuminates the grave. Significantly, the moon rises from its figurative place of interment "on the third day after the full" (LJ, 220). Although use of the number three in Lord Jim has been correlated with Christ's resurrection, this seems unneces- sary.[72] It is more to the point that at the time when the moon seems to be reborn "as if escaping from a yawning grave in gentle triumph" (LJ, 221) it is already subtly in decline. The same correspondence that relates the first day of the new moon (the dark of the moon) to the full moon symmetrically relates the first appearance of the crescent (which, as every navigator knows, occurs roughly three days after the onset of the dark of the moon) to the time three days after the full moon. Thus, just as the crescent after three days without lunar illumination negates the dark of the moon, so the evening three days after a full moon inaugurates in parallel fashion the cyclical cancellation of moonlight. By causing the moon to rise from its "grave" behind the cleft mountain at this particular time in the lunar cycle and then connecting this emblematic event with the particular moment in the evolution of Marlow's consciousness when he contemplates a grave that threatens to engulf all he knows, Conrad is masterfully conjoining oppositions at two levels, to the detriment of Aristotelian logic and Western teleology. Only inscrutable Orien- tals like Captain Whalley's serang, with a conceptually vacant "unspeculating mind" whose "knowledge [is] absolute and precise" (ET, 228), or the one Malay helmsman from the Patna, with his marvellous abrogation of con- sciousness—"He says he thought nothing" (LJ, 98)—would be able to do justice to such a scene.

Marlow, however, ultimately remains bewildered and cowed by his enigmatic Eastern world. He finally asks Stein to explain to Jewel her lover's inexplicable suicide and then takes psychic refuge in the surface fact of the natural vitality apparent in a nearby bamboo grove, behind which the perplexing Jewel and Stein appropriately vanish: "For my part, I was fascinated by the exquisite grace and beauty of that fluted grove, crowned with pointed leaves and feathery heads, the lightness, the vigour, the charm as distinct as a voice of that unperplexed luxuriating life. I remember staying to look at it for a long time, as one would linger within reach of a consoling whisper" (LJ, 351). Such consolation is figured forth earlier in the same novel by a "garland of leaves and flowers . . . woven about the heads of the slender posts" surrounding the grave of Jewel's mother, and its "whisper" provides relief from frightening terminal places, signaled by fragments of white coral that look like "a chaplet of bleached skulls," where "all sound . . . in the world seemed to come to an end" (LJ, 276, 322). Although he speculates about "a faith mightier than the laws of order and progress" (LJ, 339), Marlow remains aligned with Occidental beliefs, whose more zealous proponents, such as Doramin, use their pieces of white coral constitutively, to build mosques (see LJ, 358), rather than to demarcate the abyss. Hence, he chooses to make the affirmative gesture of speech, even if it is finally to "affirm nothing" since all statements are inevitably written on "greyish foolscap" (LJ, 339–40), a fact that perhaps only Conrad's "delicate Oriental style"[73] can render with grace.

And, indeed, in his correspondence Conrad mockingly invokes a "chinaman of letters" to provide Western minds with the wraith of absolute resolution which they crave, and this fictive sage obliges by making a redemptively nonsensical pronouncement: all human constructs are "transcendental symbolico-positivist with traces of illuminism."[74] This includes the following experimental and revisionary analysis of Typhoon, which attempts to apply with some specificity and thoroughness several of the general concepts presented in the foregoing pages.

Storm and Ship, Circle and Line, East and West

As Ian Watt observes, "Sacred cows invite bull . . . until some contumelious infidel arrives."[1] For Conrad critics there exists no higher bovine divinity than Tom MacWhirr, "a hero in truth, a real, a genuine, and . . . an admirable hero," an "upholder and defender of civilization in its manifest ideals . . . , right on every count."[2] Perhaps MacWhirr is even "the image [of himself that] Conrad wanted to leave behind him,"[3] since, like MacWhirr, the author himself was supposedly an "intellectually simple" man who "didn't theorize . . . because his mind was not equipped to do so."[4] It is well over a decade since a number of excellent synthetical studies of Conrad began to demonstrate the sophistication of his thought,[5] thereby partly correcting the simplistic formulations of Conradian ontology that were long ago presented by M. C. Bradbrook and Thomas Moser, who suggest that Conrad's talent lies in "reducing the complex to the simple" and that his primary ethical concerns can be rendered by essentially platitudinous phrases like "Humanity is important; fidelity is the highest virtue."[6] Yet Tom MacWhirr continues to remain largely secure from contumelies.[7]

The Author's Note to *Typhoon* is an effective aegis, for in it Conrad states, "MacWhirr is not an acquaintance of a few hours, of a few weeks, or a few months. He is the product of twenty years of life. My life" (*T*, vi). This assertion seems firmly to identify the character of MacWhirr with the personality of the hallowed author and to ground the events of the story upon the facts of his personal history. *Typhoon* consequently can be regarded merely as "personal experience *per se*, without that forging of fact and fiction into an art form," an unusually accessible tale that "requires no elaborate interpreting." [8] However, Conrad's prefatory remarks must be understood not as a revelation of definitive sources analogous to Milton's "omnific Word," but rather as only a link in the "chain of displacements" in terms of which J. Hillis Miller defines all novels. Conrad's "displacement of the 'origin' of the story (in historical events or in the life experience of the author) into the fictitious events of the narrative" demonstrates merely that he is operating in the tradition of the Western novel, a tradition in which "works of fiction . . . must always present themselves as what they are not, as some nonfictional form of language . . . validated by its one-to-one correspondence to psychological or historical reality." [9]

Victor Shklovsky suggests that "every work of art comes into existence as a parallel and a contrast to some sort of model."[10] If it is a valid concept that "imagination . . . begins, not where a model is imitated, but where it is deformed,"[11] the well-established critical principle that Conrad's prefatory remarks cannot be taken at face value [12] locates in Conrad's prefaces a high degree of aesthetic innovation insofar as these prefaces depart purposefully from the definitive tradition of "affirm[ing] for . . . [a] novel that . . . solid basis in pre-existing fact, which is associated with the idea of history." [13] Specifically, far from providing reassurance to readers who would identify him personally with a certain mode of behavior, Conrad constantly insulates his art from his personal history. With typical cosmic doubt as to the nature of authenticity itself, Conrad assures the reader that MacWhirr "is perfectly authentic," while asserting "the same of every aspect of the story," a story which dwells upon the presence of a typhoon that is "not a typhoon of my actual experience" (*T*, vi). Conrad thereby insists that his tale be regarded only as an aesthetic fabrication by denying readers comforting biographical sources, just as he firmly resists formulaic reductions because of his acknowledgment of constantly shifting perceptions, as he indicates in a letter to Edward Garnett: "All is illusion—the words written, the mind at which they are aimed, the truth they are intended to express, the hands that will hold the paper, the eyes that will glance at the lines. Every image floats vaguely in a sea of doubt—and the doubt itself is lost in an unexplored universe of uncertainties." [14]

Conrad's indeterminate relationship with his own works has been best summarized by Edward W. Said: 'In each tale . . . Conrad's autobiographical presence plays numerous roles: first as man to whom events happened, as speaker, as listener, then finally as author who at one moment *presents* narrative, negates it by pretending it is speech, then negates that (in his letters) by sounding like Everyman's Favorite Old Novelist."[15] To use Miller's terminology, as Conrad dismantles "the basic metaphor by means of which prose fiction has defined itself, that is, a certain idea of history," he demonstrates his participation in "the practice of prose fiction in its modern form. . . ."[16] Concomitantly, as Conrad reveals his work to be only a "margin-haunted and liminal discourse"[17] that eludes reification, he frees the figure of Tom MacWhirr from the aura of sanctity that a past generation of critics erected around it. No longer to be regarded as an unimpeachable animation of an ethic serving "to remind us of what ought to be, the standard by which Conrad vigilantly judges and condemns what *is*,"[18] when challenged analytically MacWhirr's personality and conduct reveal an obtusely fallible and complexly inconsistent humanity.

Gerard Genette proposes that "all narratives, regardless of their complexity or degree of elaboration . . . can always be considered to be the development of a verbal statement such as I am walking,' or 'He will come,' or 'Marcel becomes a writer.' "[19] If the usual interpretation of MacWhirr's character is accepted, *Typhoon* must be regarded as an elaboration of the following sentence: "An excellent captain runs his vessel directly into a hurricane." Surely this statement contains an internal contradiction. Either the typhoon must be of a particularly treacherous and subtle variety so as not to be detected in advance or the captain must not be an excellent one. The first of these two propositions can be dispensed with quickly. Hurricanes are not one of nature's more elusive phenomena; moreover, the meteorological signs that MacWhirr encounters are sufficiently lucid so as to make impending events obvious to Jukes, to the ship's steward, who brings "without orders the Captain's sea-boots and oilskin coat up to the chart-room" (*T*, 32), and to laymen readers. The world of the novel is one which admits little epistemological confusion. There is no need to fabricate elaborate Marlovian responses under the assumption that "the meaning of an episode [is] not inside like a kernel but outside, enveloping the tale which brought it out only as a glow brings out a haze" (*HD*, 48), for in *Typhoon* there is little question of locating "meaning" since "the earth is the kernel" (*T*, 29), and it can be adequately interpreted, although it is an exacting text. In such a world if the captain of a ship runs into a hurricane he must be a remarkably lousy first officer.

MacWhirr's gross inadequacies can be understood in the light of the simple fact that he commands one of the "wretched steamboats" that Conrad condemns for having negatively altered the "whole psychology of sea travel" (*LE*, 30, 35). By subverting the necessity for true craftsmanship in the handling of a vessel, the "dreary steamboats" (*LE*, 87) cancel "the redeeming and ideal aspect of this bread-winning . . . , the attainment and preservation of the highest possible skill on the part of the craftsmen" (*MS*, 24). Men who know how to handle a sailing vessel well are "masters of the fine art" of getting "the best and truest effect from the infinitely varying moods of sky and sea . . . , an art whose ultimate result remains on the knees of the gods" (*MS*, 31), an art always operating at the edge of annihilation as "the sailing ship's machinery . . . seems to draw its strength from the very soul of the world, its formidable ally, held to obedience by the frailest bonds, like a fierce ghost captured in a snare of something even finer than spun silk" (*MS*, 37). In marked contrast, a steamboat allows "machinery" to annul man's relationship with the elements and "makes her passages on other principles than yielding to the weather and humoring the sea" (*MS*, 72). Steam travel imposes no need for that "intimacy with nature, which is an indispensible condition to the building up of an art"; moreover, the "incertitude which attends closely every artistic endeavour is absent from its regulated enterprise" (*MS*, 30), which "is not so much a contest as the disdainful ignoring of the sea" (*MS*, 72).

The worst influences of a steamship involve a dulling of awareness. A sailing vessel demands that its master live with it in such "intimacy . . . that his senses [are] like her senses, that the stress upon his body [makes] him judge of the strain upon the ship's masts" (MS, 38); to "the man of the masts and sails . . . the sea is not a navigable element, but an intimate companion" (MS, 71). On the other hand, a steamer manifests "simply the . . . use of a captured force, merely another step forward upon the way of universal conquest" (MS, 31). It is a form of transportation that discourages skill on behalf of almost everyone involved. Even stevedoring, "which had been a skilled labor, is fast becoming a labor without the skill" since the cargo of the "modern steamship" is "not stowed in any sense; it is simply dumped . . . through . . . hatchways" (MS, 74). The steamship makes possible only an increase of human arrogance and irresponsibility as a fatuous, "incorrigible mankind hardens its heart in the progress of its own perfectibility" (MS, 72) by depriving itself of occasions in which skills are tested and self-knowledge is gained. It is for these reasons that Conrad, in a document crucial to a proper understanding of Typhoon,[20] vehemently insists that "a voyage . . . out by the Cape and round by the Horn" in a medium-sized sailing vessel of the sort in which the "greatest achievements of Merchant Service seamen have been performed," equipped with "no labor-saving appliances in the shape of steam winches and so on," would be the best training for the men who are "to be perfected as future officers of the finest modern steamships," even if they are "destined never to be out of sight of land for more than a few days in . . . future professional life" (LE, 66, 69, 70).

Conrad to his sorrow knows such advice will appear only shocking to the uncomprehending "minds of men who own and manage fleets of large steamships" (LE, 67), for these men, in "blind trust in material and appliances" and "in deference to commercial and industrial interests," promote what Conrad devastatingly calls "a new kind of seamanship": "If you see anything in the way, by no means try to avoid it; smash it at full tilt" (NLL, 218–19). Conrad's indignation springs from his awareness that the crews and officers of the merchant steamers "have been put by the commercial employers in the impossibility to perform efficiently their plain duty"; indeed, "this is not a problem of boats at all. It is a problem of decent behavior" (NLL, 224–42). Conrad defines "the new seamanship" in an essay entitled "Some Reflections on the Loss of the Titanic," written a decade after Typhoon. The pathetic absurdity of MacWhirr running headlong into a hurricane owing to his lack of respect for "breezes" and "the winds of heaven" and owing to his fear of an unexpectedly large coal bill should he change course (T, 34) is an uncanny, insightful, and definitive anticipation of the causes of one of modern man's most shameful tragedies: "the fatuous drowning of all these people who put their trust in . . . the reckless affirmations of commercial men and mere technicians . . ." (NLL, 214).

An important indication as to the direction Conrad's inquiry takes in Typhoon is this tale's inversion of many of the significant details in The Nigger of the "Narcissus." Having dramatically tested the personality of the laconic but thoroughly perceptive Captain Allistoun, who "know[s] everything . . . of [the] ship's life" (NN, 125), who plies the North Atlantic, where the "best sailors in the world have been born" (MS, 94), who sails (not steams) into ugly weather as a clearly anticipated necessity in order to round the Cape and reach his destination at all, and who must actively and shrewdly resist the irrational disintegration of his crew and make decisions involving the delicate handling of his vessel, Conrad chooses in *Typhoon* to take the measure of Allistoun's alter ego, Tom MacWhirr. MacWhirr is an imperceptive clod who takes command initially as a shuttle-captain put in charge of the *Nan-Shan* on a one-way trip from England to the China Sea, where it and he remain, embedded placidly within "the eternal peace of Eastern sky and sea" (LJ, 13). In marked contrast to the situation on the *Narcissus*, aboard the *Nan-Shan* the captain is the least intelligent member of the crew; his dullness exceeds even that of Singleton, who reads books and profoundly grasps the concept of temporal perspective. MacWhirr is a perfect example of the sort of mariner Conrad feels is a product of the irresponsible commercial interests that fill the sea with steamships supervised by ill-trained officers, for MacWhirr's life is devoid of every experience that Conrad prescribes as necessary for proper training. Never having been "out by the Cape and round by the Horn" (LE, 66) in a meaningful sense, MacWhirr has never encountered anything but "very fine weather" (T, 5) and ships that were "the floating abode of harmony and peace" (T, 4). His life, and consequently his mind, are as dull and static as the quiescent surfaces they traverse, a reflection of the steam-powered vessel that he directs in a simple linear fashion, independent of the winds, which are the sole potential source of aggressive complexity. Just as mountains are used by Conrad in other novels in order to define the protagonists' mental states—the volcano on which Heyst broods, the mountain on Patusan that Jim admires, the rocky height where Renouard proposes to Felicia Moorsom on Malata, and the peak of Higuerota at which Giorgio Viola stares—so MacWhirr's vessel in the same way figures forth his mentality, for *Nan-Shan* means "southern mountain." [21]

The assertion has been made that "*Typhoon* cannot [involve] a symbolic descent into self and into the preconscious" because MacWhirr "remains to the end incapable of genuine introspection. So this storm at least cannot be called an inward one."[22] But the matter is not so simple. C. G. Jung's suggestion that "nothing endangers . . . connection [with the unconscious] more in a man than a successful life"[23] is more pertinent, for it implicitly provides for the possibility that such a connection may in fact dangerously occur. Of course, physical commotion appropriately can operate in Conrad's works as an emblem of unconscious irruption regardless of the respective protagonists' capacities for psychological inquiry and insight. Although MacWhirr may indeed remain insulated from conscious confrontation with inner darkness, the very fact that he purposely runs his ship into a hurricane is a clear dramatization of the extent to which in such an unaware individual irrationality can usurp control of the mind under the guise of prudence and reason.

Devoid of functional abstract concepts of time and probability, MacWhirr is incapable of acting in terms of future possibilities. Were he forced like Captain Allistoun to deal with a nebulous creature named Wait and the confusing moral and temporal situations such a figure precipitates, MacWhirr probably would crack. Fortunately, his crisis evolves as an obvious meteorological analogue of his psychic incapacity, and thus MacWhirr can meet it successfully. Like Jim, who can only deal with adversity in the manner of "a charging bull" (LJ, 3), and the narrator of The Shadow-Line, who early in the novel conceives of life as a line on a chart, a matter only of "blessed simplicity" (SL, 53), MacWhirr, unlike Conrad, is too stupid to recognize how "perplexing are . . . end-on approaches, so infinitely more trying to the men in charge than a frank right-angle crossing" (NLL, 257); thus MacWhirr insanely refuses to avail himself of any intellectual aid to be derived from the accumulated experience of his kind. He distrusts his barometer, a "fundamentally honest" instrument (MS, 97), and rejects his navigation manual because the information it offers does not respond to his definition of "certitude"—a definition as crazily limited as the experience of its formulator, who has only seen "fine weather," and who cannot interpret cosmic signs that suggest the world is about to run at right angles to his expectations, as the ominous "cross swell" does relative to his course (see T, 7, 33). This analogy is further justified by a letter in which Conrad himself cites the phenomenon of a cross swell as a figurative means of denoting the demands made by language for semantic sophistication, the very talent MacWhirr lacks: "words, words, words" are often recalcitrant like "an unruly choppy sea running cross-wise in all the endless shifts of thought." [24]

MacWhirr's rejection of his book defines the extent to which he is out of touch with the community of responsible seamen; and his indifference to the flag under which he sails is of parallel significance. Even the harlequin in Heart of Darkness treasures Towson's manual, although living in a hut over which flies a flag of "unrecognizable tatters" (HD, 98). MacWhirr's apathy toward the absurd Siamese white elephant dramatizes his remoteness from the white, birdlike sailing craft (see NN, 57, 161) that sustain true seamen, who perceive in the "piece of red bunting" a symbol that [holds] up the Edifice" of "stability and purpose [and] continuity of effort" (NLL, 202–4), and who venerate the "Red Ensign [that] prevailed on the high seas to such an extent that one always experienced a slight shock on seeing some other combination of colours blow . . ." (NLL, 202).

Unwilling, and thus not able, to recognize the legitimacy of communal tradition and human emotive responses, MacWhirr stifles both Jukes's negative reaction to the silly appearance of the Siamese flag and his early concern for the coolies' welfare and comfort, and cannot even comprehend a contrary-to-fact grammatical construction (see *T*, 10, 25, 31). Recent linguistic theory elaborates upon precisely what sort of psychic cripple MacWhirr is. In an effort to relate linguistic structures to the act of conceptualizing social relations, Basil Bernstein has distinguished two linguistic codes which he terms *elaborated* and *restricted*. Only the latter is relevant to MacWhirr's use of language:

> When a child learns a restricted code he learns to perceive language . . . not as a set of theoretical possibilities which can be transferred into a facility for the communication of unique experience. Speech is not . . . a means for a voyage from one self to the other. In as much as this is so then areas of the self are not likely to be differentiated by speech and so become the object of special perceptual activity [nor will] the motivations of others . . . serve as starting points for inquiry and verbal elaboration. Of some importance, the identity of the individual will be refracted to him by the concrete symbols of his group rather than creating a problem to be solved by his own unique investigations. . . .[25]

According to Bernstein, the restricted code is likely to be operant in working-class families in which social relationships are founded upon autocratic hierarchy. This code "does not facilitate the verbal elaboration of meaning; it is a code which sensitizes the user to a particular form of social relationship which is unambiguous where the authority is clear-cut and serves as a guide to action."[26] This is precisely the sort of linguistic usage one would expect of a "petty" grocer's son, who is incapable of the most rudimentary understanding of human emotion (MacWhirr fails entirely to anticipate his parents' worry after he leaves home), whose father even thinks him "an ass" and a half-wit (*T*, 5), and who suffers from "an excess of the empirical."[27] MacWhirr suffers, that is, from a limitation that Roman Jakobson calls a "similarity disorder" and describes in the following manner: "Patients of this type 'grasped the words in their literal meaning but could not be brought to understand the metaphorical character of the same words.'"[28]

MacWhirr's obsessively organized life will tolerate no ambiguous categories, no crooked lines. Thus, he is seriously threatened by unpredictable door latches that may permit a sudden violation of neat compartmentalization (*T*, 8, 35), unlike the mystic in *The Shadow-Line*, Mr. Burns, who must always have doors kept open (*SL*, 74, 77).[29] As a result, he is disproportionately annoyed by any suggestion of altering course, since deviations from strict linearity connote to him sailing craft, which he unwarrantably identifies with physical weakness; and his loathing for the book, with its "semi-circles" and "curves," is similarly motivated, for he prefers volumes containing pictures of flags, which permit immediate and absolute solutions to obvious questions. Indeed, he heatedly asserts to Jukes that even if the *Nan-Shan* were powered by sails he would rather let the masts go over the side than change course to meet the swell (see *T*, 32)—an ominous and appropriate echo of the crew under Donkin's influence desiring to cut the masts and turn the *Narcissus* into a drifting hulk (see *NN*, 59, 108; cf. use of *drift*: *NN*, 125, 172), for Mac-Whirr is about as responsible a leader at this point as Donkin would be. An agent of chaos whose very name denotes the offspring of an undifferentiated, primal noise (MacWhirr means "son of whirr"), the captain of the *Nan-Shan* is genealogically related in a psychic sense to that experience of the whirling tempest (see *T*, 64, 77) that he forces himself and his charges to endure at great risk because of what he feels is an unacceptable lack of certitude in barometers and texts, as he steers his "southern mountain" toward the "mountains of water" (*T*, 64, 74) that nearly destroy them all.

Conrad's male protagonists typically employ female analogies [30] when struggling to orient themselves toward that dark, elusive otherness that is their experience of the phenomenal world; and consequently their personal limitations in or near the bedroom become indices of the various directions taken by their flawed ontologies. The letters that frame the main storm narrative in *Typhoon* seem an unimportant aspect of the novel at first, in spite of their prominence as a structural feature. However, these epistles prove to be a significant key to the main characters' respective psychic capacities and susceptibilities. Specifically, MacWhirr's vulnerability to irrationality (amusingly manifested particularly as a resentment of curves) can be traced causally to his inability to develop a vital relationship with femininity; and this problem is revealed in his sterile letters to his wife.

MacWhirr is obsessed by superficial organization. He cannot deal as ship's captain with probable tempestuous eventualities even though barometers are falling, but, absurdly, he never goes ashore without an umbrella (*T*, 4). Like Captain Beard in "Youth" crazily salvaging junk for the underwriters as the *Judea* burns, MacWhirr broods over a coal bill while risking an entire ship, a direct extension of his concern with maintaining the neighbors' opinion of his wife as a being who is "quite superior" (*T*, 14) by renting her an expensive home while at the same time letting the entire human relationship degenerate into meaninglessness. His impotent pedantry is perhaps most effectively dramatized by his decision to give up even the most rudimentary echoes of domestic comfort that are available in his stateroom in order to sleep "in the chart-room," whence, fittingly, "he indited . . . his home letters" (*T*, 15). Just as the rationalistically unbalanced Charles Gould uses the study of mines as a medium for structuring a human relationship while courting Emilia and eventually ends up sleeping at the San Tomé mine rather than at home, so Mac-Whirr marries Lucy upon the occasion of receiving his first command, thus necessarily making a thoughtless choice of wife, and thereafter sleeps among charts, comforting reductions of the phenomenal world to a symmetrical grid, instead of with her. Wedded by preference to navigational facts and inflexible schedule rather than to the unfathomable alterity of womanhood, MacWhirr when writing home can only account "in minute detail each successive trip" of the *Nan-Shan* (*T*, 14). Thus, he talks ultimately only to himself about himself and perverts any potentially genuine emotive remarks, through the empty chronological fidelity of his monthly missals, until his formulaic reiterations become "worn-out things . . . of a faded meaning" (*T*, 13). Surely none of the fittings on the *Nan-Shan* would be allowed to become nearly as shoddy as the verbiage of his letters. Indeed, MacWhirr reveals beyond question where his commitment lies when he immediately discovers a flawed lock on the cabin door but consistently fails even to think of locking the desk in which he keeps his intimate correspondence (*T*, 8, 15).[31]

Solomon Rout, on the other hand, has "enough imagination to keep his desk locked" (*T*, 15), and his communication with his wife contains the sort of philosophical speculation that is reminiscent of the biblical Solomon and that elicits "joyous," responsive shouts from the "jolly woman of forty" (*T*, 15) to whom he is married. Unlike MacWhirr, he refuses to discuss shipboard matters with his wife and omits specific mention even of the great typhoon. Most significant, however, is the "increased longing for the companionship of the jolly woman" (*T*, 97) that Rout expresses by letter after having experienced the storm. Although his wife does not understand the reason for such a statement and can only judge sympathetically that if he still wants her "he's well" (*T*, 97), it is clear that the chief engineer confronts his mortality during the voyage, realizes that "we are not growing younger" (*T*, 97), and consequently desires even closer communion with his wife while there is still time. Rout's vital marital relationship indicates that he both acknowledges the legitimacy of strong emotion and is capable of acting effectively in terms of visceral urgency. Appropriately, he controls the potent breast of the ship meticulously, working among "skeleton limbs" (*T*, 69) and firelight glowing "like a pool of flaming blood" (*T*, 70), antipode of MacWhirr's chart-room and wheelhouse, the ship's "head" (*T*, 64).

Jukes has no women whatsoever in his life, and in this way stands in partial contrast to MacWhirr, with a mercenary wife and "her abject terror of the time when her husband would come home . . . for good" (*T*, 14) and a dreary, "colourless" daughter (*T*, 95); and in direct contrast to Rout, who has positive relationships with his humane and committed wife and mother. Jukes is given to spontaneous and uncomprehended irrational outbursts, as the emblematic absence of feminine influence in his life suggests would occur. However, his imaginative sophistication causes his outbursts to have different occasions and take different expressive directions from those of MacWhirr, thus preventing the two from understanding one another. For Jukes, language is indeed a medium for "a voyage from one self to the other," a way of defining and grasping "areas of the self," and consequently he can elaborate on experience for hours, an ability that only exasperates MacWhirr (see *T*, 17–18). Yet Jukes cannot employ his refined conceptual abilities in order to cope with his own and others' manifestations of irrationality. He conceives of his personal behavior as eminently intelligible and judges those who fail to comprehend him as ultimately lacking in reason and intellect, therefore as being "stupid" (*T*, 102), just as MacWhirr feels his decision to ignore all warnings and continue on a straight course is a function of sane reasoning and therefore condemns accepting the conflicting advice of others as akin to "listening to a crazy man" (*T*, 35).

But the plight of Jukes and MacWhirr is extended even further in the personality of the second mate, whose one-dimensional rationality coupled with a self-pitying imagination makes him even more vulnerable than Jukes to the assaults of inner and outer disorder. An exaggerated composite of Jukes and MacWhirr, the second mate writes letters to no one and refuses to speak (see *T*, 28–29). Appropriately, the violence of uncontrolled unconscious dynamism is constantly at the surface of his personality to the extent that he seems always to be "raging inwardly" (*T*, 28) like "a mean little beast" (*T*, 29). But his animalism reflects more his attitude and conduct than his physique. He is recalcitrant and eventually assaults his captain (*T*, 68). Relative to life at sea he is a physical and spiritual eunuch; like Chaucer's Pardoner, he has "no hair on his face" (*T*, 27). Exemplifying a psychic dead end, the second mate's sterile bestiality connects him in a contrasting manner with the boatswain, who significantly has a wife and daughters to whom he is quite attached (*T*, 61), yet who crawls "on all fours" resembling "an elderly ape" with "paws," "furry forearms," and "grizzled pelt on his chest," and a "menacing demeanour" (*T*, 49); and with the second engineer, who descends to his post by "dropp[ing] into the dark hole with a whoop" (*T*, 24), and who passionately "curses . . . all things on earth including his own soul, ripping and raving, and all the time attending to his business" (*T*, 71). These parallels make possible delicate psychological distinctions. Like Solomon Rout, the boatswain and second engineer contribute greatly to the ship's welfare because they are able to indulge in irrational behavior while consistently refusing to surrender their humanity. Thus, they transmute vital disorder into an essential support for rational ends, and stand in varying degrees of contrast to MacWhirr, Jukes, and the second mate, men who have primarily negative relationships with their own irrational energy and the world's external immensities.

Lacking any viable understanding of the alogical elements within the human soul, MacWhirr is doomed to collide with an external upheaval of the elements in the form of the typhoon, for the meeting is merely a reenactment in the phenomenal world of MacWhirr's unrealized, and therefore potentially destructive, irrationality. Apparently Conrad is intuitively aware of the

> psychological rule [that] says that when an inner situation is not made conscious, it happens outside, as fate. That is to say, when the individual . . . does not become conscious of his inner contradictions, the world must perforce act out the conflict [since] when a part of the psyche is split off from consciousness it is only

apparently inactivated; in actual fact it brings about a possession of the personality, with the result that the individual's aims are falsified in the interests of the split-off part.[32]

It is clear that MacWhirr constantly loses his control in many minor but revealing ways. For example, he piously resents the second engineer's cursing and snobbishly condemns him for a "profane man," saying, "The heat does not make me swear," whereupon he continues: "Damme! I'll fire him out of the ship if he don't look out" (*T*, 25). On another occasion, frustrated by his inability to find "at once the opening for inserting his foot" in his boots, he kicks "viciously" at his shoes for daring to be "scurrying from end to end of the cabin . . . playfully" (*T*, 36), all the while never sharing Marlow's essential insight that "a boat on the high seas . . . bring[s] out the Irrational that lurks at the bottom of every thought, sentiment, sensation, emotion" (*LJ*, 121). Consistently blind to the disorder latent within the simplistic logic he uses to define acceptable conduct, MacWhirr rejects his navigation manual. He scorns the authors' supposed fear of "breezes" and "the winds of heaven . . . [which] seem[s] to [him] the maddest thing" (*T*, 34), while he orders his vessel into a hurricane because of bullish resentment of curved lines and his own fear of an unexpectedly large coal bill, thus following with devastating precision the dictates of Conrad's "new seamanship: when in doubt try to ram fairly—whatever's before you" (*NLL*, 220). This is rationality in the service of madness, as Conrad indicates by revealing the slippery foundations of MacWhirr's logic as analogous merely to superstition when the captain's condemnation of his book is mockingly described as a "confession of faith" (*T*, 35).

Far from being a redemptive "voice of reason,"[33] MacWhirr is scarcely fit for command, and his ship survives the typhoon through no fault of his own. The captain's decision to quell the disturbance that breaks out below decks when the coolies grow desperate and struggle to keep their balance and preserve the hard-earned contents of their sea chests is commonly lauded, for example, as a defense "of civilization in its manifest ideals,"[34] a suppression of a "threat . . . posed from below" to the ship's welfare.[35] But the facts of the matter differ radically from these interpretations. MacWhirr's obsession that the coolies be restrained is entirely irrelevant to the survival of the ship, for the disorder is limited to the virtual prison where the coolies have been confined and has no effect upon the crew, who know nothing about it. Moreover, the coolies are not actually pitted against one another in combat, but rather are "fighting only for their footing" (*T*, 78); they offer "no resistance" (*T*, 78) to the crew and harm Jukes not at all when he accidentally falls into their midst (see *T*, 77). MacWhirr's supposed preservation of cultural order is a function merely of the captain's acceptance of wrong information, for he believes the coolies to be battling to the death and cannot bear the idea of such a situation aboard his ship even "if [he] knew she hadn't five minutes to live" (*T*, 88).

No better dramatization than this exists in Conrad's writings of the way

Conrad conceives of the standards of civilization to be only a version of the legendary emperor's clothes, "a vain sticking up for appearances, as though one were anxious about the cut of one's clothes in a community of blind men."[36] To praise MacWhirr as a protector of civilized values in the face of his conspicuous responsibility for both the external and (therefore) internal uproars is about as amusingly invalid as to offer condemnation of the tumbling coolies for having rejected "civilized judicial procedure,"[37] as if it is an index of their corrupt and riotous nature that they do not halt all physical motion and redistribute hundreds of coins during a hurricane in a manner fulfilling the best traditions of Western middle-class prudence.

Just as MacWhirr is ignorant of his own madness, so he fails to notice the characterological changes the typhoon forces upon him.[38] Perhaps the most obvious of these behavioral shifts is MacWhirr's sudden propensity to talk. As he approaches the ontic center that the eye of the hurricane figures forth, Mac-Whirr is dispossessed of lingual stability by the typhoon's alinguistic vortices: "Circles [that] do not speak, they tell only of the inconceivable . . . , they enclose a blankness even as they seem partly to be excluding it."[39] MacWhirr also finds that casually appropriated meaning "will not do precisely because you have not had to bear the pain and responsibility of creating it."[40] Like others of Conrad's characters in the midst of an orientational crisis, MacWhirr is becoming acquainted with a mode of language that has been defined as "the only proper response to unspeaking nature and to the essentially preverbal character of all experience." [41]

MacWhirr must discover that Merleau-Ponty calls that "constitutive language which emerges when the constituted language, suddenly . . . out of equilibrium, reorganizes itself."[42] This is achieved when he becomes a "voice, forced and ringing feebly, but with a penetrating effect of quietness in the enormous discord of noises" (T, 44). From "some remote spot . . . beyond the black wastes of the gale" (T, 44), that is, MacWhirr in his sheer persistence forges what to Merleau-Ponty is "the meaning of words [which] must be finally induced by . . . a kind of deduction from a gestural meaning, which is immanent in speech."[43] MacWhirr can now meaningfully use the subjunctive form of verbs to measure doubt in terms of alternate versions of futurity (see use of may: T, 48, 60), a feat the captain who initially set out on the voyage would not have been capable of because of a conceptual imprisonment within superficial definitions of actuality and present time (see T, 4, 6, 9). Moreover, he discourses at length with Jukes, who regards the event as "a miracle" (T, 34); mutters to himself (T, 86) as he discovers that things he "wouldn't have believed" (T, 84) have in fact occurred; and develops as an outgrowth of his modified relationship with language a stronger trust in "the books" (T, 81) and an ability to seriously consider probabilities that earlier he would have dismissed summarily. That is, the primary test MacWhirr undergoes is semiotic, a matter of conceptualization. His skills as administrator or navigator are largely irrelevant. This is why the disorder within the ship remains ever remote from his physical presence and understanding, and why he has no navigational options whatsoever once he makes the initial gross decision not to change course.

An even more significant change that involves but ultimately transcends MacWhirr's character is MacWhirr's allowing the course of the *Nan-Shan* to alter without his awareness in spite of his previous absolute refusal to change the course voluntarily. Conrad presents the relevant details in such a way as to cause them to be easily overlooked, and this is thematically appropriate, for the alteration of the ship's course is another example of how the storm very subtly qualifies MacWhirr's absolutism and reveals him to be personally out of control in spite of his rationalistic pretentions. While brooding resentfully over his navigational manual, MacWhirr discovers that "the centre of the [typhoon] bears eight points off the wind" (*T,* 33), which defines the Coriolis force. As yet there is no wind, but when it arrives it fortuitously strikes the ship "right ahead," without any change in course having been made to compromise with the weather (*T,* 38). This means that the eye of the hurricane is about eighty degrees to the starboard side of the ship, and the *Nan-Shan* is running at a dangerous tangent to the center of the circular storm. Due to the uproar, however, there is great uncertainty as to the vessel's precise bearing, for "the compass-card [swings] far both ways . . . and sometimes seem[s] to whirl right around" (*T,* 64). Consequently, by the time the enormous "wall of water" (*T,* 74) running ahead of the typhoon hits the ship, the course has deviated gradually so as now to be oriented directly toward the center of the storm; and this is the sole reason why the *Nan-Shan* survives. In order for his ship to live, MacWhirr's trite, absolutist Occidental dictate that one must keep "facing it—always facing it" (*T,* 89) is forcibly qualified by a storm that follows a linear course but is defined by violent circular winds that blow at almost a right angle to its linear progress. Thus, to face one thing is not to face another, although MacWhirr never consciously realizes this; and Conrad's masterfully conceived symbolic collision between a static and simplistic human fixation and a multidimensional upheaval of the elements emphatically asserts that flexibility is a prerequisite for survival in an ambiguous cosmos that by definition must assault and nullify dogma.

This thematic concern is typical of Conrad's Eastern tales that examine the psychic fate of Western man when the "ideals of modern civilization . . . , out of key with the fundamental relativism of the phenomenal world" and sanctioned only by "a spurious philosophy of progress and linear historicism," [44] are challenged. Unlike Almayer and Willems, MacWhirr never is blighted by a recognition of the discrepancy between "his intellectual ability to plan the future and his actual power to control its course"[45] because he gets through the typhoon (Almayer and Willems must sit and wish for redemptive linearity while staring at a river), and because MacWhirr's wooden mind is practically invulnerable.

The initial Genettean proposition can now be modified into a logically consistent statement: "An inept captain runs his vessel directly into a hurricane." But this formulation is only partially adequate, for it fails to take into account the specific temporal setting of the novel: the action of the story takes place on Christmas Eve (see *T*, 94). Since the date of MacWhirr's passage through the hurricane cannot be incorporated functionally into the foregoing analysis, the parameters of the analysis clearly need to be made more inclusive.

Reduction of a conflict to a direct collision between two neatly defined, physical entities is a rarity in Conrad's fiction and in the case of *Typhoon* functions as a trope for the impercipience the tale examines. The complexity of MacWhirr's unconscious, compulsive motivation is qualified by his conscious mind, which is nearly as dull and vacant as the elements it obstinately resists. MacWhirr is capable only of understanding oppositions in terms analogous to solstitial extremes, writing, " 'The heat here is very great.' Or: 'On Christmas day . . . we fell in with some icebergs' " (*T*, 5). Attempts to identify such behavior as the dramatization of an ethic that Conrad heartily approves have extended the specifics of MacWhirr's irresponsible and helpless triumph in the wrong direction, however. He is not an allegorical representation of personalistic standards. Rather, he functions, along with his vessel and crew, as the protagonist in a modern reworking of the myth of *sol invictus* confronting the threat of the winter solstice.[46] For this reason Conrad models the character of MacWhirr after a common heroic anti-type the most famous example of which is perhaps Parsifal, the "pure fool," who is able to accomplish amazing physical feats precisely because he is free from nearly all challenges arising from inner sophistication. The consequent discrepancy between the absurdly limited (human) and awesomely unconquerable (mythic) dimensions of MacWhirr, "a hero who triumphs by virtue of deficiency,"[47] demands a highly complex response from the reader, who is never permitted to separate these conflicting characterological attributes after the convenient fashion of the present analytic distortions. Ultimately, the most useful definition of MacWhirr's paradoxical character is provided indirectly by Conrad himself in a letter in which he admits his "love [for] the marionettes that are without life, that come so near to being immortal," that are "heroic, super-human, fascinating" with their "impassibility in love, in crime, in mirth, in sorrow." [48]

In *Typhoon* Conrad examines the clash between conscious simplicity and undifferentiated chaos in terms of the most uncomplicated paradigm of all: the struggle of light with darkness. In order to establish this mythic foundation Conrad causes the action of his story to occur on Christmas Eve (see *T*, 94), the *natalis mundi*, the time of the sun's yearly battle with the *draco caelestis* which seeks to extinguish it. And he creates the *Nan-Shan*, its wheelhouse and chart-room managed by the impotently rational MacWhirr and its innards controlled by the vital and passionate engineers, as a symbol of human consciousness whereby stubborn rationality and dynamic intuition are rendered by means of the spatial metaphor of the ship's various levels and their respective functions. This composite representation of psychic structure is then imperiled by chaotic, unconscious usurpation in the form of the hurricane and its effects upon the ship and crew. Thus, *Typhoon* is a work of art in which distinctions between internal and external are deprived of conventional significance, and the novel's entire cosmos is reconstituted analogically so as to figure forth Conradian psychology. As in his other Eastern tales, Conrad "locates his [protagonists] in psychological environments where their thoughts and feelings are anatomized . . . ; his backgrounds are not objective recreations of tropical realities" but rather are "containing worlds [that define] distinct modes of existence."[49] By assimilating every aspect of *Typhoon* into the category of psychic events Conrad can dramatize figuratively, through the effects of a gale that is "a composite symbol of both natural and human evil,"[50] the irruption of the disorderly unconscious that MacWhirr experiences personally.

This idea can be further clarified by briefly applying Jung's assertions that "water is the commonest symbol for the unconscious" and "the sun . . . usually denotes consciousness," for the story then suggests a dramatization of the diligent confrontation of the ego with its subliminal sources, a process Jung terms *individuation:*

> The conscious mind does not embrace the totality of a man, for this totality consists only partly of his conscious contents, and for the other and far greater part, of his unconscious, . . . is of indefinite extent with no assignable limits. . . . (I have called this process of realization the "individuation process.") So far as the personality is still potential, it can be called transcendent, and so far as it is unconscious, it is indistinguishable from all those things that carry its projections[;] . . . the unconscious personality merges with [the] environment in accordance with [a] *participation mystique.*[51]

The crucial psychological law that activates this process (of which MacWhirr remains ever oblivious) is "the necessity of reconciling the conscious and the unconscious parts of the psyche,"[52] of discovering "a right relation to the nonpersonal energy that manifests itself . . . in . . . instincts, and in all those experiences, arising either in [the] environment or within [the self], which have . . . power to . . . arouse . . . unruly or compulsive emotions." [53]

The blurring of confines separating subjective from objective events can best be seen by observing how the novel's narrative perspective makes no consistent rhetorical distinctions between the crew, the ship, and the storm. MacWhirr ridiculously kicks "viciously" (*T,* 36) at his shoes as the squall strikes with "startling viciousness" (*T,* 39). Supporting one another in the wind, Jukes and MacWhirr seem like "two hulks lashed stem to stern together" (*T,* 46), while the ship is assaulted with "hate" by the sea and is "like a living creature thrown to the rage of a mob" (*T*, 47), "no longer struggling intelligently" (*T*, 53), "gone mad with fright" (*T*, 39). The coolies are connected imagistically with the very elements when, as a "raging" (*T*, 56) mob, they cause "sounds of the tempest" and cry out in a "gust of hoarse yelling" (*T*, 57) and "roll . . . [about] like a boulder" (*T*, 78) because of the "mountains of water" (*T*, 64, 74) that hit the *Nan-Shan* like "an avalanche" (*T*, 39) and the "darkness [that is] absolutely piling itself upon the ship" (*T*, 90).

MacWhirr and his ship share a common destiny as they are tested by elemental forces that figure forth the menacing unconscious as archetypal feminine: the sea is both etymologically and phonetically connected with the nouns *mother* and *fate* and the verb *to die*,[54] facts that reveal ancient analogical relationships that are congruent with Conrad's symbolic contrivances. Moreover, the very word *typhoon* is linked with the destructive Typhon,[55] the *aqua abyssi*, a legendary opponent of the solar hero [56] and inversion of Tryphon, the healing sea deity.[57] Appropriately, therefore, the approach and presence of the storm are presented primarily by means of descriptions that involve apocalyptic annihilation of celestial light: the sun initially is "pale and without rays," shining with "a strangely indecisive light" (*T*, 21) like "a queer white misty patch in the sky" (*T*, 6), appearing "unnatural" (*T*, 24) and "lurid" while casting "faint and sickly shadows" (*T*, 22) "as if millions of centuries elapsing since the morning had brought it near its end" (*T*, 26); and the *Nan-Shan* sails toward the tempest also "floundering . . . like an exhausted creature driven to its death" (*T*, 26), a descriptive mode suggesting that the two entities suffer a common assault from the primordial "blackness ahead of the ship . . . the starless night of the immensities beyond the created universe" (*T*, 29) that descends "like the sudden smashing of a vial of wrath" (*T*, 40; cf. Revelation, chap. 15f.), "a catastrophic disturbance" of such potence "that the end of the world [is] to be finally accomplished" (*T*, 20).

Clearly, Conrad wishes the elemental uproar in *Typhoon* to connote not only a classic epic-descent on behalf of MacWhirr and his ship, but also the possibility of a cosmic eradication of all meaningful form as the distinction between the firmaments seems about to vanish and the stars appear "to hang very near the earth" (*T*, 26) and are "blurred . . . , as if returning to the fiery mist of [their] beginning" (*T*, 88), while "the whole atmosphere" seemingly "roar[s] away from the tenebrous earth" (*T*, 46). The logical necessity for this is dictated by the previously mentioned depiction of the entire physical universe (men, ship, and storm) as a composite symbol of human psychic structure, a convention that forces a correlation between successful usurpation by the unconscious and a return through an inverse creation event to chaos.

Amidst the clash of opposites in *Typhoon* emphatic threats are presented to all of the major archetypal icons of consciousness, "the light, the sun, the head, and the eye."[58] The voyage of the *Nan-Shan* toward the north at the winter solstice, of course, confirms astronomically the figurative assaults on the sun that Conrad fabricates as perceptual analogues to describe the appearance of the approaching storm. But the lights on board are also attacked by "the black wastes of the gale" (*T*, 44). No sooner does the typhoon strike than all exposed members of the crew are trapped in darkness: "a tongue of air scurrie[s] in and lick[s] out the flame of [MacWhirr's] lamp" (*T*, 37) at the same time that "the sailors, dazed and dismayed," take shelter in a "very black, cold, and dismal" alleyway and "whine after a light" (*T*, 54); later even below decks where the coolies are confined "one of the lamps had gone out" (*T*, 62), and still another is extinguished in the very heart of the ship, the engine room, during the crisis when "she dip[s] into the hollow straight down, as if going over the edge of the world" (*T*, 74). The temporal progression is significant. As the vessel draws ever nearer to the center of the hurricane, the influences negating light penetrate ever more deeply into the vitals of the *Nan-Shan*, but with only partial success, a sign of the ship's ultimate invincibility.

The struggle to preserve luminescence during the night of 24–25 December defines a major motif in the novel and directly recalls the paradigm of *sol invictus* in combat with the annihilatory celestial dragon. Although driven downward by the storm, the light persists both in the coolies' chaotic chamber and in the "vastness, peace and brilliance of the engine-room" (*T*, 71), lair of chief engineer Solomon Rout and his cursing, passionate second. However, the lamps among the coolies are not practically accessible to the crew and are dominated by the typhoon's influence in the form of the surrounding riot even though they continue to shine. Indeed, it is as if the very darkness itself were actively seeking to keep these sources of illumination from aiding the crew, for the entrance to the " 'tween-deck" limbo where the tumbling, incomprehensible Chinamen are held in suspension is guarded by a coal bunker, a veritable condensation of negation, "being perfectly and impenetrably black" (*T*, 55), and containing a deadly threat in the form of "a heavy iron bar" that, like "a wild beast" (*T*, 55), is viciously "striking here and there, always in the neighbourhood of [the] head" (*T*, 56). Like other chthonic guardians such as Cerberus or the Hydra (both offspring of Typhon and Echidna, the "she-viper"),[59] the consuming darkness defends its stronghold aboard the *Nan-Shan* and vigorously opposes human effort to renew the light. Bestially endangering (see *T*, 22, 23, 55) men's heads both on deck ("The wind would get hold of [Jukes's] head and try to shake it off" [*T*, 49]) and in the coal bunker, the storm assaults consciousness in an archetypally significant manner. Even the boatswain's original determination to "get a light, if he were to die for it" (*T*, 55), from the coolies' chamber, is nullified by the impact of his discovery of a shipboard chaos which seemingly equals the one raging outside, as the darkness overwhelms still another rational intent.

Illumination appears topside only briefly when MacWhirr strikes several matches to check his instruments (see *T*, 84–85). Although his serenity amidst the storm exists for the crew as a figurative means of sustaining the light, Mac-Whirr's "quietness like the serene glow of a halo" (*T*, 46) is not adequate in itself to the task of preserving the crew's rational stability and the vessel's life. Only in the company of the engineers, who strive mightily within the ship's vitals to maintain motion and control, is the light truly available for meaningful use. These men, significantly, are supervised by a giant of lively persistence, Solomon Rout, who is "almost invariably the tallest man on board every ship he join[s]" (*T*, 11). Rout is not intended primarily to be an echo of the biblical wise man, for the chief engineer feels that "wonders will never cease" (*T*, 96), whereas the traditional Solomon supposedly made the famous assertions that "all is vanity" and "there is no new thing under the sun" (Ecclesiastes 1:2, 9). Not called Solomon but rather "old Sol" and "Father Sol" (*T*, 11, 96), precisely the names that have been assigned to the sun for eons in Western culture, the chief engineer in his vital pugnaciousness typifies the primordial solar hero, as his last name implies, for he fearlessly and wisely engages with and routs (see *T*, 40) the darkness and the storm, making possible the attainment of "a bright sunshiny day" (*T*, 91).

Typhoon is a remarkable part of the Conrad canon because of the high degree of congruence between trope and literal fact which its narrative technique makes possible. When Lingard feels himself, under the influence of Mrs. Travers, "whirled high in the midst of an uproar and as powerless as a feather in a hurricane" (*Res*, 179), General Santierra perceives a "hurricane of stampeded men" (*SS*, 64), and James Wait coughs "like a hurricane" (*NN*, 24), an unfathomable semantic gap between the vehicles and tenors of these figures of speech must be crossed in the act of interpretation, for at the moments when the comparisons are made no literal tempests exist. To an indeterminate extent each reader must search his own stock of attributes for the category of "hurricane" in an effort to apply several of these attributes in a selective and distorted manner to the categories of "emotional response," "mob," and "cough" and thereby restore a measure of the semantic coherence that was originally fractured by the tropes. On the other hand, when the boatswain of the *Nan-Shan* discovers the struggling Chinamen as "a tempestuous tumult" with "gusts of screams . . . and the tramping of feet mingling with the blows of the sea" (*T*, 77), the metaphoric content of the description is validated literally by a direct casual connection between the external storm and the uproar on board; and this causality is emphasized rhetorically at the outset of the passage when the appearance of the passengers' struggles suggests that "an eddy of the hurricane, stealing through the iron sides of the ship, had set all these bodies whirling like dust" (*T*, 77).

Conrad seldom permits such convenient solution of interpretational enigma. Applications of the concept of "darkness" to the text of *Heart of Darkness* can be perhaps infinitely varied owing to the indeterminacy of metaphoric limits. But light literally vanishes from both the heavens and the exposed portions of the ship in *Typhoon;* and if the men experience a resultant demoralization, their mood vanishes with the departure of the storm and the rising of the sun. State of mind and meteorology are causally related and thus saved from the limitless polysemy generated by merely analogical relationships. As their letters and conduct reveal, the crewmen of the *Nan-Shan* are stable in the sun after the tempest. Unlike Marlow, they suffer no haunting perceptions of a figurative darkness in broad daylight. Although *Typhoon* "rehearses the familiar scenario of man's plunge into the abyss" that Conrad employs "at least once in every Eastern tale . . . to mediate some encounter with nothingness—to evoke . . . a fall out of time,"[60] the descent of the *Nan-Shan* into "the awful depth" (*T,* 74) is an event of primarily physical import. It is that impalpable Conradian point of "uncomplicated coincidence between intention, work, and deed [where] the ghost of a fact . . . can be put to rest."[61] The bodies of the crew follow the ship "into the hollow straight down, as if going over the edge of the world" (*T,* 74), but their minds remain largely unscathed by the sort of debilitating figurative plunges that ruin, for example, Almayer, who feels "year after year, he had been falling, falling, falling" (*AF,* 99); Willems, who feels 'like one . . . falling down a smooth and rapid declivity" (*OI,* 78); and Whalley, who discovers fatally that "all his spotless life had fallen into the abyss" (*ET,* 319).

When regarded according to interpretational criteria provided by modern psychology, the very physical structure of the typhoon correlates with a departure from insightful conscious growth. According to Jung, the circle motif or "mandala" is the archetype of psychic wholeness. Its severe restricting pattern provides compensation for psychic disorder by relating the often contradictory contents of the circle (or totality of the self) by means of concentric arrangement, to a central point, which, to the extent that the mandala renders a successful integration of conscious and unconscious, is typically defined by an intense light.[62] Moreover, a mandala will often incorporate a pattern suggesting that the circle is revolving about its center. When present, this is a most important detail, for "in general, a leftward movement indicates movement toward the unconscious, while a rightward (clockwise) movement goes toward consciousness."[63] Thus, MacWhirr's nocturnal passage through the center of a storm revolving in a counterclockwise direction (as all hurricanes do in the northern hemisphere) is a symbolic configuration indicating that the journey of the *Nan-Shan* is not productive of any profound increase of awareness.

In this respect, Conrad violates in *Typhoon* both the classical and modern psychological models of a *nekyia,* for after his descent and emblematic return "somewhere from the bottom of the sea" (*T,* 91) MacWhirr, a solstitial but not soular hero, reaps few lasting refinements in understanding. His mind echoes that of the idiot boy, Stevie, who compulsively draws circles (*SA,* 187) but fails to partake of their visionary potential, quite unlike Ansell in Forster's *The Longest Journey*, who draws "with the square a circle, and with the circle a square, and inside that another circle, and inside that another square," and who locates transcendence in "the one in the middle of everything, that there's never room enough to draw." Upon his "southern mountain," with the sea below, clouds on all sides, and moonlight gilding all visible surfaces, Mac-Whirr presides unthinkingly over a setting that parallels the one that occasions Wordsworth's vision on Mount Snowden. Of all Conrad's characters, Mac-Whirr is the one, comically, who has most direct access to a traditional ontic center-point as he sails through the mystic dome-shaped eye of the hurricane. This adventure corresponds significantly with Don Quixote's plumbing of Montesinos' cave and Bottom's confrontation with the fairies, for MacWhirr is similarly incapable of recognizing his situation or of commenting upon it; and this is epistemologically appropriate, since there is in Conrad's universe ultimately nothing to be said anyhow. Unlike Marlow, who is frustrated at his own inability to talk about his experience of the edge of the abyss into which he envisions Kurtz mentally falling (see *HD*, 149), MacWhirr and Jukes share the intuitive and sad response of the drab Davidson at the end of *Victory*, recognizing, indeed, there is "nothing to be done" (*T*, 45; see *V*, 412).

Although intellectually ludicrous personally, the inarticulate MacWhirr within his typhoon is perhaps the most clear dramatization extant of the ultimate implications of the Conradian metaphysic, which typically purges its fictional world of the redemptive presumptions of Western linear inflexibilities by immersing them in an obscure and cyclical resiliency that reveals them to be mere insubstantial psychic pollutants, indeed, no more than "a dark smudge, a cross-shaped stain, upon the shifting purity of the mist" (*TU*, 116). Everyone aboard the *Nan-Shan* forgot the Nativity.

GENERIC CONTEXTS
Some Versions of Romance

Many a man has heard or read and believes that the earth goes round the sun; one small blob of mud among several others, spinning ridiculously with a waggling motion like a top about to fall. This is the Copernican system, and the man believes in the system without often knowing as much about it as its name. But while watching a sunset he sheds his belief; he sees the sun as a small and useful object, the servant of his needs and the witness of his ascending effort, sinking slowly behind a range of mountains, and then he holds the system of Ptolemy. He holds it without knowing it.

—Conrad, *Notes on Life and Letters*

Toward Defining a Fundamental Intrageneric Tension: Teleological and Dysteleological Romance

Abstract definitions of any genre are often practically useless because of the high degree of interpretational variability made possible by generalities. By their very existence such definitions imply distortively that the complicated temporal and conceptual relationships that must be sustained between an evolving form and a descriptive terminology attempting to specify and account for that form can be captured paradigmatically. Moreover, the postclassical and coincidental origins of the romance genre lie concealed amidst a welter of linguistic accidents that prevent the location of any primal inception. There exist only semantic variables as the Old French *romans* evolves into a generic concept:

> The term "romance" in the early Middle Ages meant the new vernacular
> languages derived from Latin, in contradiction to the learned language, Latin itself.
> *Enromancier, romancar, romanz* meant to translate or compose books in the ver-
> nacular. The book itself was then called *romanz, roman,* romance, *romanzo.*
> Then the meaning of the word extended to include the qualities of the literature in
> these tongues, in contrast to Latin literature or works composed in Latin. Thus, in
> old French, *romant, roman,* means "courtly romance in verse," but literally
> "popular book." [1]

That is, definitive emphasis was gradually displaced from the linguistic medium to the content. The act of writing in the vernacular, *en romanz,* began, around the time of Chretien de Troyes, to pale in significance before the act of writing a *romans,* a narrative with a certain kind of content.

Interestingly, what began as an emphatically secular medium rapidly became identified as perhaps the most effective means whereby man's understanding of cosmic absolutes can be clarified, sustained, and celebrated. The works of Ariosto and Spenser are, of course, definitive of the way Christian romance typically dramatizes human limitations in the presence of demonic, mutable inauthenticity. To accomplish this end, the

> romance vision [is] almost inevitably [founded upon] a foreground world of "the
> Actual," which [is] full of . . . confusion; but its structure [is] completed by a sure
> sense of "the Real," the abiding . . . , a world of certain truth and order, tradition
> and logic, [evoked] at the precise moments that [the] foreground action [is] pre-
> senting in all its folly the world of the merely "actual" — the particular and the con-
> tingent, dominated by the absurd. [2]

Such penetration of the mortal "actual" by the transcendent "real" is typically anatomized and solemnized in romance. A naive protagonist frequently must be measured against an ultimate presence as he participates in a varying sequence of mundane psychological experiences that in their modulations suggest fallen seasonal cycles, and from which he finally must emancipate himself at the same moment he learns how to leave behind cyclical, earthbound mutability. It is at this moment that, in the words of Northrop Frye,

> the hero of romance [becomes] analogous to the mythical Messiah or deliverer who comes from an upper world, and his enemy is analogous to the demonic powers of a lower world. The conflict however takes place in, or at any rate primarily concerns, *our* world, which is in the middle, and which is characterized by the cyclical movement of nature. Hence, the opposite poles of the cycles of nature are assimilated to the opposition of the hero and his enemy. The enemy is associated with winter, darkness, confusion, sterility, moribund life, and old age, and the hero with spring, dawn, order, fertility, vigor, and youth.[3]

Frye's comments are most relevant to romances composed in an effort to dramatize traditional Christian values. However, such comments are inadequate when they are applied to many romances composed since the seventeenth century. This inadequacy is due to a radical shift in Western ontology that in effect prevents the sort of work Frye describes from being written during modern periods of cultural history. Earl Wasserman summarizes this shift as well as anyone:

> There [once] was sufficient intellectual homogeneity for men to share certain assumptions, or universal principles, outside the structure of discursive language, that tended to order their universe for them. In varying degrees, ranging from conviction to faith and to passive submission, man accepted, to name but a few, the Christian interpretation of history, the sacramentalism of nature, the Great Chain of Being, the analogy of the various planes of creation, the conception of man as microcosm, and, in the literary area, the doctrine of the genres. These were cosmic syntaxes in the public domain; and the poet could afford to think of his art as imitative of "nature," since these patterns were what he meant by "nature." He could expect his audience to recognize his employment of these cosmic syntaxes . . . and could survey reality and experience in the presence of the world these syntaxes implied. . . .
>
> By the nineteenth century these world-pictures had passed from consciousness for the purpose of public poetry, and no longer did men share in any significant degree a sense of a cosmic design.[4]

A common modern problem consequently appears: familiar modes of signification survive the demise of the old signifieds. It is no longer possible to make traditional affirmatory statements about supposedly reified nouns like *God*, in spite of the fact that the forms through which these statements once were made still exist, though now hollow and ineffectual. Since "God has become a mere empty form in a man-centered universe . . . the continued use of motifs and structures" once thought to be directly related to God is "also merely an empty form."[5] One response to this cultural situation is especially relevant to dysteleological transformations of traditional romance. Many artists employ the now empty forms as a means of demonstrating the abolition of ideas and values that used to be associated with these forms, creating thereby cannibalistic narratives that "thrive like parasites on structures whose ruin is the source of their life."[6] Thus, for example, in William Godwin's *Caleb Williams*, pre-Kantian "Things As They Are" (the original title) dissolve amidst a multitude of potentially false facts as the protagonist struggles futilely to order his life according to the moribund conventions of quest-romance, discovering at last that even his own personality has become arbitrary and fictionalized and that the only direction for his narrative lies in the illusion of completion: "I began these memoirs with the idea of vindicating my character. I have now no character that I wish to vindicate: but I will finish them that . . . the world may at least not hear and repeat a half-told and mangled tale."[7]

Frederic Jameson suggests the medium of romance particularly makes possible a revelation of the phenomenologists' "world" or "gestalt," that "overall organizational category within which the various empirical inner-worldly phenomena are perceived and the various innerworldly experiences take place." In semiotic structures such a gestalt is almost always invisible. It cannot itself be "the object of experience or perception, for it is rather that supreme category which permits all experience or perception in the first place and must thus lie outside them as their own first condition." However, romance is a literary form that uniquely makes possible deep ontic revelations, and that therefore can be called "that event in which *world* in the technical sense of the transcendent horizon of my experience becomes precisely visible as something like an innerworldly object in its own right, taking on the shape of *world* in the popular sense of nature, landscape, and so forth."[8] In many modern romances there are as many gestalt-landscapes as there are characters, and they all exist in a world that is at once dispossessed of messiahs and grails, and of any human potency sufficient to join validly and harmoniously the many conflicting subjectivities that strive futilely to assign meaning to a neutral panorama of experience. No longer is the world a locus in which verbal constructs are sustained noumenally. Consequently, in place of theologically triumphant meditational or physical linear quests there exists only a directionless flicker of interpolated narratives, the modern culmination of a once important romance convention, the *entrelacement*. It is in this dysteleological form that the genre of romance is inherited by Joseph Conrad.

"Sentimental articles with ferocious conclusions": The Parameters of Conradian Romance

The genre of romance has long been paradoxically regarded both as an aesthetic medium that has great and lethal potential to deflect attention from redemptive observation of divinely ordained values, and as the medium uniquely suited to the metaphysically necessary enterprise of continued renewal and celebration of transcendent order. Such an absolute opposition is typical of Western thought, and has made possible works as different as the *Roman de la rose* and *The Faerie Queene*. But the cultural situation in recent centuries has not supported teleological absolutisms philosophically. More intellectually useful and more relevant to Conrad is the example of Charles Dickens, who in the Preface to *Bleak House* asserts his achievement of an unusual union: "I have purposefully dwelt upon the romantic side of familiar things." Conrad read and enjoyed *Bleak House*,[1] and in the important Author's Note to *Within the Tides* he makes a statement that generalizes, in terms like those used by Dickens, his efforts to let "the romantic feeling of reality [which] was in me an inborn faculty" operate upon "hard work and exacting calls of duty, things which in themselves are not much charged with a feeling of romance" (*WT*, v; cf. *PR*, 135).

There is little doubt that the author of works like *Romance—A Novel* (co-authored with F. M. Ford) and *The Rescue—A Romance of the Shallows*, as well as many other works, Author's Notes, and letters in which the words *romance* or *romantic* appear repeatedly in important passages, maintains an important conceptual relationship with the romance genre. Indeed, Conrad's aesthetic milieu contains many examples of writers who naively perpetuate in their prose fiction conventions of character and physical action that derive from inherited traditions associated with this genre. One need think only of the works of Haggard, Marryat, Kipling, and Stevenson for confirmatory examples, whose special attributes can be summarized as "a concatenation of faraway places, bizarre characters, sea voyages, mysterious benefactors, abductions, duels, endless flights from hostile pursuers, and seemingly endless quests for unattainable goals."[2] Yet Conrad consciously resists this milieu, which he disparagingly terms "super-literary,"[3] and his earliest readers seem to sense this, for they contrast *Almayer's Folly* and *An Outcast of the Islands* emphatically and advantageously with contemporary examples of naive romance even while implicitly acknowledging certain affinities in Conrad's works with hackneyed popular conventions. H.G. Wells's remarks in the London *Saturday Review* are typical: "Compare Mr. Conrad's wonderful Aissa with the various combinations of Mr. Hope's Duchess and Mr. Weyman's fitful lady that do duty in contemporary romance. How she lives and breathes . . . !"[4] But what then is Conrad's relationship with the romance?

To Conrad romance is less important as a literary form than as an abstract concept that is related to past experiences recaptured and modified by a mind whose current attitudes differ greatly from previous perspectives. Although he knows "romanticism in relation to imaginative literature . . . in its early days was associated simply with medieval subjects, or . . . with subjects sought for in a remote past," Conrad modifies these traditional associations and greatly reduces temporal vistas. Therefore, he concludes, he may legitimately fabricate romances even though the enterprise necessarily involves past time, since "my subjects are not medieval and I have a natural right to them because my past is very much my own" (*WT*, vi). Formal connections with medievalism are dispensed with quickly, leaving Conrad's primary interest, "romanticism in relation to life," a relationship that "may be a curse but when disciplined by a sense of personal responsibility and a recognition of the hard facts of existence shared with the rest of mankind becomes but a point of view from which the very shadows of life appear endowed with an internal glow" (*WT*, v–vi). Although Conrad can assert within the tidy security of an Author's Note that "such romanticism is not a sin" (*WT*, vi), the fate of Axel Heyst, at once known as "Heyst the Romantic" and "Hard Facts Heyst," suggests a fundamental difficulty exists with regard to simultaneously achieving "romantic feeling" and "hard facts" within practical experience (*WT*, v). Shadows "endowed with an internal glow" may be useful verbal constructs to aid in the analogical description of another's "inconclusive experiences," the meaning of which envelopes "the tale which brought it out only as a glow brings out a haze" (*HD*, 51, 48), but people who cannot tell dark from light are apt to fall into holes. This is why romance in Conrad is so frequently a perspective with lethal consequences, although, at times, a fortunate survivor serves as narrator, "an old man talking of the days of his youth" (*SS*, vi), securely established within relatively tranquil, domesticated surroundings. Only this kind of setting allows a character to luxuriate, without endangering his life, in the sort of solipsism that assigns human qualities and values to an essentially amoral and disinterested cosmos while the mind surveys a past it somehow has survived and therefore pretends was at least partially benevolent.

"Youth" exemplifies this pattern with precision by dramatizing a traditional mentality that was similarly depicted in medieval works (cf. *The Interlude of Youth*, ca. 1513).[5] Trapped within Western obsessions with fulfillment in linear time, Marlow's auditor can only regret that his life has amounted at best to a parody of quest romance, his "weary eyes looking still, looking always, looking anxiously for something out of life" (*Y*, 42). Yet as a mature man he must acknowledge that the very consciousness of the quest implies the inaccessibility of its goal, which is a certain perceptual capacity that is identified exclusively with the state of being young. Marlow describes this perceptual mode in a way that parallels precisely Conrad's own analogical description of the "romantic" mentality as one that makes shadows glow: to Marlow it is like "fire . . . throwing a magic light on the wide earth . . . like the flames of the burning ship surrounded by an impenetrable night" (*Y*, 30). From the point of view of an elegiac alcoholic impasse experienced among supportive friends, a past of potentially deadly "hard facts" (a leaking and burning ship supervised by a stupid first officer) takes on teleological qualities derived merely from the human ability to create pathetic fallacies through contrary-to-fact grammatical constructions: when the grossly unseaworthy *Judea* finally sank, "a magnificent death had come *like* a grace, *like* a gift, *like* a reward to that old ship at the end of her laborious days." Similarly, the vessel's destruction can be seen as a victory: "The surrender of her weary ghost to the keeping of stars and sea was . . . *like* the sight of a glorious triumph" (*Y*, 35; italics mine). And thoughtless, youthful solipsism becomes to Marlow "a moment of strength, of romance," sentiments echoed at the conclusion of the story by the narrator as he wistfully celebrates "the romance of illusions" (*Y*, 42).

The above examples indicate briefly that Conrad is indeed concerned with "romance." But before any more rigorous investigation can be conducted it is necessary to define theoretically the assumptions about human psychology that Conrad seems to anatomize in his narratives when rhetoric derived from traditional romance conventions appears. The following behavioralist generalizations by Morse Peckham provide a useful theoretical framework:

> In any situation in which our senses give our minds messages about the world, two elements are present. On the one hand is the real world, the public world. . . . On the other is the pattern in the mind, the Gestalt, the neural path, the orientation, with which we organize these public data. . . . Any given orientation, or psychic "set," or Gestalt, works in two ways. It screens our minds from receiving everything, so that we may act on what we do observe; it also prevents our minds and our nervous systems from breaking down under the strain of excessive stimulation, including stimulation from within the mind itself. But at the same time . . . a psychic set prevents us from responding to those stimuli which it screens out. There is always a disparity between an orientative set and the data of the real world. On the one hand the drive toward equilibrium preserves the set; on the other, the drive to engage the mind with the real world must break the set down, show up its weaknesses, reorganize it, introduce new material.[6]

Conrad's art commonly explores through many different characters and settings the incompatability of these two drives and the resultant psychic instability, which is definitive of the human condition. To Conrad any perception is a "lie" insofar as this event must necessarily be distortive due to the active projection onto data perceived of the interests of the perceiver. As Conrad recognizes, such interests are culturally determined. In the Christian West they are characterized by a compulsive quest through an illusion of linear time for an experience that will seem to offer some evidence that the perceiver's needs are sustained noumenally by a benevolent providence. As J. Hillis Miller puts it: "People in Conrad's world are in an intolerable situation. The Apollonian realm of reason and intention is a lie. The heart of darkness is the truth, but it is a truth which makes ordinary life impossible." It is therefore "a mistake to define Conrad's solution to the ethical problem by the phrase the 'true lie.'"[7] All perceptual events are steeped in falsehood. In an epistemologically inaccessible world that consequently can only elude the successful and durable imposition of any orientation, a Conradian character is nevertheless fated to attempt survival the only way open to him: by forcing the world, through an active process of selective and distortive perception, into the shape of his current orientation, thereby engendering comprehensibility. And if

> the situation is one in which he can produce or innovate no instrumentally successful pattern of behavior, he will employ a completely inappropriate pattern: whether it is called psychosis or religious illumination depends upon the culture [he] is part of and upon its sanctions and behavioral status systems. His purpose is to reduce the tension elicited by the disorienting effect of a problem.[8]

The most common means whereby Conrad makes the lie visible is in the forceful imposition by his characters of various conventions derived from naive Christian romance upon their world. Both *Heart of Darkness* and "The Planter of Malata," for example, end with a lie. In both cases a woman has lost a man she loves, and the death occurred under circumstances that the woman is incapable of assimilating without abandoning her sentimental, absolutist romance categories, without radically and painfully reconstituting her orientation. In the first instance, Marlow takes the responsibility upon himself for telling the overt lie that enables Kurtz's fiancée to maintain intact the latent lie she is living. He tells the ignorant woman the melodramatic nonsense that "the last word [Kurtz] pronounced was—your name" (*HD*, 161). In this sentence lurks Conradian romance, just as in Marlow's description of the Intended's "great and saving illusion that shone with an unearthly glow in the darkness" (*HD*, 159) lurks the very imagistic analogy whereby Conrad describes "the romantic feeling of reality" as "a point of view from which the very shadows of life appear endowed with an internal glow" (*WT*, v–vi). In the second instance the situation is more complex. After Felicia Moorsom discovers that her unwelcome suitor, Geoffrey Renouard, has been lying in telling her that her lover still lives, she knowingly generates the compensatory and sustaining lie that she "found her betrothed in Malata only to see him die in her arms" (*WT*, 84). By means of this lie she preserves intact her inauthentic "fashionable" surface. Thus, like Kurtz's betrothed as seen by Marlow, Felicia Moorsom as seen by Geoffrey Renouard participates ominously in the definitive iconography of Conradian romance, "glowing mysteriously in the dark background" (*WT*, 47; cf. again v–vi). In fact, of course, the abused object of Felicia's quest, her lost Master Arthur, died in a most unmasterly way. Previously victimized at once by imprudence, by a false charge of embezzeling, by a "woman who wouldn't believe in that poor innocence of his" (*WT*, 75), and by a "horse" that hurt him somewhere "up-country," Master Arthur, unlike his legendary namesake, was indeed "not a steel-tipped man," and "his poor soul . . . gave way very soon" after "a mere slip and tumble of ten feet into a ravine" (*WT*, 74). Ignominiously planted by the Planter of Malata, he lies buried on a hill beside a burlesque monument, the island's central rock, a meaningless axis, "weather-worn, grey, weary of watching the monotonous centuries of the Pacific" (*WT*, 73).

Central to Conrad's disapproval of teleological romance is the way such perceptual categorization necessitates the creation of unnecessarily distortive metaphysical dualisms. The world too easily becomes a locus wherein antipodal forces of black and white magic seem to strive to frustrate or fulfill human needs. To illustrate this idea more specifically it is useful to analyze further "The Planter of Malata," which fittingly takes place in the Southern Hemisphere in the area of "the Antipodes" (*WT*, 14). To this location Felicia Moorsom comes with her father in search of her absconded lover, whom she wronged and to whom she seeks to do "reparation." This desire she conceives as a "sacred debt—a fine duty" (*WT*, 76), and she harbors it in a desperate effort to live out a romance paradigm that already has been deeply challenged once when Master Arthur failed her prediction that "he will come back to claim me, and I'll marry him" (*WT*, 20). Felicia is indeed on a "sentimental pilgrimage," indulging in "dangerous trifling with romantic images," feeding "a sacred fire," as her father accurately judges (*WT*, 40–41) while he warns Renouard of his socialite daughter's pampered impercipience:

> But you don't know what it is to have moved, breathed, existed, and even tri-umphed in the mere smother and froth of life—the brilliant froth. These thoughts, sentiments, opinions, feelings, actions too, are nothing but agitation in empty space—to amuse life—a sort of superior debauchery, exciting and fatiguing, meaning nothing, leading nowhere. She is the creature of that circle.
>
> (*WT*, 41)

The warning comes too late, however, for Renouard is already under a "radiant spell" cast upon him in old Dunster's garden by the impact of Felicia's uniquely vital physical presence (*WT*, 29) among a group who "looked to [him] like people under a spell" (*WT*, 8). From the moment he first sets eyes on her, his every orientation is dominated by her disconcerting "persistence in getting between him and the solid forms of the everyday material world"

(WT, 12). In the company of a lovely woman who is determined to act out a soap opera, Renouard promptly falls prey to his own version of romance.

Accordingly, he imposes upon her his own absolutist, antipodal categories. As Renouard quests for supernal renewal (cf. French *renouer*), he sees "her splendour . . . absolutely unconquerable in its perfection," a "splendour, almost absurd in its lavishness . . . perhaps, divine," and he fantasizes "that the love of such a woman [is] enough to pull any broken man together—to drag a man out of his grave" (WT, 22, 23, 40). In contrast to her sheltered origins amidst the British aristocratic world of "the two big F's" (WT, 17), Renouard is "almost ill-famed for his ruthless daring, the inflexible leader of two tragically successful expeditions" (WT, 43) and a raiser of silk plants, raw material for Felicia's world of fashion and finance. In contrast to her "divine" essense as a "helmet[ed]," "striking," "amazon" of a "tragic Venus" (WT, 23 and 77, 10 and 31, 12, 42, 36), stands his own "miserable mortal envelope." Subject to her "penetrating" presence "like a sharp arrow," he is a vulnerable, foolish "Pallas" who "fears disenchantment more than sortilege" (WT, 44, 23, 33, 38 and 75, 30). Indeed, Renouard even creates for himself his own alternate world of "big F's." He is a "Fool" in quest of a perfect "felicity" (WT, 18, 77), which he learns too late amounts only to "froth and fraud" (WT, 45), whereupon he accuses Felicia climactically of failing to meet his eidetic requirements, of being not at all

> like the men and women of the time of armours, castles, and great deeds. Oh, no! They stood on the naked soil, had traditions to be faithful to, had their feet on this earth of passions and death. . . . They would have been too plebian for you since they had to lead, to suffer with, to understand the commonest humanity. No, you are merely the topmost layer, disdainful and superior, the mere pure froth and bubble on the inscrutable depths. . . .
>
> (WT, 77)

Of course, in making such an accusation Renouard continues to maintain, by means of the absolutely opposed categories of past authenticity and modern "froth," his simplistic romance perceptions. He is only disillusioned with the personality of Felicia and has gained no insight into his own crude and awkward perceptual mode. Thus, it is fitting that the above accusation is made while he and Felicia, the two liars, are in the midst of an absurd argument as to which of them is in possession of "truth" (see WT, 75–78). Only the cynical and cautious Professor Moorsom (from *meerschaum*, a kind of coral originally though to be solidified foam; cf. his hair "whiter than anything . . . except the broken water" [WT, 65]), a "man full of doubts and hesitation," who counsels, "*Spe lentus, timidus futuri*" (WT, 40), is able to come to terms with the elusive essence of experience. As his name suggests, he can cope with paradox, with both the froth and the rock, unlike Felicia, who is all froth, and Renouard, who with "stony eyes" (WT, 18, 40) seeks the rock, and sinks. Professor Moorsom knows indeed that the antidote to teleological romance is a recognition of "the Impermanency of the Measurable" (*WT*, 45), which subverts both hope (*spēs*) and quests for "truth." [9]

Throughout the story Renouard conceives of Felicia as "Venus," "the eternal love itself" (*WT*, 36, 77), a deity originally born from the bloody, spermatic foam raised when Uranus's severed genitals fell into the sea (Aphrodite means "foam-born"). She floated ashore on a scallop shell, and, after stopping briefly at Cythera and the Peloponnese, she took up permanent residence on Cyprus, where she was incarnated in a brilliant white aniconic image. [10] Conrad consciously fashions Renouard's perception of the physical appearance of Felicia Moorsom after the traditional iconography of Aphrodite. Her emasculating, frothy essence needs no further elaboration. Her hair is consistently described as red like "burnished copper," highlighted with "coppery gleams" (*WT*, 10, 45; Cyprus was famous in the ancient world for its great resources of copper, the element from which the Cyprian goddess and island both take their names: Greek *Kupros*, "copper," the ancient sign for which is ♀). [11] Moreover, Felicia has an "ivory face" that is "fairer than Parian marble" (*WT*, 59, 32), and her complexion is "dazzling" with "whiteness" (*WT*, 36 and 45, 75). Altogether she looks like an animated idol "made of ivory and precious metals" before which Renouard kneels "in silence," but an idol that is strangely aniconic, "a figure without shape, a face without features" (*WT*, 10, 77, 46).

In an impermeable cosmos Renouard's pursuit of transcendent felicity through the ultimately shapeless figure of Felicia, the "sphinx" (*WT*, 76), can only culminate in his death beneath the "enormous and melancholy confusion" (*WT*, 72) of the sea. Throughout the story he has associated water with an amniotic release from tension at once in the girl, "a misty and fair creature fitted for . . . the *murmurs* of waters," in the bewildering "cool whirlpool" she engenders emotionally, and in the "gentle, voluptuous heave" of the sea, whose "breast swung him up and down" and which "*murmured* in his ears" (*WT*, 34–35, 71, 60; italics mine; see also 43–44, 85).

Indeed, he thinks of Felicia as residing beyond mutability in "the seventh heaven" (*WT*, 78), the sphere of the fixed stars. But like Professor Moorsom, Conrad is aware of "the Impermanency of the Measurable," and in his world there are no ontic fixtures, no seventh heavens. The implacable Renouard can only fatally pursue the cynosure of traditional romance, for "The Planter of Malata" is set in the Southern Hemisphere in "the Antipodes," where there is no celestial or psychological polestar whatsoever. Nevertheless, like Tennyson's Ulysses, the sinking Renouard follows "a sinking star / Beyond the utmost bound of human thought," and in a masterful stroke Conrad makes possible the probable identification of this star. The story takes place in the autumn (*WT*, 57), which season corresponds to the vernal months in the Northern Hemisphere. The skies south of the equator have many conspicuous stars, but the unusually vacant galactic latitude visible from April to July contains only one star of any prominence that would be setting in the late evening: Spica, the "ear of wheat" borne by Virgo, the cosmic virgin. Moreover, Renouard's terminal westward decrescence occurs beneath Arcturus, located near Spica and the only other bright luminary in the sky at this time of year. No longer a celestial reminder of the redemptive hero who dominates Arthurian romance, Arcturus in the present context only suggests with definitive Conradian ironic indirection the perpetually superior import of the late Master Arthur, now a permanent dweller among "the islands . . . westward," to the starry-eyed Felicia, steadfast director of the "department of sentiment" (*WT*, 64, 38). Indeed, Renouard's watery death after the copper-haired Felicia scorns him confirms absurdly Spenser's description of an important attribute of the Cyprian goddess, "that Venus [who] of the fomy sea was bred; / For . . . the seas by her are most augmented" (*Faerie Queene*, IV, xii, 2).

The radical difference between pre-nineteenth-century teleological romance and the bleak variations of this paradigm that are fabricated by writers like Tennyson and Conrad can be exemplified with precision and efficiency through a simple comparison of the celestial figure of Virgo-Astraea as employed by Spenser (*Faerie Queene*, V, i, 11) and Pope (*Pastorals*, "Winter," 69–76) and the allusions to this same figure in "The Holy Grail" and "The Planter of Malata." What exists as a stellification of a transcendent absolute for Spenser, rising with redemptive impact simultaneously in the east as well as in the shepherds' consciousness for Pope, is for Tennyson and Conrad alike only a means of illustrating deadly extremes of pious delusion. In westward decline and operant dysteleologically, the modern Virgo signifies only the ability of fatally deluded mortals to destroy their lives by pursuing solipsistically and inflexibly an impossible personal fulfillment. It is to Renouard's misfortune that he insistently perceives the world as if it were fraught with a cloudy but accessible feminine meaning after the allegorical manner of a medieval heraldic design: Malata appears "charged with heraldic masses of black vapours . . . , showing here and there its naked members of basaltic rock through the rents of heavy foliage" (*WT*, 57). It is only fitting, therefore, that he should depart from this configuration as he abandons both life's "sinister riddle" (*WT*, 76) and his island to swim to his death toward the stars of Virgo, a parallel feminine personification "showing here and there" from out the sable chaos of the night sky. In Conrad's works, the pursuit of an adamantine order culminates in an annihilatory revelation of its adamant absence.

This absence is never more effectively made apparent in Conrad's works than by the author's subversions of characters' fervent and often public efforts to achieve triumphant signification. The ultimately lethal effect of Renouard's projection of the conventions of medieval heraldry is a good example. Another appears at the outset of "An Anarchist," where by means of a com-

plex ecphrastic image the narrator is made to analyze negatively the osten-
tatious advertisements distributed by a "famous meat-extract manufacturing
company." He describes the company's iconic depiction of itself as follows:

> B.O.S. Bos. You have seen the three magic letters on the advertisement pages
> of magazines and newspapers, in the windows of provision merchants, and on
> calendars for next year you receive by post in the month of November. They scat-
> ter pamphlets also, written in a sickly enthusiastic style and in several languages,
> giving statistics of slaughter and bloodshed enough to make a Turk turn faint. The
> "art" illustrating that "literature" represents in vivid and shining colours a large and
> enraged black bull stamping upon a yellow snake writhing in emerald-green grass,
> with a cobalt-blue sky for a background. It is atrocious and it is an allegory. The
> snake symbolizes disease, weakness—perhaps mere hunger, which last is the
> chronic disease of the majority of mankind.
>
> (SS, 135)

The narrator is offended by the extremist semiotics of the "modern system of
advertising" because "it proves to my mind the wide prevalence of that form
of mental degradation which is called gullibility" (SS, 135, 136). Significantly,
what the narrator finds "degrading" is the human propensity to believe that a
selfless Providence is preparing an apocalyptic event whereby will be purged
all reptilian recalcitrance to the cosmic fulfillment of human needs. So long as
the human race is not weaned from its infantile need for a redeemer it is
vulnerable to manipulation by unscrupulous, vulgar, commercial interests
that promise implicitly in the very gesture of offering disgusting products for
sale a "love" for their "fellowmen" like "the love of the father and penguin for
their hungry fledglings" (SS, 135). The narrator is only too aware of the way
in which advertising takes advantage of the cultural predominance of Christian teleology. He ironically remarks that as far as he can recall commercial
interests "make no promise of everlasting youth . . . , nor yet have they
claimed the power of raising the dead for their estimable products. Why this
austere reserve, I wonder!" (SS, 136).

Yet such claims are nearly made. The company chooses to call itself
"B.O.S." (Latin for "ox": bos), a name Conrad probably invents as a nasty
pun on the well-known British "meat-extract" company that markets "OXO."
The "three major letters" bear a hidden import, the discovery of which can
only be satisfyingly reassuring (cf. "the four magic letters" of Rita's name [AG,
242]). Due to the overwhelmingly strong human tendency to hypostatize its
teleology, obscure religious associations connected with the sacred number
three plus traditional identification of "Bossy" as a willingly sacrificial
domestic beast are sure to dispense with the grossly obvious inauthenticity of
a meat-extract manufacturing company that has pretentiously adopted as its
name the Latin word for its victims. Moreover, the heraldic bearings blazoned
on company literature aggravate this tendency toward "mental degradation."
The entire cosmos is clearly resolved into only two contrasting locations and

animate creatures, a simplistic pairing that responds easily to the imposition of an absolutist dichotomy. The pathetic fallacy is triumphantly reified as a morally enraged Bull of Nourishment, silhouetted against a blue sky (sign of its supernal ally), attacks a contemptibly expressionless and earthbound Serpent of Hunger. Temporal process is canceled, and a complex struggle as old as the world is summarized and solved in an instant. Allegorical creatures fight in a semiotic field that admits no ambiguity regarding the identification of the actants or the outcome of the struggle, just as all the colors in the picture are monochromatically consistent and densely brilliant, permitting no areas of mottled signification. In addition, this icon is surrounded with a shrill verbal gloss, "written in a sickly enthusiastic style in several languages," and this babel is even itself glossed with "statistics," the nonverbal import of which presumably cannot be misunderstood.

In this composite configuration Conrad schematizes the assumptions about semiotics that provide the foundation for the sort of teleological romance he loathes. These assumptions can be quickly summarized in the following way. The Logos entered unimpeded into the phenomenal world through Adam's prelapsarian assignation of words to things: "I named them, as they pass'd, and understood / Thir Nature" (*Paradise Lost*, VIII, 352–53). But due to the Fall the original Order has been obscured, though it is still present in a diluted and discontinuous form. Divine Presence can no longer be detected directly, though, as Michael promises Adam, in natural order at times one can discern "of his steps the track divine" (XI, 354). It is possible therefore to focus attention upon certain creatures and objects, radically intensify a conceptual relationship with their presences, and thereby discover external moral significances. Often this results in the translation of these phenomena into redemptive art. Inside a frame of some sort, with perspective, coloration, postures, attitudes, and subject under rigorous control, it is possible further to clarify the immanent Order and thereby distill primal purpose and proportion from a presently imperfect world.

Such an aesthetic field need not be limited to strictly religious art, since, given the assumptions just summarized, all art (and, more generally, all fatuously reverent perception) is loosely religious, preoccupied with the transcendent reification of human significances through a pasteurized definition of the phenomenal world. Thus, the seventeenth century books of emblems, the preface of one of which asks "What are the Heavens, the Earth, nay every Creature, [but] *Hierogliphicks* and *Emblemes* of His Glory?" [12] Thus, Renouard's heraldic perception of an obscure but promising femininity in the geology and flora of Malata. Thus, the preposterous bull rampant and serpent couchant of the B.O.S. meat-extract manufacturing company. And although words no longer consistently reveal the Logos since they have degenerated into "several languages," numbers remain. It matters little that the Augustinian numerology, whereby "the mind is raised from the consideration of changeable numbers in inferior things to unchangeable numbers in unchangeable truth,"[13] has been displaced by "statistics of slaughter and bloodshed" supplied by modern technology, since both purport to be the source of a metaphysical arithmetic that one way or another will kill the "snake" and redeem time. The B.O.S. company under this pretense can even anticipate the abolition of the old almanac, according to which the New Year begins in January, and make possible a contemplation of the promised *annus mirabilis* each November through its subtly revisionist calendar bearing "three major letters" and delivered (coincidentally) by the post in plenty of time to allow for efficient ordering of meat-extract for the holidays.

As Conrad sees it, the human propensity to rage for order is seldom content with anything less than simplistic hyperbole; and in the compulsive assignation of significance to experience absolute dichotomies abound, the most common of which is derived from the hackneyed Christian metaphysical filibuster involving God and the Devil. Due to this propensity the intellectual differences between Conrad's characters often blur, since the rhetoric of a cosmic moral melodrama usually predominates whether is involved the perception of a credulous, priest-ridden South American peasant or a verbally more sophisticated ship's captain. Even though the peasants in *Nostromo* regard the static blackness within the Golfo Placido at night as capable of frustrating both divine omniscience and demonic maleficence, the familiar devices of personification and absolutist rhetoric remain, summarized with condescension by the narrative voice:

> Sky, land, and sea disappear together out of the world when the Placido—as the saying is—goes to sleep under its black poncho. . . . The eye of God Himself—they add with grim profanity—could not find out what work a man's hand is doing in there; and you would be free to call the devil to your aid with impunity if even his malice were not defeated by such a blind darkness.
>
> (*N*, 6–7)

Similarly, oppressed by disease, darkness, and delay, the narrator of *The Shadow-Line* seeks security and regards his (nonexistent) quinine as a concoction obtained directly from the Great Physician. His perceptual mode is less valid even than that of the peasants, who are subtle enough to admit the presence of potent metaphysical vacancies in their constantly insecure world:

> I believed in it. I pinned my faith to it. It would save the men, the ship, break the spell by its medicinal virtue, make time of no account . . . , and, like a magic powder working against mysterious malefices, secure the first passage of my first command against the evil powers of calms and pestilence.
>
> (*SL*, 88)

It is such rhetoric that typically calls forth from critics statements that Conrad writes "romances." Gillian Beer suggests that "the use of the 'marvellous' and the supernatural" is a "hallmark of romance," which "occurs in a muted . . . form in . . . Conrad's *The Shadow-Line*."[14] And John Stevens, in *Medieval Romance*, comments at some length upon *The Shadow-Line* as definitive of what he calls the "romance of integrity, of the idealized Self," a type of romance which exhibits the following characteristics: "the call, youthful aspiration engaged by a sudden vocation of a challenging kind; the quest, culminating in the great *adventure* (here, the crossing of the dead man's latitude); the sense of an evil to be conquered, a death to be encountered, a plague to be dispersed."[15] Stevens's comments are useful because of their inadequacies, because they focus exclusively and misleadingly upon externals. It may be advantageous to analyze Medieval and Renaissance romances by attending primarily to attributes of character and setting, for in works like *The Faerie Queene* even when the point of view modulates to first person it can be assumed that the transcendent First Person is inspiring the narrator, and as a result the narrative perspective has not plunged into the Wood of Error. However, Conrad contrives to make the narrator's words the only fact of the narrative in *The Shadow-Line*; and if the tale contains the paraphernalia of divine and demonic supernaturalism it is because the narrator's prejudiced perceptions are manifested in his rhetoric by means of this burdensome paraphernalia.

To Conrad, romance is identified with a capacity needfully to violate amoral external phenomena by imposing a dichotomous mode of perception that in effect charges everything with significances like those encountered in Christian allegory. This way of seeing is at once the source of comprehensibility and self-justification and the reason for inevitable, solipsistic, and often fatal misapprehension. To attain and sustain a practical sanity one must be purged of inflexible and naive yearning for external validation of one's needs, and this purgative process is described in *The Mirror of the Sea* in the chapter on "Initiation" where Conrad tells of the negation of his own "romantic" absolutes by a corrosive awareness of "duplicity":

> On that exquisite day of gentle breathing peace and veiled sunshine perished my romantic love to what men's imagination had proclaimed the most august aspect of Nature. The cynical indifference of the sea to the merits of human suffering and courage, laid bare in this ridiculous, panic-tainted performance extorted from the dire extremity of nine good and honorable seamen revolted me. I saw the duplicity of the sea's most tender mood. It was so because it could not help itself, but the awed aspect of the early days was gone. . . . In a moment . . . I had looked cooly at the life of my choice. Its illusions were gone. . . .
>
> (*MS*, 141–42; cf. *LE*, 17)

The illusions associated with a specific realm of experience may be gone, but the structures of thought that breed specific illusions remain as vital as ever. Personification laced with moral judgment lingers. The sea is not just "indifferent," but also "cynical." It has moods like any sentient creature, and if an event occurs that seems inappropriate to a certain mood, the sea bears responsibility for being "duplicit" and permitting such things to go on even though paradoxically "it could not help itself." Indeed, Henry James's definition of the "autobiographical form" (first-person narrative perspective) as "the darkest abyss of romance"[16] is more relevant to Conrad than most abstract critical theories about the romance genre. This is particularly true with regard to Conrad's most sustained acknowledgment of the inevitability of the moralistic pathetic fallacy (and in turn of romance), the "Rulers of East and West" section of *The Mirror of the Sea*, where for many pages the oceans of the world are depicted in detail as if they were human personalities. Such an exercise the enlightened Conrad could perform with relative safety in the tranquil physical and temporal remove of his study, but this is not an indulgence recommended for those at the masthead, something the narrator of *The Shadow-Line* and "A Smile of Fortune" learns belatedly and reluctantly.

Works of fiction that repeatedly anatomize the perceptual mode outlined above (which typically fabricates and sustains a world masked sometimes providentially, sometimes satanically, always humanly) are responsive to the theoretical constructs of Tzvetan Todorov, who notes that although there has "never been a literature without genres," at times there may seem to be "no intermediary between the particular, individual work and literature as a whole, the ultimate genre."[17] Given this generic openness, it may not seem overly outrageous to suggest that Conradian "romance" fits with some convenience into the genre recently defined in the following manner by Todorov in his book *The Fantastic: A Structural Approach to a Literary Genre:*

> The fantastic . . . lasts only as long as a certain hesitation: a hesitation common to reader and character, who must decide whether or not what they perceive derives from "reality" as it exists in the common opinion. At the story's end, the reader makes a decision even if the character does not; he opts for one solution or the other, and thereby emerges from the fantastic. If he decides that the laws of reality remain intact and permit an explanation of the phenomena described, we say that the work belongs to another genre: the uncanny. If, on the contrary, he decides that new laws of nature must be entertained to account for the phenomena, we enter the genre of the marvelous.
>
> The fantastic therefore leads a life full of dangers, and may evaporate at any moment. It seems to be located on the frontier of two genres, the marvelous and the uncanny, rather than to be an autonomous genre.[18]

Conrad's fiction commonly presents characters who demonstrate their fatal humanity by imprisoning themselves within various, often conflicting, allegorizations of the phenomenal world. They have no choice, and neither does the reader, though he is not expected to accept uncritically any of the characters' perceptions. On one hand, Conradian romance depicts characters who exist immersed in their respective autotelic lies, who try to justify these lies noumenally, and who therefore live out a Todorovian fantasy that yearns toward the marvelous. On the other hand, Conradian romance requires a reader who will resist the fictional characters' lies, who will see that super-natural rhetoric is simply a needlessly hyperbolic way of describing amoral phenomena, and whose experience of the literature thus begins in the realm of the fantastic but quickly tends toward the uncanny. But finally, and most crucially, Conradian romance requires a reader able to admit that whatever criteria he uses to establish "'reality' as it exists in the common opinion" are ultimately just as inauthentic as the characters' autotelic lies that he demystifies, that he is captured irredeemably in the epistemological vacancy of Todorov's fugitive fantastic—as indeed was Conrad himself, who, according to Wells, stalked about projecting a *"persona* of a romantic adventurous unmercenary intensely artistic European gentleman carrying an exquisite code of unblemished honour through a universe of baseness." [19]

With these ideas in mind it is expedient to discuss in some depth *The Shadow-Line* and "A Smile of Fortune," two tales in which the rhetoric of tor-rid supernaturalism and humid sentiment is used consistently as a means whereby the protagonist seeks to impose upon disorderly, amoral experience the dyads of his teleological assumptions.[20] The pointless passage of time (especially if devoid of linear physical activity) has always been anathema to the Christian West. This prejudice is ingrained even in agnostic characters like the narrator of *The Shadow-Line.* Although for him God has been displaced by the "supreme authority" of "the Harbour-Master," who is designated mockingly by means of the sacrilegiously capitalized pronouns "He" and "Him" (*SL,* 29), and Jesus is at best "a mad carpenter . . . convinced that he was King of Jerusalem" (*SL,* 101), fear of temporal process remains strong and lurks as a deep emotional problem that surfaces rhetorically. Consequently, youthful lack of awareness is idealized aesthetically as "beautiful," a useful evasion, since in the West, obsessed by activity, technique, and accomplish-ment, the absence of self-consciousness can scarcely be justified practically. The perception of units of time is not a problem for the young, who have "no moments" and who live in the "beautiful continuity of hope which knows no pauses and no introspection." The experience is prelapsarian, one of amniotic, timeless origins like "an enchanted garden" where the "very shades glow" (*SL,* 3; cf. Conrad's definition of the "romantic feeling of reality" as a mode of perception that makes the "very shadows . . . appear endowed with an inter-nal glow" [*WT,* vi]).

Given such assumptions, temporal process, which is unavoidable, can only bring "always something disagreeable as opposed to the charm and innocence of illusions" (*SL,* 65). Appropriately, a metaphoric discontinuity accompanies the growing perception of temporal discontinuity, and the static garden tropes give way inevitably to linear compulsions, to a "path" leading to a harbor from which one is doomed to set forth on the sea and confront "a shadow-line," sign that the security of an ontic anchorage is forever to be abandoned and "the region of early youth . . . must be left behind" (*SL,* 3). Now metaphorically at sea for the duration of his existence, the narrator experiences life as a fallen parody of the "enchanted garden." Like the garden, the sea is ultimately static; but in marked contrast it provides a medium through which time acts constantly in the form of wind and wave (or the absence thereof). Like the garden, the sea has no "path"; but one is nevertheless forced to strive for linear travel within its structureless labyrinth in accordance with the demands of precise scheduling, all the while literally navigating to survive.

Although he has lost much of his youth, the narrator verbally preserves the romance analogues in terms of which he envisions youth. Aboard Captain Kent's ship he "could not have been happier if [he] had had the life and the men made to [his] order by a benevolent Enchanter" (SL, 5), an existence with which one breaks "as one parts with some enchanting company" (SL, 44). And he takes the rhetoric of youth with him to his new position as captain, which had come "as if by enchantment" (SL, 39), and to his new ship, which in its moorings looks "like an enchanted princess," "spellbound, unable to move, to live, to get out into the world (till [he] came)" (SL, 40). But the ambiguities of life at sea in "the world" are not responsive to simplistic role models learned from tales of the Brothers Grimm (see reference to Cinderella [SL, 40]), as the latent inconsistency in the narrator's use of the idea of "enchantment" suggests. He conceives of desirable events as the work of some "benevolent Enchanter" who has power over him, while naively assuming that the negative "enchantment" under which his "princess" of a ship suffers is of negligible potence and can be dispelled by his mere presence. He imagines the ship as a living thing in need of a redeemer because he identifies life with physical motion. But mere successful and practical physical activity alone is not sufficient to justify existence. Motion must have a goal, and for a goal nothing less than "truth" will suffice. Thus, he abandons Captain Kent's ship because the "past eighteen months, so full of new and varied experience, [appear] a dreary, prosaic waste of days. [He feels] . . . that there [is] no truth to be got out of them" (SL, 7).

The narrator tells his tale at some temporal remove from the original experiences, but he has still not outgrown his propensity to see experience as a sequence of events each of which can be categorized according to the predominance of black or white magic. In this respect he prolongs the experience of the fantastic, not allowing it to dissipate into the following polarization outlined by Todorov:

> The I apparently comprehends two distinct persons: a character who perceives unknown worlds (and lives in the past), and the narrator who transcribes the former's impressions (he lives in the present)[;] . . . the fantastic does not exist here: neither for the former, who regards his visions not as due to madness but as a more lucid image of the world (he is thus in the realm of the marvelous); nor for the latter, who knows that the visions are the product of either madness or dreams, not of reality (from his viewpoint, the narrative is merely uncanny).[21]

The Shadow-Line is fraught with an enduring supernaturalism: "divine (pagan) emanation," "deputy-Neptune," "benevolent Enchanter," "enchanted princess," "magic," "sorceress," "semi-mystical bond with the dead," "evil spirits," "unknown powers," "a miraculous shrine," "evil spell," a "fatal circle," "ghosts," "bewitched," the "fever-devil," and "that Thing" are only a few examples. The narrator clearly has not profited from his experience with his delerious mate, Mr. Burns, who is obsessed with a dead captain's supposed homicidal power at latitude 8°20' North. The narrator never recognizes in Burns's insistent perceptions of supernatural evil merely an exaggerated, single-minded version of his own propensity to force the world into absolute definition by imposing upon it rhetorically a slightly more complex, if no more sane, fiction. The naive concepts of his youthful "enchanted garden" such as truth, timelessness, and perfection are not abolished. Rather they are simply displaced into alternate contexts. Truth resides analogically at the end of Captain Giles's watch chain, which the old man raises "like solid truth from a well" (*SL*, 27). Time vanishes, albeit outside the primal "enchanted garden," in the "monotony of expectation, of hope, and of desire" (*SL*, 97). And the ideal of perfection, maintained negatively in the "perfect silence, joined to perfect immobility, [which] proclaimed the yet unbroken spell of our helplessness" (*SL*, 115), is regained at the end of the tale in the harbor, where a redemptive "perfect stillness reign[s] in the ship" (*SL*, 127). Appropriately, therefore, unlike the sagacious Captain Giles, the narrator never masters the art of "intricate navigation," in spite of his discovery of "the inwardness of things and speeches" (*SL*, 12, 26).

Due to the fever that has deprived him of an active crew, he can manage his ship only through abandonment either to extremes of "deadly stillness" (*SL*, 119) or the wind's caprice: "If the wind shifts round heavily after we close in with the land she will either run ashore or get dismasted or both. We won't be able to do anything with her. She's running away with us now. All we can do is to steer her" (*SL*, 123). This is why the narrator's journey through the story is circular. At the conclusion he is back where he was at the beginning, having gained scarcely any mastery of the intricacies of physical or intellectual navigation, as his vocabulary reveals. Through the absolutist rhetoric of teleological romance he continues to impose upon the phenomenal world the same sort of preposterous supernatural categories in terms of which he earlier defined his youthful lack of awareness. Indeed, he appropriately speaks as if he actually participates in Burns's delusions, though he deprecates them through much of the story: "By the exorcising virtue of Mr. Burns's awful laugh, the malicious spectre had been laid, the evil spell broken, the curse removed. We were now in the hands of a kind and energetic Providence" (*SL*, 125).

This sort of vulnerability to romance conventions continues to trouble the captain when, years later, still in the company of Mr. Burns, he encounters in

"A Smile of Fortune" a physical configuration that is receptive to the imposition of these conventions, a literal garden full of beautiful flowers that serves as a prison for an attractive young woman. In *The Shadow-Line* the captain in the "enchanted garden" of youth sought to lose his "feeling of life-emptiness" in a "romantic reverie" that involved relating to his ship "like a lover," perceiving it "like some rare women . . . , one of those creatures whose mere existence is enough to awaken an unselfish delight," moored in a "spellbound" immobility like "an enchanted princess" from which the captain "like a king in his country" would triumphantly release it (*SL*, 49, 48, 46, 49, 40, 62). Likewise, in "A Smile of Fortune" the captain is oppressed by "horrid thoughts of business" that are forced upon him in "this infernal hole of a port" by a hateful world that demands one "kill and traffic on it, pursuing aims of no great importance." Trying to elude these thoughts and demands, he allows himself to become "entranced" by a garden wonderland that makes the port seem "miles away" and that contains Alice, "captive of the garden" in "long immobilities," for him to try to rescue as if she were "a castaway . . . wrecked on a desert island" (*TLS*, 3, 42, 6, 43, 42, 62, 59).

Although he insists glibly that "life [is] not . . . a fairy tale," he immediately proceeds to speculate eagerly about having discovered on this lovely "astral body of an island" an "enchanted nook . . . where wealthy merchants rush fasting on board ships before they are fairly moored" (*TLS*, 7, 3). That is, he preserves the unrealistic hope that somehow one can do business in a manner free of duplicity and selfish motivation in the company of "fasting," self-abasing merchants, who inhabit an island that will be pleasing at once to both the aesthetic and moral sensibilities. And the duplicitous ship's chandler, Jacobus (Latin for James and a traditional reference to the "Old Pretender"), is quite capable of conjuring an ambiguous situation in which the narrator for a while can luxuriously live a fantasy in which it is absolutely possible to distinguish selfish motivation from "unselfish delight," for indeed "a Jacobus on his native heath" is "a bit too much of a Jacobus" (*TLS*, 75). In other words, due to his need to separate concepts that he regards as opposites (the conventions of business dealings from the conventions of romance), the narrator allows himself to be seduced by "my Jacobus" (*TLS*, 29, 36) long before he ever sees Alice. Jacobus contrives to greet the young captain his very first morning in port with a hearty breakfast of fresh produce, an important course of which consists of a common folklore aphrodisiac, "a dish of potatoes" (*TLS*, 8).[22] Some days thereafter Jacobus returns bearing "a beautiful bunch of flowers in his thick hand," a gesture that makes the narrator "feel as if I were a pretty girl" (*TLS*, 22). Jacobus indicates he is "a lover of gardens," and the narrator admits "I too take extreme delight in them" (*TLS*, 32).

Most intriguing of all, Jacobus has a personal history that is extremely impractical and unbusinesslike, and that fascinatingly approximates the plot of a naive romance. Years ago "when a wandering circus came to the island" he "became suddenly infatuated with one of the lady-riders" and abandoned wife, daughter, home, social position, and economic enterprise to follow "that woman to the Cape." The narrator willingly perceives in this folly "an unholy love-spell," and "listen[s] open-mouthed to the tale as old as the world, a tale which had been the subject of legend, or moral fables, of poems" (*TLS*, 36). Thus, by the time the narrator meets Alice, Jacobus's illegitimate daughter by the circus performer, a very peculiar, if latent, emotional attachment already draws the captain toward the girl's father. This strange attachment is fittingly displaced by overt attention to Alice when the narrator, by studying her face, sees in her Jacobus's features and decides suddenly the father is attractive, "rather handsome . . . after all" (*TLS*, 47).

There is, of course, a disagreeable dimension to Jacobus the ship's chandler, a confrontation with which the narrator tries to avoid due to his need for one-dimensional perceptual categories. All the while Jacobus is seducing the captain with food, flowers, a garden, and the presence of Alice, he subtly introduces commercial issues. Jacobus feeds the narrator potatoes with the immediate goal of persuading him to buy tons of them. He brings the narrator fresh flowers in hope of encouraging him to have Jacobus's own "skilled workman" fit a shelf "all round the skylight for flowers in pots to take . . . to sea," and naturally Jacobus "could produce . . . two or three dozen good plants" as well (*TLS*, 23). Worst of all, after having learned the narrator is not married and after having fed him well on potatoes, Jacobus offers to the narrator the pleasures of his home and garden, remarking disarmingly, "There's only my girl there" (*TLS*, 32), in full knowledge of the sexual deprivation necessarily suffered at sea and with full intention of trapping the narrator into marriage. The captain, however, prefers to sustain the "romantic view" of Jacobus and his daughter, seeing them as "a lonely pair of castaways, on a desert island; the girl sheltering in the house as if it were a cavern in a cliff, and Jacobus going out to pick up a living for both on the beach—exactly like two ship-wrecked people who always hope for some rescuer to bring them back at last into touch with the rest of mankind" (*TLS*, 39). He can only preserve this perspective by ignoring the obvious, Jacobus's corpulent and unheroic "bodily reality" (*TLS*, 39), just as he ignores Jacobus's overt efforts to entangle him in various economically and emotionally compromising situations.

This kind of distortive and selective perception is facilitated by the fact that Jacobus has a brother, whom he resembles very much in physical appearance. But, in marked contrast to the ship's chandler, the manners of "the wealthy merchant" are visibly, even obnoxiously, aggressive; and he offends the narrator immediately by "spitting" at him, "If you won't sit down and talk business you had better go to the devil" (*TLS*, 27). Such offensively direct allusions to commercialism reinforce in the captain's mind his own irrational association of subhuman selfishness with the marketplace. He concludes "the wealthy merchant" is a "beast" that exhibits the "odiousness of the human brute" (*TLS*, 26), and takes as a result a "kindlier view of the other Jacobus" that even resembles "partisanship" (*TLS*, 29). Thus, the narrator can pretend that the external world reifies his emotional needs, preserving an obvious and absolute differentiation between the romantic and the mercantile in general, and between the brothers Jacobus in particular, so long as he maintains his perverse ignorance of the fact that both are businessmen and were once professionally associated.

In his compulsive visits as rescuer to Alice, the "castaway" in her *hortus conclusus*, the narrator is really trying to rescue a cumbersome perceptual mode that is weighted with impractical, eidetic absolutes. He typically frequents the garden at sunset, when the "*shady* nooks . . . had an extraordinary magnificence of effect" and the "shadows blazed with color" (*TLS*, 43, 48; italics mine; cf. again Conrad's "shadows . . . with an internal glow" [*WT*, vi]), and he quickly establishes by extension a "*shady*, intimate understanding" with Alice, the spirit of the garden (*TLS*, 51; italics mine). Within the dim intaglio of the "gorgeous maze of flower-beds," "dark water," and "the massed foliage of varied trees" (*TLS*, 42), the captain finds insular respite among "castaways" from the rigorous demands of social respectability and commercial and nautical "regular habits" (*TLS*, 34). Like the shady garden, Alice's physical appearance suggests a delightfully disorderly alternative existence relaxingly deprived of brilliant light. She has "magnificent black eyes" that seem perpetually to be "half closed, contemplating the void" (*TLS*, 45, 59), and above "the black depths of her fixed gaze" (*TLS*, 57) looms "a mass of black, lustrous locks, twisted anyhow high on her head, with long, untidy wisps hanging down on each side of the clear sallow face; a mass so thick and strong and abundant that, nothing but to look at, [sic] it gave you a sensation of heavy pressure on the top of your head and an impression of magnificently cynical untidiness" (*TLS*, 44).

Amidst this scented darkness "like a voluptuous and perfumed sign" (*TLS*, 54) the narrator can with some efficiency act out his chivalric fantasy. However, when in the interest of professional obligation to his ship's owners he accepts a favor from Jacobus, who somehow obtains quarter-bags that have been "impossible to buy" (*TLS*, 41), the captain can no longer avoid acknowledging that his relationship with Alice's father is predicated upon business. And in a gesture of guilty self-castigation he purchases several hundred bags more than he needs: he originally requested "eleven hundred quarter-bags" but eagerly assents when Jacobus asks, "It's fourteen hundred your ship wanted, did you say, Captain?" (*TLS*, 41, 52). That night walking to Jacobus's house he must admit to himself concomitantly that his visits to Alice probably stem from visceral motives that would not be at all welcome in a romance: "I became aware that it was not mere gratitude which was guiding my steps towards the house with the old garden. . . . Mere gratitude does not gnaw at one's interior economy in that particular way. Hunger might; but I was not feeling particularly hungry for Jacobus's food" (*TLS*, 53).

Consequently, he apparently lingers along the way and arrives later than normal at the garden, which, now atypically devoid of all light, seems blighted, owing to his inner awareness of moral complexity. An autumnal melancholy predominates and the fact of mortality seems manifest: 'The garden was one mass of gloom, like a cemetery of flowers buried in the darkness, and she . . . seemed to muse mournfully over the extinction of light and colour. Only whiffs of heavy scent passed like wandering, fragrant souls of that departed multitude of blossoms" (*TLS*, 53). Within this tainted context he appropriately offers food to Alice with "the murmur of a pleading lover" (*TLS*, 54), in a climactic inversion of Eve's gesture in the primal Edenic seduction scene. At the same time Alice's physical appearance becomes troublesomely ambiguous. She no longer fits easily into the romance category of "a spellbound creature with the forehead of a goddess" for she looks also like "a gipsy tramp" (*TLS*, 59), and he perceives in her "indifference" a projection of unpleasant qualities which he fears lurk within himself, "ingratitude doubled with treachery" (*TLS*, 69).

If one expects gratitude from a love relationship, one is implicitly desirous of a return for past investment. As might be expected, within "A Smile of Fortune" rhetorical ambiguities mingle eros and mammon. The very title contains the word "fortune," which can denote material wealth as well as, more generally, a chance occurrence, and which is personified mythically by the frustratingly detached goddess Fortuna. A "smile of fortune" takes place when prosperity and chance are uniquely and fortuitously combined, and an indifferent cosmos appears to reflect and fulfill human needs, as in this tale Fortuna's fatal femininity responds affectionately with a bag of loot. These ambiguities stand remote from an ideal love relationship. But the narrator, caught in a duplicitous world, must confirm them rhetorically because, for example, the same words signify both endearment and love as well as capitalistic scheming, both love affairs and "commercial affairs" (*TLS*, 80). Thus, he asks "Are the provisions generally *dear* here?" upon his arrival in port, and later laments that "outward decency may be bought too *dearly* at times" (*TLS*, 9, 74; italics mine). These rhetorical ambiguities are forced into the narrator's consciousness when he can no longer deny to himself that his relationship with both Jacobus and Alice is predicated upon self-interest of one sort or another. Consequently, the captain articulates in the following manner his resentment of Alice's "black fixed stare" that is "not even aware . . . of my presence": 'I felt as though I had been cheated in some rather complicated deal into which I had entered against my better judgment" (*TLS*, 68).

The unexpected rhetorical merger of ideas that the narrator originally sought to keep separate causes disorientation of sufficient potency to subvert the simplistic object of his quest-romance, the rescue of Alice. The girl's enigmatic "tragic and promising, pitiful and provoking" (*TLS*, 78) physical

appearance now only stimulates "an unrealizable desire," a "strange provoking sensation . . . of indefinite desire . . . which had made me . . . dread the
prospect of going to sea" (*TLS*, 59, 73). Having experienced a shocking con-
tamination of his naive assumptions and their rhetorical implementation, the
narrator contemplates a cosmic betrayal, as a perverse Fortuna and Jacobus's
island seem to intersect:

> The remembered vision at sea, diaphanous and blue, of the Pearl of the Ocean at
> sixty miles off; the unsubstantial, clear marvel of it as if evoked by the art of a
> beautiful and pure magic, turned into a thing of horrors too. Was this the fortune
> this vaporous and rare apparition had held for me in its hard heart, hidden within
> the shape as of fair dreams and mist?
>
> (*TLS*, 74)

He begins at last to talk like a modern-day Coheleth, an exemplary opponent
of linear quests, declaiming in "a world buried in darkness" a "weary conviction of the emptiness of all things under Heaven" (*TLS*, 79), for he has been
caught by Jacobus in the act of assaulting Alice physically and buys his con-
science clear "with every single sovereign of . . . ready cash" by agreeing to
purchase personally tons of aphrodisiac potatoes from the girl's father. So
attraction turns to resentment, rescue to ravishment, and the originally intended cargo of sugar to starch, as humanly pleasing delusions and aesthetic
surfaces are reduced to their rooty, commercial fundaments and "whiffs of
heavy scent" from "the garden [like] an enormous censer" are displaced by
"whiffs from decaying potatoes . . . , an atmosphere of corruption" (*TLS*, 76,
82). The narrator, who earlier had objected to having a "mess of mould and
dead vegetable matter" aboard ship (*TLS*, 23), sails away with precisely such a
mess, while his dehumanizing "bargain with all its remotest
associations . . . [is] everlastingly dangled before [his] eyes" (*TLS*, 82).

And when to his amazement he learns that, due to a drought at Port Philip
Heads, he can make a profit from his cargo, the "atmosphere of corruption"
becomes a conclusive psychic "plunge . . . into corruption" (*TLS*, 82, 84),
from which depths he conceives of himself figuratively as a moral sexton:
"That night I dreamt of a pile of gold in the form of a grave in which a girl was
buried" (*TLS*, 84). In this case, the smile of Fortuna is only "the demon of
lucre" (*TLS*, 85). Just as the narrator exchanged Alice's humanity for mammon after kissing her, so he can only exorcise this state of demonic "possession" by seeing to it that the "kiss . . . be paid for at its full price" (*TLS*, 85,
87). If he is to regain his integrity, the selfish sacrifice of one love demands the
selfless sacrifice of another. The captain can do no less than quit "the ship I
had learned to love" and thereby banish from his life (temporarily at least) all
opportunity to live out a linear fantasy, whether the quest be for love or fortune, "seeing all my plans destroyed, my modest future endangered" (*TLS*,
88). The captain thus departs from Conrad's pages, irrationally throwing
away an excellent position, precisely the way he initially entered Conrad's

works, quitting Captain Kent's ship at the outset of *The Shadow-Line*. The penalty eventually exacted by an ambiguous world for indulgence in the naive assumptions and rhetoric of teleological romance is a traumatic deconstruction of the very ability to perceive the world "romantically," as the starchy, fetid roots that in a sublunary realm must support all bowers of sweet flowers are brutally revealed.

"Freya of the Seven Isles" is a superior story wherein Conrad continues to anatomize the psychology of arrogant, distortive, libidinous perception by means of a technical repertoire derived from the tradition of Western European romance. For these reasons it merits close consideration. The tale examines at length the "state of perpetual elation" (*TLS*, 163) occupied by the protagonist, Jasper Allen, as he anticipates his marriage to Freya Nelson, a "Lady of the Isles," whose erotically suggestive pagan Christian-name only amplifies the promise of unearthly fulfillment extended by her physical appearance, "charming in a complex way" though "perfect" (*TLS*, 149). To the extremist Jasper, the entire world is animate with Freya's subtle participation:

> The beauty of the loved woman exists in the beauties of Nature. The swelling outlines of the hills, the curves of a coast, the free sinuosities of a river are less suave than the harmonious lines of her body, and when she moves, gliding lightly, the grace of her progress suggests the power of occult forces which rule the fascinating aspects of the visible world.
>
> (*TLS*, 210)

And just as his brig, the *Bonito*, is his swift and efficient means of entering this world and sampling phenomenal delights, so it is to be the vehicle of accomplishing and sustaining the bliss Jasper anticipates he will enjoy upon his marriage to and penetration of Freya, the "ship-child" who "loved Jasper" only through "the brig, your brig—our brig. . . . I love the beauty!" (*TLS*, 167, 190). Indeed, the moment Freya becomes his wife will initiate for Jasper an experience of ontic completion paralleling the mythic unions in romance of mortals with goddesses, through which conjunctures the physical world itself is made congruent with human desire (a representative example is Keats's *Endymion*). The wedding and elopement will consolidate with himself the two extreme values of Jasper's life (the girl, "Scandinavian Goddess of Love," and the *Bonito*; the empyreal and the hyaline), thus forming a triune transcendence that mingles a sentient femininity and fatuous masculinity with an insensate object, the brig, "the floating paradise which he was gradually fitting out . . . to sail his life blissfully away with Freya" (*TLS*, 195, 152).

Jasper's attention is consequently focused upon the *Bonito* with pathological intensity. He must keep reconfirming the emblematic significance of the vessel by adding ever more precious substance to its physical structure. As a result, the hull is covered with "the very best white paint" rivaling "costly enamel such as jewellers use for their work" and gilded with "nothing less than the best gold-leaf" (*TLS*, 157–58). These extreme decorations are primarily symptomatic, as the narrator understands when he recounts as a "new instance of Jasper's lunacy . . . that he was distressed at his inability to have solid silver handles fitted to all the cabin doors" (*TLS*, 174). In "fitting out" the *Bonito* as a "paradise" Jasper fails to see that a fragile floating bower cannot long survive in a world that is not itself fitted out in like manner. And this failure is a function of his myopic projection of Freya's presence onto the entirety of the phenomenal world. Not only does the "beauty of the loved woman" vitalize "the beauties of Nature." Jasper's "feelings for the brig and for the girl were as indissolubly united in his heart as you may fuse two precious metals together in one crucible" (*TLS*, 210, 158). Thus, when the narrator cautions Jasper, "Mind you don't come to grief trying to do too much," the rash youth replies, "Nothing, nothing could happen to the brig" (*TLS*, 167–68). He is as sure of his ship's safety as he is confident of the benevolence of the world surrounding the *Bonito* (from Latin *bonus*, "good"), since Freya's essence animates and unites in psychic alchemy all things. This is why Jasper placidly takes what appear to others as unconscionable chances with his vessel, imprudently "shoot[ing] the brig through" an opening "between two disgusting old jagged reefs" and "always anchor[ing] foolishly close to the point" near Nelson's cottage, wherein he would remain during even a violent storm "stock still on the verandah" in confident adoration of Freya "while the brig, down at the point there, surged at her cables within a hundred yards of nasty, shiny, black rock-heads" (*TLS*, 152, 151, 152). Perceiving all the world fraught with "the image of Freya," Jasper courts disaster by charting his life through contrary-to-fact grammatical constructions,

> as if the winds had to wait on his future, the stars fight for it in their courses; as if the magic of his passion had the power to float a ship on a drop of dew or sail her through the eye of a needle—simply because it was her magnificent lot to be the servant of a love so full of grace as to make all the ways of the earth safe, resplendent, and easy.
>
> (*TLS*, 168)

Within the mind of Jasper Allen, that is, the seductive forest bowers encountered by Dain and Willems, and the debilitating garden of Jacobus the ship's chandler are expanded so as to include the earth itself. A boundless *locus amoenus* is fabricated. But Jasper is dangerously unaware in his tropical stasis of the necessary flux of world-weather, be it a function of solar motion or the soul's own zodiac.

Because the "image of Freya" permeates all Jasper's apprehensions of all things, thereby conjuring a vision of an impossibly congenial cosmos, she controls the extent to which for Jasper a Paphian utopia seems attainable. By merely withdrawing she can crush her lover utterly: "the fellow actually suffered. . . . His voice failed him, and he sat there dumb, looking at the door with the face of a man in pain" (*TLS*, 153; cf. 215). Nevertheless, Jasper usually experiences "a degree of bliss too intense for elation" mingled with a "soothing certitude of happiness already conquered" (*TLS*, 164, 210). For someone in this state of mind, no doubt, "the very shadows of life appear endowed with an internal glow," Conrad's figurative definition of "the romantic feeling of reality" (*WT*, vi, v). As might be expected, given Freya's psychological impact, she is described in precisely these terms. A goddess of love, with a "perfect" face, violet eyes, and a "golden crown" of luxuriant, thigh-length hair, she regally apportions romance as she glows in the dark: "This wealth of hair was so glossy that when the screens of the west verandah were down, making a pleasant twilight there, or in the shade of the grove of fruit-trees near the house, it seemed to give out a golden light of its own" (*TLS*, 149, 195, 150). Fittingly, Jasper's spellbound mentality is summarized by means of the same sort of analogy. He behaves "as if the flame of his heart could light up the dark nights of uncharted seas, and the image of Freya serve for an unerring beacon amongst hidden shoals" (*TLS*, 168).

Such rhetoric is familiar. It might well have been excerpted from "Youth," a tale centrally concerned with "the romance of illusions" (*Y*, 42). But there is an important difference between Jasper Allen and the middle-aged Marlow. The former is youthful, impulsive, irresponsible, unwilling to anticipate danger, eluding all doubt through "his immense activity" reminiscent of "a flashing sword-blade perpetually leaping out of the scabbard" (*TLS*, 154, 158): that is, the young Marlow, of course. The latter, in marked contrast, is one who has gained a dark maturity, who is (at the time of the telling of "Youth") completely removed from physical action, and who can now perceive a figurative significance in the radiant holocaust of the dying *Judea* that provides a blighting context for the successful race to Java. Marlow realizes that youth is primarily a mental state laden with self-consuming illusions, whose fires, "leaping audaciously to the sky," limit the perceptions of the young to their own "magic light." But the aging Marlow can also understand a temporal extension of youth to the point where it is "quenched" by time, more cruel, more pitiless, more bitter than the sea" (*Y*, 30). Such an understanding evades Jasper and Freya. As a result they are trapped eventually in a sterile emotional revulsion from the very world that seemed once to guarantee "a blissful future," but which in fact destroys the vessel that "seemed to have the secret of perpetual youth" (*TLS*, 188, 157). Apparently, neither survives to maturity.

No "kid" like Jasper (*TLS*, 185), the narrator who regretfully tells the tale has survived, probably due to an early discovery of the relevant wisdom that "a state of perpetual elation fit, perhaps, for the seventh heaven [is] not exactly safe in a world like ours" (*TLS*, 163). Thus, he can caustically and self-consciously insert the subversive but necessary "as if" qualifiers into the description of Jasper's arrogant, trusting behavior "as if the winds had to wait on his future" (*TLS*, 168), qualifiers that Jasper ignores in his preference to collapse "might" into "is." One reason such circumspect qualification is necessary is that in Conrad's works love and elation are not eidetic states existing statically and safely. In each human instance there are prior and unique characterological limitations of which these states are symptoms, limitations that may be perpetual and at the same time incomprehensible to the persons who are thereby confined.

For instance, both Freya and Jasper grew up deprived of affection from a parent of the opposite sex. Until she was twelve Freya "sailed about with her parents in various ships." But after her mother's death she was abandoned by her father to the care of a "kindly old lady in Singapore" for the next six crucially formative years, during which time her father's personality altered radically. After a period of "dumb grief and sad perplexity" that led to the abandonment of his daughter, old Nelson left his previous way of life of "sailing in all directions" and, becoming obsessed with property, "established himself on his island." At this point he reluctantly accepts Freya's company once again, largely because the girl's keeper, "the kind old lady," has gone "away to Europe" and there is no alternative to assuming responsibility for the girl, who becomes "my Freya," just more property (*TLS*, 147–50, 238). Similarly, Jasper, an "old man's child, having lost his mother early, thrown out to sea out of the way while very young . . . , had not much experience of tenderness of any kind" (*TLS*, 183). Once these two deprived persons meet, a fatal attraction is promptly generated, for each to each manifests necessarily a fascinating, needful otherness. Conrad typically imposes such a context upon eros. To recall merely one other example, Yanko falls in love with the lethally stupid Amy Foster when, in despair in an alien land, he finds a kind stranger who uniquely brings him "such bread as the rich eat," whereupon suddenly "he drop[s] the bread, sieze[s] her wrist," and, integrating manna and manikin, he "imprint[s] a kiss on her hand." His love is returned in similar manner by Amy, who, long fascinated with "outlandish" things, at last has found for herself an outlander and becomes "haunted and possessed by a face, by a presence, fatally, as though she [were] a pagan worshipper of form under a joyous sky" (*T*, 124, 110).

For Conrad teleological romance and eidetic love are always just pathology because only human beings with experiential, fluxile histories are involved in his fictions. Such is not the case for a writer like Spenser, who peoples his narrative with characters of various ontological status. As Isabel MacCaffrey notes,

> Paradigmatic figures [like Belphoebe and Amoret] who embody humanity's recurrent dreams of perfection must be distinguished from personifications, and such distinctions can conveniently be made with reference to modes of temporality. The personified characters produced by analytical allegory refine our understanding of concepts by allowing us to observe them in action, but within Spenser's fiction they have only a local life. Their *ad hoc* incarnations sink beneath the narrative surface and are reabsorbed as it moves along; they are left behind, killed,

forgotten, or otherwise disposed of—the most visible and comic instance being the evaporation of Orgoglio. Certain other personages in *The Faerie Queene* disappear and reappear, and in them Spenser is pointing to philosophical absolutes which have a "real" non-subjective status; they "exist" whether or not any mind is attending to them. Such personages are eternal and therefore, in the fiction, immortal: Duessa, Archimago, Despair, Acrasia. Ensamples or paradigms, on the other hand, are implicated in time, particularly the history of imagining, and their temporal dimension is normally indicated by attaching them to history, pseudo-history, or legend. . . .[23]

Specifically, the embrace of Amoret by Scudamour at the conclusion of Book III (1590 version) provides a useful contrast to similar scenes as handled by, say, Tennyson in "The Holy Grail," or by Conrad. Scudamour

> clipt her twixt his armes twaine,
> And streightly did embrace her body bright,
> Her body, late the prison of sad paine,
> Now the sweet lodge of love and deare delight:
> But she faire Lady overcommen quight
> Of huge affection, did in pleasure melt,
> And in sweet ravishment pourd out her spright:
> No word they spake, nor earthly thing they felt,
> But like two senceles stocks in long embracement dwelt.
>
> Had ye them seene, ye would have surely thought,
> That they had beene that faire *Hermaphrodite*,
> Which that rich *Romane* of white marble wrought,
> And in his costly Bath causd to bee site:
> So seemd those two, as growne together quite. . . .
>
> (*Faerie Queene*, III, xii, 45–46)

Spenser's lovers embrace prototypically and timelessly, free of neuroses. But such is not the case when Tennyson in "The Holy Grail" describes the nun closely embracing Galahad at Arthur's court with a belt made of her own hair and "saying, 'My knight, my love, my knight of heaven, / O thou, my love, whose love is one with mine, / I, maiden round thee, maiden, bind my belt / Go forth, for thou shalt see what I have seen' "(157–60), because, as the poem makes quite clear, the nun is erotically frustrated and obsessed with courtly scandal. For her to see a throbbing red cup in her chamber and to bid Galahad "break thro' all" and find it is not to assert the ontological validity of grail or quest, but rather to question the sanity of visionaries and questers alike. The hermaphrodite tropes of Plato's *Symposium*, the Bible (see Genesis 2:24), and *The Faerie Queene* (see IV, x, 41) are no longer innocent vehicles for efficient communication. Thus, when Freya and Jasper sit "as close together as is possible in this imperfect world where neither can a body be in two places at once nor yet two bodies can be in one place at the same time" and exchange "discourses, apparently without sense, which . . . become pregnant with a diversity of transcendental meanings" (*TLS*, 182–83), the couple's communion exists within a context that insists their love be subjected to analytic scrutiny in the demystifying light of past events in their personal histories, a light which reveals in turn only the sorry impossibility of traditional communion or transcendence.

Characters reacting compulsively against some form of disorientation experienced in the past are not unique, nor are they particularly to be held morally responsible for their compulsions. Conrad's world is radically flawed. Epistemologically inaccessible and phenomenally uncontrollable, it is therefore recalcitrant to efforts to reform it into a *locus amoenus;* and to those who are sufficiently perceptive it reveals evidence of this recalcitrance, which most often takes the form of semiotic discontinuity. That is, human signs that comfortingly signal teleological progress are typically negated by a chaotic world whose absolute, albeit sometimes latent, disorder becomes specifically apparent during moments when it seemingly acts in opposition to these signs. Indeed, "Freya of the Seven Isles" is a tale that limits its technique largely to subverting the precious coherences of teleological romance by means of just such discontinuity.

Jasper Allen is an erotically elated lunatic. He would have even practical and mundane objects like door handles transformed to silver (the lunar metal); he sees in the "full moon . . . perfect and serene . . . the glance of Freya's eyes," and would transmute all the world into an extension of his miniscule *locus amoenus,* the "private foliage-embowered verandah" that is a continuation of Freya's bedroom on the north side of the cottage (the side toward "the everlasting sunshine of the tropics" in the Southern Hemisphere), where he experiences "felicity" (*TLS*, 174, 210, 183, 188). And as a result of his perceptual rapine in "a world that itself seem[s] but a delicate dream" he finds "everything in the world remind[s] him of [Freya]" (*TLS*, 212, 210). A synecdoche for Jasper's transformative efforts is the manner in which the *Bonito* changes color. Of unknown origins, the brig was previously possessed by a "middle-aged Peruvian, in a sober suit of black broadcloth, enigmatic and sententious," and was itself "all black and enigmatical" like its "saturnine" master (*TLS*, 156–57). After purchasing the vessel, Jasper treats it "like a lover" and covers its cryptic nigrescence with "the very best white paint," triumphantly transfiguring a sinister absence into a tropological assertion of a felicitous futurity: "The white sails of that craft were . . . the white pinions of [Jasper's and Freya's] soaring love." Without the brig "there would have been no future" (*TLS*, 157, 156). Significantly, the new chromatic program of the *Bonito* parallels precisely the appearance of Freya. The ship's "brasses flashed like gold, her white body-paint had a sheen like a satin robe" and a "martial elegance"; Freya has a "golden crown" of hair and dresses "all in white," looking like a "martial statue" (*TLS*, 163, 195, 164). Jasper clearly seeks to forge a supportive coherence between all aspects of his experience, but a cosmic pathetic fallacy eludes him: the very coral reef on which his beloved *Bonito* dies is white too.

The *Bonito* strikes the reef because Jasper cannot banish all recalcitrant darkness from his world. Though he can change the color of his sailboat from black to white after obtaining it from the dusky Peruvian, and he can skillfully avoid "nasty, shiny black rock-heads" and "points of land stretching out all black," he cannot for long defy the sable ontic essence of both land and sea. The steam-powered *Neptun* also is "black," the disfiguring smoke from its "short black funnel roll[s] between the masts of the *Bonito*" and obscures "the sunlit whiteness of her sails, consecrated to the service of love" (*TLS*, 152, 171, 164); and it is commanded by a swarthy, ponderous Dutch naval officer, Heemskirk, "forty years of age," with "black hair" and "unpleasant eyes [that] were nearly black, too," who appears ultimately "like a black beetle" (*TLS*, 208, 159–60, 162). Just as Heemskirk amuses himself by going about knocking down the navigational beacons which Jasper erects, so ultimately Jasper, the "flashing sword-blade," is crushed, ironically becoming "a skeleton in *dirty white* clothes," (*TLS*, 158, 236; italics mine), thus confirming the narrator's decisive doubts: "It is very fine and romantic to possess for your very own a finely tempered and trusy sword-blade, but whether it is the best weapon to counter with the common cudgel-play of Fate—that's another question" (*TLS*, 167).

And, again, just as Heemskirk destroys Jasper's navigational beacons, so a more subtle force is at work to annul "the image of Freya" that serves Jasper as "an unerring beacon amongst hidden shoals," for "events [are] mysteriously shap[ing] themselves to fit the purposes of a dark passion" (*TLS*, 168, 228). Stated simply, Freya is not permanently an imposing divinity clad in white. Her appearance parallels that of the *Bonito* only in the early parts of the story. Freya dons "her dark dressing-gown" (*TLS*, 203) the morning after she has violently slapped Heemskirk in revenge for his gross amorousness. Now clad in umbral hues, she eagerly sends kisses at sunrise across the anchorage to the departing Jasper (who claimed "I could run with you in my hands . . . without stumbling—without touching the earth") while the enraged Heemskirk, who is constantly stumbling, watches from concealment (*TLS*, 189; see 184, 196, 205). Although Freya's affections have not at all been diverted consciously from Jasper and his *Bonito*, toward which she stares in an "attitude of supreme cry" (*TLS*, 204), she has initiated the fatal enmity that will undo all possibility for "matrimony and 'ever after' happiness" (*TLS*, 178), and the fact of this undoing is revealed by the definitive semiotic discontinuity that now distinguishes her darkened appearance from that of her lover and his alabaster vessel. Put differently, Freya's altered guise is a sign that the world-weather is degenerating, that for Jasper and his lady the global *locus amoenus* is beginning a terminal dissolution.

This impending dissolution indicates how the narrative climactically inverts Northrop Frye's general specification for the plot of a typical comedy: "What normally happens is that a young man wants a young woman, that his desire is resisted by some opposition . . . , and that near the end . . . some twist in the plot enables the hero to have his will."[24] Like a light comedy, "Freya of the Seven Isles" is laden with laughter as characters repeatedly find one another amusing. An exhaustive list would be impractical, but the following are representative examples. The narrator finds it "funny" that Jasper is so easily desolated by Freya's absence; he also finds "funny" the great contrast between the physiognomies of Jasper, the Nelsons, and Heemskirk; and he calls old Nelson a "comedy father," "pathetically comic," and the maid a "comedy camerista" (*TLS*, 153, 165, 176, 177, 178). Freya's maid mocks Heemskirk by making "funny and expressive grimaces" behind his back, and Freya herself finds the Dutchman "ridiculous" and "funny" and once "laughed outright" at him (*TLS*, 178, 187, 191 and 200, 192). Jasper laughs at the narrator's efforts to urge caution upon him, finds Heemskirk's shadow "comical," and cannot even take seriously having the *Bonito* towed—to Jasper it is only "the beetle's little joke" (*TLS*, 167, 216, 218).

This pattern of amusement is a function of the characters' unjustifiably optimistic assumptions, "a soothing certitude of happiness already conquered" (*TLS*, 210). They fail to notice the profoundly ambiguous nature of hilarity: Heemskirk, who is "repulsively comical," causes Freya to make a "smiling grimace" and "faint, spasmodic sounds of a mysterious nature, between laughter and sobs," just as thoughts of having Freya aboard the *Bonito* cause Jasper to make "an inarticulate sound, something like a moan wrung out by pain or delight" (*TLS*, 187, 199, 190). Due to their impercipience, a cruel trick is played upon them by the only secure joker in the story, "fate, which . . . wears the aspect of crude and savage jesting" (*TLS*, 231). And the cosmic joker strikes, of course, at the precise moment when the amenable world-weather seems most completely to encourage and justify human trust in its inherent benevolence:

> It was at that moment, in this peace, in this serenity, under the full, benign gaze of the moon propitious to lovers, on a sea without a wrinkle, under a sky without a cloud, as if all Nature had assumed its most clement mood in a spirit of mockery, that the gunboat *Neptun*, detaching herself from the dark coast under which she had been lying, invisible, steamed out to intercept the trading brig *Bonito* standing out to sea.
>
> (*TLS*, 210)

Hereafter, taken unawares by the destruction of his vessel, Jasper "would never laugh at anything in his life" again, and Freya, dying "sometimes . . . would laugh a little" in unrelieved despair (*TLS*, 221, 237). Conrad's comedies are not for mortals to divine with merriment.

Just as sustained, one-dimensional hilarity permeates the story only until a tragic inconsistency in the nature of comedy is revealed, so the area around "the Seven Isles is a particularly calm and cloudless spot as a rule" (*TLS*, 151), but storms occasionally occur: "Now and again, an afternoon thunderstorm over Banka, or even one of those vicious thick squalls, from the distant Sumatra coast, would make a sudden sally upon the group, enveloping it for a couple hours in whirlwinds and bluish-black murk of a particularly sinister aspect" (*TLS*, 151–52). During these storms "Freya would sit down to the piano and play fierce Wagner music in the flicker of blinding flashes" (*TLS*, 152). By means of this "fierce piece of love music" the ominous weather is seemingly bridled; its potent tonalities have "been tried more than once against the thunderstorms of the group" (*TLS*, 206). But when Freya tries to use this same music as a means of deterring the amorous efforts of the "black" Heemskirk (himself a metaphoric tempest), it fails, another indication that the world-weather is negatively altering. And when at last Freya, now "very erect," viciously strikes Heemskirk, temporarily limiting him to the use of only one "black, evil, glaring eye" (*TLS*, 196, 197),[25] she threatens to displace his masculinity and leaves him predisposed to respond in kind to her lover.

At this point the Wagnerian context of this scene must be invoked specifically. Conrad uses partial plot parallels from Richard Wagner's *Der Ring des Nibelungen* to emphasize the central thematic concern of "Freya of the Seven Isles": a revelation of the existence of a central cosmic flaw, "Fate" (*TLS*, 167, 169), which appears specifically as an irreconcilable tension between a need to accumulate power and property and an ability to love. In *Das Rheingold* Freia, goddess of love, controls and dispenses the source of eternal life for the gods, the golden apples in her garden: "Ohne die Äpfel, / alt und grau, / gries und grämlich, / welkend zum Spott aller Welt, / erstirbt der Götter Stamm."[26] Similarly, Conrad's Freya is committed to the transcendence of time: in a realm of "everlasting sunshine" she pursues "'ever after' happiness" aboard a vessel that, "like some fair women . . . , seemed to have the secret of perpetual youth" (*TLS*, 209, 178, 157). But in Norse mythology divinities are limited by time and fate. In Conrad's story this fact makes appropriate the previously discussed degeneration of world-weather, violations of the comic sensibility, and resultant semiotic discontinuities, as well as, more specifically, the predicted betrayal of Jasper by Schultz, a betrayal "as sure as Fate" (*TLS*, 169).

In *Das Rheingold* a lethal cosmic resistance to order is manifested in terms of the inability of the gods to reconcile the possession of great power with an ability to love. Wotan initially makes a bargain with the giants, Fasolt and Fafner, that grants them Freia, goddess of love, in exchange for them using their vast strength to build the fortress of Valhalla. But when, their task complete, the giants carry Freia off, Wotan deeply regrets the deal and schemes to recover her. Meanwhile, in Nibelheim the benighted Nibelung, Alberich, is hoarding a great treasure. Through power derived from a magic ring he has had forged from gold stolen from the Rhine maidens, he enslaves others and forces them to gather riches. Wotan plans to steal the treasure from Alberich and use it to purchase Freia from the giants. The plan works. Freia is returned. The gods are, temporarily at least, saved. But a horrid possibility has been loosed upon all creation. The Rhine maidens Wellgunde and Woglinde first articulate the proposition:

Wellgunde

Der Welt Erbe
gewänne zu eigen,
wer aus dem Rheingold
schüfe den Ring,
der masslose Macht ihn verlieh'.

Woglinde

Nur wer der Minne
Macht entsagt,
nur wer der Minne
Lust verjagt,
nur der erzielt sich den Zauber,
zum Reif zu zwingen das Gold.

Earlier, Alberich heard and accepted, in a rage because the nixies mercilessly mocked his coarse offers of love: "Ich . . . / schmiede den rächenden Ring; / denn hör' es die Flut: / so verfluch' ich die Liebe!"[27] And when Wotan and Loge later trick him into surrendering at once the treasure, the Tarnhelm, and the ring, Alberich reiterates his curse, making it fatally applicable to all:

Die in linder Lüfte Weh'n
da oben ihr lebt,
lacht und liebt:
mit goldner Faust
euch Göttliche fang' ich mir alle!
Wie ich der Liebe abgesagt,
alles, was lebt,
soll ihr entsagen!
Mit Golde gekirrt,
nach Gold nur sollt ihr noch gieren! [28]

All this is relevant to "Freya of the Seven Isles" because this tale directly concerns the qualification, and even abandonment, of love for the sake of power. In marked contrast to Wagner's Freia, Freya Nelson is no goddess; and since she is no animate abstraction, she too is culpable. For example, unwilling to acknowledge that maturity is a "shadow-line," she insists that she will not accompany Jasper aboard his brig to be his wife until her twenty-first birthday. Freya arbitrarily creates an absolute situation as a way of reassuring herself of her own power over her lover. This might be expected of a young lady who had little if any influence with her father while growing up, and who remains under the dominion of a man concerned primarily with property and therefore willing to subvert his daughter's affection for Jasper. Due to his fear of Heemskirk and consequent "fright about his 'little estate,'" the old man disregards "sense, feeling, and ridicule" (*TLS*, 166). Appropriately, Freya resents any suggestion that a man might have the ability to control her, and resists the "delightful giddiness" of Jasper's erotic embrace in order to insist that only her own decisions govern her activities: 'I've promised you—I've said I would come—and I shall come of my own free will. You shall wait for me on board. I shall get up the side—by myself. . . . And then—and then I shall be carried off. But it will be no man who will carry me off—it will be the brig, your brig—our brig. . . . I love the beauty!" (*TLS*, 190). Freya experiences love essentially as a function of power, control, and property. She arrogantly disregards contingency as well as her lover, and too late recognizes she was "conceited, headstrong, capricious" (*TLS*, 238). As one might anticipate, Freya is irrationally threatened by the frustrated Heemskirk's offer to carry her away. Moreover, Jasper had just proposed the same thing, so when Heemskirk shouts 'I will lift you off that stool" and then kisses her, Freya strikes without thinking.

Like Alberich in his thwarted efforts to embrace the Rhine maidens, and the giants in their fruitless attempts to carry Freia away, Heemskirk is devastatingly humiliated, and he decides to forsake his affection for the girl in order to seek revenge. Wagnerian echoes abound, though they are sporadic and indicate that Conrad is not emptily mimicking the plot of the Ring-cycle. Heemskirk is squat, dark, and awkward, an Alberich indeed, casting an "inky shadow" (*TLS*, 215). And when Freya hits him he becomes one-eyed, like Wotan, who also forgoes love for power and who in order to win a wife "mein eines Auge / setzt' ich werbend daran."[29] By momentarily merging the infernal and supernal (Alberich and Wotan) in the human Heemskirk, Conrad is able to demonstrate his primary interest lies in emphasizing the motif of the sacrifice of love, rather than in playing superficial intellectual games by means of barren and precise character parallels. Obsessed with revenge through exercise of power, Heemskirk ghoulishly destroys Freya and Jasper by annulling their respective illusions of potency, which are attached to the brig. The *Bonito* signifies to both the lovers Jasper's "power to snatch the calm, adorable Freya to his breast, and carry her off" (*TLS*, 218). Through the destruction of Jasper's brig just after Jasper has lost all his firearms, the predatory Heemskirk, who always sought to "devour" Freya "with his eyes," emasculates Jasper and reduces him to "a skeleton," and, in turn, Freya to an anemic corpse (*TLS*, 160, 236). The "immovable" Heemskirk in his "sinister immobility" has fixed the soaring brig in "desolated immobility" and fatally paralyzed the lovers (*TLS*, 193, 188, 229).

It is appropriate to the present discussion to note that Northrop Frye calls romance "the mythos of summer" and suggests that the "complete form of the romance is . . . the successful quest," a "search of the libido or desiring self for a fulfillment that will deliver it from the anxieties of reality but will still contain that reality," during which search "the opposite poles of the cycles of nature are assimilated to the opposition of the hero and his enemy."[30] Conrad's acknowledgment of this paradigm appears through his obvious and repeated subversive modifications of it. Freya as "an unerring beacon amongst hidden shoals" who was capable of "transcendental meanings" is terminally displaced. A decisive change in the world-weather substitutes for her the inhuman beacons of "pale lightning . . . , faint, mysteriously consecutive flashes, like incomprehensible signals from some distant planet." And this change culminates both in the lethal triumph of Heemskirk, "a grotesque specimen . . . from some other planet," who ironically enjoys "a transcendental, an incredible perfection of vengeance" (*TLS*, 192, 165, 228), and in the demonic midwinter setting that ends the story, on "one of those January days in London, one of those wintry days composed of the four devilish elements, cold, wet, mud, and grime, combined with a particular stickiness of atmosphere that clings like an unclean garment to one's very soul" (*TLS*, 233). Thus is negated the usual ontologically confirmative June marriage of romance tradition that reflects the victorious congruence in an earthly *locus amoenus* of reigning celestial harmonies. Jasper's brig struck the reef "On the very top of high-water, spring tides," when he had slightly more than two months to wait for his wedding (*TLS*, 221, 207). The Seven Isles are located in the Southern Hemisphere. This means the union probably would have taken place in January, a sunny summer fulfillment that the swarthy Heemskirk as well as the climactic spatial shift of the narrative decisively prevent.

The Fundament of Paradise

The topos of the *locus amoenus* (often a beatific garden), has existed in Western literature for two thousand years as a figure through which intellectual concord is rendered apparent by physical analogy. An early example is Odysseus's experience in Calypso's cave (*Odyssey*, bk. V); Theocritus in Idyll VII details more thoroughly the visual and auditory constituents of this trope: "Many a poplar and elm murmered above our heads, and near at hand the sacred water from the cave of the Nymphs fell plashing. . . . Larks and finches sang, the dove made moan, and bees flitted humming about the springs. All things were fragrant of rich harvest and of fruit time."[1] Traditionally, this is a life-sustaining spot harboring those "aspects of nature that are not only recreative, but generative . . . , tied to nature in its numinous aspects . . . , a vessel for essentially religious feelings."[2] Thus, it is often correlated with redemptive locales like that which conceals the "silver flood, / Full of great vertues," the "Well of Life,"which revives the Red Cross Knight (*Faerie Queene*, I, xi, 29), and the landscape of Pope's "Spring" that is psychologically re-created with compensatory impact by the shepherds in "Winter." As E. R. Curtius suggests generally, the portrayal of environmental features in such a way as to indicate that the phenomenal world validly reflects human needs (a descriptive technique definitive of the *locus amoenus*) usually involves "harmonies of opposites" employed as "emotive formulas."[3] But in the modern world such portrayals are foredoomed. What seems to be an amenable place is often only a medium through which the ultimate absence of order appears. In works like "A Smile of Fortune" and "Freya of the Seven Isles" (to cite only two brief examples) Conrad redefines for his fictional purposes an ancient topos and demonstrates thereby the tendency of teleological romance to degenerate, within the consciousness of a single character, from a deceptively triumphant pathetic fallacy to a definitive revelation of incomprehensible asympathetic process.

Such revelations are not uncommon in the nineteeth century. In *Almayer's Folly* Dain and Nina, two enraptured narcissi, float in their canoes "quietly side by side, reflected by the black water in the dim light struggling through a high canopy of dense foliage; while above, away up in the broad day, [flame] immense red blossoms sending down . . . a shower of great dew sparkling petals that [descend] rotating slowly in a continuous and perfumed stream . . . over them, under them, in the sleeping water . . ." (*AF,* 71). The solipsistic triumph of *Eros armata* is here figured forth by means of a loss of the distinctions that normally isolate the opposing categories of darkness (with "sparkling" stars) and light (with "flam[ing]" sun), while up and down, verticality and horizontality, all mingle in a "rotating" vertigo of "over," "under," and "in." Precisely the same sort of externalization of a tragically temporary narcissistic deliverance occurs within the *locus amoenus* depicted in Shelley's *Alastor.* At noon (traditional moment when opposites conjoin in the Creation as Logos becomes phenomenon, according to Augustine) the doomed Poet discovers a "still fountain" in which "his eyes [behold] / Their own wan light," as all around in "night's noontide clearness" opposites commingle: "pyramids / Of . . . cedar . . . frame" their own contrasting shapes, their branches' "solemn domes," while the "ten thousand blossoms" of "parasites" seem only "gamesome infants' eyes" with "most innocent wiles" as their tendrils fold in lethal embrace the "wedded boughs" of their hosts amidst the "noonday watch" of "Silence and Twilight" and a "soul-dissolving odour" (see 420–68).The "stagnant" yet elfin lagoon replete with a "fleecy pink cloud" where Arsat and Diamelen seek an escape from time through eroticism is still another locale (*TU,* 189). Though an apparent talisman due to its surface of sacred lotus blossoms, like Jacobus's garden it can only betray human demands for a sustained redemptive function.

The tropical landscape in *Almayer's Folly* and *An Outcast of the Islands* resists physical and metaphysical human tampering. Unlike a manicured garden, it cannot be compelled to conceal its alarming necrophagous vitality,

> where lay, entombed and rotting, countless generations of trees, and where their successors stood as if mourning, in dark green foliage, immense and helpless, awaiting their turn. Only the parasites seemed to live there in a sinuous rush upwards into the air and sunshine, feeding on the dead and the dying alike, and crowning their victims with pink and blue flowers that gleamed amongst the boughs, incongruous and cruel, like a strident and mocking note in the solemn harmony of the doomed trees.
>
> (*AF,* 167)

By depicting such lethal entanglements Conrad suggests the dependence of the illusion of love upon dangerous and morbific neuroses and at the same time subverts a familiar and traditional marriage topos.[4] Only to peer closely at the *danse macabre* of the forest, its "exulting riot of silent destruction" (*AF,* 165), is to risk being "touched by the breath of Death itself" (*AF,* 167), being entrapped mentally inside a mordant "magic circle," a "great silence full of struggle and death," with "Death everywhere—wherever one looks"(*OI,* 157, 326, 342). Such consciousness dissolves mental and physical identity in an anxious anticipation, such as Willems suffers, of the day when he will lie

> stretched upon the warm moisture of the ground, feeling nothing, seeing nothing, knowing nothing; he would lie stiff, passive, rotting slowly; while over him, under

him, through him—unopposed, busy, hurried—the endless and minute throngs of insects, little shining monsters of repulsive shapes, with horns, with claws, with pincers, would swarm in streams, in rushes, in eager struggles for his body . . . till there would remain nothing but the white gleam of bleaching bones in the long grass that would shoot its feathery heads between the bare and polished ribs. There would be that only left of him; nobody would miss him; no one would remember him.

(*OI*, 331–32)

Such a landscape and such thoughts reproduce with precision the mental spaces behind Spenser's House of Pride, where the Red Cross Knight "scarce could . . . footing find in that fowle way, / For many corses . . . / of murdered men, which therein strowed lay" (*Faerie Queene* I, v, 53), within Orgoglio's castle, where ". . . all the floore (too filthy to be told) / With blood of guiltlesse babes, and innocents trew . . . / Defiled was" (I, viii, 35), and before the Cave of Despair, where ". . . carcases were scattered on the greene, / And throwne about the cliffs" (I, ix, 34).

But in Conrad these spaces provide only an occasion for exposing the failure of heroic pretensions, as red-faced knights like Dain Waris and Willems discover. Dain promises transcendence, a means whereby Almayer can eventually "live rich and respected . . . and forget this life, and all this struggle, and all this misery," a means whereby Nina can sever herself at last from the commercial jungle, "the atmosphere of sordid plottings for gain, of the no less disgusting intrigues and crimes for lust and money" (*AF*, 18, 42). To someone like the deracinated Nina, who knows of "no heaven to send her prayer to," "a Son of Heaven" like Dain is indeed captivating. The apparent "embodiment of her fate, the creature of her dreams . . . the ideal Malay chief of her mother's tradition," he integrates both future and past in a delusive deliverance (*AF*, 118–19, 51, 64). Similarly, Willems appears to Aissa "as necessary as the sun that gives life," "so great that his presence hides the earth and the water from my sight!" (*OI*, 248–49). But like the "doomed trees" that had "lost faith in their strength," Dain "had lost faith in himself" and hides furtively in the forest with the timid swine that greet him, as he bends down to seek more thorough concealment, with an "angry grunting, and a sounder of wild pig [that] crashed away in the undergrowth" (*AF*, 167, 165, 168, 167). Willems too is suspiciously like a "Pig! Pig! Pig!" and though "he had been a man once," his "strength was a lie" (*OI*, 94, 253). Irremediable degradation, whether intensely private or disconcertingly public, defiles the knight in Conrad's fiction one way or another this side of the grave. In the face of an omnipotent yet evanescent extinction, martial conduct is pointless. Doing battle "with the impalpable . . . with the shadows . . . with the darkness . . . with the silence," Willems can only strike "futile blows, dashing from side to side; obstinate, hopeless, and always beaten back" (*OI*, 157). And Dain can only humiliate himself: "Carried away by his excitement, he snatched the kriss hidden in his sarong, and . . . rushed forward, struck at the empty air, and fell on his face" (AF, 168).

Just as there is no enemy, there is no Una, only "the high dignity of lifeless matter . . . , incurious and unmoved," onto which one indecorously tumbles (OI, 242). Nevertheless, Conrad's questers typically search for a oneness that lives and reflects their respective desires: "mankind" has an intense "desire for singularity" (OI, 202). It is enlightening to observe how in Conrad's works the definite article functions in passages wherein is described a character's deepest wish. Willems, for example, thinks there is such a thing as "*the* scheme of creation," "*The* road to greatness" (OI, 11, 65; italics mine). Singularity promises a neatly focused salvation. Plurality subverts and absorbs, "vague, disgusting, and terrible . . . like a band of assassins in the darkness of vast and unsafe places" (OI, 265; italics mine). In its fractious presence there can only be "unknown things," a "horror of bewildered life where he could understand nothing and nobody round him; where he could guide, control, comprehend nothing and no one" (OI, 149). For Conrad's characters a haven from multiplicity, a "refuge from . . . thoughts" (OI, 65), can be found (temporarily) in erotic love. Willems recovers singularity through his infatuation with Aissa: "*She* seemed to him to be some*thing* loud and stirring like *a* shout, silent and penetrating like *an* inspiration," and "*all* his sensations, his personality—*all* . . . seemed to be lost in . . . *the* priceless promise of that woman," who now is "*his only* thought, his *only* feeling," "*the* luminous fact" (OI, 69, 128–29, 76; italics mine).

A place of pure order, pure value, and identity free from threat in a Christian world is heaven; in Conrad's world such singularity and immutability is inherently inauthentic, a premature path to the tomb. To indicate this Conrad fittingly invokes Spenser's Bower of Bliss, a locus of delusive, destructive feminine gratification, for both writers dramatize in their own terms the way a woman's gaze "whips the soul out of the body, but leaves the body alive and helpless, to be swayed here and there by the capricious tempests of passion and desire" (AF, 171), the way a "faire witch" like Acrasia typically disarms and consumes verdant knights:

> And . . . right over him she hong
> With her false eyes fast fixed in his sight,
>
> . . . .
> And oft inclining downe, with kisses light,
> For feare of waking him, his lips bedewd
> And through his humid eyes did sucke his spright,
>
> . . . .
> Wherewith she sighed soft, as if his case she rewd.
>
> (*Faerie Queene*, II, xii, 73)

Similarly, "bewitched" by the dominant, emasculating Aissa (significantly, one of the names Achilles assumed when seeking to avoid the Trojan War),[5]

Willems mistakenly identifies "true life" as the "dreamy immobility" he experiences as "she [draws] the man's soul away from him through his immobile pupils" (OI, 157, 146, 140; cf. the way Renouard feels in the presence of Felicia "as if his soul were streaming after her through his eyes" [WT, 64]). Aissa also exerts her ocular potence upon Lingard as she seeks to mould his will to her own: "From her staring black eyes . . . a double ray of her very soul streamed out in a fierce desire to light up the most obscure designs of his heart" (OI, 246). Indeed, so there will be no mistake as to the lethal nature of the delusion of total and singular fulfillment, Conrad causes Willems's *initial* surrender to Aissa, when "he gave up as a tired swimmer gives up . . . , because the night is dark and the shore far—because death is better than life" (OI, 81), to decisively echo the recommendation of suicide, the *final* act of life, that Spenser's Despair gives to the Red Cross Knight:

> "Is not short payne well borne, that brings long ease,
> And layes the soule to sleepe in quiet grave?
> Sleepe after toyle, port after stormie seas,
> Ease after warre, death after life does greatly please."
> (*Faerie Queene*, I, ix, 40; cf. epigraph to *The Rover*)

The inappropriate search for a final deliverance on the part of many characters in nineteenth century literature is typically arrested in passages fraught with iconography used by earlier and more optimistic writers of romance, such as Spenser, to indicate the kind of dangerous self-enclosure that distracts persons from an entirely appropriate quest for salvation. In Sonnet 35 of the *Amoretti* Spenser's infatuated narrator complains:

> My hungry eyes, through greedy covetize
> Still to behold the object of their paine,
> With no contentment can themselves suffize,
> But having pine, and having not complaine.
> For lacking it, they cannot lyfe sustayne,
> And having it, they gaze on it the more:
> In their amazement lyke Narcissus vaine,
> Whose eyes him starv'd: so plenty makes me poore.
> Yet are mine eyes so filled with the store
> Of that faire sight, that nothing else they brooke,
> But lothe the things which they did like before,
> And can no more endure on them to looke.
> All this worlds glory seemeth vayne to me,
> And all their showes but shadowes, saving she.

The speaker suffers because he regards his lady as a final goal, whereas she can never be more than a medium through which divine perfection is revealed. Consequently, he lives among "shadowes," like Britomart, who (mistakenly) feels:

> But wicked fortune mine, though mind be good,
> Can have no end, nor hope of my desire,
> But feed on shadows, whiles I die for food,
> And like a shadow wexe, whiles with entire
> Affection, I doe languish and expire.
>
> *(Faerie Queene, III, ii, 44)*

The mental states dramatized in these passages are pauses along the way to deliverance and therefore are not denotative of lethal error but rather only of a frustrating partiality that eventually will be made whole. But in Shelley's *Alastor* the youthful poet's pursuit of an absolute revelation is absolutely terminated in a dream of a shadowy feminine enigma that vanishes even as he seizes it:

> . . . she drew back a while,
> Then, yielding to irresistable joy,
> With frantic gesture and short breathless cry
> Folded his frame in her dissolving arms.
> Now blackness veiled his dizzy eyes, and night
> Involved and swallowed up the vision; sleep
> Like a dark flood suspended in its course,
> Rolled back its impulse on his vacant brain.
>
> (184–91)

The "dark flood" that overwhelms Shelley's visionary youth is the counterpart of the figurative waters that engulf Conrad's amorous Willems when he surrenders to Aissa "as a tired swimmer gives up" (*OI*, 81), and, in turn, all Conrad's sinking absolutists. Both writers operate in terms of a tradition that defines desire as analogous to the (auto)eroticism of the mythic Narcissus, trapped into hopeless and lethal groping for his own unrecognized watery image, which in his case is connotative as well of plenary sources since his mother, Liriope, was imprisoned in the waters of Cephisus when he was forcefully conceived. All narcissi are doomed, though Spenser treats his "foolish *Narcisse*, that likes the watry shore" (*Faerie Queene*, III, vi, 45) gently, if ironically, assigning the sterile self-lover a place in the Garden of Adonis, the origin of all physical life, where he can exist forever yearning for the impossible in a "state of consciousness which walls out death and pain, which is unrelated to generation on the one hand or chastity on the other." [6] Refusing to provide a transcendent arbor for his inflexible quester, Shelley in *Alastor* demonstrates that narcissism can at last only commemorate and futilely consecrate the absence of supernal plenitude and clarity, while suggesting the tragic vulnerability of minds that seek to elude in a solipsism of limited potency the "colossal Skeleton" in its "devastating omnipotence" (611, 613).

The modern etiology of need does not get beyond Shelley's *Alastor*. The culminant embrace can only be "dissolving," for through the very existence of an image of desire is predicted the paucity of gratification. Irreconcilable tension between mind and world is dramatized metaphorically in terms of a masculine quest for a female soul-mate after the familiar pattern outlined by Aristophanes in Plato's *Symposium*. But a transcendent fusion is frustrated because the world perpetually resists and eludes the mind's presumptuous formative powers. Feminine personifications of Nature have always been veiled, from Apuleius's vision of Isis, through the mythic Psyche at her wedding and the Shulamite in the Song of Songs, to Blake's Vala. As usual, Spenser best summarizes a traditional icon: "great dame Nature" is

> far greater and more tall of stature
> Then any of the gods or Powers on hie:
> Yet certes by her face and physnomy,
> Whether she man or woman inly were,
> That could not any creature well descry:
> For, with a veile that wimpled every where,
> Her head and face was hid, that mote to none appeare.
>
> (*Faerie Queene*, VII, vii, 5; cf. IV, x, 41)

At the outset of *Alastor* the narrator metaphorically describes his unsuccessful search for ultimate knowledge as a failed attempt at seducing the "Mother of this unfathomable world" (18), who "ne'er yet" has "unveiled [her] inmost sanctuary" (37–38). The narrator's tragically visionary friend dreams of "a veiled maid" (151) who seems more receptive to solipsistic imposition, who has a "voice . . . like the voice of his own soul" (153), and who speaks "thoughts the most dear to him" (160). Connoting the evanescent surfaces of phenomenal nature, the maiden's "sinuous veil / Of woven wind" (176–77), of "woven sounds of streams and breezes" (155), fatally entangles "his inmost sense suspended in its web / Of many-colored woof and shifting hues" (156–57), and ultimately "veil[s] his dizzy eyes" with "blackness" (188) when the feminine revelation so tantalizingly concealed behind the veil decisively evades the young poet's ardent psychic embrace.

It is primarily this well-established romance tradition rather than constitutional peculiarities[7] that determines the impalpable and eidetic qualities of Conrad's women. In the manner of Spenser's "dame Nature" with her "veile" and Shelley's "veiled maid," these women appear as does Aissa, "an apparition behind a transparent veil—a veil woven of sunbeams and shadows," to Willems, who partially penetrates the sanctum of "Nature's workshop" and sees an imposing female presence "standing above him, her head lost in the shadow of broad and graceful leaves" (*OI*, 70, 74, 76). This same tradition also determines that Conrad's women, like Shelley's superlative and elusive female wraith in *Alastor*, shall so consistently be able to slip away from the fervent arms of their lovers. The opposition of mind and world in Conrad's works cannot be canceled beneficently in a *hieros gamos*. Thus, at the climactic moment when Karain stands face to face with Pata Matara's sister, of whom he has dreamed for years, and whose life he has just saved, she denies his identity, saying, "I never saw him before" (*TU*, 39). Thus, when in "The Informer" Sevrin, asserting to his mistress "I have felt in me the power to make you share [my] conviction" (cf. epigraph to *Lord Jim*), stoops "low as if to touch the hem of her garment," the girl "snatche[s] her skirt away from his polluting contact and avert[s] her head" (*SS*, 95–96). Thus, only when Gaspar Ruiz is at the point of death does the puritan Erminia,[8] "a supernatural being, or at least a witch," tell him she loves him (*SS*, 48, 66). Thus, Felicia Moorsom, "a wraith, cold mist, stuff of dreams, illusion," claiming to "stand for truth," ignores both the fervent embrace and kneeling adoration of Renouard (*WT*, 77–78). Thus, when M. George has at last "pressed a long kiss into the hollow of [Rita's] throat," he finds that "with a stifled cry of surprise her arms fell off [him] as if she had been shot" (*AG*, 224). Thus, in "A Smile of Fortune" when the narrator assaults Alice Jacobus in the garden with a kiss "vicious enough to have been a bite," and a "storm of haphazard caresses," and a mighty "circle of my arms," he is shocked to find that "instead of trying to tear [his] hands apart she flung herself upon [his] breast and with a downward, undulating, serpentine motion, a quick sliding dive, she got away from [him] smoothly. It was all very swift . . ." (*TLS*, 69–70). Thus, "the steady" Freya Nelson, whose conversation with Jasper Allen is "pregnant with . . . transcendental meanings," "closed her eyes and smiled in the dark, abandoning herself in a delightful giddiness, for an instant to [Jasper's] encircling arm. But before he could be tempted to tighten his grasp she was out of it, a foot away from him . . ." (*TLS*, 193, 189). Even when the sinuous surface is seized and apparently lifted, only a void appears. Thus, in the midst of an exalted appreciation of "the triumphant delight of sunshine and of life," Willems dies by Aissa's hand at Aissa's feet: "Missed, by Heaven!" indeed (*OI*, 360). And Jim expires "unflinching," (*LJ*, 6, 416), "tearing himself out of the arms of a jealous love . . . to celebrate his pitiless wedding with a shadowy ideal of conduct," having "beheld the face of that opportunity which, like an Eastern bride, had come veiled to his side" (*LJ*, 416–17).

These patterns coalesce in *Chance*, where a similar dangerously feminine yet barren *locus amoenus* exists, "the enchanted gardens of Armida" (*C*, 396), the trope that in this novel schematizes the process of solipsistic self-seduction that characterizes love relationships in Conrad's works. This sort of metaphor has been badly misunderstood in the past. Consider briefly an article that purports to deal specifically with the reference to the gardens of Armida. Gerald H. Levin in "An Allusion to Tasso in Conrad's *Chance*" observes erroneously that "in connecting Armida with Flora, Anthony senses that Flora is like Armida in her mysterious fascination."[9] By making this remark Levin shows that he refuses at all to acknowledge the most critical hermeneutic issue in *Chance*: due to the many layers of narrative perspective and their often indeterminate boundaries and relationships, characters like Anthony and

Flora do not exist at all in an epistemologically independent and definitive way.[10]

It is Marlow, not Anthony, who offers the allusion to Tasso, to elucidate his own speculations about Anthony's conceptual relationship with Flora. These speculations, moreover, concern (1) events which transpired aboard the *Ferndale* even before Young Powell first joined the ship (*C*, 376), and about which Young Powell learned later indirectly from Franklin, the outraged mate, and possibly from Flora; (2) events about which Marlow in turn learned much later from Young Powell while chatting on Young Powell's "five-ton cutter" (*C*, 258) in the Essex marshes; (3) events about which the "I" learns later still from "out the shadows of the bookcase," in his apartment, where Marlow, his informant, suddenly appears "one evening rather early, soon after dinner" and, "his eyes fixed on vacancy," proceeds to talk (*C*, 325, 257, 283); and (4) events that the "I" subsequently passes on to the reader in the form of the novel itself. Conrad's aesthetic fabrication of such a radical subjectivity frustrates the very rhetoric of traditional criticism. It is not possible legitimately to discuss anything in *Chance* but what the "I" says. There are no characters or events as they are customarily conceived, and in the following discussion of Marlow's allusion to Tasso such a disclaimer must implicitly preface every statement made. Whatever coherences are discovered in the characters of Anthony and Flora are no more than patterns created and imposed by those who have, in the previous layers of narrative and for whatever unknowable reasons, caused certain attributes to accumulate around these two proper nouns. It is precisely the reluctance of critics like Levin to acknowledge the blighting epistemic openness in Conrad's fiction that, amusingly, makes of them "knights" according to Marlow's mocking definition in *Chance* of this "masculine" mentality that constantly fabricates "well-known . . . illusions, without which the average male creature cannot get on" (*C*, 94).

In order to understand Marlow's invocation of the gardens of Armida it is first necessary to elucidate Marlow's conception of human psychology and the sexual metaphors he uses to explain it. To Marlow a woman archetypally partakes of "a force of nature, blind in its strength and capricious in its power . . . not altogether trustworthy like all natural forces which, for us, work in the dark because of our imperfect comprehension" (*C*, 327). Like the phenomenal world, the potent essence of woman partakes of a disorienting unity of opposites: "All the virtues are not enough for them; they want also all the crimes for their own. And why? Because in such completeness there is power" (*C*, 63). Marlow goes on to make a crucial distinction. The threatening "completeness" of woman must be isolated conceptually from that aspect of a woman's psychic composition (her "femininity") which prevents the destructive application of this threat to a precious masculine world: 'What prevents women . . . from 'coming on deck and playing hell with the ship' generally, is that something in them precise and mysterious, acting both as restraint and as inspiration; their femininity, in short . . ." (*C*, 63). It is "femininity" that causes women "to spare the stupid sensitiveness of men":

> The women's rougher, simpler, more upright judgment, embraces the whole truth, which their tact, their mistrust of masculine idealism, ever prevents them from speaking in its entirety. And their tact is unerring. We could not stand women speaking the truth. We could not bear it. It would cause infinite misery and bring about the most awful disturbances in this rather mediocre, but still idealistic fool's paradise in which each of us lives his own little life—the unit in the great sum of existence. And they know it. They are merciful.
>
> (*C*, 144)

A cosmos primarily responsive to woman would be to men an incomprehensibility because it would be devoid of sentimental, delusory order imposed by the "Imagination," and therefore a place dominated "fantastically" only by the arbitrary disorder of "the Irrelevant" (*C*, 93). Men are protected against experiencing such shattering perceptual anarchy by "femininity," woman's capacity and willingness to maintain "the fine tissue of the world" that veils its deeper discontinuities, "certain well-known, well-established, . . . almost . . . hackneyed, illusions, without which the average male creature cannot get on" (*C*, 94).

Plainly, Marlow chooses to discuss the discontinuities that he regards as definitive of "the very nature of things" (*C*, 146) by means of a metaphoric tension between two radically different hypothetical modes of perception that he terms "masculine" and "feminine." Mobile and aware minds owe their superiority to a conjunction of these opposites that results in a mentality resembling Marlow's own "composite temperament," which stands in marked contrast to the "pedestrian" character of someone like John Fyne, for example, who "was purely masculine to his finger tips, masculine solidly, densely, amusingly—hopelessly" (*C*, 146). Of course, the very structure of the novel reflects Marlow's all-inclusive tropology. *Chance* is divided figuratively and literally into two parts, "The Damsel" and "The Knight." The interaction of these two tropes is minimized through rigid, formalized, categorical separation only in the Table of Contents, the textual site least dominated by "chance" and therefore most clearly reflecting the sentimentalized and sharply defined sexual roles that require a *flourette* to be rescued from evil by an ontic warrior (i.e., the teleological dualities of Western European romance). Marlow's presence serves to compromise and complicate just such conceptual tidiness. As his "truth-seeking rhetoric" and "skeptical intellect" are "set in tension with an archetypal romantic affair," Marlow proceeds to "knock apart the shell of conventional opinion surrounding such universal institutions as love, marriage, and filial obedience, an effort which obligates him to undertake a certain amount of cynical reductionism."[11] More specifically, because of Marlow's emphatic discussion of perceptual and epistemological issues by means of a sexual metaphor it is not possible to analyze his allusion to Rinaldo's experiences in the gardens of Armida, or Rinaldo's eventual redemption of Armida, according to conventions that would be appropriate to an analysis of a traditional Christian romance like Tasso's *Gerusalemme Liberata* (1575). The figurative composite structure of human consciousness, which partakes of both the "masculine" and the "feminine" according to Marlow, renders irrelevant the customary conception of an heroically moral protagonist who is imperiled by seduction owing to persons or powers that are entirely external to him and that bear a metaphysical responsibility for the seduction. In *Chance*, therefore, Marlow uses the metaphor of the gardens of Armida to figure forth the human mind, lush and vital with perceptual events: everyone is both Rinaldo and Armida, and the struggle is amoral and endures as long as the perceiver lives.

The temporal sequence in which Anthony's relationship with Flora is presented in *Chance* complexly refashions the liberating and linear episodic plot of *Gerusalemme Liberata* that permits Rinaldo to save Armida from physical and metaphysical suicide at the end of the poem when, amidst the ruins of a lost battle, he reclaims her from both despair and Islam. This scene parallels the setting in which the *initial* encounters of Anthony and Flora are related to Marlow by Flora herself while she stands "on the pavement" (the title of the chapter) near "the rounded front of the Eastern Hotel at the bifurcation of two very broad, mean, shabby thoroughfares" (*C*, 197). The pervasive ugliness and cacophony, "senseless as things of the street always are," with a "meanness of aspect, in its immeasurable poverty of forms, of colouring, of life" (*C*, 86, 204), echoes the dismal surroundings "with those shadows brown" from which Rinaldo climactically saves Armida. Such a location invokes the "ugly shade / Fit place for death, where naught could life persuade" (XX, 122) of Tasso's poem,[12] a place denoting the same sort of spiritual dreariness that Spenser locates near the Cave of Despair, which Anthony denounces as "life on shore" (*C*, 221), and which drives Flora to repeated contemplations of suicide. Having eloped with Anthony, she is eager to escape from her "ugly pilgrimage" in a deplorable "world [that] existed only for selling and buying" (*C*, 209–10) and deprived its inhabitants of human dignity and awareness, as Marlow understands when he looks around:

> Every moment people were passing close by us singly, in twos and threes: the inhabitants of that end of town where life goes on unadorned by grace or splendour; they passed us in their shabby garments, with sallow faces, haggard, anxious or weary, or simply without expression, in an unsmiling sombre stream not made up of lives but of mere unconsidered existences whose joys, struggles, thoughts, sorrows and their very hopes were miserable, glamourless, and of no account in the world.
>
> (*C*, 208)

But Flora's escape, unlike Armida's, is only physical. Her suffering con-

tinues. Although Anthony prevents the despairing Flora from voluntarily taking a fatal plunge into a quarry when he interrupts her walk on the quarry
road and asks, with no awareness of the figurative impact of his question,
"Are you going far this morning?" (C, 216), he does not act altruistically. In
spite of his "chivalrous instincts," which eventually make of him "the rescuer
of the most forlorn damsel of modern time" (C, 208, 238; cf. 247), Anthony is
no Rinaldo by any stretch of the imagination. Rather, he is a kind of emotive
lamia (from Greek *lamos*, "gullet"), who has "no appetite" for dinner at the
Fynes after he experiences "tenderness of the fiery predatory kind" and grows
"ravenous" and "rapacious" for Flora (C, 222, 331, 327, 223). Indeed, it is
important to realize the way in which he generates and populates his own
"gardens of Armida," as his complex character conspires with chance to cause
him to become an aggressive suitor "with the eagerness, with the recklessness
of starvation" (C, 208).

An elucidation of this conspiration is crucial to an understanding of
Anthony's attraction to Flora. It is significant that Anthony arrived at the
home of his older sister, Mrs. Fyne, already unusually annoyed, disappointed,
and confused because one of the sustaining routines of his existence had
recently failed. As the "confirmed enemy of life on shore" tells Flora, "the
worst was that on arriving in London he found he couldn't get the rooms he
was used to, where they made him as comfortable as such a confirmed sea-
dog as himself could be anywhere on shore" (C, 220–21). Moreover, while at
the Fynes' home, subject to the overbearing Zoe, who never "felt the slightest
compunction at her treatment of her sea-going brother," and suffering from
"the sincerities of his sister and of his dear nieces," Anthony "had his loneliness
brought home to his bosom for the first time of his life, at an age . . . when
one is mature enough to feel the pang of such a discovery" (C, 159). This
means that Anthony is very lonely indeed, since the isolation and unhappiness
he experiences with the Fynes are apparently greater than that which he suffered at the hands of his "massive, implacable" father, "Carleon Anthony, the
poet [who] sang . . . of the domestic and social amenities of our age." The
schizoid sire had a "primitive cave-dweller's temperament" and "arbitrary and
exacting [manners] with his dependents" (C, 38), which caused his sequestered
son after his mother's death to flee desperately and somewhat suicidally to the
ocean: "His boy, whom he persisted by a mere whim in educating at home,
ran away in conventional style and, as if disgusted with the amenities of
civilization, threw himself, figuratively speaking, into the sea" (C, 39).

This means of escape helps determine the extent of Anthony's infatuation
with Flora when, beset by a novel extreme of loneliness, he begs her: 'Trust
yourself to me—to the sea" (C, 227). Anthony assumes there is "no rest and
peace and security but on the sea," and he projects these expectations onto the
girl, a "wreath of mist," with eyes like "a stretch of water," like "the
sea—which is deep like your eyes" (C, 221, 226, 231, 227). Predictably, he

fashions an oceanic version of Flora for himself and then plunges into it, directly echoing his previous mode of escape from abuse and loneliness as a youth. Indeed, Anthony proclaims with climactic appropriateness to Flora, "Don't speak. I love it" (C, 226–27), revealing that he is enraptured by the aura he himself has fabricated, not by her human presence.

But if Anthony synthesizes from "magic signs" (C, 217) his own Armida, Flora in like manner creates her own Rinaldo, since the sea holds a number of potently seductive associations for her also. She is "a sailor's granddaughter," and the love-starved girl vaguely but affectionately recalls the "clean-shaven man with a ruddy complexion and long, perfectly white hair [who] used to take her on his knee, and . . . talk to her in loving whispers" (C, 237; cf. 385). Moreover, she remembers one of the very few times she ever was happy with her father as an experience that is inseparable from the prevalence of the sea, which provided the original setting:

> She thought with the tenderest possible affection of that upright figure buttoned up in a long frock-coat, soft-voiced and having but little to say to his girl. She seemed to feel his hand closed round hers. On his flying visits to Brighton he would always walk hand in hand with her. People stared covertly at them; the band was playing; and there was the sea—the blue gaiety of the sea. They were quietly happy together.
>
> (C, 229; cf. 336)

When she first meets Anthony, Flora is "at the same time inert and unstable, and very much at the mercy of sudden impulses" (C, 223), a mental state that parallels Anthony's own disorientation and vulnerability. She is impressed favorably by his air of "a hermit withdrawn from a wicked world," which "appealed straight to [her] bruised and battered young soul" (C, 221). She has long thought of abandoning the world, and whether she leaps literally to her death in a quarry or takes "this other leap" (C, 209) into marriage is of little consequence to her, for the peace offered by the "hermit" hopefully resembles the "peace and rest in the grave" (C, 221).

Thus, she does not differentiate significantly between Anthony and annihilation, and it is of course fitting that she is to meet him in the garden the night she resolves suicidally to go to the quarry and "do it now—in the dark," for she eagerly anticipates Anthony's violence at her planned rejection of his love, thinking "should he get into ungovernable fury from disappointment, and perchance strangle her, it would be as good a way to be done with it as any" (C, 229). As a result Conrad can invoke with devastating irony at the inception of this relationship, which is "the tryst of death—not of love" (C, 235), Rinaldo's auspicious, redemptive union with Armida, summarized with far different semantic import by Tasso at the end of Gerusalemme Liberata: "Thus death her life became" (XX, 136). Even though she literally does not die, Flora in wedding Anthony initiates a "fatal marriage" with a man who soon makes her consider suicide once again. Despairingly, she evaluates the "placid sheet of water close at hand" from aboard the *Ferndale,* a ship whose name is a parody of the pastoral, storybook "field sprinkled profusely with white sheep" where, though ignorant of "the bucolic mind" and of "the sheep-like impulses by which our actions and opinions are determined," she first talked with her future husband of life's alternatives (*C,* 307, 336, 220, 45, 145).

Conrad again undermines the paradigms of traditional romance by insistently inverting assertions that once bore a legitimate message "in the nature of a fairy-tale with a 'they lived happy ever after' termination" (*C,* 228). Due to the unavoidable solipsism of all perception, it is not possible for anyone to escape from the "rank growth of memories" (*C,* 354), from his or her own self-generated "gardens of Armida," although one can drag another into such a psychic territory and thereby share it willfully. In Conrad's works these forceful appropriations are made summarily visible in scenes in which one character aggressively pulls another into closer physical proximity. This is a traditional gesture paralleling precisely the nontraditional psychological significance of many quite dangerous and violative embraces in more modern romances like, say, Tennyson's "The Holy Grail." Conrad confirms this significance rhetorically through his frequent and ambiguous use of the idea of being "carried off." This ambiguity is best exemplified by the statement made by the narrator of *The Shadow-Line,* who observes, "The green sickness of late youth descended on me and carried me off. Carried me off that ship, I mean" (*SL,* 5; cf. "carry on" and "carry away" [*MS,* 43–45]). The narrator plainly is conscious that the phrase "carried me off" can denote both infatuation and death, and he is anxious to limit his context to the former meaning, although his "green sickness" leads him directly from a search for "truth" and a ship "like an enchanted princess" to an unnecessarily close encounter with death by shipboard epidemic fever and superstitious dis-ease, both of which concenter in the eerie Mr. Burns, "with his greenish eyes" (*SL,* 7, 40, 101).

Attempting to escape from their subjective prisons, many of Conrad's characters grope and snatch about themselves with typically negative consequences. In *Chance* when Mrs. Fyne sees Flora run "out into the street—with the haste of . . . despair and to keep I don't know what tragic tryst," she precipitously "pulled her in" (*C,* 176–177), just as Anthony, interrupting Flora's suicidal walk to the quarry in order to "get hold of her" (*C,* 224; cf. "the girl 'who had got hold of the captain'" [267]), "unlatched the gate in silence, grasped her arm and drew her in" (*C,* 223). Similarly, the fatally enraptured Renouard fantasizes about "seizing [Felicia] in his arms" and "carrying her off" (*WT,* 45); his life threatened, Ramirez boasts "he will carry [Giselle] off from the island" (*N,* 551); and the doomed Jasper Allen feels "as if [he] must carry [Freya] off now, at once. [He] could run with [her] in [his] hands . . . without touching the earth" (*TLS,* 189; cf. also 218; the deluded Belfast's cry, "I pulled him out," and Lingard's violent embrace of Mrs. Travers as he "pulled [her] through with an irresistable force" [*NN,* 158; *Res,* 394]).

But like Spenser's "great dame Nature" and Shelley's "veiled maid," other human beings are forever epistemologically inaccessible to the perceiving subject and perpetually defy the assimilative pressure of a psychic hug. As Freya declares, "It will be no man who will carry me off" (*TLS*, 190), and this paradigmatic declaration portends the terminal deportations suffered by so many of Conrad's autotelic knights. Shared or not, the quest for a Wordsworthian ontic marriage in (and therefore with) a "ferndale" and its vernal goddess, Flora, where the "intellect of Man, / When wedded to this goodly universe / In love and holy passion shall find," to its satisfaction, 'Paradise, and groves / Elysian, Fortunate Fields—like those of old / Sought in the Atlantic Main,"[13] is for Conrad a search for the grave, the only place where self can merge parabolically and statically with itself. Indeed, the appropriately moribund Rinaldo achieves just such a merger in Armida's reflective person, as the temptress herself affirms to him:

> painted in my heart and portray'd right,
> Thy worth, thy beauties, and perfections be;
> Of which the form, the shape, the fashion best,
> Not in this glass is seen, but in my breast.

> And if thou me disdain, yet be content
>   At least so to behold thy lovely hue,
> That while thereon thy looks are fix'd and bent,
>   Thy happy eyes themselves may see and view.
> . . . .
> O let the skies thy worthy mirror be,
> And in clear stars thy shape and image see!
>   (*Gerusalemme Liberata*, XVI, 21–22)

The gardens of Armida with their central and immobilizing reflex are, of course, located beyond both "the Isles Fortunate" and "the Fields Elysian" (XV, 35, 36), a territory overwhelmingly defined by the topos of the *locus amoenus*, which is much reiterated by Tasso (see, e.g., XV, 35–36, 46, 53–54). It is into precisely this sort of sun-drenched psychic geography that the honeymooners in *Chance* immediately attempt to sail aboard the *Ferndale* on their "short trip—to the Western Islands only," which indeed very soon comes "to an end" (*C*, 382), like life itself, "that rapid blinking stumble across a flick of sunshine" (*C*, 283).

Marlow is quite aware of the psychological significance of his metaphor of "the enchanted gardens of Armida" (*C*, 396); of Anthony's and Flora's mutual attraction being primarily due to their respective abilities to project onto one another oceanic associations; and of the potentially fatal implications of a solipsistic love founded upon such desperate and watery tropes. This is why Marlow perceives in Flora's eyes "a night effect," a "glance, night-like in the sunshine" (*C*, 215), in marked contrast to Anthony, who associates them with "the sea—which is deep like your eyes" and into which at an early age the despairing Anthony "threw himself, figuratively speaking" (C, 227, 39). When Anthony gazes into Flora's eyes, that is, he concentrates upon the irises, "the rings of sombre blue" into which he "plunged . . . breathless and tense, deep, deep, like a mad sailor taking a desperate dive from the masthead into the blue unfathomable sea," and which seduce him into keeping always "his eyes turned to the sea away from his ship," thereby compromising his sense of command (C, 215, 332, 313).

But the more profound and skeptical Marlow, with his "ghastly imagination," is primarily influenced by the transcendent blackness within the oceanic blue, the "unexpressed menace in the depths of the dilated pupils" (C, 102, 215). It is necessary to cite the qualities that Marlow associates with nocturnal blackness in order to make clear the precise significance of the ophthalmic brine in which Anthony is submersed, Flora's eyes, which typically are "gazing at nothing" (C, 383). Early in the novel, while Marlow and Fyne search in vain for Flora one night, Marlow describes the heavens:

> It was one of those dewy, clear, starry nights, oppressing our spirit, crushing our pride, by the brilliant evidence of the awful loneliness, of the hopeless obscure insignificance of our globe lost in the splendid revelation of a glittering, soulless universe. I hate such skies.
>
> (C, 50)

Plainly, the chaotic and remote scintillations of the night sky, unrelieved by any dominant luminosity (such as the moon) that would provide an orientational base, signify for Marlow a revelation of the ontic absence that is the absolutely humbling context for all human activity when it exists as a function of a narrative presented by Marlow, "his eyes fixed on vacancy" (C, 283). As Marlow knows, for Anthony to dive into Flora's eyes is for him to participate actively in an insidious destiny that eventually culminates in his death by drowning when the Ferndale, struck by the Westland, "[goes] down like a stone and Captain Anthony [goes] down with her" (C, 440). Thus, Anthony by means of the Westland at last is translated ironically to "the Western Islands" (C, 382), the territory where Armida's gardens are situated and where he now is a permanent denizen.

The same sort of psychological determinism explains a great deal about Flora. On the way to committing suicide, she instead elopes with Anthony after perceiving in him her own Neptunian analogues (see C, 227, 229), thus "let[ting] herself be carried along by a mysterious force which her person had called into being" (C, 264; italics mine). This subtle undertow leads her directly to the Ferndale, a ship that proves not to be a rustic pastoral landscape like the "big field sprinkled profusely with white sheep" (C, 220) where she and Anthony got acquainted, but rather a watery abyss, figurative conjunction of the quarry and the sea. Here she perceives her countenance reflected in a mirror "distant, shadowy, as if immersed in water," looking "far off like the livid face of a drowned corpse at the bottom of a pool" (C, 265, 384). Predictably, here too she again considers killing herself, contemplating the "placid sheet of water close at hand" and, on another occasion, planning to "jump into the dock" (C, 336, 370). Even when Anthony at last claims her completely she languishes in his arms like "a drowned woman" (C, 430).

But unlike Anthony, Flora survives, to preside over still another tempting *locus amoenus,* "the fragrant darkness of the garden" (C, 445) into which she lures Young Powell and, later, Marlow, who responds to the pleasures of the amenable place with a rhapsodic prediction of the world-weather: "Breathing the dreamless peace around the picturesque cottage . . . , it seemed to me that it must reign everywhere, over all the globe of water and land and in the hearts of all the dwellers on this earth" (C, 442). Like the repressed Maggie Tulliver, whose "tall figure and old lavender gown" are visible only "through an hereditary black silk shawl of some wide-meshed net-like material," Flora's "white face" gives scant evidence of "the rich blood of life and passion" so long as her carmine vitality is kept under funereal trammels, her "heliotrope silk facings under a figured net" (C, 205). Yet, having spent much of her mature life "like a creature struggling under a net," an innocent and uncomprehending Acrasia/Armida suffering under the meshed repressions of an "idiotic" and "supra-refined" Guyon-like "knight" (C, 140, 328), she lives to blossom comfortably and liberate her colors, as Marlow observes: "The lamp [by which Flora sat] had a rosy shade; and its glow wreathed her in perpetual blushes, made her appear wonderfully young as she sat before me in a deep, high-backed arm-chair" (C, 443).

Conrad remarks in his Author's Note, "It is a mighty force that of mere chance; absolutely irresistible yet manifesting itself often in delicate forms such for instance as the charm, true or illusory, of a human being" (C, vii). Obviously, the word *chance* is of some thematic importance to the novel *Chance,* wherein it functions in a way that annuls its significance in Christian romances such as *The Faerie Queene,* which provide an "eternall God that chaunce did guide" (I, xi, 45). In Conrad's novel the word is subjected to such excessive use that *chance* is quickly stripped of all but the most nebulous of connotations. These wisps of meaning are then allowed to survive primarily to emphasize the epistemological frustration of intellects that are forced to operate within the context of mere cosmic accident. Indeed, Sir Thomas Browne's assertion in the epigraph, " Those that hold that all things are governed by fortune had not erred, had they not persisted there," provides merely an important echo of the threadbare ontology that Conrad attacks.[14]

If for characters like Flora the universe seems to be "fine," this coincidental and inconclusive appearance is made possible by chance, which also determines the temporal durability of such an appearance. Conrad stresses this point by causing Marlow, for instance, to distort his syntax so as to make his friends' surname, Fyne, denote an amenable perceptual event that certain characters meet projectively at certain moments under the guise of an attribute of phenomenal nature. Thus, Marlow remarks, "At the proper season you would meet in the fields Fyne" (C, 37). And the extent to which the novel ends "happily" is a function of the extent to which the solipsistic "charm" of such perceptual events can be sustained. Flora's claim to "have had a fine adventure. . . . The finest in the world!" (C, 444) is definitive. Throughout the novel the word *fine* is reiterated by many characters, and an extreme of semantic overdetermination is established because the word is used by all in the same manner. Consequently the denotations of *fine* are artificially narrowed, and then condensed, primarily by means of personification. The family whose surname is Fyne is presided over by "a good, stupid, earnest couple . . . with the usual unshaded crudity of average people," who are "commonplace, earnest, without smiles and without guile" and "strangely consistent in their lack of imaginative sympathy" (C, 57, 61, 143). There are obvious implications: the word denotes the sort of world-view that might be entertained by such simpletons, a world-view fraught with easy optimism and chivalric virtue. For example, the day Young Powell passed the first of his seamanship examinations he designates as "the finest day in my life," and Marlow mockingly calls "honour . . . a very fine mediaeval inheritance" and summarizes the purpose of Carleon Anthony's poetry as an attempt "to glorify the result of six thousand years' evolution towards the refinement of thought, manner, and feelings" (C, 6, 63, 38). By means of such a world-view is created the "idealistic fool's paradise in which each of us lives his own little life" (C, 144).

A recognition of the universal nothingness is thereby evaded in a manner akin to the way Anthony evades the black abyss of Flora's pupils by gazing at the blue of her irises. Marlow makes this quite clear as he describes, with an intentional pun on "fine" and "Infinite," a particularly pleasant meteorological coincidence: "It was a fine day; a delicious day, with the horror of the Infinite veiled by the splendid tent of blue; a day innocently bright like a child with a washed face, fresh like an innocent young girl" (C, 64). As a result, when Flora insists upon the "fine" nature of her marriage to Anthony she admits unwittingly that she is a member of the global family of impercipient "Fynes" who reduce experience to silly clichés, indeed as she does herself when she declares at the end of the novel, "Truth will out, Mr. Marlow" (C, 444), still having gained no awareness of the elusive and problematic essence of such a word. Clearly, what Conrad calls elsewhere "the romantic feeling of reality," which can charge "the sober hue of hard work and exacting calls of duty . . . with a feeling of romance" (WT, v), in *Chance* is made possible primarily by a "Fyne" opacity whereby "the horror of the Infinite [is] veiled" (C, 64), as is confirmed when Flora asserts, "All the world, all life were transformed for me. . . . The most familiar things appeared lighted up with a new light, clothed with a loveliness I had never suspected" (C, 444).

Yet, ever profoundly distrustful of romance, Conrad causes Flora's affirmations to appear in a chapter entitled ". . . A Moonless Night, Thick with Stars Above, Very Dark on the Water." This phrase is part of a sentence that is apparently uttered originally by Young Powell as part of a simple description (see C, 406) but is elevated in significance by the author, foreshortened to "A Moonless Night," and employed as the conceptual framework wherein the ending of the novel takes place. It is precisely such "starry nights" that Marlow, in the manner of Van Gogh, earlier established in *Chance* as an analogy for a frightening "revelation of a glittering, soulless universe" (C, 50). Consequently, "A Moonless Night" bleakly and appropriately surrounds Flora's and Young Powell's "fine" and "lighted" rejuvenescence just as in "Youth" Marlow's "fine," "dazzling," and juvenile "romance . . . of glamour" is "surrounded by an impenetrable night" (Y, 30, 42). Ever unable to alter the population of her own "gardens of Armida," Flora remains susceptible to timid knights: 'The eyes of the Flora of the old days [remain] absolutely unchanged" (C, 443). She now loves a man who amounts only to a surrogate Anthony and who demonstrates ominously "in the sanctuary of his heart . . . a devotion as pure as any vestal" (C, 441). For Flora it seems that the "inward light" of the refined and "vestal" Young Powell must finally prove finite. To investigate Conrad's morose manipulation of traditional romance conventions is indeed to trace what Marlow calls an "anti-sentimental journey" (C, 150).

Yet, this most deceptive of novels does seem to end in a sentimental affirmation of the possibility of attaining at least a limited joy: Young Powell and Flora have begun a relationship that Marlow, now acting the part of a "knight" himself, warrentlessly anticipates will culminate in a felicitous marriage. Such an arbitrary cessation of plot at a point that potentially conflates finality and human value qualifies one of Conrad's most pervasive themes, the impossibility of such conflation, and indicates the author's willingness to temper even his own characteristic pessimism. This intellectual honesty, which acknowledges the chance for a temporary and minimal happiness, can only lend plausibility to Conrad's perceptions. A triumphant spiritual integrity like that indicated in Sidney's *Arcadia* by the heroine's motto, "Yet still myself," and by her wearing an emblematic diamond set in black horn is not possible in Conrad's works because the Iron Age blightingly prevails. Nevertheless, Conrad does admit that the cheerless gray metal, repugnant in itself, can be teased at certain points into providing a context that is at variance with its normal ferrous gloom. And the dreariness of human experience is similarly discontinuous, subject to occasional displacement by a pleasing and priceless glitter, as Jack Kemp observes: "Suffering is the lot of man, but not inevitable failure or worthless despair which is without end—suffering, the mark of manhood . . . , bears within its pain a hope of felicity like a jewel set in iron" (Rom, 541).

But Kemp is a dubious spokesman, for he uniquely has attained and possessed the "unattainable," a seraphic "revelation," an "apparition of dreams," the girl Seraphina, who sends him to "the seventh heaven" due to her "transcendental grace," and to whom he clings "as men cling to their hope of highest good—with an exalted and selfish devotion" (*Rom*, 157–59, 191, 259). No other character in Conrad's works lastingly gains the sort of integrity of personality that is experienced by Kemp as he conjoins past and future by contemplating the physical immediacy of a young woman whom he only recently met, but whom he "seemed to have known . . . for years": "Every movement of hers affected me with an intimate joy; it was as if I had been waiting to see just that carriage of the neck, just that proud glance from the eyes, just that droop of eyelashes upon the cheeks, for years and years" (*Rom*, 98, 91). Only Stein has a similar experience, and it lasts merely for "that day" on which he "had nothing to desire" (*LJ*, 211). His enjoyment of psychic wholeness is a matter of capturing and transfixing a butterfly in quest of which he "took long journeys and underwent great privations": "I had dreamed of [it] in my sleep, and here suddenly I had [it] in my fingers" (*LJ*, 211). Immobile winged insects are the real "treasures" of Stein's life (*LJ*, 207), and their "lifeless tissues displaying a splendour unmarred by death" (*LJ*, 207) cannot rival the vitality of Seraphina, "a conquered and rare treasure, whose possession simplifies life into a sort of adoring guardianship" (*Rom*, 256; cf. 142, 335). Because of such exceptional experiences, Kemp perceives a world that does not force him to abandon his metaphors, unlike the suicidal Renouard, who fatally wishes to "wear [Felicia] for an incomparable jewel on my breast" (*WT*, 78); Jim, who names his woman a "jewel" but finds her terminally insufficient (*LJ*, 278); Nostromo, who wants to sequester Giselle Viola "like a jewel in a casket" (*N*, 541; cf. 218, 552); and M. George, who is entranced by the "priceless" Rita's eyes, "like melted sapphires," and her words, to be "caught up and treasured" (*AG*, 59, 200, 124), but who loses Rita to time and later her jeweled arrow of gold to the sea (just as Mrs. Travers willfully tosses Hassim's potent emerald ring into the water [*Res*, 467]).

Kemp's dangerously extremist lexicon is uniquely validated. Literal wealth merges with the intangible value he assigns to his supernal Seraphina, thereby making possible the apparent elimination of tragic discrepancies between subjective need and the stubborn resistance of the external world to the satisfaction of that need, and explaining why the original title of *Romance*, indeed, was *Seraphina*. That is, chance unites with tropology in *Romance* to make the phenomenal world become a Wordsworthian "home" for Jack Kemp. Seraphina, as her brother Carlos observes, "will be very rich" when she inherits "all our lands, all our towns, all our gold," and Kemp fittingly regards her as a "radiant presence facing me across a table furniture that was like a display of treasure," for she is herself a "rare treasure, whose possession simplifies life into a sort of adoring guardianship," a girl who through the "inexhaustible treasure of her feelings . . . appease[s] every uneasiness of my heart" (*Rom*, 79, 142, 256, 335). Such an integration of antithetical temporal dimensions (dreams with prospects) and semiotic fields (Logos with phenomena) is indeed the "pearl of a great price," a search for which typically cripples Conrad's questers, who, like the narrator of "A Smile of Fortune," usually discover an elemental corruption within "the astral body . . . of the pearl" (*TLS*, 3), a disenchanting divergence of word from world.

The existence of a jewel or a hoard of some sort of precious metal is an age-old device in myth and romance narratives by means of which an ultimately meaningful finality, a positive ontic closure, can be figured forth. Such a device is

> a materialization of the fantasy-creation, which appears in the place of physical nature, of the world as we know it. A different reality is created . . . which then becomes a "ground," "transparent and shining." With this "ground" an immutable, absolutely real foundation has been created.

> The content of all such symbolic products is the idea of an overpowering, all-embracing, complete or perfect being, represented either by a man of heroic proportions, or by an animal with magical attributes, or . . . some other "treasure hard to attain," such as a jewel, ring, [or] crown.[15]

Although in most of his works Conrad repeatedly emphasizes the ruination consequent upon quests for just such crystalline completion, in an experimental novel entitled *Romance*, for the content of which he can only partly be held accountable, Conrad seems willing to permit the intrusion of an eidetic closure into his fictive world. Thus, Kemp, apparently thriving and unthreatened in his retrospective narrative, luxuriates in the belief that "journeying in search of romance," he has been able to "catch the horizon," that in the company of the "always unattainable and romantic" Seraphina he has won the "jewel set in iron" (*Rom*, 62, 158, 541).

But in *Nostromo*, a novel written exclusively by Conrad at the same time he was collaborating in the composition of *Romance*, there are no possibilities for a fulfillment like that enjoyed by Jack Kemp, in spite of the similar availability of both literal and figurative "treasures" (the silver of the San Tomé mine and Emilia Gould). Indeed, this novel conclusively exhibits Conrad's opposition to nearly all redemptive efforts that maintain a sense of cosmic purpose, whether the scope is personal or international. To Conrad such efforts are at best inane variations of a compulsive, unenlightened, fatuous scenario that can only endlessly and destructively repeat the fierce collision of antipodes according to which the very forms of Western thought are made possible. It is precisely these forms as they are specifically manifested in the rhetoric and activities of Charles Gould that Decoud mockingly condemns for imposing upon experience the distortive melodrama of "a moral romance derived from the tradition of a pretty fairy-tale" (*N*, 218):

> Mrs. Gould, are you aware to what point he has idealized the existence, the worth, the meaning of the San Tomé mine? . . . He cannot act or exist without idealizing every simple feeling, desire, or achievement. He could not believe his own motives if he did not make them first a part of some fairy-tale.
>
> (N, 214–15)

But such is the essence of most perceptual events that lead to qualitative judgments, for, as the narrative voice remarks, "The popular mind is incapable of scepticism" (N, 420). To perceive is to "believe," to "discover a treasure," to "tell a fairy-tale."

In *Nostromo* the *loci* of romance are the various characters' deific and figurative elaborations of their own desires and of the physical facts of the San Tomé mine and its silver bullion. Giorgio Viola disperses his energy "in the worship and service of liberty" and claims, "A good name . . . is a treasure" (N, 29, 257). Don Juste Lopez "believed in parliamentary institutions" (N, 367). For Guzman Bento, the "power of supreme government had become . . . an object of strange worship, as if it were some sort of cruel deity," and Father Corbelán's faith lies in the eventual restoration of the Church's lost property and wealth: "He had not been able to keep out his fixed idea of an outraged Church waiting for reparation from a penitent country" (N, 137, 195). Similarly, Decoud measures his love for Antonia both against Father Corbelán's metaphysical "treasure" and against Charles Gould's visionary valuation of the San Tomé Concession: "She is more to me than his church to Father Corbelán [or] than his precious mine to that sentimental Englishman" (N, 238). Indeed, a high level of human awareness is no protection against being human.

Dr. Monygham's skepticism is pointed and separates him from the community of Sulaco, since "the doctor did not believe in the reform of Costaguana" (N, 370). Nevertheless, he maintains with perseverance "an ideal conception of his disgrace" for having been disloyal to friends when he was tortured by Father Beron. Paradoxically he thereby nurtures the "great fund of loyalty in [his] nature" that "he had settled . . . all on Mrs. Gould's head," a woman "he believed . . . worthy of every devotion" (N, 376):

> The doctor was loyal to the mine. It presented itself to his fifty-years-old eyes in the shape of a little woman in a soft dress with a long train, with a head attractively overweighed by a great mass of fair hair and the delicate preciousness of her inner worth, partaking of a gem and a flower, revealed in every attitude of her person.
>
> (N, 431)

Although Dr. Monygham succeeds in "living on the inexhaustible treasure of his devotion," such a living is, like all human activities, cosmically illicit, "like a store of unlawful wealth" (N, 504; cf. 526). The perils of such fanciful tropology are delineated by the narrative voice:

As the dangers thickened round the San Tomé mine, this illusion acquired force, permanency, and authority. It claimed him at last! This claim, exalted by a spiritual detachment from the usual sanctions of hope and reward, made Dr. Monygham's thinking, acting individuality extremely dangerous to himself and to others, all his scruples vanishing in the proud feeling that his devotion was the only thing that stood between an admirable woman and a frightful disaster.

(N, 431)

It seems that most of the characters in *Nostromo* find it remarkably easy to project their respective needs onto the landscape of Costaguana, a landscape unique for its receptivity, for the degree to which it invites re-formation and seemingly exists at the brink of becoming a modern earthly paradise in spite of its bloody history. It is therefore important to define more precisely the contents of this landscape, for it nurtures the subjective tragedy of the novel by seductively counterfeiting a *locus amoenus* at the same time that it provides the literal physical support whereon this tragedy is murderously enacted. To begin with, the idea put forth by Frederick Jackson Turner that the frontier is "the meeting point between savagery and civilization" located at "the hither edge of free land"[16] can be utilized to suggest the extent to which the Costaguana of Charles Gould and his mining enterprise departs from primitive frontier conditions. There are few savages evident in Conrad's fictitious nation (see *N*, 194–95); for many years there has been no free land; and, most crucially, the country is governed according to totalitarian metaphysics and politics that have been imported from Europe without significant alteration. In marked contrast to the colonial frontiers of Asia or Africa, which are culturally agressive due to their ancient and alien political, social, and philosophical forms, the Latin American landscape of *Nostromo* is dangerous precisely because it requires someone raised in the context of Western European culture to cope with almost no challenging otherness. Consequently, human experience in such a setting can be transformed with ease into a fulfilling and hyperbolic romance narrative such as the narrator of *Chance* mocks, "one of those Redskin stories where the noble savages carry off a girl and the honest backwoodsman with his incomparable knowledge follows the track" (*C*, 311).

It is true that Antonia Avellanos, "born in Europe and educated partly in England," is said to have "foreign upbringing and foreign ideas" (*N*, 140). Yet, Costaguanans do not perceive something that is foreign to be threateningly different, but rather similar and superior since derived from an admired primary source in the Old World. Thus, Martin Decoud's outlandish character is valued, his written communications are sought eagerly and with approbation, and his Continental messages are printed promptly on paper made in the United States (*N*, 158). He

was seldom exposed to the Costaguana sun under which he was born. His people had long been settled in Paris, where he had studied law, had dabbled in literature, had hoped now and then in moments of exaltation to become a poet like that other foreigner of Spanish blood, José Maria Heredia. In other moments he had, to pass the time, condescended to write articles on European affairs for the *Semenario*, the principal newspaper in Sta. Marta, which printed them under the heading, "From our special correspondent," though the authorship was an open secret.

(*N*, 151–52)

Similar European connections are urgently affirmed by many other characters. Don Vincente Ribiera, the "President-Dictator," claims "a doctor of philosophy from the Cordova University" (*N*, 144). The idiotic "provincial Excellency" boasts of "my profound studies in Europe," and judges a "military band . . . braying operatic selections" from Mozart to be "Exquisite, delicious" (*N*, 90–91). And Pedro Montero emerges from "the garrets of . . . Parisian hotels," where he "had been devouring the lighter sort of historical works in the French language, such . . . as the books of Imbert de Saint Amand upon the Second Empire," to aspire to become "a sort of Duc de Morny to a sort of Napoleon" (*N*, 387, 237). Moreover, as might be expected, physical as well as mental forms are derivative. Near Sulaco the road looks "like an English country lane" (*N*, 359). Father Roman has a "presbytery" that is "an unmistakable American white frame house" (*N*, 103). Nostromo wears "the checkered shirt and red sash of a Mediterranean sailor," the "eldest Miss Lopez" sports shoes with a "high French heel," and her father and friends don "European round hats" and at the Amarilla Club drink "Swedish punch, imported in bottles" (*N*, 96, 234, 366, 161).

The residents' determination to emulate that which is foreign is particularly bizarre when it is ritualistically manifested in abstract, self-congratulatory acknowledgment of militarism, commerce, or social concord. General Montero looks like "a cruel caricature," and evinces "the fatuity of solemn masquerading, the atrocious grotesqueness of some military idol of Aztec conception and European bedecking, awaiting the homage of worshippers" (*N*, 122). The obtuse Captain Mitchell inflexibly schedules the coastal movements of vessels belonging to the pretentious Oceanic Steam Navigation Company, vessels like the *Juno* and *Minerva*, whose degraded names "became the household words of a coast that had never been ruled by the gods of Olympus" (*N*, 9). After the Sulacan secession Mitchell happily announces plans to supplement an impoverished mythos by means of a monument to a corporate Astraea in the form of "a marble shaft commemorative of Separation, with angels of peace at the four corners, and a bronze Justice holding an even balance, all gilt, on the top" (*N*, 482). With characteristic obtuseness, Mitchell thereby unknowingly predicts the further degradation of Pax and Justitia, which virtues are indeed to be supported by a square shaft, unintentionally denotative of the lucre that maintains them and the republic and is mined from "the square mountain" (*N*, 135).

Clearly, the frontier in the Americas as experienced by Charles Gould is a place where there is little resistance to the abstractions from which European civilization derives its validation in the past and direction for the future. What feeble alien cultures were aboriginal to the territory have long since been subdued physically and conceptually, so that the military is controlled by men like Guzman Bento, the "Citizen Savior of his Country," who shamelessly appropriates Christian rhetoric, and who as a former herdsman is well qualified to lead the pious "flock" of natives (*pastor* means shepherd, of course) toward a lethal parody of millennial communion, "a united land wherein the evil taint of Federalism could no longer be detected in the smoke of burning houses and the smell of spilled blood" (*N*, 138; cf. also the other "spiritual and temporal pastors" [*N*, 102]). This abortive romance of Christian reclamation is inherited by Montero and Barrios, who lead an army of natives bearing European weapons and encouraged through propaganda fabricated by Decoud, "the adopted child of western Europe" (*N*, 156).

The only barriers to a rampant imposition of Continental eidolons are environmental, the ontic absences of Golfo Placido, the Campo, and the Cordillera, where the chairman of the railway board "utterly lost touch with the feeling of European life" (*N*, 37). But such opposition is rendered passive because of its location within a culture that has long been converted to bourgeois perceptions; and in any case the "hostility" of "nature . . . can be always overcome by the resources of finance" (*N*, 39). Moreover, the recent development of steam power has made it possible for merchant ships "to violate the sanctuary of peace [and] variable airs" (*N*, 9), the primal vacancy of the placid *gulf* that resisted for so long the ordure of European order. Indeed, the Sulacan coast was once "an inviolable sanctuary from the temptations of a trading world [owing to] the solemn hush of the deep Golfo Placido as if within an enormous semicircular and unroofed temple open to the ocean . . ." (*N*, 3). The displacement of this "temple," which is sacred to nothingness, by Mitchell's silly commercial shrine, the "new customhouse, with its sham air of a Greek temple" (*N*, 530), is a sure sign of that disastrous "trust in . . . the reckless affirmations of commercial men and mere technicians" (*NLL*, 214) that Conrad regards as a consequence of the invention of steam power.

Such technology makes the entire phenomenal world vulnerable to the imposition of the most muddled thought. The chief engineer, "inoculated . . . with . . . faith in 'pronunciamentos,'" asserts, amusingly, the unreality of the very earth that he transforms with his railway, saying: "*Upon my word . . . things* seem to be worth nothing by what they are in themselves. I begin to believe that the only solid *thing* about them is . . . spiritual value" (*N*, 316, 318; italics mine). The physical elements are abolished by a mathematician who swears upon his own inept semantics, whereby he locates solidity within the category of the "spiritual," a conceptual regression that goes far beyond the initial absurdity of "things" with a "thing about them." The submissive and uncluttered Latin American frontier, "the dreamy expanse of the Campo" (*N*, 203), offers an opportunity for people like the chief engineer, Holroyd, and the Goulds to believe they can accomplish a material translation of goals that in a physically and conceptually congested Europe exist primarily in the form of eidolons. Since "a millionaire has unlimited means" (*N*, 317), drawing-board innovations like steam power and refined mining techniques can be embodied through selective application of sufficient capital and energy. As a result, to uncritical and illogical men the semantics of redemptive moral and social stability appear to be subject to a similar incarnation.

The Europeanized local cultures seem to provide an openness and passivity that is analogous to the culturally determined rectangular form receptively embodied in the virgin sheet of paper that awaits on one's desk the order and linearity of a significant inscription. That is, the essence of the frontier in *Nostromo* is the wilderness both of a *tabula rasa* and of a dreamer's inarticulate and (therefore) immaculate abstractions. This is why, for example, the idealist Giorgio Viola has a "white mane," as "white as the snows of Higuerota," hangs the sacred icon of his idol, Garibaldi, on a "dazzlingly white" wall, and spends most of his time in his "usual position, leaning back in the doorway with an upward glance fastened on the white shoulder of Higuerota far away" (*N*, 32, 166, 23, 170); why at the moment he decides that "old Giorgio . . . is right" Nostromo (owner of a white horse) faces "the white misty sheen of Higuerota" (*N*, 418); why the equestrian statue of a dead king is "dazzlingly white in the sunshine" (*N*, 385) and the walls of the drawing room of the "King of Sulaco" as well as the walls of his private lair are "white" and almost "completely bare" (*N*, 51, 70); why Sir John, chairman of the railway board, appears "pale in a silvery mist of white hair" (*N*, 35); why the superficial and starry-eyed Antonia has a "wide, white forehead," her father a "perfectly white" head of hair, Dr. Monygham a capitulatory "white jacket" (his "concession to Mrs. Gould's humanizing influence"), and the pliable peasants and Sulaco ladies "white clothing" and faces "smothered . . . with pearl-powder" (*N*, 140, 51, 45, 89, 49); and, lastly, why the inquisitor, Father Beron, signals his role as the terminator of human life by means of a "cross embroidered in white cotton" and the modern and sacrosanct telegraph wire terminates "abruptly in the construction camp at a white deal table" (*N*, 138, 135). Only within such a conceptual whiteout can a decrepit fifty-eight-year-old like Holroyd pretend he is "eternally young" and chase his "dream" worthy of "a youthful enthusiast," the "introduction of a pure form of Christianity" (*N*, 317). This is indeed an amenable place, a narcissist's utopia. Only such chromatic openness can receive the many significances imposed upon it by pioneering Occidental visionaries, for whom historically the frontier's "colossal meaning ranged from personal and national destiny to human destiny itself" and the very "*process* of civilization . . . itself came to mean progress." [17]

Yet, although the white vacancies of the Europeanized frontier can be inscribed with almost any ideals, the inscriptions never accomplish more than an unsatisfactory formative condensation of the originary receptive pallor. The context of the following vignette illustrates this well. As Sotillo is preparing to hang Dr. Monygham, one of the O.S.N. Company's transport ships under the command of Barrios's troops appears and closes in swiftly, deluging Sotillo's vessel with gunfire. Dr. Monygham, who, in Mitchell's words,

> had given himself up for lost . . . , kept on yelling with all the strength of his lungs: "Hoist a white flag! Hoist a white flag!" Suddenly an old major of the Esmeralda regiment, standing by, unsheathed his sword with a shriek: "Die, perjured traitor!" and ran Sotillo clean through the body, just before he fell himself shot through the head.
>
> (N, 484)

This is the second time the paranoic "old major" has attacked his own comrades, and he persists in lying about the certitude with which he detects fraud: "I can smell a traitor a league off. . . . You deserve to be run through the body with my sword" (N, 289). If there is anyone present who fits his categories of traitor and perjurer it is surely he. But Sotillo himself has lied in claiming that Hirsch "confessed everything" about the location of the silver, a lie Sotillo invented in order to forestall, ironically, his men from proceeding "to plunge their swords into his breast" (N, 449). And, of course, Dr. Monygham is lying all along to Sotillo concerning the fate of the treasure.

Such insoluble ambiguity resists the power of language to describe or dissect it as well as the ability of a social order to incorporate it. At best "a white flag" can signal merely a momentary truce with part of the ambiguity and a resultant temporary triumph of an illusion of staunch clarity. But in fact there can never be the sort of ontic "surrender" needed to stabilize society and semantics: "before the lawlessness of the land" there can only be the bewildering neutrality of "equals" such as is dramatized by means of the inert Sotillo, killed by his own comrade and lying beneath a white flag beside his now fallen murderer, or by means of the transformation of "a bandit into a general," the "memorable last act of the Ribierist party, whose watchwords were honesty, peace, and progress" (N, 360, 352–53). The whiteness cannot be effectively articulated or stabilized. As a result, meaning is manifested as a confounding diversity of elusive scintillations against the backdrop of primal darkness that is revealed by such luminous condensations. Thus, Linda Viola, infatuated with Nostromo "like a sleep-walker in a beatific dream," concentrates her "passionate . . . whiteness" until it takes the form "in the depths of her paradise" of "the white light-house" that she tends "far above the shames and passions of the earth": "The whole refracting apparatus, with its brass fittings and rings of prisms, glittered and sparkled like a dome-shaped shrine of diamonds, containing not a lamp, but some splendid flame, dominating the sea" (N, 531–33, 543, 552). But her lucid fantasy, figured forth in the beacon she tends, is futile, shining perpetually to the west, the grave of all light (see *N*, 533, 495). It is ultimately just as ambiguous to others as are the "lights of San Tomé . . . suspended in the dark night between earth and heaven," in spite of her own petrific fixation which causes her face to appear "as set and white as marble" (*N*, 486, 566); and appropriately only the uncomprehending and cynical Dr. Monygham hears her piercing cry, "I cannot understand" (*N*, 566).

Such passages as these plainly invoke the iconography of Conradian romance, "shadows . . . endowed with an internal glow" (*WT*, vi). But in *Nostromo* the peril of such romance is not dramatized in terms of a character's inflexible idealization of a woman whom he pursues to his own detriment (as in the cases of Geoffrey Renouard and Jasper Allen, for example). Quite to the contrary, Charles Gould, like Jack Kemp, in fact weds a sublunary seraph, Emilia the "angel" (*N*, 513), a "white figure" with "white hands" who appears "luminous" and rides behind "always white mules," herself a romance icon, "small and dainty, as if radiating a light of her own in the deep shade of the interlaced boughs" (*N*, 114, 481, 520). Although Conrad frequently draws his idealistic and solipsistic "knights" to a self-destructive end by preventing them from consummating a relationship with the woman onto whom they have projected their ideals, the rapid degeneration of the Goulds' once potentially vital and cheerful marriage clearly shows that it is largely irrelevant whether or not the desired consummation ever occurs. The Lady can only seem successfully to incarnate the ideals which have become Cupid's vehicle as long as she remains frustratingly remote. But to possess her is merely to discover with even greater frustration that the values she apparently harbored are infinitely displaced: "A man who has had his way is seldom happy, for generally he finds that the way does not lead very far on this earth of desires which can never be fully satisfied" (*C*, 396). Discord is the fatal rule in Conrad's world, and to win the Lady is merely to postpone the necessity of recognizing this rule.

Conrad as usual locates the grounds of such inevitable discord in the compulsive human process of resolving into moral dualities the morally neutral cosmos, the serpent's paradise, which can never be authentically or thoroughly humanized. In *Nostromo* the Goulds attempt a resolvent transformation with divisive results. What was once a vital ambiguity, "a flood of tropical vegetation" flourishing by a "waterfall, with its amazing fernery, like a hanging garden," is altered by Charles Gould's trenchant mining enterprise into "an accomplished fact fulfilling an audacious desire" (*N*, 54, 105–6). The "slender waterfall [that] flashed bright and glassy through the dark green of the heavy fronds of tree-ferns" sustaining "the very paradise of snakes" has been polarized into Emilia's "*water*-color sketch of the San Tomé gorge" and Charles's "proclamation thundered forth over the land" in the form of the "growling mutter of the mountain pouring its *stream* of treasure under the stamps" (N, 209, 105–6; italics mine). Their error lies in their assumption that the eternally fluxile, aqueous world circumscribed "within the perfect circle of the horizon, its clumps of heavy timber motionless like solid islands of leaves above the running waves of grass" (N, 203), can ever be conclusively and harmoniously contained by a sentimentally dualistic lexicon. As a result, Charles Gould's life scarcely fulfills the requirements of traditional romance, in spite of his marriage to "the lady of the medieval castle," or the "comic fairy-tale" of the political success of the Sulacan secession and the consequent great material success of the Sulacan Republic, itself like "a fairy tale . . . from another world" (N, 68, 315, 487).

He lives in silent isolation from his wife, who now "hate[s] the idea of that silver from the bottom of [her] heart" and who ultimately annuls the literal and figurative value of the treasure by calling it "nothing" when, "full of endurance and compassion," she lies to Dr. Monygham at the close of the novel (N, 558–60). Emilia Gould, who once seemed to share in her husband's metaphoric transformations of the silver, finds that the "idea" that was "the inspiration of their early years" is itself no longer a unity or a basis for domestic unification. Emilia and Charles disagree, as the "idea" fragments and discordantly alters its metaphoric essence, becoming a "fetish," a "wall of silver bricks . . . between her and her husband," who seems "to dwell alone within a circumvallation of precious metal" (N, 221–22). For Emilia Gould the perception of this wall signifies in effect the closing of her conceptual frontier, a painful and often tragic psychological event, which Harold P. Simonson describes nicely:

> When a nation, like a person, comes of age, it recognizes that limitation is a fundamental fact of life. Painfully it admits that possibilities can only be finite and progress only limited, that solutions to problems are found more often through compromises than crusades. . . . It also abandons the dream that a second chance mollifies responsibilities here and now. Coming of age means awakening to the tragic realities . . . that truth comes chiefly through ambiguity and paradox; and that the old inheritance of pride still carries its inexorable consequences. . . . To come of age is to recognize no exceptions, no annulments, and, most importantly, no escape from the cycle of genesis and decay. The existentialism symbolized by a closed frontier replaces the idealism engendered on an open frontier. Instead of a limitless frontier there is a wall. The tension comes from the illusory prospect of the one and the certitude of the other. Existence in this tension is the heart of tragedy.[18]

Emilia therefore suffers an awareness that her husband apparently never gains. Although she once optimistically insisted that the only "real" aspect of the mine is "its immaterial side," Emilia now must confront, due to her altered perceptions, an equally "immaterial" but blighting "wall," and with no sense of irony she eventually complains bitterly that "there is an awful sense of unreality about all this" (N, 75, 207).

The "unreality" that causes such anxiety in Emilia Gould stems from the same sort of experience that characters like Karain, Geoffrey Renouard, M. George, and Jasper Allen have when, at the moment of anticipated consummation, they discover the spectral essence both of the objects of their desire and (consequently) of their own needful identities, and are denied fulfillment as once-suppressed ambiguities urgently reassert themselves. In *Nostromo* Emilia Gould has such an experience while lamenting "We have disturbed a good many snakes in that paradise, Charley," as she passes from a "white glaring room" into a "dimly lit corridor" that has

> a restful mysteriousness of a forest shade, suggested by the stems and the leaves of the plants ranged along the balustrade of the open side. In the streaks of light falling through the open door of the reception-rooms, the blossoms, white and red and pale lilac, [come] out vivid with the brilliance of flowers in a stream of sunshine. . . .
>
> (*N*, 209–10)

As the crestfallen Emilia articulates her disillusionment and alarm she appropriately departs from the "glaring" whiteness of the Gould's house, wherein is figured forth the "noonday" albedo of the ideals they used to share while courting (see *N*, 61). She then enters a dim corridor, a transitional space that is described analogically as a forest, and that invokes equivocally the originary glade recorded in her painting, the very "paradise of snakes" that at present she wishes had never been disturbed. For her the domesticated white intensity of her husband's *idée fixe* has begun to deconstruct, to lapse back into an aboriginal and incoherent splash of light and dark. Now the "clear patches of sun" can at best only seem to "checker the gloom of open glades in the woods" (*N*, 210; cf. the "checkered" areas that disorient Willems, Marlow, and M. George [*OI*, 70; *LJ*, 348; *AG*, 68, 284–87]). At the same time Emilia's hopes for inaugurating an amenable place in Costaguana are dashed as her world is destructively polarized into an equally uninhabitable and incomprehensible serpent's Eden and "Treasure House of the World," which promise to "weigh as heavily upon the people as the barbarism, cruelty, and misrule of a few years back" (*N*, 522, 511). Yet she survives "the withering suspicion of the uselessness of her labors, the powerlessness of her magic," the degeneration of her rejuvenescent romance, by remaining ever a "fairy," ever in a "dream . . . lying passive in the toils of a merciless nightmare," ever able to deny "the greatest fact in the whole of South America," as she proves by her decision to return Nostromo's treasure to the earth, saying "Let it be lost forever" (*N*, 520, 522, 214, 560).

Emilia Gould's ultimately debilitating personifications of the San Tomé mine can be traced to her youthful courtship with Charles, who, in marked contrast to the understanding expressed by the novel's narrative voice (see *N*, 62), attributes volition and moral responsibility to an inert hole in the ground by judging the mine to have been the cause of his father's death when he remarks to Emilia, "It has killed him" (*N*, 61). In Charles's case, a tendency to categorize human experience melodramatically seems to be an inevitable psychic legacy. He is the culmination of a long line of reformers. His grandfather fought for Bolivar. In the days of the Federation his uncle was provincial president of Sulaco and was finally shot by Guzman Bento. His father drove himself to distraction and eventual death over the manner in which he was granted "eternal" possession of the San Tomé Concession by various abortive governments in order that they might extort money from him. The family history, in other words, anticipatively incorporates most of the extremisms that still punctuate the societies of Costaguana, from militant revolutionary idealism (e.g., Giorgio Viola) through enlightened aristocratic political leadership (e.g., Don José Avellanos and Don Vincente Ribiera, Ph.D.), to Don Carlos Gould, silver magnate and the "King of Sulaco" himself. Most importantly, this historical sequence outlines the way in which the Gould family becomes ever more deeply entangled in the dishonest verbiage wielded by piratical and ephermeral governments whose invocations of morality and eternity are inversely proportional to their respective scorn for these ideas. As long as the Goulds remain soldiers of abstract notions (like "liberty") they can do battle in refreshingly physical and absolutist terms (the pull of a trigger). But the more involved the family becomes in struggles over obvious materialism (control of the silver mine), the less subject are the struggles to clarification and resolution according to sentimental finalities. Although "to be robbed under the forms of legality and business" may indeed be "intolerable" (*N*, 56), it is also inevitable.

At an early age "the fourteen-year-old boy Charles, then away in England for his education" (*N*, 57), is deeply influenced by hysterical letters from his outraged father, who finds himself caught in precisely such an intolerably ambiguous situation. The elder Gould repeatedly exposes his son to self-indulgent and compensatory efforts to resolve confusion rhetorically. These efforts take the form of a moral melodrama that involves various personifications of metaphysical absolutes, "the Old Man of the Sea, vampires, and ghouls . . . , a grewsome Arabian Night's tale" dominated by the "iniquitous Gould Concession" (*N*, 56–57). The youth grows "more and more interested in that thing which could provoke such a tumult of words and passion," and he naively responds in a markedly inconsistent manner "in such moments as he could spare from play and study." On the one hand, Charles concludes that at last "he managed to clear the plain truth of the business from the fantastic intrusions" (*N*, 57–58). On the other hand, he conceives of the distant tragedy according to the very rhetoric and romance categories of the "light literature" that his frantic father employs to describe the "eternal character of that curse" (*N*, 55–56). The problem seems ultimately to be a kind of fairy tale, with all the easy answers of a fairy tale if only the proper approach were discovered.

Consequently, by "the time he was twenty" Charles Gould had "fallen under the spell of the San Tomé mine. But it was another form of enchantment, more suitable to his youth, into whose magic formula there entered hope, vigor, and self-confidence, instead of weary indignation and despair" (*N*, 57, 59). Young Charles is thus introduced to the human activity of inscribing resolvent narratives upon confusion by the elder Gould, who writes his fantastically elaborative letters about the mine in an effort to warn his son "never to claim any part of his inheritance . . . because it was tainted by the infamous Concession" (*N*, 57). Yet the "calm and reflective" youth can only contemplate the "unfortunate affair" detachedly, "without bitterness," since "it is difficult to resent with proper and durable indignation the physical or mental anguish of another organism, even if that other organism is one's own father" (*N*, 59). And after years of thinking simultaneously of human emotions and the mine, young Charles fatally commingles the categories of animate (human) and inanimate (mines), collapsing the former into the latter:

> Mines had acquired for him a dramatic interest. He studied their peculiarities from a personal point of view, too, as one would study the varied characters of men. He visited them as one goes with curiosity to call upon remarkable persons. . . . Abandoned workings had for him strong fascination. Their desolation appealed to him like the sight of human misery, whose causes are varied and profound. They might have been worthless, but also they might have been misunderstood.
>
> (*N*, 59)

Unable to sustain the sophisticated mode of perception that is necessary to enable him simultaneously to nurture two importantly different kinds of emotional involvement, Charles cannot separate the categories of animate and inanimate and remain committed in different ways to both. Thus, just as he treats mines as if they were human, so upon his initial encounter with Emilia, his future bride, he reacts extremely in an opposite manner: "The two young people had met in Lucca. After that meeting Charles Gould visited no mines" (*N*, 60).

Conrad typically assigns causal potency to a character's past when he anatomizes that character's indulgence in the resolvent conventions of traditional romance; and he predictably describes this potency analogically while invoking his definitive romance icon, "shadows . . . endowed with an internal glow" (*WT*, vi). He presents his own experiences aboard the *Tremolino* in this way:

> After many years, on looking back from the middle turn of life's way at the events of the past . . . , we may see here and there, in the grey throng, some figure glowing with a faint radiance, as though it had caught all the light of our already crepuscular sky. And by this glow we may recognize the faces of our true adventures. . . .
>
> (*MS*, 156)

Marlow in precisely the same manner describes among "dark-skinned bodies" the "white figure" of Jim, the man who continues to enthrall him in spite of temporal and spatial remoteness:

> He was white from head to foot, and remained persistently visible with the stronghold of the night at his back. . . . The twilight was ebbing fast from the sky above his head, the strip of sand had sunk already under his feet, he himself appeared no bigger than a child—then only a speck, a tiny white speck, that seemed to catch all the light left in a darkened world. . . . And, suddenly, I lost him. . . .
>
> (*LJ*, 336)

Such analogies as these elucidate the repeated descriptions in *Nostromo* of the San Tomé mine at night "high up on the sheer face of the mountain, dotted with single torches, like drops of fire fallen from the two great blazing clusters of lights" (*N*, 104). The mine, illuminating the darkness, preserves all the potency of Charles Gould's past, all the captivating adventure and simplistic concepts that he derived as a youngster from his father's letters. Moreover, it fittingly looks "like a lighted palace above the dark Campo," since it is a conceptual extension of the ancestral house, the Casa Gould, whose windows nightly "flung their shining parallelograms" (*N*, 485, 184). Appearing himself "like a tall beacon," Gould distributes the power of the mine as he similarly idealizes and luminously advocates other technological developments, such as the telegraph, "its poles like slender beacons" (*N*, 205, 135), and the railroad, whose spectral trains pass in the night like "a mysterious stirring of the darkness" in which "nothing [is] clearly visible but, on the end of the last flat-car, a negro, in white trousers . . . swinging a blazing torch-basket incessantly" (*N*, 229). Thus, capital, electromagnetism, and steam filch most available utopian radiance from its former hosts, religion and monarchy, which now glow weakly: "high up, like a star, there was a small gleam in one of the towers of the cathedral; and the equestrian statue gleamed pale against the black trees . . . like a ghost of royalty" (*N*, 357).

And, of course, love, likewise a traditional site of eidetic radiance, suffers as well. Charles Gould's decision to visit no more mines after he meets Emilia does not abolish utterly the psychic presence of the mine, but only disguises it as a seemingly innocuous means for promoting the ends of flirtation and lovemaking: "They discussed [the mine] because the sentiment of love can enter into any subject and live ardently in remote phrases. For this natural reason these discussions were precious to Mrs. Gould in her engaged state." Indeed, the very establishment of the San Tomé mine as a means of social redemption is determined initially by its association in the minds of Charles and Emilia Gould with the heady sensations of youthful love:

> These two young people remembered the life which had ended wretchedly just when their own lives had come together in that splendor of hopeful love, which to

the most sensible minds appears like a triumph of good over all the evils of the earth. A vague idea of rehabilitation had entered the plan of their life. That it was so vague as to elude the support of argument made it only the stronger. It had presented itself to them at the instant when the woman's instinct of devotion and the man's instinct of activity receive from the strongest of illusions [love] their most powerful impulse. . . . . It was as if they had been morally bound to make good their vigorous view of life against the unnatural error of weariness and despair.

(N, 74)

But almost immediately Charles's love is compromised as the San Tomé Concession subtly reasserts itself and he is drawn to "some marble quarries, where the work resembled mining" (N, 60).

While in such a hazy mental state Gould decides that "the mine had been the cause of an absurd moral disaster; its working must be made a serious and moral success" (N, 66). By means of a single muddled sentence, he equates the death of one man with the moral reclamation of an entire country, two events that can scarcely be assigned the same magnitude. Just as crucial is his parallel transformation of a specific concept into an active and morally responsible indefinite pronoun, an inanimate excavation into a numinous "it." Charles Gould enjoys at this point a dangerous perceptual and semantic license that he maintains hereafter by means of a raw intensification of will: "Charles Gould's fits of abstraction depicted the energetic concentration of a will haunted by a fixed idea. A man haunted by a fixed idea is insane. He is dangerous even if that idea is an idea of justice" (N, 379). The power of Gould's abstraction is precisely equal to the energy latent in the protean indefinite pronoun that once signified only a mine. This enables the "King of Sulaco" to "believe . . . in the mine" and to attach his "faith to material interests" (N, 75, 84). Furthermore, such reverence for semantic openness allows the pronoun, during the rare moments when "it" assumes a specific form, to signify to Gould one of the cardinal virtues, Justitia. According to his "mystic view" the "Gould Concession was symbolic of abstract justice" (N, 402). As a result, Gould's incandescent and needful gaze becomes capable of denying the very existence of the Separationist proclamation (he "would not even glance at it when it was finished" [N, 278]), and of igniting autotelic "letters of fire upon the wall at which he was gazing abstractedly" (N, 379). Similarly, his urgently chaste affair of "subtle conjugal infidelity" with Justitia becomes a sufficiently volatile form of nympholepsy to justify the explosive transformation of "half of Sulaco into . . . air" (N, 365, 204) should any alien words threaten to penetrate and defile his pristine tunnel.

The fatal displacement of Emilia by the mine begins the day Charles learns of his father's death and embraces his ghoulish birthright. He goes straight to Emilia, "the first person to whom he opened his lips after receiving the news," and encounters his beautiful fiancée after walking in the transcendent blaze of "the noonday sun on the white road" that is covered with "white dust" (*N*, 61). Now that the crazy old man is dead, Charles unwittingly confronts the most important emotional crisis of his life. He can free himself from the lethal dementia of obsession with the San Tomé mine by establishing a commitment to ambiguous human life and the possibilities for feeling compassion and despair (as manifested in Emilia). Or he can fall prey to an isolating and vitiating passion to exhume that which is "incorruptible" and therefore exanimate, preserving thereby his father's romance fantasies, the categories derived by the old man from "light literature." These alternatives are expressed symbolically in the shaped column bearing an urn that is present in the barren room where Charles and Emilia talk. The room is "furnished with exactly one gilt arm-chair with a broken back, and an octagon columnar stand bearing a heavy marble vase ornamented with sculptured masks and garlands of flowers, and cracked from top to bottom" (*N*, 61). Little domestic comfort can be derived from a chair with a broken back, to be sure. But even more foreboding is the octagonal columnar stand with its cracked marble vase, for this aesthetic configuration is clearly bleak parody of a traditional baptismal font, a sacred source which is almost always supported by an octagonal base, denotative of transcendence.[19] In this case, however, the customary receptacle for holy water (the *uterus ecclesiae*) is replaced by a fractured and funereal marble urn (cf. "the light of the eight candle-flames" amidst which Lena performs her futile redemptive ritual [*V*, 392]). Thus, the alternative that claims Charles Gould, implicit in his earlier visit to the marble quarry, becomes explicit during his conversation with Emilia when he fails ever to look at her, contemplating instead all the while "with a penetrating and motionless stare the cracked marble urn as though he had resolved to fix its shape forever in his memory" (*N*, 62). Moreover, the displacement by the marble urn figuratively of the *uterus ecclesiae* and literally of the opportunity offered to Charles Gould in the supernal white noontide that enshrines Emilia, "small in her simple white frock" (*N*, 62), anticipates with precision at once the couple's ultimate childlessness and the eventual interment of Charles Gould's humanity in the seductive vacancies of the Costaguana frontier that coalesce in the San Tomé mine where he goes "at midnight" to sleep "in subtle conjugal infidelity" (*N*, 208, 365).

The metaphor of adultery by means of which the narrative voice describes Charles Gould's devotion to his fantasy of power and order reveals that in Conrad's fiction it is no more possible to be faithful to an idea than it is to be faithful to a woman. Indeed, people wed one another when their respective abstractions momentarily seem to find a fleshly embodiment in a person of the opposite sex. But this delusion soon passes, the abstractions on which it was founded migrate to other hosts, and the marriage that once seemed ontologically conclusive must tolerate a "subtle infidelity," if not literal adultery. No human being, however "faithful," is sufficient to the task of meeting the requirements imposed by another's chaste and pristine solipsism. Charles Gould is truly human, but scarcely culpable, when he allows his youthful romance icon, Emilia, the "kindest, most gracious woman the sun ever shone upon," who seems to glow with "a light of her own in the deep shade" (N, 481, 520), to be overwhelmingly counterfeited by the remote and inhuman "lights of San Tomé, that [seem] suspended in the dark night between earth and heaven," that "[twinkle] night after night upon the great, limitless shadow of the Campo" from their places "high up on the sheer face of the mountain, dotted with single torches, like drops of fire fallen from the two blazing clusters of lights above" (N, 486, 135, 104). As Marlow knows, after all, "however insane was the view [another] held, one could not declare [him] mad" (C, 243). For Charles Gould the receptivity displayed by the slowly closing frontier landscape of Costaguana is, understandably, far more seductive than a woman who can talk and act on her own and resist conceptual impositions. Ever preferring things more than people, therefore, he ironically supports with his gilding idealism the fundamental "general atrocity of things" (N, 439), as territory that once seemed to be an amenable place asserts inexorably its stinging, serpentine essence, its "Thorns and Arabesques" (TU, 179), indeed, the guano of Costaguana.[20]

The Rescue, "that damned and bloody romance"

The novel evolves as an art form in an era when, after Descartes and Locke, the "general temper of philosophical realism has been critical, anti-traditional, and innovating [and] its method has been the study of the particulars of experience by the individual investigator. . . ."[1] Hence, for instance, Samuel Richardson's Pamela deprecates romances for their lack of practical "instruction . . . for the conduct of common life," their depiction of "extravagant things, in order to show the mad strength of a passion [one] ought to be ashamed of," their tendency to "make parents and guardians pass for tyrants" and to drown "the voice of reason . . . in that of indiscreet Love." Fanny Burney warns readers of Evelina (1778) in her Preface that her work is devoid "of Romance: where fiction is coloured by all the gay tints of luxurious Imagination, where Reason is an outcast, and where the sublimity of the Marvellous rejects all aid from sober Probability." And Anthony Trollope in a letter of 1853 to George Eliot asserts proudly, "I have shorn my fiction of romance" in order to "confine myself absolutely to the commonest details of commonplace life among ordinary people allowing no incident that would be even remarkable in everyday life."[2] That is, expectations and perceptions that are fostered by traditional romance are frequently disparaged because their glamorous extremes pose a threat to the sort of judgment that is predicated upon the bourgeois reality-principle, which, as Joyce's disillusioned narrator in "Araby" knows, is "most hostile to romance."

But Joyce's narrator is a Catholic. In his weary condemnation of the "vanity" of earthly quests he maintains, nevertheless, his exorbitant teleological assumptions, and simply transfers them to a realm that is remote from chance and temporal flux. Such an intellectual position is not markedly different from that occupied by writers like Richardson, Burney, and Trollope, who maintain essentially Christian presuppositions even as they oppose an everyday perception that is actively predicated upon these presuppositions because such perception encourages a departure from the "commonest details of comonplace life." These writers insist upon the redemptive function of facts, and therefore are radically different in their condemnations of romance from Conrad, an author for whom

> what once seemed objective fact . . . is now transformed into a figment of man's imagination. And . . . change from traditional literature to a modern genre like

the novel can be defined as a moving of once objective worlds of myth and romance into the subjective consciousness of man. . . . The ideal world still exists, but only as a form of consciousness, not as an objective fact. The drama has all been moved within the minds of the characters, and the world as it is in itself is by implication unattainable or of no significance.[3]

Such emphasis upon subjectivity suggests that Conradian romance represents what Alastair Fowler calls "a tertiary phase" of generic evolution, since "tertiary development seems often to constitute an interiorizing" as "an author uses a secondary form in a radically new way." Moreover, there are concomitant "changes in the dignity of genres themselves" because the "status of a genre . . . depends on current evaluation of its whole conventional subject matter."[4] The problem of the genre's dubious dignity explains Conrad's typical bewilderment over the categorization and aesthetic evaluation of those of his works that most prominently utilize, albeit subversively, the conventions of traditional romance, a genre that Conrad dismissed as amounting to little more than "a boy's book of adventures."[5] For example, he denigrates a good piece of short fiction, "Freya of the Seven Isles," insisting he only meant to create "a magazine-ish thing with some decency. Not a very high purpose; yet it seems I've failed even in that!"[6] Similarly, he declares with regard to *The Rescue* that he is writing merely "a kind of glorified book for boys," and therefore "all my ambition is to make it good enough for a magazine— readable in a word." [7]

Of course, Conrad's work is consistently not only "readable" but great art. If the author himself is unable finally to authenticate and dignify his Stygian variations of teleological narrative, recent criticism can supply an advantageous context. In his important essay "The Internalization of Quest Romance," Harold Bloom provides a generalization that is as applicable to Conradian as it is to Shelleyan romance: "The quest is to widen consciousness as well as intensify it, but the quest is shadowed by a spirit that tends to narrow consciousness to an acute preoccupation with self. The shadow of imagination is solipsism."[8] It is this "shadow" that compels Conrad's characters to become ineffectual parodies of the Coleridgean "eternal act of creation in the infinite I AM," muttering, like Lingard, "I am what I am," all the while remaining confused by "the madness of a fixed idea" that is ever unintelligible, yet insisting urgently "I must have meant something" (*Res*, 323, 215, 102). The only authentic perception is no perception. Thus Conrad's affection for the brilliant, desolating, unrevelatory flash of an explosion, which he names, paradoxically, "the most lasting thing in the universe"[9] because it conjoins absolutely and eternally the subject and the object in a parody of that Wordsworthian transcendence that occurs ". . . when the light of sense / Goes out, but with a flash that has revealed / The invisible world" (*The Prelude*, VI, 600–602).

In "The Informer" Conrad provides a concise dramatization of the properly calm, Oriental acceptance required by a glimpse of this "world of eternal oblivion [where] all things were settled once for all" (*Res*, 382). An uncomprehending and timid English narrator, whose experience of the Far East is limited to his activity as a collector of weighty and substantial Chinese bronzes, cannot stomach Mr. X, the aristocratic anarchist who can sit quietly in an elite restaurant and "impassively" eat a *bombe glaceé* while discussing the use of "an agency for Stone's Dried Soup" (a formless, powdery "cosmestible article") and a "Variety Artists' Agency" operated by a "fellow called Bomm" as fronts for destructive anarchistic aggression (*SS*, 82). Indeed, Mr. X is a kind of cultural cannibal who knowingly consumes the very structures that generate his identity. But he pursues this activity with a refreshing consciousness, and therefore stands in marked contrast to a character like Falk, who in fact commits a cannibalistic act without ever accomplishing that sagacious transcendence of his culture's prim coherences upon which Mr. X placidly expounds at dinner. To make possible the intellectual or physical detonation of such coherences an analytic detachment is required that is perhaps equaled only by that necessitated during the disjointing of a human body for culinary purposes (see *SA*, 88). Hence, Stevie explodes into "a heap of rags, scorched and bloodstained, half concealing what might have been an accumulation of raw material for a cannibal feast" (*SA*, 86), precisely the sort of deconstructive feast the narrator of *Falk* finds "impossible to swallow" because it "brought forcibly to one's mind the night of ages when the primeval man . . . scorched lumps of flesh at a fire of sticks" (*T*, 145). Indeed, this "romantic" narrator remains ever a "friend" of Hermann (Mr. Man) and deeply appreciates the sort of rigorously maintained cultural musculature that can be found only aboard "world proof" vessels like the *Arcadia* and the *Diana*, where "The skipper has his wife on board" and "roaring lusts" are tempered by "arcadian felicity," and where, as a result, one can depend upon getting only innocuous and nourishing "jolly good dinners" (*T*, 160, 146–47, 156, 158). Such ships define truly amenable places where metaphysical detonations go unrecognized along with "the general atrocity of things" (*N*, 439) that demands one grow, like Jaffir, "accustomed . . . to be eaten alive" (*Res*, 372).[10]

But the "saving dullness" (*LJ*, 276) of nonrecognition can only postpone, not prevent, a terminal blast. As the Professor knows, "Every taint, every vice, every prejudice, every convention must meet its doom" (*SA*, 303). Time itself is the "perfect detonator" of earthly paradises, of the "transcendent belief in felicity as the lot of all mankind," of "all the fabulous tales of enchanted gardens where animated flowers smile at bewitched knights" (*TU*, 152–53). Synchronic "Thorns and Arabesques" (*TU*, 179) provide the bier for teleological romance. This is why Conrad emphasizes sunrises and sunsets so often at moments in his works when the "cruel futility of things [stands] unveiled" (*N*, 364) and eidetic radiance, indeed, "fade[s] away from the Hope

Reach" (*T*, 147) owing to an inexorable "oncoming shadow" of such totality "that one might have fancied oneself come to the end of time" (*Res*, 425). The sun moves ever westward regardless of its proximity to the eastern horizon, and consequently the sky for Conrad's knights must be always "blood-red, immense, streaming like an open vein" (*LJ*, 413). In *Nostromo*, for instance, a bitter day dawns for Charles Gould just after the victory of Gamacho and his nationals, when, upon returning very early in the morning to his home, Gould "in the light of failure" confronts "the cruel futility of lives and of deaths thrown away in the vain endeavor to attain an enduring solution of the problem" (*N*, 364). Moreover, this confrontation occurs within a frame narrative that serves even more to accentuate mortality. Before Gould's bleak meditation, a native youth is described by a fountain strumming a guitar for two girls who dance and hum along with the music, while in "a dark corner" there is "a mortally wounded cargador with a woman kneeling by his side . . . trying . . . to force a piece of orange between the stiffening lips of the dying man" (*N*, 364). After Gould discovers that the fight for order is a "senseless" and "irremediable folly," and that he himself is morally a pirate, potentially no better than "a buccaneer throwing a lighted match into the [powder] magazine" (*N*, 366), death moves into ascendancy and the rites of life, the music and dance by the fountain, cease: "Down below, in the patio, the wounded cargador breathed his last. The woman cried out once. . . . The practicante scrambled to his feet and, guitar in hand, gazed steadily in her direction. . . . The two girls, sitting now . . . , nodded at each other significantly" (*N*, 366).

Furthermore, the sunset of this most inauspicious day is later elaborated upon by the narrative voice in such a way so as apparently to create an apocalyptic annulment of substantiality itself as elemental opposites, fire and water, interpenetrate in a Wagnerian *Götterdämmerung:*

> The sun had set. For a time the snows of Higuerota continued to glow with the reflected glory of the west. . . .
>
> Tints of purple, gold, and crimson were mirrored in the clear water of the harbor . . . ; and beyond, the Placid Gulf repeated those splendors of coloring on a greater scale with a more sombre magnificence. The great mass of cloud filling the head of the gulf had long, red smears among its convoluted folds of gray and black, as of a floating mantle stained with blood. The three Isabels, overshadowed and clear-cut in a great smoothness confounding the sea and sky, appeared suspended, purple-black, in the air. The little wavelets seemed to be tossing tiny red sparks upon the sandy beaches. The glassy bands of water along the horizon gave out a fiery red glow, as if fire and water had been mingled togethér in the vast bed of the ocean.
>
> At last the conflagration of sea and sky, lying embraced and asleep in a flaming contact upon the edge of the world, went out. The red sparks in the water vanished, together with the stains of blood in the black mantle draping the sombre head of the Placid Gulf. . . .

(*N*, 411)

This spectacle invites humanization as the regal colors of "purple, gold, and crimson" seem to figure forth "a floating mantle stained with blood." But, alas, The Robe (cf. *N*, 218) that seems to hover above the empty gulf was worn by no Christ, and it can only confirm the final futility of faith. In such a cosmos, a theological Fall is as irrelevant as a Redeemer. Appropriately, it is to this gory sunset that Nostromo awakens, amid "ruined bits of walls and rotting remnants of roofs and sheds," where he first sees the vulture, "patient watcher for the signs of death and corruption," which is cautiously sizing up "the promising stillness of [his] prostrate body" (*N*, 413; Conrad's allusion to the eating of human flesh in this context is appropriate). Nostromo is beginning a new life, and therefore seems "as natural and free from evil in the moment of waking as a magnificent and unconscious wild beast." But he is now isolated from the social conventions he formerly manipulated in ritualistic confirmation of his identity. As a result, when the capacity for introspection returns, his "suddenly steadied glance" can only be "fixed upon nothing" as he arises to "the end of things," to "the dust and ashes of the fruit of life" (*N*, 412, 414, 416). He is beginning what will be a terminal decline beneath the sanguine menace of a "band of red in the west" that bodes ill for many since it is as well the "sun of Pedrito's entry into Sulaco, the last sun of Senor Hirsch's life, the first sun of Decoud's solitude on the Great Isabel" (*N*, 415, 468).

The annihilatory effect of these diurnal cycles of light and dark is usually concealed from characters like Nostromo because of the languorous and extended temporal scale to which these cycles conform. But their detonative effect can be perceived directly in moments when brilliant luminescence and blackness alternate rapidly. Visual sensations during an electrical storm, for example, can accelerate these periodic alternations until they become a deconstructive coruscation, a phenomenon Marlow interprets as he sees Jim vanish:

> Suddenly a searching and violent glare fell on the blind face of the night. The sustained and dazzling flickers seemed to last for an unconscionable time. The growl of the thunder increased steadily while I looked at him, distinct and black, planted solidly upon the shores of a sea of light. At the moment of greatest brilliance the darkness leaped back with a culminating crash, and he vanished before my dazzled eyes as utterly as though he had been blown to atoms.
>
> (*LJ*, 177–78)

When familiar and leisurely rhythms such as solar presence and absence focus to a dazzling intensity, time approaches infinity, intimating the "ages elapsed between sunrises" (*TU*, 168; cf. *Res*, 163), which typically explode illusions about the durability of physical substance. Thus occurs "the most lasting thing in the universe," which Mrs. Almayer, watching "all she held dear on earth . . . drift away into the gloom in a great roar of flame and smoke" (*AF*, 21), experiences remotely, but which no human being can experience directly and live.[11] Hence, when the suicidal Jörgenson one morning blows up the *Emma* and destroys Lingard's friends, possessions, and plans, the cataclysm is described as if sunrise and sunset were conjoined in a wierd celestial annulment: "A sudden dreadful gloom fell . . . [and] the morning sun, robbed of its rays, glow[ed] dull and brown through the sombre murk which had taken possession of the universe" (*Res*, 442).

Of course, this understanding is an antidote for romance, and, predictably, the protagonist of *The Rescue—A Romance of the Shallows*, the vapid Tom Lingard, a "descendant of the immortal hidalgo errant upon the sea," does not share this understanding (*Res*, 142; cf. *PR*, 36–37, 44; *N*, 171; *Rom*, 253). He sees "flickers" and sunsets in his own uniquely optimistic manner. His eyes, "as if glowing with the light of a hidden fire," transform the "charming and heartless shores of the shallow sea" into a dangerously seductive romance icon fraught with "a glowing and serene half-light" derived from the "regions charming, empty, and dangerous" where he spends "wasted moments" during his frequent psychic excursions "above the interesting cares of this earth" (*Res*, 9–11; cf. *WT*, vi). Through these eyes, while relaxing aboard his "perfect" brig, his "kingdom," Lingard personifies the sun and teleologically restructures the spectacle of sunset:

> The falling sun seemed to be arrested for a moment in his descent by the sleeping waters, while from it, to the motionless brig, shot out on the polished and dark surface of the sea a track of light, straight and shining, resplendent and direct; a path of gold and crimson and purple, a path that seemed to lead dazzling and terrible from the earth straight into heaven through the portals of a glorious death.
> (*Res*, 14; cf. *N*, 537)

A man capable of seriously entertaining such a linear violation of the circular horizon, the ecliptic, and the globe of the sun, "King Tom" understandably succumbs later to "the madness of a fixed idea" (*Res*, 215; cf. *N*, 379). Like other victims of the illusion of cosmic linearity (such as Captain Whalley, who sees a setting planet making a "gold trail . . . upon the roadstead" [*ET*, 213; cf. *Res*, 303]), Lingard is unaware of the ease with which the same luminescent phenomenon that seemingly defines an enticing celestial pathway upon unsupportive waters can, through a slight shift in spatial orientation, figure forth the psychic entrapment consequent upon the pursuit of stability and certitude, love and power.

Before he is shot, Nostromo's fatal entanglement with passion and treasure is emphasized twice by means of the same sort of optical illusion; linear reflections form figurative snares demonstrating that the simple *capataz* is susceptible to the same tension that ruins Charles Gould, whose "heart" is "very full . . . of his life with that girl [Emilia], and his mind of the San Tomé Concession" (*N*, 64). The same night on which Nostromo, already engaged to Linda, is overwhelmed by lust and unexpectedly declares his love to Giselle, an omnious spectacle seems to imprison him in "the dusk and gloom of the clouded gulf, with a low red streak in the west like a hot bar of glowing iron laid across the entrance of a world sombre as a cavern" (*N*, 536), a sultry,

Platonic cave of generation whose incandescent entrance is sealed absolutely. Similarly, on the evening of his death, when Nostromo, the "slave of the San Tomé silver," returns to the Great Isabel for treasure even after Giselle has warned him about her murderous father, the moon is setting, and its reflex defines a dank Cave of Mammon: "The moonlight in the offing closed as if with a colossal bar of silver the entrance of the Placid Gulf—the sombre cavern of clouds and stillness in the surf-fretted seaboard" (*N*, 539, 552). The only escape from the trap of wanting "a palace on a hill crowned with olive trees—a white palace above a blue sea" (*N*, 541) is through an explosive trajectory beyond time and illusion. For Nostromo, whose mistress, Giselle, seems to vanish into the "densest blackness of the Placid Gulf" even as he speaks to her, the gunpowder in Giorgio's rifle provides the psychic detonation, and it occurs by the "tree under which Martin Decoud spent his last days" beholding "life like a succession of senseless images" spinning by the place where "the shade was blackest" (*N*, 541, 553–54). Indeed, Decoud, watching sunrise after sunrise, sunset after sunset "flaming up to death in solitude," voluntarily participates in such a detonation, as does Jörgenson, whose "mad scorn . . . , flaming up against the life of men" as the *Emma* explodes, makes "all . . . as if it had never been" (*N*, 537; *Res*, 451).

Tom Lingard, torn also between past and prospect, passion and power, accepts the ominous Carter aboard his ship on "The darkest night I have ever known" and prowls likewise "Where it's darkest," by "the big tree" near Belarab's settlement, "through the deep obscurity made by the outspread boughs of the only witness left there of a past that for endless ages had seen no mankind on this shore," while across the lagoon his ally, Jörgenson, prepares to blast himself, Lingard's native friends, and most of Lingard's earthly goods to synchronic bits (*Res*, 326, 413–14; cf. Hassim's talk with Daman where "the darkness seemed denser than any he had known before" [p. 224]). Significantly, Lingard, "that man of infinite illusions," cannot control time to his own satisfaction, just as he cannot control Belarab, "that man of infinite hesitations" (*Res*, 466, 434). He stares at the "gold" sunset "path that seem[s] to lead . . . into heaven" trying to fix the precise moment of the sun's disappearance in order to set the ship's chronometer. But the sun frustratingly parodies Lingard's very name and then effortlessly betrays his assiduous concentration: "It lingered, and all at once—without warning—went out as if extinguished by a treacherous hand. . . . Lingard, who had watched intently . . . missed the last moment" (*Res*, 14; cf. "lingered" [35, 92, 138, 165, 229, 280, 342, 434, 464]).

This passage, appearing at the outset of *The Rescue*, defines summarily the futility of Lingard's "contest with heaven's injustice," his "passion to make a king out of an exile" (*Res*, 346, 405), since unless time can be managed thoroughly there is only disaster in store for those who seek to "follow the yellow-brick road" under the assumption that Lingard made: "There was something to be done, and he felt he would have to do it. It was expected of him. The seas expected it; the land expected it. Men also" (*Res,* 87). The "eternal ebb-tide of time" ensures that Lingard, urgently linear yet lingering, is perpetually "too late," for the very nature of things works against cosmic knights and navigators: 'The darkness he [has] to combat [is] too impalpable to be cleft by a blow," yet "the currents don't begin till it's dark, when a man can't see against what confounded thing he is being drifted" (*Res,* 200, 82 and 342, 202, 9). There is no solution to crucial questions such as 'Fight—or no fight? Weapons or words? Which folly?" for night or day there is only "a darkness, a darkness," and it matters not at all that "the tide has turned" in a world defined by aimless cycles, "the mass of green leaves that are forever born and forever dying" and the "struggle of the rocks forever overwhelmed and emerging, with the sea forever victorious and repulsed" (*Res,* 199, 373, 245).

Such cyclical variations are cheerless parodies of the once sacred circle that in prior romance worlds figured forth eternal stability by defining an ontologically substantial center of human meaning. Spenser's graces on Mount Acidale dance around Pastorella, whose axial beauty resembles "a precious gemme / Amidst a ring most richly well enchased," and this earthly circle reflects its source in a cosmic and humane completion that is revealed in the constellation Corona Borealis, the *diadema coeli,*[12] ". . . the crowne, which Ariadne wore / Upon her yvory forehead that same day / That Theseus her unto his bridale bore / . . . And is unto the starres an ornament, / Which round about her move in order excellent" (*Faerie Queene,* VI, x, 12–13). Such is the rose window that Captain Whalley sees, "the glass of the rosace above the ogive glow[ing] like fiery coal in the deep carvings of a wheel of stone" and injecting "grave thoughts of heaven into the hours of ease" (*ET,* 198). Of a far different figurative import is the circle Lingard observes, "a mass of white foam whirling about a centre of intense blackness [that] spun silently past the side of the boat" (*Res,* 245), harbinger not of the fugitive "order excellent" that is briefly sustained by Hassim's potent emerald ring, but rather of "the ring of disasters narrowing round men's fading hopes" (*Res,* 111; cf. *T,* 147).

Hope can "fade" only because it is initially manifested figuratively as a radiance that is most dramatically apparent against an "intense blackness." Thus, Lingard's sense of transcendent purpose reaches an extreme one night when, having arrived at Wajo with the simple intent of paying a visit to his new friend, Hassim, he suddenly is offered an opportunity to participate in the fate of a dynasty, and proceeds to save Hassim and Immada from death. Fittingly, Lingard first perceives Wajo during a violent electrical storm of the very sort that seems to blow Jim "to atoms" before the cynical Marlow's wearied eyes (*LJ,* 178), though the bolts of lightning naturally affect the buoyant Lingard in an opposite manner:

At every dazzling flash, Hassim's native land seemed to leap nearer the brig. . . . Next moment, all . . . vanished utterly from his sight, as if annihilated and, before he had time to turn away, came back to view with a sudden crash, appearing unscathed and motionless under hooked darts of flame, like some legendary country of immortals, withstanding the wrath and fire of Heaven.

(Res, 79–80)

Instead of focusing upon the annihilation that the flickering and intense illumination seems to cause, Lingard concentrates primarily upon the illusion of triumphant invincibility that is generated by apparitions of the landscape emerging repeatedly from the night. When subjected to such myopic perception, the phenomenon of an island assaulted by a "heavy gulf thunderstorm" expeditiously takes on enticing significance: "Its immutable aspect of profound and still repose, seen thus under streams of fire and in the midst of a violent uproar, made it appear inconceivably mysterious and amazing" *(Res, 80)*. This spectacle is infinitely seductive to Lingard, who, though a slum child, fancies himself a deific manipulator of thunderbolts and destinies, and who has long hypostatized his identity in a bogus coat of arms that he carries aboard his ship: "A circular shield hung slanting above the brass hilts of the bayonets. On its red field, in relief and brightly gilt, was represented a sheaf of conventional thunderbolts darting down the middle between the two capitals T.L." *(Res, 32)*. Moreover, these heraldic abstractions achieve incarnation in the very vessel that bears them, as the creator and owner proudly announces: "The brig's name is *Lightning*" *(Res, 32;* Lingard built the ship himself [p. 10]). Lingard initially decided to go to Wajo "By heavens!" and upon his tempestuous arrival there he hears himself seemingly addressed as a deity by Jaffir's "voice of a child speaking in a cathedral" that says, "Praise be to God" *(Res, 79, 80)*. Small wonder that he eagerly involves himself and his brig in the war Jaffir proceeds to describe. The melodramatic situation, suspended in the recurrent "flickering bluish flash" *(Res, 79)* of Lingard's psychic corposants, seems to externalize and therefore engage irresistibly the Jovian fatuousness that is such a prominent part of his personality: "The story of war and of suffering; Jaffir's display of fidelity, the sight of Hassim and his sister, the night, the tempest, the coast under streams of fire—all this made one inspiring manifestation of a life calling to him distinctly for interference" *(Res, 87–88)*. And when he surrenders to the conflict the potent noun that summarizes and contains his identity, Lingard's seduction by "the crashing flares of light" and the "repeated swift visions of an unknown shore" *(Res, 85, 80)* is complete. He dictates to Jaffir "magic words that make all safe": "So let your hail be *Lightning!*" *(Res, 47, 85)*.

But lightning, the "fire of Heaven," only signals metaphorically the moments when the world seems to acknowledge Lingard's "flaming impulses" *(Res, 80, 163)*. Except for the miraculous night of his first sighting of Wajo, "when there was such a thunderstorm as has been never heard of before or since," Lingard's "intoxication" and "idealism" are "shadowy impulses" *(Res, 86, 106, 11)* and are figured forth in the stars of the night sky. The night he decides to sail for Wajo he paces the poop of the brig till morning while surrounded by a cosmic glitter: 'The riding lights of ships twinkled all around him; the lights ashore twinkled in rows, the stars twinkled above his head in a black sky; and reflected in the black water of the roadstead twinkled far below his feet" (*Res*, 78). After rescuing Hassim and Immada, Lingard plans his course of action immersed in stardust: "All that night Lingard had talked with Hassim while the stars streamed from east to west like an immense river of sparks" (*Res*, 92). And while he and Belarab discuss these plans, Lingard "look[s] with a fixed gaze at the stars burning peacefully in the square of the doorway" (*Res*, 111). This is just the sort of gaze against which Marlow warns as he cautions his auditors concerning the "starlight that would make the best of us forget we are only on sufferance here and got to pick our way in cross lights" (*LJ*, 35), the very starlight that is condensed figuratively in "the mass of white coral on the roof of the mosque [that] shone like a white day-star" (*Res*, 367).

In the very same manner Lingard's eidetic stellar hosts can signal the momentary triumph of romance by concentrating their light into a single resplendence. According to the mythic version of Hassim's and Immada's flight from Wajo, a supernatural vessel appeared, and above it hovered a great luminary: "the lightning played between her masts which were as high as the summits of mountains; a star burned low through the clouds above her. . . . No flame of man's kindling could have endured the wind and rain of that night" (*Res*, 86). Of course, this "traditional account" (*Res*, 86) of the exiled pair's dramatic escape from death aboard a magic ship is factually inaccurate, having been fabricated by credulous natives. It is therefore revelatory of Lingard's inexcusably naive mentality that he views the *Lightning* in a manner precisely paralleling the perceptions of mystified savages:

> The fore-end of the brig was wrapped in a lurid and sombre mistiness; . . . her masts pointing straight up could be tracked by torn gleams and vanished above as if the trucks had been tall enough to pierce the heavy mass of vapours motionless overhead. . . . His loving eyes saw her floating at rest in a wavering halo, between an invisible sky and an invisible sea, like a miraculous craft suspended in the air.
>
> (*Res*, 203)

Conspicuous by its absence from the above description, however, is the mythic stellar ally. Like Lingard's fortunes, it has been in gradual decline for some time, and now seems very close to the earth and vulnerable to mortal vicissitudes. The night D'Alcacer and Mr. Travers are kidnapped by Daman it climactically vanishes. Having recently been shocked from a reverie "as if she had fallen down from a star" (*Res*, 153), Mrs. Travers from aboard the stranded yacht notices that "the brig's yardarm light . . . tremble[s] distinctly, and she [is] dumbfounded as if she [saw] a commotion in the firmament. With her lips open for a cry she [sees] it fall straight down several feet, flicker, and go out" (*Res,* 168). And, indeed, the counterpart of Lingard's private cynosure, the "stern lantern of the yacht," also threatens to subside, as "very low in the black void of the west" it shines only "feebly like a star about to set, unattainable, infinitely remote" (*Res,* 203), and "the shadow of the outer darkness, the shadow of the uninterrupted, of the everlasting night that fills the universe, the shadow of the night so profound and so vast that the blazing suns lost in it are only like sparks" is in the ascendant, leaving only a "trembling gleam, faint and sad, like a vanishing memory of destroyed starlight" (*Res,* 151, 42).

Yet, if one form of stellar inspiration seems to fail, the fertile optimism of knights and maidens can always fabricate alternatives. Both Lingard and Mrs. Travers perceive one another's forms outlined against the starry sky (see *Res,* 153, 463), a sign of the extent to which they idealize each other. And upon his arrival at Darat-es-Salam, the Shore of Refuge, Lingard happily observes from the brig the signals with which Jörgenson greets him from ashore. Fittingly, these signals are rockets that appear to be astral bodies under human control: one by one "a new star soar[s] noiselessly straight up from behind the land, take[s] up its position in a brilliant constellation—and go[es] out suddenly" (*Res,* 51). Ultimately, three rockets are fired in all, and their number insists upon and perpetuates the significance of the three shots Hassim fired two years before while saving Lingard's life "in the splendid light of noonday," traditional moment of transcendent harmony (*Res,* 72–76; cf. *N,* 61, 540). But there exists another stellar triad that seems to go unnoticed by Lingard. The "immense scintillation of the universe" parodies with eternally meaningless luminaries the ephemeral assertions of human order: 'To the northward, low down in the darkness, three stars appeared in a row, leaping in and out between the crests of waves" (*Res,* 46, 45). These stars can be identified with some certainty as the belt of Orion, the stellified goliath whose very existence makes pathetic Mrs. Travers's vision of Lingard in "the shape of a giant outlined amongst the constellations" (*Res,* 463). The *Hermit* runs aground "at the top of high water, spring tides" (*Res,* 32). This means that the action of the novel is probably set sometime in October, since the geographical location of the Shore of Refuge is south of the equator, and therefore the familiar calendrical and seasonal associations of the Northern Hemisphere must be reversed. Orion rises late in the evening in October, and the belt would stand out conspicuously to the north above the sea in just the way Conrad's narrative voice describes.

The apparition of Orion, the celestial giant and warrior, for thousands of years has been linked consistently with nautical disaster,[13] and this presence fittingly provides the astral context for Lingard's tragic failings. But there is more. When Mrs. Travers sees "King Tom" in "the shape of a giant outlined amongst the constellations" (*Res,* 463), she of course perceives him walking upright. Yet south of the equator Orion appears suspended upside down in the heavens, and Conrad correlates this fact with an important imagistic and psychological pattern. The human sense of value and direction, which is founded upon distortively coherent perceptions of the phenomenal world, is as open to the world's own distortive and confusing reflections as are the phenomena themselves. *The Rescue,* therefore, offers appropriately in the early pages the following decription:

> On the unruffled surface of the straits the brig floated tranquil and upright as if bolted solidly, keel to keel, with its own image reflected in the unframed and immense mirror of the sea. To the south and east the double islands watched silently the double ship that seemed fixed amongst them forever, a hopeless captive of the calm, a helpless prisoner of the shallow sea.
>
> *(Res,* 5)

A mirror image is not a congruent reflection of the object or person before the glass, but rather involves a subtle and disorienting reversal of the depth (front-back) axis while preserving the original orientation of the perceiver relative to the height and width axes (although if the sea is the mirror, as in most of Conrad's fiction, the reversal occurs in the axis that normally is regarded as governing vertical dimensions).[14] Lingard, "in the long intoxication of slowly preparing success," assumes the "sea [is] all his own" *(Res,* 106, 50). That he could somehow become entrapped by it is inconceivable to him. But, like a mirror image, the seemingly simple world rapidly grows "full of contradictions" *(Res,* 188) once Lingard gets "drunk with the deep draught of oblivion" served him by Mrs. Travers, a woman "whose life's orbit [is] most remote" from his, yet a woman who nevertheless is a strange rhetorical reflection of the "shallows [which are] the shelter of his dreams" *(Res,* 431, 276, 245). Her unruly "abundance of pale fair hair, fine as silk, undulat[es] like the sea" *(Res,* 139), the very sea which he once felt he owned. She comes from the aristocratic, "shallow glitter" of "the restless eddy and flow of a human sea" to Lingard's watery domain which, "reflecting the color of her eyes, was tinged with a sombre violet hue," to "the shallow sea which, like her gaze, appeared profound, forever stilled, and seemed, far off in the distance of a faint horizon . . . to lose itself in the sky" *(Res,* 140, 148, 125). Moreover, Mrs. Travers insistently wears a veil (see, e.g., *Res,* 399, 401, 443). She thereby appropriates an appearance that formerly was associated exclusively with those of Lingard's allies whom she displaces: the sea has a "veiled face," Hassim's eyes express "dreaminess like a . . . veil," and Immada has "eyelashes . . . like a veil" concealing her "veiled eyes" *(Res,* 64, 66, 135, 234). This tragic appropriation is made most clear by the fact that Mrs. Travers's veil is given to her by Lingard from the very sea-chest full of the precious clothes that Immada is to wear after she is "sent back to her land with all possible splendour" to reign once again as "the Princess" *(Res,* 288).

Of course, the conventional and obtuse Shaw, whose "grandfather was a preacher," vehemently resists what he calls "bottom-upwards notions" *(Res,*

22, 12). However, in order for one to survive the maddening reflexes of Conrad's world precisely such notions are often invaluable, for without them the surface that seems to be so firmly supportive can become a terrifying void, as Mrs. Travers discovers: "By looking over the side of the ship she could see inverted in the glassy belt of water its massive and black reflection on the reflected sky that gave the impression of a clear blue abyss seen through a transparent film" (*Res*, 285; cf. 56). The corpulent Shaw's myopic vision defines Lingard's own vulnerability, for he was hired by Lingard, and at the end of the novel he is borne away with Mrs. Travers on the *Hermit*. Lingard in his fatuousness remains, like Shaw, perpetually unprepared for the unexpected, for the disorienting "abyss seen through a transparent film" that for him is ultimately embodied in Mrs. Travers, who lurks aboard the *Emma* "within the transparent shelter," the "enchanted cobweb," the "white haze . . . of transparent muslin," like an enigmatic Acrasia gradually enfeebling Lingard's commitment to the conflicting "fixed dreaminess like a transparent veil" of Hassim's eyes and ideas (*Res*, 285, 277–78, 66).

A victim of "that responsive sensitiveness to the shadowy appeals made by life and death, which is the groundwork of a chivalrous character," Lingard is astounded when suddenly it becomes "impossible to say who in this shadowy warfare was to be an enemy, and who were allies," when, because of his consequent bewilderment, his umbral certitudes begin to abandon ship: "The shadows on the deck went mad and jostled each other as if trying to escape from a doomed craft" (*Res*, 74, 188, 192). Originally, the "cocksure" Lingard experienced coherent "shadowy appeals" cast by "the splendid light of noonday" when he and Hassim shook hands, and by the garish "fire of Heaven" seen off the coast of Wajo the magic night he rescued Hassim and Immada (*Res*, 40, 72, 80). He is unprepared for the conflicting shades that gather as a result of perplexing conceptual reflections. There is an alternate "fire from heaven," love, and this discordant emotion threatens and finally prevails during the alternate "noon" when Lingard sights, at the conclusion of a voyage that began at midnight, the "black hull of the yacht," which is "heeling over, high and motionless upon the great expanse of glittering shallows," and which, significantly, is immobilized pointing in a direction opposite to the heading of the agile *Lightning* (*Res*, 130, 46, 53, 55).

These bewildering situational reflections are supplemented by verbal echoes. Twice Lingard is told through Jaffir by Hassim to "depart and forget" (*Res*, 81, 450). And, in spite of Lingard's insistence, "I don't forget," he in fact does forget Hassim and Immada twice (see *Res*, 135, 259), long before they are blown to smithereens by Jörgenson when Mrs. Travers fails to convey Hassim's emerald ring to Lingard with the accompanying message from Jaffir, ironically, "to forget everything." Similarly, Lingard gets entangled in two conflicting vows in spite of his naively insisting "I am King Tom, Rajah Laut. . . . I have my name to take care of" (*Res*, 338; cf. Mr. Travers's significantly parallel assertion [354]). To Hassim he declares, "If ever you and Immada need help at once and I am within reach, send me a message with this ring and if I am alive I will not fail you," but this declaration is soon compromised by his promise to Mrs. Travers: "Not a hair of your head shall be touched as long as I live" (*Res*, 93, 164). Lingard's problem is summarized by Jaffir, who "bear[s] weighty words between great men," and who skeptically observes, "You are a white man and you can have only one word" (*Res*, 331, 333). And, indeed, amidst this echolalia Lingard is rapidly "deprived . . . of the power of speech" and is "confounded," able only to jabber at the silent Mr. Travers "You—You—" as he "stammered and stared," and to Mrs. Travers he likewise offers a "confused stammering" of " 'You . . . you . . .' deliriously repeated" (*Res*, 122, 138, 394). Such an impediment conclusively shows the heroic narrative that formerly constituted Lingard's life is broken, as he regretfully admits, saying "I am nothing now" (*Res*, 328). After encountering the Traverses, "there was nothing of a conqueror of kingdoms in his bearing" (*Res*, 249). He therefore prates confusedly because "there's nothing to tell anymore," even as he is propelled by his own urgent fantasy toward the moment when he "look[s] at nothing" after the "shock of the explosion had robbed him of speech and movement" (*Res*, 233, 426, 443).

A world that fragments redemptive singleness of purpose into discontinuous glitter and reverberation, into distracting and imprecise reflections and echoes, is indeed an "immensity of contradictions" (*Res*, 432). One way of maintaining teleological coherence in such a world is to follow scrupulously and ruthlessly D'Alcacer's advice to Mrs. Travers, "I would suppress anything I could not understand," a perceptual mode Lingard summarily describes when he observes that "people . . . go about the world with their eyes shut" (*Res*, 407, 121). Like Whalley hiding behind his "great white beard . . . like a silver breastplate over the awful secret of his heart" (*ET*, 303), such people must grip life in a chivalrous manner, gingerly and punctiliously, "as one may hold some highly explosive and uncertain compound" (*Res*, 336), though this approach to experience can only ever be partially successful.[15] Given the deceptive nature of reflections and echoes, one cannot be certain that all the perceptions that are allowed to penetrate one's suppressive defenses are in fact going to be supportive of one's precious continuities.

And to discover that a particular impression is subversive after it has been dignified and valorized is to undergo a ghastly surprise that shatters the familiar cohesions upon which identity itself is founded into a figurative "rain of shattered timbers and mangled corpses" (*Res*, 442). Thus, Conrad's world resounds constantly with the outraged cries of characters who find that "every day that passes is more impossible to [them] than the day before" (*Res*, 308), who in effect repeat impotently the protest of Chaucer's Dorigen that Conrad so fittingly uses as the epigraph to *The Rescue*: " 'Allas,' quod she, 'that evere this sholde happe! / For wende I nevere by possibilitee / That swich a monstre or merveille myghte be!'" ("The Franklin's Tale," 1342–44). This is the "moment of dumb dismay" when are discovered the "events, contacts, glimpses, that seem brutally to bring all the past to a close," when "the wanderings must begin again":

> the painful explaining away of facts, the feverish raking up of illusions, the cultivation of a fresh crop of lies in the sweat of one's brow, to sustain life, to make it supportable, to make it fair, so as to hand intact to another generation of blind wanderers the charming legend . . . of a promised land, all flowers and blessings. . . .
>
> (*TU*, 134)

Such shocks are defined as an ontological necessity by the very rhetoric of Conrad's narrative voice. For example, the simple approach of an equatorial storm from the north is described in terms of the arrival of "an immense cloud" whose darkness, "as if to prove the impossible," deepens to "an incredibly blacker patch outlined on the tremendous blackness of the sky" that "left nothing free but the unexpected" (*Res*, 42).

This principle is manifested on the human level by various characters' discoveries and consequent admissions that their respective conceptions of the possible have been violated. To Hassim and Immada the aristocratic Europeans aboard the grounded *Hermit* are "inconceivable existences" (*Res*, 135). To Mrs. Travers, Lingard is beyond comprehension, as she admits: "I can not . . . imagine him at all. He has nothing in common with the mankind I know. There is nothing to begin upon. How does such a man live" (*Res*, 149). And her husband, who petulantly protests against his suddenly exceptional circumstances, also finds Lingard impossible to understand: "The existence of such a man is a disgrace to civilization. . . . I won't admit the possibility of any violence being offered to people of our position" (*Res*, 147). Although Mr. Travers previously lived in such a coherent manner that "there were never any empty moments in [his] day," he now confronts the same sort of "unexpected solutions of continuity, sudden holes in space and time" experienced by the "high official" in *The Secret Agent* (*Res*, 337; *SA*, 85). Lingard, too, discovers something radically new, "something he had never known before," a "conflict within himself," and in astonishment recognizes "the subtle traitor": "Why! It's myself!" (*Res*, 329; cf. Willems's similar recognition, "Why! Himself!" [*OI*, 145]).

Obviously, it is not possible to maintain indefinitely an illusion of existential continuity by practicing D'Alcacer's perceptual principle of "suppress[ing] anything [he] could not understand" in a world that "left nothing free but the unexpected" (*Res*, 407, 42). Lingard sustains such an illusion for an unusually long time simply because by leaving England he can physically abandon all the wretchedness and vulnerability, the "poverty, hard work—and death" (*Res*, 218), which constituted his youth and which stand to undermine the new and compensatory identity as "King Tom" that he fabricates in the Orient. Indeed, he unwittingly confirms the validity of D'Alcacer's cynical dictum "Englishmen, when worsted . . . , travel extensively" as he proudly remarks, "I left home sixteen years ago and fought my way all round the earth. I had the time to forget where I began" (*Res*, 123, 158). But Lingard's role is only as safe as are his plans for decisive and successful action. Although he confidently affirms, "The thing simply can't fail. I've calculated every move. I've guarded against everything," the "unexpected" fatally asserts itself in the form of a stranded yacht carrying British aristocrats (*Res*, 104).

This vessel and its passengers awaken a long-suppressed dimension of Lingard's experience, "his youth . . . the distant shores of early memories" of past humiliation and powerlessness in England (*Res*, 129). They also defy "the fatal inanity" of his "impossibly wild projects" that resemble the opera libretto Lingard recalls, in marked contrast to his disaffirmed youth, as being "more real than anything in life" and having "carried [him] away" (*Res*, 96, 301, 434; cf. "carry off" [*SL*, 5; *WT*, 45; *N*, 551; *TLS*, 189, 190]). Thus taken by surprise, Lingard understandably complains indignantly:

> A yacht here of all things that float! When I set eyes on her I could fancy she hadn't been more than an hour from home. Nothing but the look of her spars made me think of old times. And then the faces of the chaps on board. I seemed to know them all. It was like home coming to me when I wasn't thinking of it. And I hated the sight. . . .
>
> (*Res*, 155)

But even more hateful is the climactic loss of identity that Lingard subsequently experiences in the face of Mr. Travers's unanticipated declaration "I don't know who you are": "Before such scepticism he was helpless, because he had never imagined it possible" (*Res*, 131, 128). And, indeed, other personalities seem to dissolve under the pressure of similar interrogations to which "there was no adequate answer" (*Res*, 154–55). Mrs. Travers asks of Jörgenson, "Who is he?" just as the spectral Norwegian later asks her, "And who are you?" (*Res*, 157, 386). Such questions even drive secure aristocrats to the brink of psychic dissolution, for when Lingard demands of Mrs. Travers "Who is he?" in regard to her conceited husband, "These three words [seem] to her to scatter her past in the air—like smoke. They [rob] all the multitude of mankind of every vestige of importance" (*Res*, 154).

Only an awareness of the profound insignificance of "all the multitude of mankind," a perspective opposed to the very form and content of teleological romance, can make possible an appropriate response to a disconcerting world that seems inevitably "to prove the impossible" at the expense of human order. Such an awareness is possessed by Captain H. C. Jörgenson, "skeleton," "phantom," and "restless shade" with an "other-world aspect," whose "expressionless eyes with an . . . unearthly detachment . . . suggested an invincible indifference to all the possible surprises of the earth" (*Res*, 95, 98, 105, 248). He therefore contrasts radically with the other characters enmeshed in this "Romance of the Shallows": "Nothing in the world could astonish or startle old Jörgenson," for he is a sojourner in "that world of eternal oblivion" where "all things were settled once for all," where men dwell who are "efficient in meeting the accident of the day, but who did not care what would happen tomorrow and who had no time to remember yesterday" (*Res*, 334, 382, 90).

Indeed, Jörgenson's demystified temporality contrasts directly with the sort of cosmic significance sought by people like Lingard and Emilia Gould, who insist that even the most spontaneous acts and events "must have meant something" (*Res*, 102), that "for life to be large and full it must contain the care of the past and of the future in every passing moment of the present. Our daily work must be done to the glory of the dead, and for the good of those who come after" (*N*, 520–21). These conflicting perceptions of time date from the earliest moments of Occidental monotheism, when primeval understanding of time as "purposeless temporal undulation" was displaced by an insistence that "temporal events move in a linear progression towards their completion in eternity."[16] Attempting to describe the magnitude of this conflict, at least one scholar notes that "no more radical revolution has ever taken place in the world-outlook of a large area." [17]

The numbing nihilism of a character like Jörgenson is a fine example of the way Conrad typically appropriates the implacable indifference of an ancient and essentially Oriental ontology by means of which to enervate Western illusions of continuity and direction. As Conrad observes, the "West having managed to lodge its nasty foot on the neck of the East is prone to forget that it is from the East that the wonders of patience and wisdom have come to the world of men who set the value of life in the power to act rather than in the faculty of meditation" (*NLL*, 88). Capable of a ghastly comprehension, Jörgenson affirms, "If you want to know anything, I can tell you," although "What I could tell you would be worse than poison" (*Res*, 91; cf. 364). And, fittingly, it is from him that "Lingard had heard of Darat-es-Salam, the 'Shore of Refuge,'" the eventual site of disenchantment and carnage (*Res*, 91–92). Moreover, he has mastered the complexities of human language: "I can speak English, I can speak Dutch, I can speak every cursed lingo of these islands." Yet there is one thing Jörgenson does not know, as he admits openly: "I have forgotten the language of my own country" (*Res*, 103). Jörgenson is from a town in Norway called Trömso (*Res*, 104; cf. German *träumen*, "dream"), and this is quite important. Conrad does not mean to suggest there is any great significance in the fact that Jörgenson cannot speak Norwegian, but rather that, unlike the other characters, he is largely immune to becoming "the prey of dreams" (*Res*, 315).

Although he is described as "the somnambulist of an eternal dream," Jörgenson's reverie is the consequence of his proximity to the *nunc stans* of cosmic emptiness: "Jörgenson looked at nothing . . . with his strange sightless gaze fixed . . . into the void" in a manner analogous to that of the "heads on stakes" surrounding Kurtz's hut "smiling continuously at some endless and jocose dream of that eternal slumber" (*Res*, 382, 250–51; *HD*, 131–31). His ability to contemplate with serenity an ontic vacancy saves him from the dreams of redemptive substance that typify the solemn and urgent perceptions of "pitiless dreamer[s]" like Lingard and his ilk, who are on "an irresistable mission" in the "forests of a dream" pursuing the "figure of [a] dream," who speak "as if in a dream," who see others as "A dream! A dream!" and who are constitutionally "unwilling to relinquish [the] dream" because of an obsessive compulsion to reify their illusions, insisting, "They are no dream to me" (*Res*, 218, 216, 259, 108, 155, 208, 265, 260). Jörgenson, the "indifferent but restless corpse," would never talk in such a manner. And for precisely this reason all the characters find that "conversation with Jörgenson was an impossible thing" (*Res*, 279). He is only too aware that the world is destructive of human order, that "the rocks forever overwhelmed and emerging" (*Res*, 245) cannot be eliminated completely in the manner of a sentimental romance like Chaucer's "The Franklin's Tale,"[18] and that "a cry of pain" is consequently in store for those deluded questers whose unwarranted confidence is analogous to "the dreamy mist that in the early radiance of the morning weaves a veil of tender charm about the rugged rock in mid-ocean" (*Res*, 23, 137).

Hence, Jörgenson has largely abolished tense and trajectory from his life, and appropriately retains as the sole vestige of his adventurous past

> a small mahogany case with a lock and silver plate engraved with the words "Captain H. C. Jörgenson. Barque *Wild Rose*."
> It was like an inscription on a tomb. The *Wild Rose* was dead, and so was Captain H. C. Jörgenson, and the sextant case was all that was left of them.
>
> (*Res*, 90)

Jörgenson's nihilistic acuity, like his vacant but finely crafted and precious sextant case, contrasts directly with the superficial pomposity of Mr. Travers, who proudly affirms, "There were never any empty moments in my day" (*Res*, 337), and with the mercenary piety of the "odious" manufacturer "on a large scale of cardboard boxes" who tortures Flora De Barral, and who remains ever ignorant of the tawdry emptiness of his pasteboard substantiality, since for him "just a little money . . . is the measure of virtue, of expediency, of wisdom" (*C*, 129, 173). Indeed, Jörgenson's terminal awareness—"He was supposed to know details about the end of mysterious men and of mysterious enterprises" (*Res*, 90–91)—enables him efficiently to terminate almost anything. He destroyed his deepest love, the *Wild Rose*, himself, rather than allow the ship to be captured by the Dutch colonial authorities (*Res*, 100). He tells Lingard it would be better to commit suicide than to meddle in native politics, and he talks repeatedly about "throwing a lighted match amongst the powder barrels" (*Res*, 103, 331). Most decisively, he is "infinitely disgusted" that Lingard is involved with a woman, and negates the possibility for his own entrapment in erotic passion by having most unromantically purchased his exceptionally devoted wife "for three hundred dollars and several brass guns," a sum that pointedly contrasts with the three shots, three barrels of powder, and three stars from which Lingard's fugitive fantasy is fashioned (*Res*, 282, 105).

Hence, Jörgenson remains unperplexed before the same patterns of reflections and echoes that drive Lingard and Mrs. Travers to distraction. For instance, he placidly observes in his letter to Lingard that he is menaced by Tengga. Jörgenson then goes on to describe the effect he has upon the militant native, who "nearly choked himself with his betel quid" when he saw the maddening indifference with which Jörgenson received his ominous observation "Even a lizard will give a fly the time to say its prayers" (*Res*, 174). Later, Jörgenson responds "with great dignity" to Tengga's offer "Will you come ashore, O white man, and be the leader of chiefs?" by observing, "I have been that before" (*Res*, 421); and he proceeds to taunt the simple Tengga enigmatically with a parody of Tengga's original threat, saying, "No, I won't fight you. But even a spider will give the fly time to say its prayers" (*Res*, 446). Far from being disoriented by situational or lexical reverberations, Jörgenson obviously can use them consciously against those for whom he feels contempt. Thus, he ends his life in a purposeful enactment of his own hyperbolic jest about "throwing a lighted match amongst the powder barrels": after a wistful look around he "put[s] the cigar in his mouth and jump[s] down the hatchway" into the powder magazine, thereby blowing up the *Emma*, with ruthless irony, immediately after he got Hassim, Immada, Tengga, Daman, and the three Pangerans to come aboard and fulfill the very conditions he himself had just set for armistice (*Res*, 331, 447; see 421–22, 445). Having decided "he had done with it all," Jörgenson, indeed, accomplishes the only true peace: "When the rain of shattered timbers and mangled corpses falling into the lagoon had ceased . . . , all strife had come to an end" (*Res*, 338, 442).

Jörgenson in his nihilism is a markedly different character from Charles Gould, who also thinks of "throwing a lighted match into the [powder] magazine," for Gould, like Lingard, remains ever a quester in pursuit of "a moral romance derived from the tradition of a pretty fairy tale," ever able to "endow [his] personal desires with a shining robe of silk and jewels" (*N*, 366, 218). Such questers must remain within time, since, as Edmund Husserl cogently observes, "Every individual in mere phantasy is temporally extended in some way."[19] But, although it is possible to sustain a subjective temporality merely by staying alive, it is excruciatingly difficult to correlate this subjectivity, defined by Hume as "perceptions which succeed each other with an inconceivable rapidity . . . in perpetual flux and movement,"[20] with other people's private experiences in order to accomplish successful communication and effective campaigns. Thus, in *The Rescue*, a novel that takes place entirely within "the hour of fate," many characters find paradoxically that in "a minute . . . years had elapsed," while concurrently "time . . . has been standing still for ever so long" (Res, 320, 163, 318). These extremes of temporal awareness are focused most clearly in Mr. Travers's punctilious compulsion to wind his watch "every evening," even though "the hands are broken off short. It keeps on ticking but [he] can't tell the time. It's absurd" (Res, 337). Men like Mr. Travers are lost without the illusion that their perceptions and activities are synchronized with the similar exertions of similar persons. Lingard's watch is also "stopped," though in his own way he likewise preserves an urgent sense of chronographic purpose and congruence by maintaining an ardent proximity to Mrs. Travers: "He couldn't spare any of her attention to any other man, not the least crumb of her time. . . . He needed it all. To see it withdrawn from him for the merest instant . . . seemed a disaster" (Res, 362, 335).

Only Jörgenson, "the man . . . so detached from the shames and prides and schemes of life that he seemed not to count at all," can in fact "count seconds correctly" (Res, 365, 363). Of course, he has no interest in synchronizing his experience with that of his fellow men, having long ago abandoned his sextant, and thereby the needs and perceptions of captain and navigator, in the knowledge that "all things pertaining to the life of men" are "uncertain" and "wrapped up in doubt" (Res, 381). Indeed, his attitude toward time parallels that of the novel's narrative voice, which describes the Lightning's "pertinacious clock [that] kept ticking off the useless minutes of the calm before it would, with the same steady beat, begin to measure the aimless disturbance of the storm" (Res, 41). And when he borrows Lingard's inert timepiece (which, significantly, stops while being overseen by Mrs. Travers), Jörgenson is "like a phantom of the dead carrying off the appropriately dead watch in his hand for some unearthly purpose" (Res, 364). The "purpose" is, of course, to measure "gravely" the meteoric fuses by means of which he will annihilate time once and for all. This is the only action Jörgenson initiates in the entire novel. As he conjures up death "he display[s] a weakness of the flesh," and is "never . . . less spectral than then" (Res, 368). A clock is useful to Jörgenson only when "there's precious little time left," and even then he is willing only temporarily to revive the ridiculous ticking, at some arbitrarily chosen moment, in order to quantify and orient only pure subjectivity until a fix can be taken upon a terminal hiatus. And precisely for this reason the key to the powder magazine aboard the Emma is kept always "fastened to the watch" (Res, 362–63).

Jörgenson is the only one who can use the "dead watch" and fatal key, because he is the "man who had done with life so completely that his mere presence robbed it of all heat and mystery, leaving nothing but its terrible, its revolting insignificance" (Res, 369). He has been to Hades, and as a "visiting ghost" on earth is only slightly troubled when he finally decides once again to cross "the water of oblivion," the river Lethe, and thereby follow his own and

Hassim's recommendations to "Drop it!" and "Depart and forget!" (*Res*, 382, 105, 100, 81). Lingard, who too late acknowledges that Jörgenson's advice is "sane," also partakes of a "deep draught of oblivion" that he obtains from Mrs. Travers, the "sibyl" (*Res*, 397, 431, 415; cf. the Dutch spy, Jewel, and Felicia Moorsom, who are seen as sphinxes [*Res*, 95; *LJ*, 307; *WT*, 76]). But Lingard's "divine emptiness of mind" is that of a "man who has had a glimpse through the open doors of Paradise," and is the consequence of "infinite illusions" (*Res*, 432–33, 466). Such a state of mind has nothing in common with the solitary Jörgenson's plutonic perspective.

This is clearly demonstrated by the propensity of Lingard, emblematic wielder of Jovian thunderbolts and occasional manipulator of pillars of smoke and flame, who at times even has "the appearance of standing upon the sea" (*Res*, 32, 59, 183, 153; cf. 367), to talk of his relationship with "Providence" and ultimately to adopt the words of Jesus: as he lavishly identifies the very creation of the world with the seven days he has known Mrs. Travers, he augurs, "It began by me coming to you at night—like a thief in the night" (*Res*, 213, 398; see Revelation 3:3; cf. I Thessalonians 5:2). This is truly a paradisiacal outlook, and makes possible Lingard's presumptuous nocturnal assertion that things are "clearer than daylight" (*Res*, 183). Overall, the world-weather seems auspicious for Lingard. It is spring, and within the "secret peace" of Belarab's *locus amoenus*, "the shade of the fruit trees, masked by the cultivated patches of Indian corn and the banana plantations," he is "lapped in the wings of the Angel of Peace" (*Res*, 32, 108, 435). He lives with "the white radiance of Eternity," in whose "desolating fury" can be detected "forms and colours fading in the violence of the light" that "devoured all colours" (Percy Bysshe Shelley, "Adonais," 463; *Res*, 297, 288). Consequently, "the Settlement full of unrestful life and the restless Shallows of the coast [ultimately] were removed from him into an immensity of pitying contempt. Perhaps they existed" (*Res*, 416). From this transcendently Platonic perspective, indeed, "if you see anything . . . it will be but a shadow of things" (*Res*, 416, 437).

Lingard's supernal clarity is made possible by a woman who has "no shadows on her face" and whose shape is "not dishonoured by any faltering of outlines" (*Res*, 214, 139). While contemplating Mrs. Travers, Lingard experiences a "vision so amazing that it seem[s] to have strayed into his existence from beyond the limits of the conceivable," and he later decides it is "inconceivable that everybody should not have loved to make that woman happy" (*Res*, 214, 304). Indeed, he has found in his female "vision" a new sense of communion that displaces his fellowship with Hassim; and, appropriately, "taking the starry night to witness," he asks of no one in particular, "Has anybody ever had a friend like this?" (*Res*, 339). In *Lord Jim* Marlow to little avail desires to cancel decisively all ambiguity, and at one point he wishes to possess as his weapon "an enchanted and poisoned shaft dipped in a lie too subtle to be found on earth," a weapon of the sort that Jim wields just before his suicide as he abandons his pen, making "the ink blot resembling the head of an arrow" (*LJ*, 316, 250). In *The Rescue* Mrs. Travers, "as straight as an arrow," is precisely such a metaphysical missile, and she elicits from Lingard an acquiescence in certitude: "And now I am sure" (*Res*, 338, 417). He dwells "in the light she seemed to shed" for she is his romance icon, appealing "to something in him that was apparently independent of his senses" and causing "the very shadows . . . [to] appear endowed with an internal glow": "Her complexion was so dazzling in the shade that it seemed to throw out a halo around her head" (*Res*, 230, 302, 139; *WT*, vi). As D'Alcacer points out to Lingard, such women are archetypes, "iridescent gleams on a hard and dark surface" (*Res*, 411).

As if to accentuate this, Mrs. Travers is depicted according to the traditional mythologem of the mystical, potent, veiled Female, which extends from the most ancient cults of the *Magna Mater* through the poetry of Spenser and Shelley, and which Conrad frequently utilizes. As Lingard transfers her in a small rowboat from the yacht to his brig, she is seen as a "dream" whose "hooded and cloaked shape" is wierdly luminous because the "ruddy glow thrown afar by the flares [on the brig is] reflected deep within the hood." As a result, "the dream had a pale visage" (*Res*, 207–8). Mrs. Travers sustains this appearance by veiling herself, "leaving little more than her eyes exposed to view" (*Res*, 288), so as not to offend the religious sensibilities of the Moslem natives. But she soon learns to defend herself also from Lingard's needful gaze by means of this costume: "Veiled . . . she confronted him boldly," and in frustration he is left "looking hard at the manner in which the scarf was drawn across Mrs. Travers' face" (*Res*, 399, 401; cf. *TU*, 140, 196). Even when the *Emma* explodes she clings to her gossamer shield, and the sole effect upon her of the apocalyptic destruction is that now "her face was half veiled" (*Res*, 443).

But Mrs. Travers the "arrow" is not only a redemptive "enchanted . . . shaft." There is necessarily a corrosive "lie" that makes highly dangerous Lingard's myopic perception of her as a type of radiant clarity and certitude. The veil of which Mrs. Travers is so fond is scarcely an attribute denotative of lucidity. Indeed, quite the opposite is the case, as is revealed more generally by the consistent use the narrative voice makes of the word "veil" to signify obscurity. Just as Mrs. Travers conceals herself "behind the veil of an immense indifference stretched between her and all men," so are "uneasy souls" cut off "from the rest of the universe" by a "thick veil of clouds" and by "the night . . . [which] spread[s] its veil over the earth" (*Res*, 125, 243, 148). Far from being a means of paradisiacal clarification, "deep feeling is often impenetrably *obscure*," and Lingard's passion for the veiled lady is echoed throughout the novel in the ever increasing opacity of his "universe" that "an *obscurity* that seemed without limit in space and time had submerged . . . like a destroying flood" (*Res*, 124, 241; italics mine). Lingard's misapprehension of Mrs. Travers is figured forth most emphatically the night she briefly bears a torch after leaving the *Emma* to visit Lingard in Belarab's stockade, for when she carries the "blazing torch on an earth that [is] a dumb shadow shifting under her feet" the same paradoxes coalesce in her veiled figure that are personified by Kurtz's "small sketch in oils . . . representing a woman, draped and blindfolded, carrying a lighted torch. The background was sombre—almost black" (*Res*, 393; *HD*, 79; cf. *LJ*, 300; *TU*, 123, 181). Mrs. Travers only seems to be a beacon. In fact, she is a harbinger of darkness. She tosses her torch away and runs forward "blindly" through the murk, and when she later is together with Lingard by a campfire in the "deepest shade of the night" suddenly he "scatter[s] the embers with his foot and [sinks] on the ground against her feet" because her eidetic impact is greatest when she is immersed in obscurity, as Lingard admits: "I never believed in you so much as I do now, as you sit there . . . with hardly enough light to make you out by" (*Res*, 413, 418, 417).

Although Lingard might entertain the fantasy that his relationship with Edith Travers will eventually encompass the passion of Paris and Helen (about which he and Shaw converse at the beginning of the novel), in fact she is incapable of leaving her husband. The etymology of her first name makes this plain. *Edith* is derived from Old English *Eadgyth*, a fusion of *ēad* ("possessions") and *gūth* ("battle") denoting "one who fights for family possessions." And appropriately this arrow-like woman, who is "the best man of them all," and who stands "only half a head less tall than [Lingard] himself" (*Res*, 182, 228), emasculates her lover with little remorse before departing with her spouse. Soon after meeting her, Lingard mutters, "it is hard—hard" while "he look[s] into Mrs. Travers' violet eyes" (*Res*, 144). But all too soon he comes to say "You . . . have taken all the hardness out of me," whereupon he becomes and remains the "*limp*id soul" his potent lady later judges him to be (*Res*, 339, 417; italics mine).

Unable to manage time to his own advantage, Lingard cannot accomplish his chivalric romance. Like James Wait, he has been content to "let all this wait; let everything wait, till tomorrow or to the end of time" (*Res*, 416). But he is revived and thrust back into uncongenial temporality by the very explosion that propels his friends and enemies into eternity. He "feel[s] . . . abandoned by the All-Knowing God," whereupon Conrad, with merciless irony, causes him to speak in the manner of the resurrected Christ when He restrains the joyous Mary Magdalene. Lingard warns D'Alcacer, "Don't disturb me. . . . I have just come back to life and it has closed on me colder and darker than the grave itself. . . . I can't bear the sound of a human voice yet" (*Res*, 444; cf. John 20:16, and Mrs. Travers's similar words [355, 467]).

Thus, as his teleological fantasy is ruined Lingard unwillingly undergoes an experience with which Conrad, suffering as he repeatedly fabricates a romance while aiming only to destroy it, is quite familiar. Indeed, having written the last page of *Victory*, Conrad pointedly speaks to his wife essentially in Lingard's words, thereby revealing the intensity of his regret after having ended still another hopeful romance in holocaust:

> "She's dead, Jess!" "Who?" I asked, suddenly feeling sick. "Why, Lena, of course, and I have got the title: it is 'Victory.'" He flung his cigarette out of the window and muttered the injunction, "Don't come near me. I am going to lie down." [21]

His feelings no doubt were the same upon completing "that damned and bloody romance,"[22] *The Rescue*, the "most representative, if not the most popular, of Conrad's novels."[23]

TECHNICAL CONTEXTS
Rendering Discontinuity

Et les mots s'envolent; et il ne reste rien, entendez-vous?
Absolument rien, oh homme de foi! Rien. Un moment, un clin
d'oeil et il ne reste rien—qu'une goutte de boue, de boue
froide, de boue morte lancée dans l'espace noir, tournoyant
autour d'un soleil éteint. Rien. Ni pénsee, ni son, ni âme.
Rien.

—Conrad to Cunninghame Graham, 15 June 1898

Discontinuous Narrative Perspectives

In recent years critics have been provided with a number of new and significant intellectual tools that bolster their efforts to determine the abstract nature
of a literary text and to respond to it adequately as interpreters of specific
passages and works. The criterion of mimetic realism particularly has been
assaulted and judged to be an unfortunate and misleading concept that has
mistakenly been imposed upon artifacts that exist apart from such comforting
epistemological assumptions. J. Hillis Miller has perhaps stated the problem
most succinctly:

> One important aspect of current literary criticism is the disintegration of the
> paradigms of realism under the impact of structural linguistics and the renewal of
> rhetoric. If meaning in language rises not from the reference of signs to something
> outside words but from differential relations among the words themselves, if
> "referent" and "meaning" must always be distinguished, then the notion of a
> literary text which is validated by its one-to-one correspondence to some social,
> historical, or psychological reality can no longer be taken for granted.[1]

Although literary criticism has long dealt with intellectual constructs derived
from metaphors that are founded upon the idea of mimesis, there is at present
a tendency to reject as futile all attempts to validate a text through references
to supposedly extralinguistic presences. And the growing awareness that one
cannot evade forests of purely verbal relationships that threaten to engulf
reassuring potential for correctness and truth has given rise to a body of
theoretical criticism that emphasizes "indeterminancy" and "discontinuity" in
literature as typical, if not necessary, aesthetic facts.[2] Joseph Conrad's point of
view devices make such facts visible and even obtrusive.

Although there is no scarcity of analytical criticism dealing with the
thematic statements made by works presented from a discontinuous point of
view, very little positive attention has been given to the artistic function of
Conrad's device of narrative inconsistency. Indeed, critics have commonly
dismissed the points of view developed in novels like *Nostromo*, *The Nigger
of the "Narcissus,"* and *Victory* as mere bungling on the author's part, which,
if anything, detracts from the aesthetic success of these works. It is a central
concept in modern criticism that the technique a writer chooses for presenting
his work is a profound intellectual tool, "the means by which the writer
himself first finds out what he is really trying to say. . . ."[3] As Mark Schorer

151

asserts in "Technique as Discovery," "The final lesson of the modern novel is that technique is not the secondary thing that it seemed to Wells, some external machination, a mechanical affair, but a deep and primary operation; not only that technique *contains* intellectual and moral implications, but that it *discovers* them."[4] Indeed, much of the resistance recent criticism has expressed relative to the device of discontinuous point of view is the result of irrelevant or overly stringent criteria. But attempts at instilling some thoughtful hesitancy into the minds of critics who tend confidently to pass decisive qualitative judgments are not lacking. In "Authors, Speakers, Readers, and Mock Readers"[5] Walker Gibson warns that the gesture of rejecting a book can imply merely that the author has required the reader, in order to comprehend the work, to adopt an attitude that the reader finds unacceptable. In other words, evaluative remarks should be made in full awareness of the sort of "mock reader" the work necessitates, and of one's own attitude toward this role.

On a more profound level, Frank Kermode and Morse Peckham both insist that the art of fiction vigorously assaults a reader's expectations, however sacred, inherently frustrating almost any "paradigmatic fiction"[6] a reader may bring to bear upon the work of art. Kermode asserts that it is entirely permissible, indeed, to be expected, for an author to create "a novel in which the reader will find none of the gratification to be had from sham temporality, sham causality, falsely certain description, clear story."[7] And in *Man's Rage for Chaos* Peckham convincingly presents an argument that artistic perception necessarily involves the experience of disorder and disorientation, since it is that "human activity which serves to break up orientations, to weaken and frustrate the tyrannous drive to order, to prepare the individual to observe what the orientation tells him is irrelevant, but what very well may be highly relevant."[8] More specifically, Wayne Booth in *The Rhetoric of Fiction* suggests that the "most important unacknowledged narrators in modern fiction are the third-person 'centers of consciousness' through whom authors have filtered their narratives."[9] Furthermore, Booth affirms that an author's creation of narrative perspective is essentially equal to the fashioning of a "character" in a literary work. Thus, a reader must be prepared to encounter, free from negative value judgments, inconsistency on all levels of the narrative.

The inconsistent point of view as Conrad uses it commonly involves a switching back and forth between a first-person, subjectively limited persona and a third-person, omniscient narrative voice.[10] This device, of course, is not unique to Conrad's works. Charles Dickens, for instance, employs essentially the same sort of discontinuity in *Bleak House*, in which the narrative perspective oscillates between that of the third-person narrative voice and that of Esther Summerson, the first-person narrator. J. Hillis Miller feels that the shifting point of view in *Bleak House* has a very specific artistic function: by juxtaposing "the succession of disconnected moments experienced by the third-person narrator" with Esther's point of view, "the vision of a person for whom events are seen in retrospect to have a continuity because the person was herself involved in them," Dickens creates a statement that demonstrates that order is a projection of human perception onto an essentially disordered world, since the "vividness and immediacy of the sections in the present tense gives them a kind of priority, and suggests that the structuring of events into a 'destiny' is a falsification, an intellectual deformation."[11] Thus, the third-person narrative voice serves as a negative qualifier of the optimistic and ordered perception of Esther Summerson; and in Conrad's novels the discontinuous point of view functions in much the same manner.

At this point a specific example is in order. Consider briefly the shifting narrative perspective manifested in the volume in which Marlow makes perhaps his most memorable appearance. It is important to realize that *Heart of Darkness* is the second story in a volume consisting of a series of three tales ("Youth," *Heart of Darkness*, and *The End of the Tether*) that Conrad insists must be read as a unified work of art. In a letter dated 7 February 1924 and addressed to F. N. Doubleday, Conrad remarks, "I told you that in my view every volume of my short stories has a unity of artistic purpose. . . ." In the same letter Conrad goes on to say that the "volume of *Youth* . . . presents the three ages of man (for that is what it really is, and I knew very well what I was doing when I wrote 'The End of the Tether' to be the last of the trio). I can't somehow imagine any of those stories taken out of it and bound cheek and jowl with a story from another volume. It is in fact unthinkable."[12] And in another letter, addressed to Alfred A. Knopf, Conrad remarks, more generally, "I don't shovel together my stories in a haphazard fashion."[13] Thus, there should be several important principles of unity operant in the *Youth—A Narrative and Two Other Stories* (1902) volume, perhaps the most significant of which is the modification of narrative perspective as the series of tales progresses.

Much has been written about the importance of the character Marlow, Conrad's most famous first-person narrator, and perhaps the best work in this area has been done by John Palmer, who writes persuasively that only with the development of Marlow was Conrad able "for the first time to draw attention to the primary object of interest in his early fiction—the processes of moral discovery and self-exploration." That is, "Marlow's meditation is itself the hard fact of the story."[14] However, Palmer goes on to make somewhat exaggerated claims about Marlow's importance as a character whose perception Conrad intends the reader to trust thoroughly: "All the Marlow tales involve such a variety of artifices tending to 'justify' Marlow as a choral voice that the reader must suppose Conrad to have been deeply concerned in gaining the reader's trust. . . ." Palmer feels that these tales "hold their narrator out as a trustworthy spiritual guide, one whose judgment about his own experience is likely to be both subtle and sound. . . ."[15] Palmer's discussion of Marlow's function as a normative voice or choral figure, whose attitudes are basically congruent with Conrad's own, needs to be qualified somewhat; and the problem of the function of the narrative inconsistency can be approached by a brief demonstration of Marlow's subjective fallibility, for it is precisely such human perceptual limitations that the third-person narrative voice reveals and censures in those of Conrad's works in which the two narrative modes clash.

In "Youth" a relatively congenial situation is established: the anonymous narrator, wallowing in his own illusions, appropriately agrees implicity with the disturbingly maudlin Marlow, who bewails the departure of the state of being (youth) that he has endowed, somewhat foolishly, with almost transcendental value, exclaiming, for instance, "Oh, the glamour of youth! Oh, the fire of it, more dazzling than the flames of the burning ship, throwing magic light on the wide earth . . ." (Y, 30). Certainly Palmer's assertion that Marlow is "a trustworthy spiritual guide . . . whose judgment . . . is . . . both subtle and sound" must be qualified in view of this story, for Marlow is so overwhelmed by the prospect of his vanished youth that he, most depressingly, must buffer his feelings repeatedly with alcohol while sentimentally lamenting "O youth!" The most blatant sign of Marlow's intellectual inadequacy, however, is that, even at a great chronological remove from his youth, he still takes seriously the pathetic and inept Captain Beard, who leaps into a rowboat without oars to save his equally inept wife when his ship is struck by another, and who must be rescued by his bewildered crew. To Marlow the incompetent old man is still admirable ("Just imagine that old fellow saving heroically in his arms that old woman—the woman of his life" [Y,9]); the motto "Do or Die" is still profound. Although he can regard youth intellectually as "silly," a lure "to joys" as well as "to perils" and "to death," he is emotionally a slave to the past and enjoys indulging in regret a good bit more than dealing with an uncongenial present.

However much Conrad may sympathize (or even agree) with Marlow's philosophical meditations, it is indisputable that Marlow is repeatedly presented as a character whose personality is warped and whose vision is colored by subjective biases just like other of Conrad's characters, and as such Marlow's voice cannot be accepted unquestioningly by the reader. In *Heart of Darkness*, for instance, Marlow's attitude toward women is openly scornful of what he considers to be their innate inability to cope with adversity. Yet, when the steamer is departing at the end of the tale and Marlow blows the whistle, in the face of the shrieking of the whistle and the crashing of the pilgrims' rifles (what to her must have been a disorienting "darkness") only "the barbarous and superb woman [does] not so much as flinch" (*HD*, 146) while the men of the tribe flee in terror, a detail which clearly undercuts Marlow's understanding. Moreover, in *Heart of Darkness* the anonymous narrator no longer assents to Marlow's tale-telling.[16] Indeed, he would rather have Marlow keep silent than suffer through "one of Marlow's inconclusive experiences" (HD, 51). And although the narrator does get interested in Marlow's story, confessing that "[he] listened on the watch for the sentence, for the word, that would give [him] the clew to the faint uneasiness inspired by this narrative . . ." (HD, 83), one cannot be sure that the "clew" ever comes (we do know, of course, that the tale has impressed him, for he retells it to the reader). The narrator's final remark is inconclusive. It could involve simply the narrator's transposition of the diction he has heard for hours from Marlow onto his relating of the fact that during Marlow's tale the sun has set and it has grown dark: "The offing was barred by a black bank of clouds, and the tranquil waterway . . . seemed to lead into the heart of an immense darkness" (HD, 162). The remark does not necessarily betray a completed "moral progress,"[17] although it may.

In *Heart of Darkness* Marlow speaks with a self-conscious aura of elite profundity that may annoy the reader even more than the maudlin triteness he displayed in "Youth." His contempt for the remainder of humanity after his return from the Congo betrays an unjustified egoism on Marlow's part that is significantly akin to Gulliver's downright insanity upon his arrival in England in book four of *Gulliver's Travels*. As he shows in works like *The Secret Agent*, Conrad is aware that the "darkness" can be encountered anywhere, within civilization or outside of it, an awareness that Marlow in his pride does not share: "I found myself back in the sepulchral city resenting the sight of people hurrying through the streets . . . because I felt so sure they could not possibly know the things I knew" (HD, 152). Indeed, one wonders whether the Director of Companies's comment at the end of Marlow's tale, "We have lost the first of the ebb" (HD, 162), is really "banal,"[18] and not an ironic qualification of the supposedly overwhelming profundity of Marlow's story.

In any case, as both the character of Marlow and his relationship with the anonymous narrator (and other listeners) alter, the narrative perspective of the volume of stories progresses significantly from a protagonist who idealizes the state of imperceptive innocence while in harmony with his companions and in a tearful, alcoholic haze himself, to a protagonist who values, to an equally exaggerated degree, a blighting recognition of what he sees as a moral darkness at the heart of Man, while his shipmates and he can relate only in a remote and discordant manner. Only the incisive third-person narrative voice of *The End of the Tether* can clear the air of the disturbing (but thematically relevant) subjectivity that has dominated the first two stories and give the reader some sort of objective, factual information and philosophical construct, even though this validity is derived only from the artistic convention of an omniscient narrative voice and functions only within the framework of the artifact in which it appears.

There are few tales in the Conrad canon that are more pessimistic than *The*

End of the Tether. The moral vision implicit in Marlow's voice and Kurtz's pronouncement is gone, and a bleakly neutral universe takes the place of the "heart of darkness" and the "whited sepulchre." In this universe darkness, as presented by the narrative voice, functions only as an aesthetic device that is devoid of moral connotations, being used only to develop an aura of disaster by means of repeated descriptions of sunset and the advance of night, and standing in marked contrast to Captain Whalley's morally connotative use of the same imagery to suggest evil as he describes the sensation of losing his eyesight as "the light . . . ebbing out of the world" (*ET*, 304). Consequently, "evil" becomes merely an evasive mental projection, and, as Sterne aptly remarks, "one man's poison, another man's meat" (*ET*, 334). The sparse objectivity of the third-person point of view repeatedly describes events and characters and uses imagery in a manner that directly echoes many details used in the previous two stories, thereby canceling out the moral vision that was imposed upon these details by Marlow's human meditation. Like Captain Beard, Captain Whalley is childlike, having a "boy's" glance (*ET*, 187) that perceives "the world is not bad" (*ET*, 174). In a somewhat absurd contrast, the Marlovian vision of a "heart of darkness" is given to Sterne ("star," a body aligned with the night), whose mental state is essentially congruent with Marlow's upon returning from the Congo, a detail that can only diminish Marlow's authority in the preceding tale. Sterne feels that there is a basic flaw in every man, and consequently "no skipper in the world would keep his command for a day if only the owners could be 'made to know'" (*ET*, 239), an attitude that is censured by the third-person omniscient narrative voice as "romantic and naive" (*ET*, 239). To continue, like Marlow in "Youth," Captain Whalley is also the product of a "dare-devil" youth, although his naively optimistic conception of man and human experience prevents him from feeling the bitter regret Marlow articulates. Marlow's prediction that after the "fire" of youth is gone nothing remains but "an impenetrable night" (*ET*, 30) establishes the imagistic darkness aligned with an implicit human moral judgment that is stripped away by the detached narrative voice of *The End of the Tether*, which does not make imagistic moral judgments, but rather signals disaster by means of the juxtaposition of objective description: "The twilight abandoned the zenith; its reflected gleams left the world below, and the water of the canal seemed to turn into pitch. Captain Whalley crossed it" (*ET*, 211).

Lastly, the structure of *The End of the Tether* echoes that of both of the preceding tales. As the plot develops we move ever farther inland, away from the open sea where Captain Whalley achieved youthful success and fame, into complex waterways, islands, and shadows of trees, much like the symbolic use of navigation problems in *Heart of Darkness*. After the ominous scraping of the bar, furthermore, the narrative becomes disorienting because of time-shifts, echoing in a sinister manner the contrasts between a congenial past and bitter present in "Youth," and between a hideous past and indifferent present in *Heart of Darkness*. Structurally, however, Whalley's successful remote past exists only as a dwindling memory, and the time-shifts contrast, in a subtle but important modification of the situation in "Youth," a recent past of loss and shocking change with a tragic present that only confirms in an unsympathetic way Marlow's prediction in "Youth" of the "impenetrable night" that lies in wait for all. By means of a shift in narrative perspective, the phenomenal world is freed from the burden of articulating human values; and whether one is a God-fearing optimist like Captain Whalley, who feels "the world is not bad" (*ET*, 174), or a subversive pessimist like Sterne matters little, for neither vision can cope adequately with the problems of human experience. In *The End of the Tether* the "strong bond of the sea, and . . . the fellowship of the craft" that the anonymous narrator celebrates in "Youth" (*Y*, 3) have vanished. An old friend like Captain Eliott cannot understand Whalley's problem; and not only do Massy and Sterne prevail, but they are more perceptive in their defensive paranoia than the conventionally admirable Whalley. Thus, the point of view in this tale has assumed the detached, ironic, and essentially amoral qualities that are displayed in Conrad's other novels employing a third-person omniscient narrative voice, either consistently, as in *The Secret Agent*, or inconsistently, as in *Lord Jim*,[19] *Nostromo*, *The Nigger of the "Narcissus"* and *Victory*.

Consider next *Nostromo*, a novel dominated by a third-person voice that only rarely (apart from dialogue, of course) permits the intrusion of a first-person utterance. In *Nostromo* the narrative voice is in essence the voice of the harsh Conradian universe, testing and evaluating men, although, being articulate, it serves as a mediator between the human and the phenomenal. As spokesman for Conrad's world, and for the history of Man's activities in this world, the narrative voice fittingly uses setting as a primary means of establishing tragically ironic symbols and imagery that underscore the mental and physical inadequacies of Man, for it is a necessity of such a cosmos that it crush Man and all his works. Thus, the use of objects in the phenomenal world as symbols of this tragic opposition is organically meaningful and passes beyond the level of mere artifice. As in *The End of the Tether*, the narrative voice in *Nostromo* is free of process and "knows," without learning. While pessimistically citing the facts of contemporary life in Costaguana it describes the depressing historical background of human civilization in this country, thereby suggesting to the reader that its essentially negative attitude is valid.

In one unusual instance, however, a markedly different attitude and descriptive mode are evident in a sequence of remarks that opens chapter eight in the section entitled "The Silver of the Mine," apparently told from the point of view of a nameless persona who was a visitor to Costaguana during the relatively pristine time before the Gould concession began to impose modern material changes upon the land. The concession was in existence, but, significantly, the railroad had not yet been constructed, and in this chapter the coming of Sir John and the railway functions as a sign of the onset of sophisticated and insurmountable complications. The situation that the first-person narrator describes presents the San Tomé mine at the very pinnacle of success, before internal military or social dissension has recommenced in the land: "Those of us whom business or curiosity took to Sulaco in these years before the first advent of the railway can remember the steadying effect of the San Tomé mine upon the life of that remote province. The outward appearances had not changed then as they changed since . . ." (*N*, 95). Although the speaker is definitely aware of the presence of negative forces in Costaguana during his visit, these forces are controlled by Nostromo's fists and revolver:

> Nobody had ever heard of labor troubles then. The cargadores of the port formed, indeed, an unruly brotherhood of all sorts of scum, with a patron saint of their own. They went on strike regularly (every bullfight day), a form of trouble that even Nostromo at the height of his prestige could never cope with efficiently; but the morning after each fiesta, before the Indian market-women had opened their mat parasols on the plaza, when the snows of Higuerota gleamed pale over the town on a yet black sky, the appearance of a phantom-like horseman mounted on a silver-gray mare solved the problem of labor without fail. . . .
>
> (*N*, 95)

During this period the miners are effectively protected from tyrannous governments and are supervised by Don Pépé, who is personally concerned with the existence of each of his men (a feat not even the humane Emilia Gould can accomplish): "Even when the number of the miners alone rose to over six hundred he seemed to know each of them individually" (*N*, 100). In the speaker's memory, the situation in Sulaco is at the peak of positive, redemptive value: the mine is saving the country financially; the miners are protected from governmental oppression and are sufficiently devoted to the mine to risk their lives later to save Charles Gould; and even Nostromo is seen as triumphant and adequate in his love affairs (a source of illusion that leads to his death at the end of the novel). As the speaker says, "The material apparatus of perfected civilization which obliterates the individuality of old towns under the stereotyped conveniences of modern life had not intruded as yet . . ." (*N*, 96–97).

After the intensely optimistic opening paragraphs, the narrative perspective shifts quietly from the first-person narration of the onetime tourist to the point of view of the novel's omniscient narrative voice; and, as one might expect, the tone changes quickly to pessimism. It is noted that the miners must live in numbered villages; the stupidity of Father Roman, the "spiritual pastor" of the "mine flock," is revealed (Guzman Bento was also a herdsman before becoming the Citizen Savior); and "the mountain" is said to "swallow one-half of the silent crowd" (*N*, 100), an ominous echo of earlier mining techniques when the mine "had ceased to make a profitable return no matter how many corpses were thrown into its maw" (N, 52). The sound of the ore being crushed under the stamps is like "a proclamation," and is a sign of the fulfillment of "an audacious desire"; this diction alludes darkly to the past of Costaguana, which was just one "long turmoil of pronunciamentos" (N, 52), and suggests the future deaths of Decoud and Nostromo, victims, respectively, of "intellectual audacity" and "audacious action" (see N, 501). The narrative voice goes on to describe the agreement that heralded the coming of the railway (something the first-person speaker who began the chapter could not know about, as he admits) and the testimonial banquet honoring Sir John and Don Vincente Ribiera, who had just been "brought into a five-year dictatorship" (N, 117), only to qualify such apparent success by mentioning the threatening presence of Montero at the same banquet and by destroying any hope in Ribiera with a statement of historical context: "Next time when the 'Hope of honest men' was to come that way, a year and a half later, it was unofficially, over the mountain tracks, fleeing after a defeat on a lame mule, to be only just saved by Nostromo from an ignominious death at the hands of a mob. It was a very different event . . ." (N, 130).

It is at first difficult to understand the reason for Conrad's brief use of the first-person speaker for the opening paragraphs of this chapter. However, a parallel in structure and subject matter between chapters eight of "The Silver of the Mine" and ten of "The Lighthouse" is powerfully suggestive. Chapter ten also begins with a first-person narration interspersed with occasional deprecating comments by the narrative voice: Captain Mitchell provides the first-person narrative as he guides a visitor on a one-day tour of Sulaco (which recalls the tourist's voice in chapter eight). The time is set just after the success of the secession movement, and to an obtuse and superficial mind like Mitchell's all things seem to indicate prosperity and stability. Like the point of time preserved in the tourist's memory in chapter eight, Mitchell's tour involves Sulaco at the peak of apparent success, the moment of greatest triumph of the redemptive plan. Indeed, the parallel is significant, for Conrad thereby indicates that the voices of success are essentially frivolous, subjective voices with little understanding or experience, which stand in marked contrast to the novel's narrative voice, the voice of transcendent awareness of tragic inadequacy.

The tourist speaking in chapter eight sees only a simple, pristine nation trembling eagerly in the face of plans to effect an economically and morally redemptive change. Mitchell can only tell of the details of the success of the military version of this redemptive movement, which he feels has prepared the way for the complete fulfillment of Gould's ideals, while emphasizing his own petty importance in the course of "historical events": "There are people of this Alameda that ride in their carriages, or even are alive at all today, because years ago I engaged a runaway Italian sailor for a foreman of our wharf . . ."

(N, 483). Just as the tourist's vision of prerailway stability is ruined by the narrative voice's pointing out the coming of the railway and the demise of the Ribierist government, so is Mitchell's simple, tourist-guide's success story undercut by the structure of the chapter, which again permits the narrative voice to have the last, dismal word. Mitchell closes his demonstration by mentioning that Nostromo had told Antonia "how Decoud had happened to say that his plan would be a glorious success" and giving his opinion: "There's no doubt, sir, that it is. It is a success" (N, 489). Nostromo lied in conveying such a message to Decoud's "intended," for Decoud fled Sulaco because he despaired of both the success of the secession movement and the possibility of ever wedding Antonia (see N, 239). Mitchell's tale of "glorious success" is likewise untrue (although Mitchell does not think so), and the narrative voice's ironic comment, that the "cycle was about to close," apparently referring to Mitchell's tour, but also clearly referring to the tragic cycle of historical process, underscores this untruth (another meaningless revolution is imminent, since the mobs are already forming under the aegis of Father Corbelan and Hernandez to turn against Gould [see N, 510–11]). Immediately thereafter, in a flashback, this voice fittingly proceeds to reveal the real Decoud, his fall into a total psychological loss of value, and his suicide, in addition to Nostromo's entrance into a state of slavery to the silver. Thus, in both chapters, which closely parallel one another in point of view, subject matter, and structure, the voice of optimism and success is the subjective human voice, which is severely limited in both instances by an abysmal lack of understanding, while the omniscient third-person narrative voice serves as the qualifier and even destroyer of the credibility of such success.

J. Hillis Miller remarks that all of Conrad's work might validly be called "an effort of demystification"; he sees the "aim of all Conrad's fiction [as an attempt] to destroy in the reader his bondage to illusion. . . ."[20] The viciously ironic third-person omniscient narrative voice that Conrad characteristically employs as an integral part of his device of discontinuous point of view is his means of demystifying the universe in which his subjects live and onto which they inherently project their respective ethical myths; that is, Conrad creates an ironic discrepancy between the world of his novels as it is formulated by the omniscient narrative voice and the same world as it is invalidly envisioned by even the most acute characters, in a manner much like the point-of-view devices used by Dickens in Bleak House. Conrad's third-person narrative voice is aware of the dark ontology toward which Miller feels the nineteenth century novel moves in its philosophical progression "from the assumption that society and the self are founded on some superhuman power outside them, to a putting in question of this assumption, to the discovery that society now appears to be self-creating and self-supporting, resting on nothing outside itself."[21] Throughout much of the Conrad canon a similar perception of a metaphysically neutral world in which ethics and values are invalid projections of the human mind serves as the normative vision against which characters' subjective fabrications of meaning and value in life must be measured and ultimately broken. The true choral voice in Conrad's fiction is the third-person omniscient narrative voice rather than any of Marlow's moral meditations, for the fictional convention of omniscience necessarily lends validity to its understanding, just as the first-person convention necessarily discredits the reliability of the speaker, be he a Donkin or a Marlow.

Of course, the omniscient third-person narrative voice derives its quality of reliability solely from the conventions governing this aesthetic device. Conrad as author does not pretend to have access to the same freedom from subjective illusion that is demonstrated by the narrative voice, which ironically, he has created. That is, within the artistic framework of the novel in which the device is used, there is no choice but to grant the narrative voice a degree of perceptual acuity which is unavailable in real life; but the attitudes that the narrative voice demonstrates were instilled in it by a human subject, the author, and therefore it must be kept in mind that these attitudes have no more validity outside the aesthetic configuration than any other subjective definition of the nature of life. The ironies arising from the reader's realization of this fact save the corpus of Conrad's fiction employing the omniscient third-person narrative voice from any annoying tendency to seem like pontificating, which would be inconsistent with Conrad's ontology.

Morse Peckham suggests that "as behavior language has two polarities, the exemplary and the explanatory." He does not mean that there are two types of statements that can be made, but rather "two opposite directions in which discourse moves. A statement is exemplary if it is explained by another statement; it is explanatory if it explains another statement." Literary interpretation is in essence "nonexemplary or explanatory discourse" that is capable of "infinite regressions, a process which is halted . . . by satisfaction on the part of the interpreter."[22] In an effort to evade the accumulation of long sequences of interpretations, the validity of which must always remain tentative, some critics have begun to plead for an increase in pure research, asserting that "interpretive critical commentary . . . cannot form the basis of sound scholarship, although serious scholarship can form the basis of sound interpretive commentary."[23] Such remarks suggest a desire to assemble a body of generative sources in order to make available a "sound" basis of knowledge that can redeem verbal behavior from the risk of a high level of uncertainty; a desire, that is (using Peckham's terminology), for achieving in a basically exemplary sort of discourse the security of referring ultimately to semantically inert things. The concomitant need, however, to devalue a response to literature predicated on the "conception of a narrative as a fabric of language generating meaning from the reference of words to other, anterior words"[24] is unfortunate. Although a reassuring division of critical activity into the categories of "serious scholarship"[25] and "critical flying-by-the-seat-of-the-pants"[26] may be appealing, it is a simplistic escape from the haunting suggestions of current literary theory that "the pre-text of a given text is always another text open in its turn to interpretation." [27] One can never penetrate to an epistemological plenum no matter how much one manipulates the language or the card catalogue.

Most readers of Conrad's novels are aware that point of view in *The Nigger of the "Narcissus"* is discontinuous, fluctuating between a first-person singular narrator (who at times makes use of the first-person plural) and a third-person omniscient narrative voice, and that the artistic quality of the work has repeatedly been questioned by reference to this device.[28] A careful consideration of the function of point of view in this novel will directly involve the problem of discontinuity in characterological presentation and in the overall structure of the book, as well as provide an opportunity to take J. Hillis Miller's advice and turn away "from our traditional concern for 'point of view,' with its overt or covert commitment to certain representationalist assumptions." [29]

When an author creates a character, be it an anonymous persona or Tom Jones himself, what is accomplished quite simply is the presentation of "a proper name [or pronoun]" and then the verbal ascription of "a series of attributes to that name [or pronoun] while presenting it in an increasing range of verbally signified situations." All one can possibly talk about in the case of named character is "a term." Mimetic criteria are of little significance, serving frequently only to pervert a properly aesthetic response into a debate as to whether a character is "believable" or not, leaving us intellectually "defenseless before the degree of our tolerance of violations of our expectancies." [30]

Since the character of the first-person persona dominates *The Nigger of the "Narcissus"* throughout, a great many attributes are constellated around it. Consequently, one can expect a high degree of discontinuity in the novel, for according to Morse Peckham, "In fiction, the prime source for . . . discontinuity is character."[31] An author achieves this quality "by continuously introducing characterological sentences (which . . . may also function simultaneously as situational and narrative sentences) in order to force the reader to abandon his effort to create a stable cognitive model whenever the presence of the character in question is indicated in the narrative sentences or even merely implied."[32] In *The Nigger of the "Narcissus"* a major source of attributional confusion is derived from the temporal involvement of the point of view. Using his excellent memory, the narrator tells his tale in retrospect; he has already passed through his initiatory experience in time and recalls the story from a timeless position—that is, he is no longer changing. The knowledge the narrator has gained as a result of his experiences on board the *Narcissus* conditions the attitude in terms of which he presents the tale, for his point of view involves futurity in the sense that only at the end of the novel is the reader finally led to (and thus able to comprehend) the state of mind that is embodied in the narrator throughout. The reader is presented the problem of learning from and about a person who has already attained a certain knowledge, yet who, by reliving the past from a point of view the reader can only understand at the end of the novel, portrays himself as learning from the events he describes in a process paralleling the reader's secondhand learning experiences. The burden that these complex requirements place upon the artistic convention of a narrator is immense. Only with great difficulty, and never with certainty, can the reader decide at a given moment whether the assumptions underlying a particular descriptive mode are exclusively part of the past as the narrator conceives it or part of the narrator's completed wisdom and projected from his physically and temporally detached position; and, moreover, the reader can properly accomplish this only after multiple experiences of the novel.

The attitudinal shift that the narrator undergoes involves primarily his relationship with the concepts he identifies with the person of James Wait. Elaborate metaphors and similes are a common intellectual device by means of which the narrator orients himself toward his perceptions. By carefully observing which qualities in the figures of speech alter and which remain unchanged one can tentatively distinguish between an awareness that is being dramatized as having been modified or newly gained during the voyage and a static attitude that the narrator imposes from the perspective of his final detachment (in which case one cannot tell whether the attitude was held even before the voyage, or acquired during or after the voyage).

James Wait's influence plainly discomposes the narrator. He at first seems only to be capable of understanding the great "nigger" by recourse to often extreme subjective elaboration, in terms of which elaboration the very structure of the novel is developed. To the narrator the physical world seems to be morally neutral; the land is a place of "perfumes and dirt," at once both "precious and disgusting" (NN, 165). The sea is likewise largely ambiguous and "inscrutable." Since the narrator's shocking initiation has primarily been a function of the confusing intellectual darkness consequent upon the ambivalent intellectual assaults of James Wait and the ocean, according to his implicit subjective logic, the narrator seems to conclude that these three ideas share a common essense; and he repeatedly applies the same descriptive mode to the night, James Wait, and the sea. Not only does Wait have black skin and materialize out of the night at the beginning of the novel; his physical appearance, a disorienting muddle of darkness and sparks of light, is presented in a manner exactly parallel to the narrator's vision of the sea and the night. James Wait is seen thusly: "He held his head up in the glare of the lamp—a head vigorously modelled into deep shadows and shining lights—a head powerful and misshapen with a tormented and flattened face—a face pathetic and brutal: the tragic, the mysterious, the repulsive mask of a nigger's soul" (*NN,* 18).

It is clear that this huge black man, whose physical appearance is so enigmatic—'The whites of his eyes and his teeth gleamed distinctly, but the face was indistinguishable" (*NN,* 17)—is beyond the literal understanding of the narrator. He is forced to rely upon an elaborate subjective fiction to cope with what he sees, talking about tragedy, mystery, and the particularly "repulsive mask" characteristic of "a nigger's soul." Thus, even before Wait's strange influence upon the crew begins, he is almost a supernatural manifestation to the narrator. In the following description of the night and the sea, the parallel with the intermingling of lights and darkness visible in Wait's face is readily apparent:

> On the town side the blackness of the water was streaked with trails of light which undulated gently on slight ripples, *similar* to filaments that float rooted to the shore. Rows of other lights stood away in straight lines *as if* drawn up on parade between towering buildings; but on the other side of the harbour sombre hills arched high their black spines, on which, here and there, the point of a star *resembled* a spark fallen from the sky. Far off . . . the electric lamps at the dock gates shone on the end of lofty standards with a glow blinding and frigid *like* captive ghosts of some evil moons. Scattered all over the dark polish of the roadstead, the ships at anchor floated in perfect stillness under the feeble gleam of their riding-lights, looming up, opaque and bulky, *like* strange and monumental structures abandoned by men to an everlasting repose.
>
> (*NN,* 15; italics mine)

Both James Wait and the night evade the narrator's ability to understand them directly. Consequently, he resorts to the device of altering his perceptual mode through simile (note the italicized instances). The tenors of the narrator's figurative comparisons are of relatively slight importance. In the above passage the tenors all are founded upon one detail of the speaker's world—the confusing interpenetration of lights and reflections in the night. Incapable of comprehending these visual sensations, the narrator extends the vehicles of his similes ever farther subjectively from experientially validated sensory data. This epistemological desperation parallels significantly the way he reacts to his initial glimpse of James Wait's face, when the description also culminates in subjective metaphoric vehicles, in a psychic imposition of concepts like tragedy, mystery, and the mask of "a nigger's soul." Like the night, the "nigger" is essentially inaccessible, a strange, ambiguous interpenetration of light and dark, a tragic and mysterious mask, and thus always at least once removed from a physical appearance that can be accepted without subjective speculation and analogy on the part of the perceiver.

An important reason for the narrator's uncertainty as to how best to conceive of James Wait and the night can be derived from the comments he makes in the following seminal descriptive sequence. While the *Narcissus* is becalmed and Wait, with excruciating delays, approaches death, the narrator offers the following visualization of the ship's appearance on a moonlit night:

> On clear evenings the silent ship, under the cold sheen of the dead moon, took on a false aspect of passionless repose resembling the winter of the earth. Under her a long band of gold barred the black disc of the sea. Footsteps echoed on her quiet decks. The moonlight clung to her like a frosted mist, and the white sails stood out in dazzling cones as of stainless snow. In the magnificence of the phantom rays the ship appeared pure like a vision of ideal beauty, illusive like a tender dream of serene peace. And nothing in her was real, nothing was distinct and solid but the heavy shadows that filled her decks with their unceasing and noiseless stir: the shadows darker than the night and more restless than the thoughts of men.
>
> (*NN*, 145)

The narrator's use of diction derived from the winter season, emphasizing frigid withdrawal and death, in an effort to render the debilitating effects of suspension and stasis, is appropriate and obvious. More significant for the present discussion, however, is his figurative alignment of light itself with both the condition of motionlessness and ideas of inauthentic transcendence. Departing subjectively from the neutral fact of a celestial body, the narrator views the moon as a source of cold, lifeless illumination, which attaches itself to the ship almost parasitically, in a manner suggesting frost, snow, and mist, quiescent forms of water that stand removed from the flux of the sea and impede physical process; indeed, even the mighty blackness of the amniotic ocean is desecrated by illusory lunar gilding.

In the face of this overwhelmingly inert glow the narrator seems orientationally distressed. He is aware that, because of its inertia, the scene he beholds warrants a negative response; and he delivers such judgment by resisting an aesthetic appeal and by interpreting the visible aspects of his surroundings as analogous to extreme yet insubstantial states of delusive subjective merit: "a vision of ideal beauty" and "a tender dream of serene peace." But, having drained value from the radiant and precisely discernible surfaces in his environs, the narrator has deprived himself of all visually concrete bases upon which he can establish the concept of actuality. Hence, like Goethe's Mephistopheles, he is intellectually compelled to stand opposed to what seems to be physical existence and assign validity only to darkness. In a climactic inversion of Platonic rhetoric, the speaker asserts that only "the heavy shadows" are substantial and reliable; moreover, his vocabulary and sentence structure imply that authenticity is derived only from the presence in the mental shadows of the qualities of apparent weight, excessive blackness, and movement; thus, they are antithetical to the illusory and deadly static radiance that assaults the narrator's eyes and tempts him to conceive of a comforting and motionless aesthetic transcendence. Only the "heavy shadows" are "real" and "solid" as they admirably fill the decks with "their unceasing and noiseless stir," being properly dark and restless, because only they partake of the attributes upon which the narrator has come to depend when he measures the reliability of an experience.

The narrator's assignation of delusive, negative values to light and glowing surfaces helps explain why the appearance of James Wait's face, as well as that of the reflecting but essentially dark waters, is so confusing. What he perceives is, in effect, a positive, reliable constellation of ideas (the darkness and its refreshing connotations of flux and authenticity) being stultified before his eyes by the imposition of light, and attempting to transform itself into an extension of humanly fabricated meaning as the act of perception takes place. The narrator is confident that he grasps the nature of the black, aqueous world surrounding the protective construct of the ship on which he sails. But when a human being appears who seems to partake of this darkness through his very physical essence, the narrator becomes disoriented, for he knows that human beings and human things tend to embody fictive "radiance," the projection of subjective models of perfection, due to man's enduring, tempting, yet debilitating, desire to envision the world as a source of fulfillment. In other words, the humanity of James Wait is at war with the connotations of his color in the narrator's mind.

At first the speaker aligns the Nigger with the "immense and hazy" ocean, implicitly focusing only upon the fact of his blackness in an effort to define his nature with satisfying rapidity. Consequently, descriptions are offered in which James Wait seems to function in a manner opposed to light according to the narrator's subjective interpretation. For instance, he extinguishes the sun as the sea does at sunset: "He seemed to hasten the retreat of departing light by his very presence; the setting sun dipped sharply, as though fleeing before our nigger; a black mist emanated from him; a subtle and dismal influence; a something cold and gloomy that floated out and settled on all the faces like a mourning veil" (*NN*, 34). Note the narrator's use of figurative elaboration, and the presence of the reliable qualities of darkness and mortality ("a mourning veil"). The "black mist" emanating from Wait contrasts significantly with the illuminated "frosted mist" (*NN*, 145) that was identified in a previously examined passage as a threatening propagation of delusive and static moonlight; "black mist," on the other hand, far from sustaining a luminous surface, can annul the sun as the watery horizon itself does at evening: "A crested roller broke with a loud hissing roar, and the sun, as if put out, disappeared" (*NN*, 75).

As the novel progresses, however, James Wait's conduct efficiently works to cancel the narrator's initial complimentary response to him. The narrator's discovery of the "nigger's" humanity, which effectively cuts Wait off from the authentication of the darkness, regardless of the hue of his skin, radically alters the narrator's rhetorical values, and therefore functions as the major structural principle of the entire work. James Wait's willful eagerness to shirk active strife gradually aligns him with the quiescence that troubles the narrator so deeply when he witnesses it occurring haphazardly in the phenomenal world. Appropriately, "Jimmy's cabin" becomes a center for the sort of stagnant, idealized transcendence that the sailcloth's whiteness of "stainless snow" in the "sheen of the dead moon" (NN, 145) suggests to the narrator at another time; and the darkness is temporarily banished by the "glare of Jimmy's lamp" in his quarters, which have significantly been "repainted white," and which fluoresce "in the night [with] the brilliance of a silver shrine" (NN, 105) in the manner of a Conradian romance icon. Moreover, unlike the inky sea, which, as interpreted by Singleton, prompts men to "Look out for yourselves!" (NN, 57) the "nigger," who is also, meaningfully, known as "Snowball" (NN, 121), urges the crew to look out only for him in a grotesque perpetuation of infantile dependence.

The narrator's interpretational struggle with James Wait reaches a climax in the description of the rescue of the helpless black from the cabin in which he is trapped underwater while the Narcissus is swamped (see NN, 66–72). The rescue project itself imposes an unwelcome redemptive occasion, causing the crew to struggle actively and forcing them to deny their wishes to surrender to the temptation of reclining "back on the poop where we could wait passively for death in incomparable repose" (NN, 67). The diction once again aligns ideal extremes with a vitiated quietude; and fittingly, the wish for such a state is routed through a temporal perspective by use of the verb "wait," thus recalling ominously the parallel behavior in fact of James Wait himself. While the narrator takes an active part in the deliverance of the "nigger" he necessarily is acutely aware of the ontological significance of the suffering he and his shipmates voluntarily bear, as the above description of their frustrated wishes for passive "repose" clearly implies, for this important word is echoed later in the narrator's visionary and thematically crucial elaboration of the "passionless repose" captivating the Narcissus (NN, 145). Consequently, James Wait's cowardly passivity as the rescue progresses is particularly outstanding to the narrator, and he begins to grasp directly the weak and merely mortal essence of the miserable "squeak[ing]" man whom up to now he had regarded as being occultly aligned with the omnipotent sea and validating darkness. The episode of Wait's delivery from the cabin where he has been trapped because of the ship's capsizing is of vital significance, therefore, because it provides the narrator with an embarrassingly direct enactment of the "nigger's" pathetic vulnerability as well as with a factual situation upon which he can handily found a metaphor that will enable him to alter his attitude toward the hitherto frighteningly powerful black man.

The sequence of events leading to the "nigger's" rescue has commonly been regarded as a presentation of "a difficult childbirth."[33] What is usually overlooked, however, is the presence of equally stressed vocabulary related to mortality. As the narrator describes the rescue, that is, he undergoes the unpleasant experience of having his two major conflicting values brought into violent collision as they constellate themselves around James Wait. Measured against death, darkness, and the sea, the "nigger" sheds his cryptic potency and appears shockingly mortal; and the narrator's mind, with its propensity to deal in figurative extremes, effects an emphatic revaluation by transforming the victim into a grotesque child. The very situation, the crew at the mercy of the storm and Wait trapped underwater in his cabin, is dominated by the threat and presence of death, and the imagery seems to support this idea: the crew hears Wait "screaming and knocking below [them] with the hurry of a man prematurely shut up in a coffin"; later, Wait becomes silent, "as quiet as a dead man inside a grave; and like men standing above a grave [they are] on the verge of tears"; when the men finally succeed in penetrating the bulkhead, they almost kill Wait with the crowbar—"suddenly the crowbar went halfway in through a splintered, oblong hole . . . miss[ing] Jimmy's head by less than an inch"; after the men get Wait out of his cabin they "[totter] all together with concealing, absurd gestures, like a lot of drunken men embarrassed with a stolen corpse."

However, the narrator balances the death images with equally prominent images and suggestions of a trying childbirth: trapped in his cabin, Wait "screamed piercingly, without drawing breath, like a tortured woman"; the place of confinement is "deep as a well," and "every movement of the ship was pain"; as the crew struggle to rescue Wait, they must contend with the sea splashing over their heads and penetrate a layer of nails barehanded—water and blood are both present in significant quantities at birth; when Wait in terror tries to come through the small hole made by the crowbar, the imagery of a human being trying to pass headfirst through an opening described very much like the female genitalia is unmistakable—"He pressed his head to it, trying madly to get out through the opening one inch wide and three inches long"; Wait is finally rescued, but only after the men, despairing because they cannot pull him out by his short hair, see him emerge unaided—"suddenly Jimmy's head and shoulders appeared"; last of all, the men climb out of the confinement of the space above Wait's cabin and, overheated, come "into icy water"—the method of inducing breathing in newborn infants by dipping them into cold water is well known. The scene is further complicated by the fact that, in the last example cited above, the birth imagery applies to the crewmen, who have functioned primarily as midwives, as well as to James Wait; just as, when the "nigger" "screamed . . . like a tortured woman," the distinction between parent and child is blurred. This ambiguity, apart from indicating clearly that a "real" analogical birth is not supposed to be occurring but rather a discontinuous figurative interpretation, indicates that in the narrator's mind the state of shrieking dependence aboard a capsized and crippled vessel is as inappropriate as a nativity scene. Although the men properly evade the seductive wish for "incomparable repose" by suffering to save James

Wait, on another level they are only perpetuating and courting infantile parasitism, and are soon thereafter derided by Mr. Baker for being "worse than children" (*NN*, 76).

The "nigger's" metaphoric birth from both himself as "tortured woman" and the sea is quite important. The old James Wait, whose physical appearance and figurative effects resembled so closely the "immortal sea . . . with a glittering surface and lightless depth" (*NN*, 155) that can potently extinguish the sun, is left behind with the sea itself. He now becomes a ridiculous and mortally ill "child" identified with the delusive, fictive light itself, dwelling in a cabin "repainted white" and shining with "the brilliance of a silver shrine" (*NN*, 105). No longer is he primeval and frightening to the narrator, almost an Anglo-Saxon *nicor* ("water monster"), but only incredibly inauthentic and "demoralizing" as he partakes directly of the essence of the "phantom rays" (*NN*, 145), becoming "immaterial like an apparition" (*NN*, 139). Furthermore, the descriptive mode in which his burial is presented clearly indicates that, far from being a source of "black mist" capable of swallowing up the sun like the waters themselves, James Wait is now, like the spectral radiance whose nature he shares, engulfed effortlessly by the sea. During the burial ceremony the narrator notes that "the whole vast semicircle of steely waters visible on that side seemed to come up with a rush to the edge of the port, as if impatient to get at our Jimmy" (*NN*, 159). The sailmaker's comment, "You don't know where it [Wait] comes from. Got nobody. No use to nobody. Who will miss him?" (*NN*, 158), and the facts that he simply disappears when he is returned to the sea ("Charley, who anxious to see Jimmy's last dive, leaped headlong to the rail, was too late to see anything but the faint circle of a vanishing ripple" [*NN*, 160]) and that he has "no papers of any kind—no relations—no trace" (*NN*, 169) are all details that the narrator cites to reinforce implicitly the flickering insubstantiality of the human essence as manifested in James Wait, whose mortal remains continue to partake of the fictive light until they vanish physically into the sea. The corpse, significantly, is stashed in "a white blanket" (*NN*, 157) and sewed into "gray sailcloth" (*NN*, 158)—sailcloth previously was an important medium for the propagation of "the phantom rays" (*NN*, 145) that threateningly connote delusive human ideals to the narrator. Moreover, as he encloses the body in canvas, the sailmaker mumbles of having "sewed in twenty men a week" and "thought nothing of it" aboard a fittingly named vessel, the *Blanche;* and, at last, the corpse climactically departs the wooden chute "like a flash of lightning" (*NN*, 160).

The point may scarcely seem worth making that the narrator and James Wait are the most important characters in the novel; and, indeed, the prospect of critical debate over the relative significance of a figure is most uninviting. Such an inquiry here may be useful, however, for Morse Peckham interestingly relates the rating of a character's consequence to the amount of discontinuity a reader can expect to experience in the presentation of that particular character. He suggests that the importance of a character can be "defined by the amount of discontinuity he displays. That is, we know that a character is unimportant precisely because he has a narrower range of responses than other characters and appears in a smaller variety of situations."[34] Certainly the number of attributes that *The Nigger of the "Narcissus"* manages to assign to the persona and to James Wait, respectively, is extremely high; one can make many merely exemplary statements about each of them, for many specific situations and details are involved. This sort of detailed characterization would be regarded conventionally as a means of severely limiting the range of interpretational responses that could be elicited by each portrayal; and on one level of reading perhaps this is true. Nevertheless, Wolfgang Iser has recently observed that "the more a text tries to be precise" through the inclusion of many "representative aspect[s]," the greater will be the potential for indeterminacy in the reader's response, since "between the 'schematized views' there is a no-man's-land of indeterminacy, which results precisely from the determinacy of the sequence of each individual view."[35] As Peckham puts it, "Characters are discontinuous according to their distance from the central character. Spear-bearers are always the same." [36]

The previously analyzed sequence of figurative interpretations of James Wait clearly reveals discontinuity in the narrator, and, consequently, in the presentation of the "nigger" as well, since the latter is largely a function of the fluctuating attitudes manifested by the narrator. Yet, James Wait is not entirely at the mercy of the speaker: the point of view of *The Nigger of the "Narcissus"* is also discontinuous, as was mentioned earlier, and alternates first-person subjectivity with third-person omniscience in order, occasionally, to present James Wait from a significantly different perspective, and thus call into doubt the human view represented by the narrator. Only after many years has this device of narrative discontinuity been received positively and not labeled an artistic blunder on Conrad's part. For instance, a recent and refreshing critical response suggests that

> the evidence of textual investigation clearly shows that Conrad consistently, deliberately, and consciously labored to establish a dual perspective in the novel by these shifts from an omniscient to a crewman narrator and back again to the omniscient. And I do not believe that these shifts represent a structural weakness. They represent, instead, one of the strengths of the novel. . . .[37]

The interpretational problems posed by such narrative inconsistency are great. Not only must the reader cope with the set of attributes gathering around James Wait as he is seen through varying perspectives of the narrator, but also the details that accrue as the omniscient narrative voice presents him must be assembled, yet all kept separate and distinct. And, if Iser is correct, interpretational indeterminacy increases accordingly, for the dynamic narrative perspective causes a blurring of differentiations among the rhetorical devices employed by the narrator as crewman, the narrator as distinct from the crew and growing in awareness, the narrator as voice of futurity telling his tale in retrospect and employing his completed wisdom, and the omniscient narrative voice.

Concerning the problems involved in the confident application of any concepts of aesthetic order, Morse Peckham has the following to say in "Discontinuity in Fiction: Persona, Narrator, Scribe":

> . . . When we are given instructions, no matter what their metaphysical explanation and justification, to look for a set of configurations, we use them constitutively when we observe and report on only what we have been told to look for, but instrumentally when we also observe what we have not been told to look for and use those observations to correct both the . . . instructions and their . . . explanations and metaphysical justifications.[38]

Thus, for instance, plainly thinking constitutively, Vernon Young and Albert Guerard, respectively, can censure the shifting point of view of The Nigger of the "Narcissus" for providing information and presenting conversations and interior monologues that "are impossibly come by,"[39] and that consequently "violate the reader's larger sustained vision of the dramatized experience." [40] The presence of the third-person omniscient narrative perspective distresses both critics, who appear troubled by the tensions that develop owing to the markedly differing view of James Wait that is thereby made available. Guerard goes on to protest that "it has been the very convention of the novel that Wait must remain shadowy, vast, provocative of large speculation. . . . The very fact that he comes in some sense to represent our human 'blackness' should exempt him from the banalities of everyday interior monologue." [41] Although Guerard's suggestion that Conrad violates his own aesthetic conventions is inadequate, it is clear that the multiple dimensions of James Wait generate an opposition, which it seems is precisely to the point.

One of the major concerns of The Nigger of the "Narcissus," as well as of most of Conrad's fiction, is the dramatization of the necessary entrapment of the human psyche as it assigns meaning to the phenomenal world in the act of perception. This theme can be demonstrated most immediately by providing the reader with a point of view that, by virtue of the very definition of omniscience, is free of subjective coloring and also able to transcend human temporal and spatial limitations to make available information that serves to qualify or even negate the attitudes of the human subjects in the work. To be specific, the reader is permitted to enter the mind of James Wait on two occasions in order to explode both the narrator's and Singleton's preposterous interpretations of him. The lengthy fantasy of death and burial at sea (NN, 113) that James Wait suffers logically results from his memory of previously having been trapped underwater while the ship was swamped. And, instead of a wierdly potent emblem, the reader discovers a mere man, terribly ill and very much afraid to die. Similarly, somewhat later the reader learns that James Wait has been a ladies' man when ashore and that his dying fantasies concern getting back to land to see the "Canton Street girl" who chose him over "a third engineer of a Rennie boat" (*NN*, 149). Here appears a weak, frightened human being who is reliving his past nostalgically, and desperately hoping for a comparably successful future. Singleton is ridiculously wrong in his opinion of Wamibo as a sorcerer who casts spells to delay the ship, and he has a similar conception of James Wait. He feels the "nigger" is working with Wamibo to impede the ship's progress because Wait does not want to get home since he knows that the presence of land will mean his death. Wait's meditation clearly proves Singleton is wrong, for the sick man eagerly anticipates returning to shore.

Although it is implied above that the omniscient narrative voice deserves a higher level of credibility than the narrator, it must be remembered that the quality of reliability is solely a function of the conventions operant through an aesthetic device. Conrad as author never claims the same perceptual abilities for himself, never pretends to be free from delusive subjectivity. The perspectives presented through the third-person narrative voice were instilled in it by a human subject, and consequently have no more authenticity outside the aesthetic configuration than any other illusory specifications of the nature of human experience. Appropriately, the omniscient narrative voice is so thoroughly suppressed in *The Nigger of the "Narcissus"* by the sheer sustained temporal dominance of the narrator's subjective struggles that until recently, if it was detected at all, critics could justify its presence only by chastizing the author for permitting an illegitimate intrusion.

And perhaps, after all, perceptive readers like Guerard are also correct. A chapter dealing with indeterminacy and discontinuity can scarcely afford to be dogmatic. As Martin Price has asserted,

> The full import of any detail remains a problem at best, just as does the structural form itself. We may easily force meanings by distortion of emphasis or failure of tact. The elements of a novel shift in function . . . as the work unfolds and as new linkages are revealed. For this reason we can never with confidence ascribe a single purpose or meaning to a detail, nor can we give an exhaustive reading of the structure.[42]

Suitably, *The Nigger of the "Narcissus"* is developed rhetorically in terms of only the narrator's subjectivity, and consequently the very structure of the novel, as well as the narrator's visionary elaborations, is brought into doubt by the qualifying function of the omniscient narrative voice. As was noted, after the rescue of James Wait from the sea and the recovery of the *Narcissus* a transformation occurs that reverses the associations built up around the black man in the early part of the novel. The change in rhetorical values was previously demonstrated by close textual analysis. It can here best be illustrated by the following comparison:

Before Rebirth	*After Rebirth*
Wait's confusing influence coincides with the perplexing "fair monsoon" and with the violent storm.	Wait's influence is still confusing, but is now supposedly (according to Singleton, whose pronouncements the narrator absurdly idolizes) the cause of calm weather, of headwinds and a high barometer.
Wait's "unmanly lie," which is seemingly told only to avoid work, is that he is sick when he really appears to be well; he uses the fact of death as a tool to shame the crew into treating him with deference.	Wait's "unmanly lie" now is that he is healthy and can work, when he obviously is dying; it is told in a pathetic attempt to deny the fact of death, whereas before he continuously told the crew that he was dying.
It is disconcerting to the crew to believe Wait ill and not be able to see any physical evidence: "He became the tormentor of all our moments; he was worse than a nightmare. You couldn't see that there was anything wrong with him: a nigger does not show" (*NN*, 44).	It disturbs the crew to see Wait fail visibly while denying that he is at all sick: "The latent egoism of tenderness to suffering appeared in the developing anxiety not to see him die. His obstinate non-recognition of the only certitude whose approach we could watch from day to day was as disquieting as the failure of some law of nature" (*NN*, 138–39).
Wait is a slick confidence-man, actively bullying and contemptuous of the entire crew, continually abusing them for his personal benefit.	Wait becomes inactive, physically declines, and gives up life (he makes no attempt to save himself even during the storm).

Plainly the transformations that form the major structural principle of the novel occur exclusively according to the perceptual contortions and distortions effected by the narrator's and Singleton's minds, and at the expense of the crucial information made accessible by the omniscient narrative voice as it gives the reader entry into James Wait's private thoughts.

The values of the third-person narrative voice never change; in its bleakly objective description it has no trouble comprehending what is presented, for it is not human. Similarly, Captain Allistoun remains unperplexed by the "nigger," although he provides no psychological aid to the crew, for the accusation he directs at James Wait before the ship's company is just the opposite of what he knows to be true: "You have been shamming sick. . . . Why, anybody can see that. There's nothing the matter with you, but you chose to lie-up to please yourself—and now you shall lie-up to please me. Mr. Baker, my orders are that this man is not to be allowed on deck to the end of the passage" (*NN*, 120). Only later does the captain reveal to Mr. Baker, in secret, that he really understands Wait's problem. Fittingly, this information is conveyed to the reader by the omniscient narrative voice, not from the subjective point of view of the narrator: "When I saw him standing there, three parts dead and so scared—black amongst that gaping lot—no grit to face what's coming to us all—the notion came to me all at once [to order Wait confined to quarters], before I could think. Sorry for him—like you would be for a sick brute. If ever creature was in a mortal funk to die! . . . I thought I would let him go out in his own way. Kind of impulse" (*NN*, 127). Although discontinuity is injected momentarily into Captain Allistoun's personality when he admits to Mr. Baker that he is not sure about the efficacy of his techniques of dealing with the "row" on board and asks "Did you think I had gone wrong there. . . ?" (*NN*, 126) and when he at the same time evasively reduces his problems with the crew to a meteorological analogy, saying, "Headwind! all the rest is nothing," the captain nevertheless maintains like the omniscient narrative voice, a static conceptual relationship with James Wait. And if Peckham's ideas are valid, these details conclusively indicate that the major characterological significance in the novel rests with the persona and James Wait, for, indeed, like the Captain and the omniscient narrative voice, "Spear-bearers are always the same."

That the dominant characters of *The Nigger of the "Narcissus"* should manifest a high degree of discontinuity, and that the normative functions, the sources of valid perception according to aesthetic convention, should be relegated to a minor and implicitly qualified position, thus causing also structural indeterminacy, brings to light an important paradox inherent in Conrad's art. If, as J. Hillis Miller suggests, the "aim of all Conrad's fiction [is] to destroy in the reader his bondage to illusion," the works are also thereby involved in an impossible task; for the attainment of the goal of successful "dymystification"[43] is not consistent with Conrad's ontology, since "we, living, are out of life. . . . The mysteries of a universe made of drops of fire and clods of mud do not concern us in the least."[44] Conrad feels, in other words, that human consciousness cannot begin to conceive of the phenomenal world validly; and he appropriately deprecates the very artistic device that provides him with the means to achieve his "demystification," the omniscient narrative perspective. Conrad growls, "Why the reading public, which . . . has never laid upon a storyteller the command to be an artist, should demand from him this sham of Divine Omnipotence, is utterly incomprehensible" (*NLL*, 18). Thus, when the definitive attitudes toward James Wait presented by the omniscient narrative voice and by Captain Allistoun are weakened tentatively owing to the remote possibility that, somehow, Singleton's absurd prophecy has come true—that indeed "the barometer had begun to fall," though whether "it [was] before or after 'that 'ere glass started down'" that Wait died "was impossible to know" (*NN*, 157)—Conrad is merely sustaining his own epistemological assumptions within the novel and insisting that a measure of indeterminacy limit subtly even the aesthetic convention of omniscience.

It is possible that the theoretical constructs of scholars like Miller and Peckham, who explore the ramifications of the presence of indeterminacy and discontinuity in verbal behavior, are most useful as tools of aesthetic response when applied only to comparatively recent works of art. As Wolfgang Iser attests, it is a "striking historical fact that since the eighteenth century indeterminacy in literature—or at least an awareness of it—has tended toward a continual increase."[45] Conrad, in any event, clearly operates in terms of an epistemology that makes his writing quite responsive to recent theoretical criticism that asserts, "Literature is an instrument of knowledge with its own unique epistemological conventions . . . committed to forms and to a species of language which tend to hold opposites in suspension . . . [and] yield . . . a heightened sense of human dilemmas, and of Man's ultimately paradoxical relation to his universe."[46] If such theoretical foundations permit no final resolution of problems of specific aesthetic function and semantic content, they echo thereby the intellectual attitudes and thematic intention of many authors, whose works, when regarded in the light of unpretentious yet sophisticated constructs, may gracefully yield a level of unity seldom anticipated previously. More specifically, if Conrad criticism is indeed "at the end of the tether" as has been lamented,[47] possibly some careful application of current theoretical scholarship, exploring "the reciprocal relation . . . between the story narrated and the question of what it means to narrate a story," [48] treating a literary text properly as a "performative utterance"[49] that in fact generates its own object, may revitalize the situation and define a critical enterprise at once free from contextually empty "new readings" and from illusions of semantically redemptive "serious scholarship."

Directly or indirectly, modern aesthetic practice has absorbed the Hegelian concept of *aufheben*, which Harry Berger, Jr., explains in the following way: "As I understand Hegel's notion, when you sublate something, you (1) transcend it or negate it, pass it by, render it obsolete, (2) recognize *that* you have transcended it, therefore, (3) you . . . bestow on it a career going beyond itself which it could not have had without you."[50] Much of Conrad's work is involved with subverting inherited forms that in the past were particularly used as means of embodying optimistic Western philosophical contents. If indeed Conrad bestows "a career going beyond itself" upon iconography, role models, and symbolic situations that have been traditionally associated with Christian and secular transcendentalism, he does so in such a way that the original significance of these forms is annulled. For example, the titular noun "Victory" becomes a parody of metaphysical affirmations that traditionally lurk behind many of the details that appear in *Victory*, for these affirmations evaporate within the context of cosmic disaster that closes the work upon a resounding "Nothing." Although it may indeed be true that during more coherent moments in cultural history there was "no fate-bound dionysiac dissolution of the individual into nothingness and night . . . but a freedom beneath the dome of that religion which affirms the freedom of the will," [51] such an option no longer is available to Conrad's world. Instead, only "the tragic or ironic rehandling of a myth which had an optimistic meaning in its original form fits the modern sensibility of disillusionment and regret." [52]

The authorial point of view employed by Conrad in his lengthy Author's Note to *Victory* provides an indication of precisely how consistently present is this modern sensibility. A detailed consideration of the attitudinal content of this prefatory essay is therefore a useful prelude, since these perceptions are preserved in the narrative perspective of the novel itself. In the Author's Note Conrad immediately establishes contrasting attitudes toward detachment and involvement. He mocks those who continually meddle with conventionally profound metaphysical issues like "the Last Judgment" and lauds the man who is made of "wonderfully adaptable cloth" thanks to "his power of endurance and . . . his capacity for detachment," for such a detached man, "with perfect propriety," will not worry about things that do not concern him personally or that he cannot remedy. Far from opposing a Heyst-like detachment in his prefatory remarks, Conrad valorizes skepticism and uses the critic as an example of the mental stance which he is praising: in the face of "the lightning of wrath" the "critic will go on criticizing with that faculty of infinite littleness and which is yet the only faculty that seems to assimilate man to the immortal gods" (*V*, x). Significantly, "the Last Judgment," "the lightning of wrath," is inescapable in Conrad's cosmos. His use of such Christian terminology is merely a further example of his characteristically ironic pose, for in Conrad's works these ideas denote only inevitable destruction and hence are stripped of consoling theological connotations.

Having described in a complimentary context the benefits of aloofness, Conrad appropriately goes on to outline the dangerous situation that can seduce "even the best representative of the race . . . to lose his detachment." The aloof man is in most acute danger when he encounters a situation into which he is able to project himself because "the catastrophe [of the situation] matches the natural obscurity of [his] fate" (*V*, x). In other words, it is the gesture of getting enmeshed which is dangerous. It may be countered, of course, that, as Heyst himself admits, all involvement is perilous, "all action is bound to be harmful" (*V*, 54), since ultimate effects are unknowable. But this objection applies equally to the act of deciding to detach oneself, an act that, within the aesthetic framework of *Victory*, Conrad lauds, while specifically rejecting involvement, saying, "There should [be] a remedy for that sort of thing" (*V*, x). More specifically, both Heyst and Ricardo destructively commit themselves to Lena precisely because they are able to project themselves into a situation or onto another character; and Conrad is defining in the Author's Note what sort of attitude the reader is to take toward such involvement.

Conrad's apparent criticism of Heyst's "fine detachment" and "habit of profound reflection" also needs to be clarified. In the Author's Note to *Victory* Conrad does not oppose detachment, although aloofness does have negative consequences regarding the character of Axel Heyst in that it causes him to lose the ability to assert himself, leaving him, indeed, with only "wretched round knives [having] neither edge, point, nor substance" (*V*, 360). But this is a criticism specifically limited to Heyst. For example, Wang is even more thoroughly detached than Heyst, yet he appropriates Heyst's revolver, sustains his marriage, and retains the power to act decisively to defend himself and others. What Conrad implicitly defines as harmful is not the attitude of detachment leading to "profound reflection." The deeply damaging mental event is the surrender to inflexibility, the formation of a habit (whatever its specific manifestation), for "all the habits formed by civilized man" are, implicitly, "pernicious" (*V*, xi).

Perhaps the most perplexing aspect of Conrad's Author's Note is his protestation of good will for his characters. There exists a marked discrepancy between the criticism the novel at times directs at Heyst and Conrad's insistence that "I wouldn't be suspected even remotely of making fun of Axel Heyst" (*V*, xi). In this instance it seems clear that Conrad is consciously being duplicitous in his prefatory remarks. However, the case of Lena is perhaps more delicate. The existence of irony is always difficult to prove because, by definition, irony remains unstated. Nevertheless, the naive and optimistic tone Conrad adopts when discussing Lena's fate is apparently meant to be ironic in the most merciless way. Although the structure of a rhetorical question puts the burden of cold-blooded awareness upon the reader, Conrad's generalization about Lena's ugly fate can scarcely be taken at face value: "In view of her triumphant end what more could I have done for her rehabilitation and her happiness?" (*V*, xvii). Had Conrad simply called her demise a "triumph" there would be little ground for claiming an ironic intent, but to ask what more could have been done "for her rehabilitation and her happiness" in view of her absurd death is outrageous.

But Conrad does not limit his craftsmanship to the caustic implications of his generously optimistic rhetorical questions. He develops his own personality at some length almost like a character in a novel, describing in detail the subjective impressions that caused him wrongly to regard the person after whom Lena was fashioned as one who might be adequate to the desperate challenges posed by human experience. Blurring the boundaries between biography and fiction, Conrad describes himself passively watching the girl as she leaves him "for her meeting with Heyst." He then notes that he remained reticent at her departure because, due to his own illusions at the time, he conceived of her as being able to handle any situation: "It was my perfect idleness that had invested the girl with peculiar charm, and I did not want to destroy it by any superfluous exertion. The receptivity of my indolence made the impression so permanent that when the moment came for her meeting with Heyst I felt she would be heroically equal to every demand of the risky and uncertain future" (*V*, xvii). Conrad realizes such an impression is wrong, of course,[53] and he definitively undercuts the seriousness of the encounter of

"Lena" with "Heyst" described in the Author's Note by naming their trysting place the "Place de la Comédie."

Consider next the epigraph to *Victory*, which consists of the following three lines from Milton's *Comus:* "Of calling shapes, and beck'ning shadows dire, / And airy tongues, that syllable men's names / On Sands, and Shores, and desert Wildernesses" (207–9).[54] These lines are spoken by the Lady soon after she has been led astray in the forest by gullibly following sounds, in spite of her better judgment, for she was ordered to remain still and wait for the return of her brothers. This context is noteworthy. Throughout *Victory* there is a pervasive motif of silence and noise,[55] although it is only revealed as especially significant when one arrives at the philosophical prescription of Old Heyst: "Look on—make no sound" (*V*, 175). An important metonymical device in this novel connects the act of speaking with the decision to relinquish detachment. For example, in each of his three fatal involvements Heyst makes the first sound, directly opposing his father's advice: he offers aid and comfort to Morrison and Lena, and the noise of his inquisitive footsteps on the wharf prompts Ricardo's call for help.

The need to make noise, to speak, is presented as an instinct. The narrative voice remarks that "all the world . . . had instinctively rejected [Old Heyst's] wisdom" (*V*, 91). Fittingly, this instinct is itself described by means of a verbal analogy: it is called "the oldest voice in the world," and is apparently shared by all human beings, for it is Adamic, an unavoidable inheritance. Meditating in dismay on his gestures of involvement, Heyst concludes "There must be a lot of the original Adam in me, after all." More importantly:

> He reflected, too, with the sense of making a discovery, that this primeval ancestor is not easily suppressed. The oldest voice in the world is just the one that never ceases to speak. If anybody could have silenced its imperative echoes, it should have been Heyst's father, with his contemptuous, inflexible negation of all effort; but apparently he could not. There was in the son a lot more of the first ancestor who, as soon as he could uplift his muddy frame from the celestial mould, started inspecting and naming the animals of that paradise which he was so soon to lose.
>
> (*V*, 173–74)

This passage is admirably illuminated by an abstract commentary on the nature of language that was written by Walter Benjamin in 1916, a year after *Victory* was published, and that employs the same biblical reference. Benjamin asserts that the fall to knowledge involves nominalization, the use of nouns. This unprecedented knowledge

> is exterior knowledge, the uncreative imitation of [God's] creative verb. The name steps away itself in this knowledge: the Fall is the moment of birth of man's language, that in which the name no longer remains intact, that which has left behind . . . the language . . . that knew its own imminent magic, all this in order for language now to make itself deliberately magical from the outside. The word

must communicate *something* new, outside itself. This is really the original sin of the spirit of language. As it communicates outside of itself the word is something of a parody, by an explicitly mediate word, of the explicitly immediate word, of God's creative word; it is the Fall of a fortunate essence of language in Adam. . . .[56]

Many of Conrad's writings explore the consequences of this fall from "a fortunate essence." Trapped in a postlapsarian babel of conflicting verbalization, Conrad offers only the two alternatives of chaos or radical solipsism: "Half the words we use have no meaning whatever and of the other half man understands each word after the fashion of his own folly and conceit," for "No word is adequate."[57] Such a dualism reveals Conrad's typically modern ontic departure from the Judeo-Christian metaphysic in terms of which *Comus* was conceived. If indeed the "*Maske at Ludlow* is a study in listening,"[58] the acoustic options available to Milton's characters are defined according to a far different and more optimistic duality than that which Conrad offers.

In the noctural forest of *Comus*, the Lady's choice of either silent inactivity or inquisitive pursuit of foreign sounds is inherited from the traditional Augustinian opposition of truth versus eloquence, things versus signs.[59] For the unfallen Eve of *Paradise Lost* and virginal Lady of *Comus*, seductive and demonic verbal aggression can only be an elaboration of that which is as yet unknown. It can arouse a dangerous curiosity, which in turn can stimulate a fatal departure from God's "omnific Word," the sole ground of Being. Perhaps the most common trope by means of which this tension is defined in Western literature is based upon music: 'There are . . . two very different kinds of 'melodye'—one the music of the spirit and the flesh in harmony with created nature, and the other the music of the flesh as it seeks inferior satisfactions as a result of its own concupiscence. Both are melodies of love, one a 'rational' love, and the other a love whose 'ratios' are illogical."[60] As might be expected, *Comus* is organized around motifs of phantasmagoric visual and melodic attempts at seduction, which are finally annulled through divine restoration of proper "ratios." [61]

By means of the epigraph to *Victory* Conrad indicates that similar tropes are operating in his novel, although the original cosmic context of *Comus* is tragically altered. In Milton's masque it is not the act of commitment that is suspect, but rather the object of one's commitment. The Lady wrongly trusts Comus and imperils her soul, but it is correct and admirable for her to engage with the metaphysically positive characters in the masque, as she does at the end. In *Victory*, however, all commitment is psychologically damaging and paralyzing, and, because Man is tragically incapable of sustaining detachment, the possibility of a morally satisfying resolution is eliminated. In view of the function of bewitching sights and sounds both in *Comus* as a whole and in the epigraph to *Victory* it is no accident that some of the most important passages in the novel describe Heyst's lethal surrender of his aloofness in a music hall.

This lapse, moreover, is appropriately due to the visual and auditory assaults upon Heyst that are effected by a teenage girl's physical appearance and voice. While awaiting Davidson's arrival prior to a return to Samburan, Heyst stays at Schomberg's hotel. His mental state is deteriorating, for he realizes that by befriending Morrison he deviated from his father's prescribed mode of life. Consequently, Heyst feels "the gnawing pain of useless apostasy, a sort of shame before his own betrayed nature; and, in addition, he also suffered from plain, downright remorse. He deemed himself guilty of Morrison's death" (V, 65). Heyst begins to pity himself while staying at the hotel. The death of Morrison has made him aware that he is utterly alone in the world. Significantly, it is only after he has enjoyed the luxury of a commitment and been regarded by Morrison as an agent of God that Heyst develops the need for human companionship. He continues to weaken, losing control of himself and of his "ratios":

> Not a single soul belonging to him lived anywhere on earth. Of this fact—not such a remote one, after all—he had only lately become aware; for it is failure that makes a man enter into himself and reckon up his resources. And though he had made up his mind to retire from the world in hermit fashion, yet he was irrationally moved by this sense of loneliness which had come to him in the hour of renunciation.
>
> (V, 66)

Heyst is made more vulnerable by his "taste for silence," which has kept him from learning how to cope with mental distress caused by great noise. Preferring "the music of the spheres" (V, 66), and thus unable to endure the orchestral storm that violently penetrates the "ring of magic stillness" (V, 66) to which he is accustomed, he is driven from the heights of his hotel room.

Conrad uses the idea of descent to signify a fall from an adequate to a vulnerable mode of life. This spatial metaphor is based upon traditional Judeo-Christian usage, although in the present context there are no absolute moral connotations associated with it. Heyst abandons his hitherto successful protective aloofness by descending from his spartan upstairs hotel room to a world of glowing lanterns, heat, raging music, colorful costumes, and swaying human limbs. Similarly, Lena, who tries to remain apart from any potential involvement by staying up on the bandstand, gets punished for her recalcitrant behavior and is driven down among the men, where she meets Heyst. At the moment they exchange their first words, a primeval Adamic lapse into language is reenacted amidst the auditory commotion of the human community that has been assembled by the aeolistic Schomberg, the "mountain of froth." In Comus the Lady responds to the "calling shapes and beck'ning shadows dire" by remarking, 'These thoughts may startle well, but not astound / The virtuous mind" (210–11). Stanley Fish perceptively observes:

The distinction between "startle" and "astound" is the basis of the definition of virtue offered in the masque. Milton conceives of virtue as a state of inner composure, a moral readiness that cannot be shaken, even by something totally unexpected. The virtuous mind may be surprised (startled) at a possibility hitherto unknown . . . without losing its balance. . . . On the other hand, a mind that is astounded has allowed the weight of external pressure to paralyse and rout it. . . .[62]

By using the verb "paralyse," Professor Fish shrewdly alludes to Milton's technique of figuring forth the moral lapse consequent upon "astonishment" in terms of a complete loss of voluntary motion. One might add that this trope is appropriate because *astonish* is etymologically related directly to the adjective *astonied,* which means "to petrify" and which is derived from *stony.*[63] In spite of her overly confident declaration concerning the protective powers of virtue, the Lady is nevertheless eventually victimized, to her astonishment, by Comus's magic seat and her own petrific posterior. Similarly, Heyst, in the presence of an outrageous "volume of noise" generated by "executants" with "stony eyes," can only "drop . . . into a chair" powerlessly, "astonished" (*V,* 68). From this moment on, Heyst is a dead man, won over to involvement in lethal communal insanity by the "executants" in the "Zangiacomo band [which] was not making music; it was simply murdering silence with a vulgar, ferocious energy" (*V,* 68). Heretofore, Heyst was "invulnerable because elusive"; his safety was "accomplished not by hermit-like withdrawal with its . . . immobility, but by a system of restless wandering, by the detachment of an impermanent dweller amongst changing scenes" (*V,* 90). Hereafter, Heyst is immobilized due to Lena's influence. Captured permanently by Samburan, he becomes the easily found "axel" of a static circle.

Like the Lady's nearly disastrous temporary alignment with Comus, Heyst's fatal surrender results from the irresistible impact of the incomprehensible. He has never encountered anything remotely resembling the "stunning" tumult of Schomberg's "concert-hall"; and he is completely disoriented by the experience of "an instrumental uproar, screaming, grunting, whining, sobbing, scraping, squeaking some kind of lively air; while a grand piano, operated upon by a bony, red-faced woman with bad-tempered nostrils, rained hard notes like hail through the tempest of fiddles" (*V,* 68). Overcome, Heyst collapses into a chair, amazed at himself for being able to tolerate what he beholds. Although he is disgusted by the spectacle and shattered by the noise, that he descended and entered the hall at all is a sign of how tragically far he has strayed from Old Heyst's prescription, and from his own successful fifteen-year compliance with the prescription. Although "triumph of song is the main thing that happens in *Comus,*"[64] only a triumphant cosmic discord dominates *Victory,* figuring forth a postlapsarian solipsism sustained by the sheer racket in which human beings need to immerse themselves. It is instructive to contrast Heyst, whom the uproar is overwhelming, with the other patrons of Schomberg's music hall, who are "sitting . . . quietly on their chairs, drinking . . . calmly out of their glasses . . . , giving no signs of distress, anger or fear" while in "terrific" heat a "horrible" man extracts "piercing clamour" from a dehumanized group of women who exude "something cruel, sensual and repulsive" (V, 68). These people, whose indifference seems an "unnatural spectacle" to the prejudiced Heyst, are immune to the situation because their senses have been dulled by frequent involvement in the illusory world of human communal activity, which is epitomized in this scene as raw, sexually tainted noise.

Having been severely disoriented by the sights and sounds of the Zangiacomo band, Heyst is vulnerable to a restructuring of his personality. This happens when the uniquely hideous experience of the band, which has already displaced his father's advice to remain aloof, is itself displaced by the uniquely pleasurable experience of "A girl, by Jove!" That is, Heyst "had the sensation of a new experience . . . because his faculty of observation had never before been captured by any feminine creature in that marked and exclusive fashion" (V, 71). Having entered the music hall in a lonely, self-pitying state of mind, Heyst is doomed to abandon his detachment once he catches sight of a fellow being upon whom he can project his own isolated state. It is necessary to recall here the following words from the Author's Note: "When the catastrophe matches the natural obscurity of our fate . . . even the best representative of the race is liable to lose his detachment" (V, x). Thus, when the Zangiacomo woman pinches Lena, "Heyst, at his table, [is] surprised into a sympathetic start" (V, 71). Worst of all, Heyst absolutely relinquishes the protective ironic tension which, up to now, he had preserved more or less intact between himself and his world: "He positively forgot where he was. He had lost touch with his surroundings" (V, 71). His vision of Lena provides him with comforting forgetfulness, and he conveniently loses sight of the pain he suffered because of his previous involvement with Morrison, pain that haunted him up to this moment and that he should have understood as an experience that validated his father's advice: "It may be said that, for the first time since the final abandonment of the Samburan coalmine, he had completely forgotten the late Morrison. It is true that to a certain extent he had forgotten also where he was. Thus, unchecked by any sort of selfconsciousness, Heyst walked up the central passage" (V, 72).

Although *Victory* does not contain the same sort of divinely ordered hierarchy of texts leading to the Logos that one finds in the Christian tradition, there nevertheless exists a textual priority founded upon simple pragmatic efficacy. Specifically, Old Heyst's advice worked for fifteen years in protecting his son from fatal involvements. And the superior validity of this advice is further indicated by Old Heyst's dying peacefully, like a child in bed, in marked contrast to the shootings, burning, and drowning suffered by those who cannot observe his wisdom. Of course, in the absence of God no priority is absolute; all knowledge is partial. Thus, Old Heyst's dwindling presence survives only in the imperfect form of books (perishable relics of his own necessarily limited, epigrammatic subjectivity), pieces of furniture, and, most significantly, a portrait rendering merely a profile view. The throbbing, frontal immediacy of Lena easily annuls these vestiges, causing Heyst to join in the fallen music and make an "overture" (V, 72), to which she offers her own melodic response in a voice with "charm" like "the tone of some instrument" (V, 74). Old Heyst's words are displaced by Lena's physical presence, which is to the enraptured beholder an open-ended text, "a script in an unknown language . . . simply mysterious: like any writing to the illiterate" (V, 222). Thus, Heyst can engage in his own Adamic play of naming Lena, having descended to the level of those who earlier were mystified by him and tried to locate his essence through the assignation of a myriad of one-dimensional epithets. Heyst is called on various occasions by various persons "Enchanted Heyst," "Hard Facts Heyst," "Heyst the Utopist," "Heyst the Spider," "Manager of the Tropical Belt Coal Company," "Naive Heyst," "Heyst the Enemy," "Heyst the Swedish Baron," "Heyst the Hermit," "Heyst the Lunatic," "Heyst the Pig-Dog," "Heyst the Vagabond," "Heyst the Romantic," "Mr. Blasted Heyst." Yet, his essence forever eludes mere adjectival exercises, for the proper name, itself meaningless, remains an enigma that engulfs all taxonomies in its semantic emptiness.

Significantly, Heyst makes no attempt to describe the girl. He simply invents, "after several experimental essays in combining detached letters and loose syllables" (V, 186), an alternate proper name. Thus, the "script in an unknown language" is nominalized and becomes Lena, but with no concomitant increase in conceptual lucidity. In Comus words are reliable to the extent that they are employed by speakers who are consciously reverent: a divinely ordained system of individual linguistic entities then permits an orderly semantic ascension from earth to heaven, from unique, unambiguous generic nouns to dissolution in the transcendently inane "I am that I am" (Exodus 3:14), verbal approximation of the total coherence which is God. But in Victory the option of resisting spectral voices that generate a morally distracting multiplicity of referents is no longer available. Like Heyst assembling a useless proper name from "detached letters and loose syllables," Conrad's characters, in a futile struggle to achieve redemptive understanding, are compelled to murmur along with all "airy tongues that syllable men's names," thereby damning themselves to the equivocal confusion that is human experience. Heyst can never conflate the transcendent and the mundane, innocence and experience, Alma and Magdalen, no matter how he may fragment and reassemble constitutive phonemes. Like Keats's Lycius trying to unravel the serpentine Lamia, who is at once "a virgin purest lipped, yet in the lore / Of love deep learned to the red heart's core" (*Lamia*, I, 189–90), Heyst remains confounded by Lena, who in spite of her new name seems "just a little child" as well as "something as old as the world" (*V*, 359).

Although Ricardo understands correctly that "a man's life hangs on sometimes—a single word," the more perceptive Heyst worries over the "power there must be in words only imperfectly heard" (*V*, 133, 214). To the extent that the entire novel is a dramatization of human beings unwisely and hastily acting upon and reacting to false information, it is thematically appropriate that the Schombergs ultimately control the action insofar as their deceptions become the conflicting grounds of belief for the protagonists. As Heyst knows, a world whose existence depends upon fallible acts of perception can only deny the validity of the verb *to be:* "Appearances—what more, what better can you ask for? In fact, you can't have better. You can't have anything else" (*V*, 204). Thus, in *Victory* a vocabulary of demonic insubstantiality, such as Milton applies in *Comus* only to metaphysically irredeemable creatures, becomes definitive of all possible human experience. Nothing is theologically wrong, though all things are myopically perceived and consequently incomplete and unreliable; and by extension, "any one world, an idea of the conditions of being, threatens—attacks or merely rejects—every other and the existence it supports."⁶⁵ This principle is most visible in *Victory* when many characters apply satanic analogues and death imagery to whatever or whomever seems threatening. To Schomberg, Jones looks like "a corpse" foreshadowing a "menace from beyond the grave" (*V*, 112) and Heyst is "the devil" (*V*, 31); Ricardo also suspects that Heyst may be "in league with the devil himself" (*V*, 238); to Lena, Schomberg is a "horrible red-faced beast," the Zangiacomo woman is a "devil-woman" (*V*, 206), and Ricardo is "the embodied evil of the world" (*V*, 298); while to Heyst action is "devilish" (*V*, 54), Wang's smiling face looks like a "conceited death's head" (*V*, 349), and Jones has "a death's head grin" (*V*, 230).

Such terminology reaches a crescendo early in the novel when Heyst is becoming ever more infatuated with Lena during late night meetings with her in the grove beside Schomberg's hotel. Their initial encounter takes place accidentally the evening they first become aware of one another. Unable to tolerate the musical uproar any longer, Heyst takes refuge among the trees outside the concert hall. He is uneasily contemplating his involvement with Lena and ominously, if appropriately, compares the threat of the bewitching young girl to his earlier experiences among the New Guinea cannibals. The trees surrounding Heyst recall "the forests at the back of Geelvink Bay, perhaps the wildest, the unsafest, the most deadly spot on earth from which the sea can be seen" (*V*, 82). From these thoughts he flees to his bedroom; but he cannot remain there, and compulsively returns to the grove to pace among deep shadows of trees where extinguished paper lanterns gently swing. Suddenly he becomes aware of a second presence. It is Lena, and she is repeatedly described as a phantom, paralleling in appearance and thematic import the Miltonic "calling shapes and beck'ning shadows dire" of the epigraph. The girl seems to be a "white, phantom-like apparition" (V, 83), a "vaporous white figure . . . in the darkness" (V, 85), and, in a manner filled with ominous connotations, "white and spectral, she was putting out her arms to him out of the black shadows like an appealing ghost" (V, 86). If, like Comus, Lena poses a threat, it is only because of the solipsistic epistemology operant throughout *Victory*. Soul at war with sense comes to signify the irredeemable opposition of subject and object. The girl's apparent insubstantiality does not indicate that she exists beyond the frontiers of Christian legitimacy but rather that she is primarily a captivating extension of Heyst's own personality, a status she intuitively defines later when she informs him, "I can only be what you think I am" (V, 187).

In a world where all men are incomprehensible texts, all men must partake of the cosmic inanity that once was reserved for a definition of the point at which language merged with God, logic with the Logos. What for Milton was a monological world is for Conrad a multilogical babel in which all men futilely parody divine self-sufficiency because they have no other choice. Thus, Heyst asserts "I am I" (V, 350) and Jones claims "I am he who is" (V, 317; cf. 376). To an isolated human being, omnipotent in his supreme subjectivity, other minds are as perplexing and inaccessible as creatures "from the higher spheres" (V, 382). Although ultimately all efforts to impose order upon the external world amount to a repetition of the primeval "I am that I am," these efforts in their multitudinous specificity must remain incomprehensible, thus ensuring only that all appear perpetually to all as "amazing strangers . . . bringing . . . gifts of unknown things, words never heard before" (V, 228).

The only way to create and maintain an illusion of shared meaning is to banish alien specificity by transcending language. Heyst accomplishes this by concentrating upon Lena's voice and ignoring the contents of her statements. Indeed, he wishes he did not even share a language with the girl, so urgently does he need to create her in his own image: "He thought that if she only could talk to him in some unknown tongue, she would enslave him altogether by the sheer beauty of the sound, suggesting infinite depths of wisdom and feeling" (V, 209). Just as Lena's physical substance earlier dissolved before Heyst's needful glance when she became "an appealing ghost," so her efforts at communication, perceived reductively by Heyst, are denuded of form and content, thus becoming a mere siren tonality. Initially, Lena's speech provides Heyst with a delightful auditory alternative. They typically converse "during the interval between the two parts of the concert" (V, 78), a time when Lena's tremulous cadences would be most likely to contrast advantageously with the band's vulgar instrumental onslaught. Moreover, as Lena speaks a transformation occurs that inverts the process of aesthetic degradation effected within the concert hall. The grim musicians take acceptable content (melodic compositions) and violate it, changing a potentially delightful experience into raw discord, while Lena's voice, in marked contrast, begins with a barely tolerable content (her foolish prattle) and transfigures it, making "silly chatter supportable and the roughest talk fascinating," and thereby competing successfully with the sad instrumentalists. Like Comus wielding his cup, Lena seduces Heyst with her voice: he "drank in its charm as one listens to the tone of some instrument without heeding the tune" (V, 74); through its medium "the words went straight to his heart—the sound of them more than the sense" (V, 221; cf. PR, xi).

This pursuit of transparent and innocent communication culminates in the physical act of lovemaking that occurs on the mountain at the center of Samburan, an act that is possibly the only means of congenially resolving a lengthy conversation between two parties, neither of whom understands the other. Because of the immediacy of an erotic clinch, all need for interpretive effort and compromise is transcended. But such moments are very rare; they cannot be controlled consciously or sustained in time and therefore are of little practical value. Heyst's perception of Lena's voice as an ideal medium only partially achieves such transcendence, for, try as he may, he can never purge her statements completely of their embarrassingly naive semantic content. Yet this is as far as Heyst can carry his solipsism, for an effort to bypass speech completely through charged eye-to-eye contact fails. Heyst discovers a primal recalcitrance as he tries to gain total access to Lena visually: "What an impenetrable girl you are, Lena, with those grey eyes of yours!" In frustration, Heyst then more clearly defines his goal by sardonically invoking a metaphoric rendition of the fulfillment that eludes him: eyes should be "windows of the soul, as some poet has said" (V, 204). This metaphor is pointedly reminiscent of certain lines from Shelley. In both *Alastor* and *Prometheus Unbound* there occur moments of erotic bliss that make possible flawless and redemptive human communion. The nameless poet of *Alastor* encounters his epipsyche in a dream, and "her voice was like the voice of his own soul" (153); in *Prometheus Unbound* Asia seeks to transcend time and space by effecting communication with Prometheus through a mediator, whom she implores, "O lift / Thine eyes, that I may read his written soul" (II, i, 110).

Additional echoes of Shelley are supplied by Jones when he discovers the second scene in the novel in which Lena becomes a means of achieving sensual transcendence: the scene in which Lena seduces Ricardo into surrendering his knife. As Jones watches, Lena pursues amidst the brilliance of eight candle flames her own morality play, seeking to enact Christ's triumph over a stinging, serpentine death by depriving Ricardo of his weapon and obtaining "the venom of the viper in her paradise, extracted, safe in her possession" (V, 399). Though Lena regards her seductive negation of Ricardo's vitality as a redemptive act, Jones, of course, finds it a destructive accomplishment. To him, Lena is a character analogous to all the fatal women of myth and literature who disarm their men by offering illusions of transcendent erotic escape. And he defines Ricardo's surrender as "serious" for "He has found his soul-mate" (*V*, 392), thereby invoking the concept of the epipsyche so frequently employed by Shelley in works like *Epipsychidion* ("this soul out of my soul" [238]; cf. also 14–15 and *LJ*, 317) and *On Love* ("a miniature . . . of our entire self," "a soul within our soul"). Indeed, the parody of a supernal moment is sustained even by the eight candles that illuminate the scene, and which, by their static radiance, seem to insulate the room from the surrounding temporal flux, the tempestuous alternations of intense darkness and flashes of lightning: "The only thing immovable in the shuddering universe was the interior of the lighted room and the woman in black sitting in the light of the eight candle-flames" (*V*, 392). Traditionally, the number seven is connected with the seven days of creation, seven seas, seven wandering stars, and seven ages of the world. Eight, on the other hand, denotes that which is just beyond seven, that which transcends corporeal existence; and is associated with the rite of circumcision (eighth day after birth) and with the resurrection (the eighth day of Holy Week).

In this scene Conrad cleverly brings together and subverts both Christian and secular transcendentalism. Christian salvation, as established by the epigraph from *Comus* and sustained within the novel through verbal and situational echoes of this epigraph, culminates in Lena's effort, as she seduces Ricardo, to fulfill a behavioral model derived from Christ's triumph over death. Secular salvation, as established by Old Heyst's philosophical prescription and sustained within the novel through Heyst's attempt to displace the paternal texts at once with the syllables of the name Lena, with the tonalities of the girl's voice purged of semantic content, and with an intuitive communion accomplished by peering deep, deep into another's eyes, culminates in the foot-licking Ricardo, disarmed, supine, discovering his soul-mate. At the moment this culminant scene is shattered by Jones's gunshot, Conrad's artistic technique assaults and subverts with finality two of the most dominant forms in terms of which the Western world has rendered the ideal of transcendence. The novel ends with death regnant in Heyst's clearing on Samburan, while the forms of civilization are upheld only by the most impercipient of persons, Davidson, who can live placidly with "Nothing" since the word has been domesticated by inclusion in the dreary context of an official report, where it offers no obtrusive metaphysical threat. If once again the "Son of David" (see, e.g., Matthew 1:1, 9:27, 15:22) redeems a world, he accomplishes the task only partially and in helpless ignorance, his very name serving only to confirm bleak ironic discrepancies that are for Conrad ontologically definitive. Concomitantly, the idea of victory, that most treasured of Western illusions enshrined obnoxiously in the name of the flagship of Lord Nelson (the "seaman of seamen" who expanded "the very conception of victory" [*MS*, 187]), is demolished by an intellectual vessel, Conrad's novel, bearing the same appellation.

This demolition is ultimately effected by means of the novel's point of view devices. As in *Nostromo* and *The Nigger of the "Narcissus,"* these devices are discontinuous; they are also skillfully and appropriately wielded by Conrad, although this fact is not widely appreciated. Albert Guerard's criticism of narrative perspective in *Victory* is typical:

> *Victory* begins with an unidentified crude jocular narrator who presently calls in the no less commonplace Davidson. The narrative difficulties, once Heyst reaches his island, are theoretically insoluble. . . . But this is only in theory, and the pretense of a narrator is soon dropped. The limited view gives way abruptly to standard omniscient narrative with Heyst as the usual post of observation. . . . The improbable appearance of Davidson at the end could be accepted with amused tolerance had it granted Conrad the detachment he needed. So far as the reader is concerned, there is no reason for Davidson to appear. The omniscient and certainly uninhibited narrator of the heart of the book could have described the holocaust just as well.

Guerard finds no aesthetic value in the unnamed speaker who narrates the first section of the novel or in Davidson, whose official report ends it. To him *Victory* only "offers a dullard within a dullard, Davidson with the 'I.' "[66] One of the few voices of dissent belongs to John Palmer, who asserts, in a uniquely complimentary response, that "it is probable that both the structure and point of view of *Victory*, Davidson included, are the best that Conrad might have devised for his special artistic purposes."[67] Indeed, Palmer's judgment anticipates the manner in which current critical theory has valorized narrative discontinuity and thereby radically redefined some of the tasks of critics of fiction. But it is no longer sufficient merely to attempt to validate such modes abstractly; rather, their aesthetic merits must be explored by means of rigorous inquiry into the function of discontinuous point of view in specific works. *Victory* contains a great deal of appropriately challenging material.

The novel opens with the voice of an anonymous persona whose presence perpetuates the authorial recommendations that were established in the prefatory essay. The speaker does not exist as a person who is intimately involved with the people and events he describes and whose personality is altered by his experiences. On the contrary, he remains a static, detached, ironic voice, gathering most of his information secondhand, a speaker who seems to use the subject matter of his narrative as a buffer between himself and his world. He can commit himself only to a tale told by someone else, which he modifies by adding his own details and then relates again, all the while engaging in a minimum of intimate and revealing personal contact. Very little can be known about the speaker's innermost feelings, for he keeps himself hidden and thereby eludes a threatening world harboring a predatory and "unnatural physics" that even dictates on occasion that "evaporation precedes liquidation" (V, 3). Indeed, he is aware of the same sort of inverse alchemy the narrative voice of *Nostromo* perceives when it notes "the silver bars were worth less . . . than so much lead, from which at least bullets may be run" (N, 219); and he concludes appropriately that a practical mode of behavior in a dangerous and contradictory world is aloofness, since an "inert body . . . provokes no hostility, is scarcely worth derision" (V, 3). That he is fond of ironic detachment is about all that can be discovered of the speaker, who dramatizes the detachment of which he approves by elaborating primarily upon the superficial epithets that constellate themselves, thanks to idle gossip, around Axel Heyst, the elusive man who "had the singular good fortune that his sayings stuck to him and became part of his name" (V, 8). It seems that the speaker is a placid echo of Old Heyst, who also preserved a veil of public statements around himself. Moreover, both these characters are equally one-dimensional, functioning essentially as attitudinal norms that emphasize the successful behavioral mode Axel Heyst followed early in his life and from which he later deviates on account of his infatuation with Lena's voice.

The speaker preserves his detachment from his tale by toying with words, so that the resultant ambiguity and irony become amusing and epistemologically definitive ends in themselves, distracting both the teller and listener, and thereby preventing the mental entrapment consequent upon a sympathetic projection of self into events and characters. He describes, for instance, how talk of "these coal-outcrops began to crop up" (V, 6) in Heyst's conversations. When a drunk, to whom Heyst suggested, "Come along and quench your thirst," calls Heyst "a . . . utopist," the speaker responds with the sarcastic hypothesis that anyone "who could propose, even playfully, to quench old McNab's thirst must have been a utopist" (V, 9). He purposefully subverts the very judgments that he allows to enter his own narrative: the "delicate, humane, and regular" Davidson, who has just visited Heyst's island, thinks Heyst has "gone mad," though the speaker without warrant asserts confidently, "He was not mad" (V, 53–54, 4). Moreover, he seems to be as contemptuous of empathetic responses as he is of conventional demands for consistency. He describes with cold amusement the moving scene in which Morrison and Heyst share confidences—"It must have been funny, because they were very serious about it" (V, 19); and he intolerantly criticizes Mrs. Schomberg for smiling vapidly, calling her "an It—an automaton, a very plain dummy, with an arrangement for bowing the head at times" (V, 40). When word reaches him that Heyst "must be starving on his island" with Lena, the speaker callously suggests that Heyst may resort to cannibalism, "may end yet by eating her" (V, 45).

This sort of irreverence is characteristic of still another dimension of the speaker's generation of intellectual distraction within his narrative: a continual manipulation of biblical references for the sake of creating preposterous contexts. For instance, echoing a famous parable of Christ (see Matthew 6:28), the persona describes Heyst's secretive way of making a living as that of a man "who didn't toil or spin visibly" (V, 16). In the Bible this state of being is a sign of God's favor to the beasts and plants, but the speaker uses the idea to undercut Morrison's view that Heyst was sent by God to lend aid: to the narrator, Heyst seems "the very last person to be the agent of Providence in an affair concerned with money" (V, 16). Another example of a contextually ludicrous biblical allusion can be seen in the speaker's deprecatory description of the omnipresence of the topic of Heyst at Schomberg's hotel due to Schomberg's obsession: "Whenever three people came together in his hotel, he took good care that Heyst should be with them" (V, 26; see Matthew 18:20).

From his vantage point of ironic detachment the nameless persona can understand the limitations inherent in Heyst's essentially congruent life style. He is quick to note that Heyst's problems seem to develop because of his inability to achieve and sustain sufficient isolation: "His detachment from the world was not complete. And incompleteness of any sort leads to trouble" (V, 31). The narrator does not mean to imply that the proper degree of detachment is necessarily only to be achieved on an island, at complete physical remove from the bustling mainland. Indeed, in Heyst's case physical withdrawal only increases the intensity of Heyst's psychic entanglement with his vision of Lena, whereas, in marked contrast, the narrator and Old Heyst are examples of detachment that are as pure as any in the Conrad canon, and these individuals have attained their mental aloofness while remaining physically connected to their respective social orders, successfully resisting the "romantic" tendencies of Axel Heyst, who vulnerably colors "the world to the tune of [his] own temperament" (V, 51).

Soon after the theft of Lena the narrative perspective modulates to a third-person omniscient point of view, probably because no first-person narrator could logically have been present on Samburan, since the novel's thematically appropriate conclusion dictates that every member of Heyst's intimate circle who might be used as the voice through which to describe events on the island be killed. It is more important, however, that a major concern of the remainder of the novel is a detailed exploration of Heyst's and Lena's respective mentalities and the consequent revelation that the two lovers do not at all understand one another. An omniscient narrative voice is the only aesthetic convention by means of which access can properly be provided to subjectivity prior to articulation by the subject. This narrative technique lends an objective quality to the novel that was pointedly lacking in the section dominated by the persona, where an entirely subjective view of Heyst was presented in terms of both vague rumors and specific tales told by identifiable characters, which view depended greatly upon spatial and temporal discontinuity to sketch the "impermanent dweller amongst changing scenes" (V, 90).

The third-person narrative voice of *Victory* is usually an omniscient voice that attacks one character after another with its ironic, perceptive analysis of these characters' respective illusory drives toward involvement. But it is not obtrusive, and enters the novel in an ontologically definitive manner only occasionally. Moreover, it is necessary to qualify the omniscience of the narrative voice, and modify thereby the traditional concept of this artistic device, because there are instances in *Victory* when this voice chooses to evade the presentation of absolute resolutions of characters' motives. This occurs most markedly in relation to the topic of Heyst's past, which was left nebulous by the nameless persona, and which the narrative voice also pointedly fails to clarify. For example, in the following passage the subjunctive mode is used by the narrative voice apparently to avoid a conclusive definition of Heyst's response to his dead father's belongings: "It seemed as if in his conception of a world not worth touching, and perhaps not substantial enough to grasp, these objects familiar to his childhood and his youth and associated with the memory of an old man, were the only realities, something having an absolute existence" (*V*, 176). After his abortive involvement with Morrison, Heyst realizes that he has abandoned the way of life recommended by his father. The narrative voice hints that it was the influence of his father's belongings, vestiges of a lost faith, that caused Heyst to remain on the island after the economic failure of the Tropical Belt Coal Company. Yet, once again, flat statements of fact are avoided:

> The manager of the Tropical Belt Coal Company, unpacking them on the verandah in the shade besieged by a fierce sunshine, must have felt like a remorseful apostate before these relics. He handled them tenderly; and it was perhaps their presence there which attached him to the island when he woke up to the failure of his apostasy. Whatever the decisive reason, Heyst had remained where another would have been glad to be off.
>
> (*V*, 177)

These lapses in the omniscience of the narrative voice are strange, but perhaps there is a reason for them. By causing this point of view to be unclear about the precise, personal motives that conditioned Heyst's past, Conrad prevents the third-person voice from contradicting the first-person speaker. Unlike the narrative technique used in *Nostromo* and *The Nigger of the "Narcissus"*, in which the omniscient third-person voice functions as a means of demythologizing the world presented by men like Captain Mitchell and the anonymous narrator who sailed as a crewman on the *Narcissus*, the technique used in *Victory* does not challenge the accuracy of the first-person narrator. The nameless speaker in the latter novel is meant to function more as a normative character than as an individual in whose opinions the reader is to be interested because they are fallible in accordance with the limitations of human subjectivity. This is not to say it is obligatory to valorize the persona's tale or to treat as trustworthy the information it makes available, as if an omniscient narrative voice were speaking. But it is to say that Conrad's interest seems not to lie primarily in dramatizing the limitations of his speaker. Rather, he paradoxically qualifies the awareness of his third-person narrative voice at times so that the persona's vague tale of Heyst's past will not be canceled to the detriment of the synthesizing human source.

Yet, in spite of the importance of the narrative voice, Conrad does not use it to end his novel. This decision is quite significant. The innocuous Davidson is permitted to relate the details of the resolution of the conflict on Samburan, an artistic choice that at least one important critic feels only contributes to a "preposterous" ending.[68] And, indeed, if the value of Davidson's appearance must rest upon his significance as a character (as F. R. Leavis thinks),[69] Conrad's decision to use him as a means of ending a complex novel may be questionable, for Davidson's character is never developed at any length, and his mind is quite uncomplicated, devoid of abstract insight into the events he witnesses. But perhaps the discrepancy between the philosophical and thematic implications of the tale Davidson relates and his own pedestrian understanding of his experiences is precisely what Conrad wishes to establish when he permits Davidson to preside over the final pages. It is entirely appropriate to the novel's ironic narrative mode that Heyst's oft-celebrated "woe to" sentimentalities be presented from a perspective of invincible dullness—and only an academic Davidson could embrace Heyst's remark as conclusive support for a thematic content that supposedly lauds the success of Lena "in extricating from Heyst at least a posthumous expression of his love. This is a victory, indeed. . . . She shakes Heyst out of his accustomed mold and almost reconciles him to the world."[70] Davidson reports that "practically the last words [Heyst] said to me . . . were: 'Ah, Davidson, woe to the man whose heart has not learned while young to hope, to love—and to put its trust in life!'" (V, 410). If Lena has indeed caused Heyst to decide that detachment is wrong, his decision must be regarded simply as another sign of the degree to which he has strayed both from his father's prescribed way of life and from the aloofness that is cited in the Author's Note as "the only faculty that seems to assimilate man to the immortal gods" (V, x). Apart from Heyst's inaccessible conscious understanding of his own meaning, however, the statement functions most significantly on a thematic level, for it is an echo of the narrative voice's earlier assertion that acute perception, by permitting freedom from much illusion, causes a profound unhappiness. To be one of the "clear-sighted" is to be "unhappy in a way unknown to mediocre souls" (V, 91–92). Anyone who escapes the "blessed, warm mental fog" (V, 92) of hope, love, and "trust in life" (V, 410) is plagued by "woe." But it does not follow that such a mental state is necessarily detrimental. As he presents his summary of the destructive events on Samburan, Davidson's voice can remain "placid" because his superficial intellect has prevented him from being abstractly "unhappy in a way unknown to mediocre souls" (V, 91); and the simple man no doubt finds it difficult, consequently, to be troubled when, after all, there is "nothing to be done" anyway (*V*, 412).

Like the other characters in *Victory*, Davidson's behavior must be evaluated primarily in terms of the previously mentioned hierarchy of detachment and involvement, which ranks Old Heyst at the top. Although very little is revealed about Davidson as a complex entity, sufficient information is provided to enable him to be placed within this hierarchy. He is the obese[71] captain of the *Sissie*, a transport ship that puts in at island ports along the Java Sea approximately once a month. His occupation insures his physical remove from the human community and also forces a certain psychological detachment, for he is employed by "a Chinese firm," and, since he only hauls natives, "he never [has] any sort of company on board" (*V*, 33). Davidson's aloofness is also prompted by his own very discreet personality, which prevents him from imposing upon others, and therefore keeps him from making acquaintances. As the narrator remarks, "He was the most delicate man that ever took a small steamer to and fro amongst the islands" (*V*, 52). Yet Davidson, like Heyst, is nevertheless a very considerate person, and Heyst is touched by the concern implicit in the captain's monthly patrol of Heyst's island.

Although perceptually the two men differ radically from one another, Davidson's manner of observation parallels that of the anonymous narrator, for both of them remain emotionally apart without totally detaching themselves physically from their society. The narrator's remove is static, however—he only gets interested in stories, which he passes on while offering ironic commentary. Davidson, on the other hand, because of his potentially destructive sympathy, moves from the isolation surrounding himself initially, to a dangerous involvement with Heyst, and back again to an essentially detached position after Heyst's death. Thus, the character of Davidson, fluctuating between detachment and commitment, serves as a measure of both the ironic narrator and the tragically entrapped Heyst. Owing to his discreet humanity, Davidson is more conventionally admirable than the rather nasty speaker, but it is precisely because of this capacity for sympathy that Davidson is drawn ever deeper into the threatening situation developing around Heyst. This is why Davidson appears illogically at the moment of greatest threat on Samburan. His involvement with Heyst has led him through alternate though converging paths to the same situation as has Heyst's involvement with Morrison and Lena; and Davidson, too, must consequently risk death.

Because Davidson's commitment to Heyst is qualified by the captain's exaggerated sense of delicacy, and because a masculine relationship does not involve the bewitching erotic potential that captivates Heyst, Davidson is able to disengage himself from the situation even when he witnesses the death of the very individual whose welfare he has come to value, unlike Heyst, who destroys himself soon after Lena's demise. Davidson is redeemed from disastrous commitment by the chance annihilation of the persons with whom he would align himself, and he ends the novel with only renewed aloofness, the sole articulate survivor of the deadly confrontations on Samburan, presenting his tale in the form of an official report immaculate in its detached narrative.[72]

The disparate modes of narrative perspective in *Victory* serve definite, though often highly specialized, aesthetic functions. Throughout the novel, by skillfully manipulating an inconsistent narrative technique that involves two human personalities and an omniscient narrative voice, Conrad establishes the bleak ontology in terms of which *Victory* must be read and validates the sustained detachment of the human narrators by causing their aloof positions to be congruent with that recommended by the Author's Note, the narrative voice, and Old Heyst. Moreover, the catastrophic events of the final pages confirm what the various points of view have implied throughout, that, indeed, "he who forms a tie is lost" (*V*, 199–200); and the novel ends with a futile human attempt to articulate negation that actually can be accomplished only "at the point where the final sentence dissolves into the blankness of the margin . . . in the silence which follows the last words,"[73] where all perspectives cease.

Discontinuous Semiotics:
Language *"in articulo mortis"*

Much of Joseph Conrad's art probes the limitations of the English language. The phrase "heart of darkness" is a pertinent, if dangerously threadbare example. Founded not upon anything that exists empirically either for Marlow or the reader, the phrase is grammatically ordered so as to suggest that the noun *heart* is the metaphoric vehicle, the noun *darkness* the tenor, thus concealing the fact that both the vehicle and the tenor are themselves tropes devised by Marlow while reminiscing in a state of epistemological confusion from which he never escapes. In such cases only a process of indeterminate imaginative regression survives the suicidal figurative inflation of the original grammatical unit. The human need to interpret then stands alone, bereft of direction and any possibility of fulfillment. Perceivers of Conrad's art are thus rendered even more powerless to achieve a definitive orientation than are his most sensitive characters. In their efforts to come to grips with human experience the characters futilely strive to discover and impose a metaphoric system that will preserve the possibilities of self-justification and action.

However, Conrad's readers must start at one remove from the open-ended array of sensory perceptions that his characters grapple with. The readers are doomed to begin their efforts to discover and impose words that will rescue meaning from the fiction by starting at the level of metaphor itself — manifested nearly every way, from tropes devised by characters like Marlow or an omniscient narrative voice to seemingly factual descriptions and situations that nevertheless must be given figurative significance. Moreover, Conrad's metaphors frequently are attracted to one of the following two poles, both of which tend to annihilate the metaphor. On one hand, metaphor may disintegrate into a multiplicity of potential specifics which may indeed be held in suspension by a grammatically valid construct, but which exist chaotically beyond even rudimentary semantic control. On the other hand, metaphor may move toward an imaginative fusion of the disparate elements it contains. A successful and complete fusion, however, destroys the metaphor by eliminating the disparities that give it life, collapsing them into a one-dimensional literalness where tropes are not possible. Thus, Conrad's texts, like his ocean, can be practically bottomless. Facts and events are refracted

---

Parts of this chapter appeared in somewhat altered form in *Nineteenth Century Fiction* 34, no. 2 (1979): 127–53, © 1979 by The Regents of the University of California. Reprinted by permission of The Regents.

through the figurative perceptions of speaking characters and/or a narrative voice; and in the process of utterance the narrating presence is in danger of falling through its own porous metaphoric structure, in the manner of Marlow and his phrase "heart of darkness." But most confusing of all, the reader necessarily is dragged along, since he may regard even his experience of inter-pretational vertigo as a trope.

Recently, Morse Peckham has written persuasively that since "there is no necessary or imminent connection between any sign and any [semiotic] matrix," the only way one can generate responses to signs is through analogy, according to the following process: "perceptual disengagement of an analogically determined recurrent semiotic pattern [e.g., statements] from an analogically determined series of semiotic matrices [e.g., situations]." This process can be frustrated when a syntactic structure is encountered that makes it difficult or impossible to "place the utterance in an analogically determined series of normal English sentences," for "without the recognition of the recur-rency of the semiotic pattern, without its disengagement, no response at all is possible."[1] Peckham's conceptual framework is a powerful means of approaching the notorious problem of Conrad's lexical indeterminacy and "failure . . . to create coherent metaphorical structures,"[2] for it at once encourages and makes possible discussion of those unhandy features of an artist's work that in the past have occasioned responses like that of F. R. Leavis, who concludes Conrad merely "is intent on making a virtue out of not knowing what he means." [3]

Conrad's tropes frequently are resistant to interpretive responses because he is purposefully deriving (and therefore isolating) these semiotic patterns from an original semiotic matrix, which he typically rejects. Conrad is involved in what Peckham terms "semiotic transformation," an inherently discontinuous process: "Because the meanings of words are not immanent . . . the connection between a verbal sign pattern and its semiotic transformation . . . is not immanent."[4] It is not accurate or very useful to read Conrad as if the aesthetic devices he uses to embody his bleak agnosticism were symmetrically opposable to similar configurations employed in earlier periods of cultural history by, say, Christian writers. Coleridge remarks, 'There is, strictly speaking, no proper opposition but between two polar forces of one and the same power." That is, difference, no matter how great, generates only heterogeneity, not opposition, which is a function of a unique kind of repetition involving a juxtaposition of several similar ideas that are symmetrically annihilatory precisely because of this very similarity. More useful than the idea of opposition with regard to Conrad's work is the mathematical concept of the multiplicative, or the genetic, inverse. According to mathematic notation, the inverse of a number is indicated by the index $^{-1}$. Thus, 2^{-1} denotes the number that when multiplied by 2^1 produces 1. The number is, of course, $\frac{1}{2}$, not the opposite of 2 but rather only the genetic inverse, only a degree of difference illuminating a certain oblique relationship.

A similar relationship exists frequently between semiotic patterns that are culturally antecedent to Conrad and Conrad's reconstitution of them in his own works. Such obliqueness frustrates "the recognition of the recurrency of the semiotic pattern,"[5] frustrating in turn, due to discontinuities in semiotic matrices, the discovery of analogical sequences, thus making very difficult the act of interpretation: George White is, indeed, the prototype of the black, James Wait, whose protean name contributes temporal connotations of indistinct import, and who is a crewman in autumnal decline aboard the ship *Narcissus,* which appellation invokes enigmatically a white vernal flower. The conceptual emptiness of one proper name leads analogically only to the similar vacancy of another proper name; and the communicative potentials of the text come to parallel each reader's capability for innovating, modifying, and sustaining analogues, since

> the refusal to create analogies, [which refusal is] accomplished by not suppressing attributional discontinuities between any two signs . . . , results in a deconstruction, not of the text, but of the individual's semiotic superstructure or behavior. This cannot be sufficiently emphasized. It is not a text that is deconstructed, for it cannot be, since meaning is not immanent; rather, it is the individual's ability to respond that is being deconstructed.[6]

Within the present context, it is useful to consider Conrad's emblematic use of the sea. Critics have stressed for decades that the ocean in Conrad denotes an indifferent force of nature against which the coherences of various characters are tested through exposure to deadly threat. But such a response is predicated upon the metaphysical opposition of order and disorder implicit in classical and Christian metaphors of vessel as microcosm, a "ship of state," existing in redemptive tension with formless primal waters. Although it was once possible to define a world of fallen mutability as a "sea of hyle,"[7] which was related in a derivative and negative way to figurative ships and a static, substantial eternity, such concept is of little use to Conrad because it is no longer valid ontologically. Instead, the entire cosmos lacks substance, amounting at last only to words (themselves merely "waves of air of the proper length, propogated in accordance with correct mathematical formulas" [*SA,* 260]) in the form of frustrated nominalization ("some-thing") and aqueous tropology: "There is no space, time, matter, mind as vulgarly understood, there is only the eternal something that waves and an eternal force that causes the waves. . . ."[8] Consequently, the very idea of literal matter survives simply as an occasion for jokes and puns, in the midst of which attention is typically drawn to the absence of any durable cosmic substrata. In *Lord Jim* one of the resident surgeons points out that a former crewman of the *Patna,* now hospitalized and subject to hysterical visions, is unfit to appear in court, and asks, "Is his evidence material, you think?" to which Marlow enigmatically replies, "Not in the least" (*LJ,* 55; cf. *Res,* 337).

And in *Nostromo,* where "material changes swept along in the train of material interests," a "material train," whose cars, absurdly, are "empty" and consequently emit "no rumble of wheels, no tremor of the ground," dematerializes, becoming a specter of quickly altering shapes that seemingly is consumed by the very demented sound waves it emits: "the shrieking ghost of a railway engine" is itself but "a white trail of steam that seems to vanish in the breathless, hysterically prolonged scream" (*N*, 504, 171–72). Having abolished the concept of matter, Conrad promiscuously mingles the attributes of solidity and insubstantiality, of land and water, until interpretational possibilities become overwhelming. The sea can appear to be solid "like a precious stone," "a buckler of steel," "polished marble," or "an adamantine surface" (*Y*, 20; *TU*, 2; *SL*, 76; *ET*, 165). Conversely, land can be liquefied and all substantiality liquidated. The following passage from *Nostromo* is a useful example:

> The declining sun had shifted the shadows upon the whole extent of the immense Campo, with the white walls of its haciendas on the knolls dominating the green distances; with its grass-thatched ranchos crouching in the folds of ground by the banks of streams; with the dark islands of clustered trees on a clear sea of grass, and the precipitous range of the Cordillera, immense and motionless, emerging from the billows of the lower forests. . . . The sunset rays, striking the snowslope of Higuerota from afar, gave it an air of rosy youth, while the serrated mass of distant peaks remained black, as if calcined in the fiery radiance. The undulating surface of the forests seemed powdered with pale gold-dust; and away there, beyond Rincon, hidden from the town by two wooded spurs, the rocks of the San Tomé gorge, with the flat wall of the mountain itself crowned by gigantic ferns, took on warm tones of brown and yellow, with red, rusty streaks and the dark-green clumps of bushes rooted in crevices.
>
> (*N*, 394)

The narrative voice describes the physical appearance of a coastal landscape bathed in evening sunlight by means of factually distortional elaborations that import concepts associated, appropriately, with both water and fire. Moreover, the description is bifurcated. Appearances presented through aqueous and igneous analogies are kept separate. The first section is composed of a single lengthy sentence, beginning with reference to shifting "shadows," and containing a sequence of tropes that join the attributes of land and water. The second section is composed of several shorter sentences, beginning with reference to "sunset rays," and containing a sequence of contrary-to-fact grammatical constructions that emphasize, through "warm" earth colors, the spectacle's aesthetic appeal.

Ostensibly, the narrative voice is describing the appearance of the landscape near Sulaco at sunset; but it is also concocting an ontological commentary by means of the bewildering rhetorical devices that are incorporated into the description. Water metaphors appear frequently in *Nostromo* and denote the novel's single enduring fact: orderless flux. Decoud's citation of Bolivar's despairing judgment "America is ungovernable. Those who have worked for her independence have ploughed the sea" (*N*, 186) is paradigmatic, for the narrative voice later notes the flooding and ebbing of the "political tide" in Gould's drawing room (*N*, 189, 192, 199) and the disruption of a meeting in Sulaco of Monterist revolutionaries, "a torrent of rubbish" (*N*, 384), as there develop "currents and eddies in the crowd" (*N*, 393). It seems that recalcitrant formlessness is ontologically definitive. Consequently, the use of metaphor in the long passage quoted above to fuse the categories of land and water is appropriate, for through such a fusion an annihilatory essence is revealed that contrasts markedly with the colors that ephemerally fulfill human demands for aesthetic delight and durable surface. Furthermore, this contrast is emphasized by the way the passing of cosmic time, which must culminate in sunset and, as a result, in the elimination of the entire vista, in this particular instance opposes juvenescence and, indeed, life itself: the narrative opens with a citation of descending shadows, a chiaroscuro landscape, and ends clinging to chromatic glories that futilely and anachronistically lend "an air of rosy youth" as the evening sun declines.

Of course, an adequate interpretive response to passages like the one under discussion probably would necessitate a mode of communication capable of transcending linear narrative and the metaphysic of binary opposition. Voyaging intellectually in an ultimately tropological (consequently aqueous and perforate) cosmos wherein "there occur unexpected *solutions* of continuity, sudden holes in space and time" (*SA*, 85; italics mine), Conrad becomes indeed "a Ulysses of the interstices," forging a "statement of units of existential mystery conceived as having a certain order, [which] is itself formulated as units of linguistic mystery accepted in a certain order."[9] Conrad's texts therefore invite interpretation at the same time they discredit it, while concomitantly admitting nevertheless that the discredited activity is inevitable. Interpretation, like all perception, involves the sporadic, alogical displacement of one word by another under the reigning illusion that the whole process involves the rational, purposeful substitution of equals for equals, opposites for opposites. Thus, while initially it may seem to make sense to say "the serrated mass of distant peaks remained black, as if calcined in the fiery radiance," conceptual discontinuities lurk when "black" rock is described as if "calcined" (from Latin *calx*, meaning "lime"; i.e., attention is called to white powder), a figurative process supposedly due to a bright light (that is only figuratively "fiery") incapable of illuminating the very "black" surfaces upon which it (perhaps) is corrosively acting. In these instances, a seemingly meaningful logical surface is subverted by the ontic vacancy of raw diversity established through a plurality of multiplicative inverses, to which the very idea of orderly and sequential monogenesis is indeed alien.

Conrad frequently correlates such interpretational depths with locations within which his characters cease horizontal, linear motion in space. These locations are often essentially circular. (We just examined a description of land as if it were water and fire that was presented from an anonymous point of view located, significantly, within the sinister circumscription of the Golfo Placido.) Such places usually signal areas of semiotic overdetermination that threaten to annul language itself. As Edward W. Said notes, "Circles do not speak, they tell only of the inconceivable . . . , they enclose a blankness even as they seem partly to be excluding it."[10] The use of the figure of a circle as a means of signifying moments of linguistic breakdown is an extension of Conrad's awareness that all language is tropological in nature and thus is forced to turn (or trope) upon itself destructively under analytical pressure. Concerning the use of circinate images in recent periods of cultural history, Georges Poulet has this to say: "let the figure of God . . . withdraw itself to the horizon of thought, let the variety of the world appear in itself, stripped of all theological signification, then the symbol of the center and the sphere will reduce itself to a simple perspective diagram. . . . The divine encyclic will become a simple encyclopedia." [11]

Accordingly, the ultimate circle is always the relative, illusory, and solipsistic horizon-line that encloses the reader along with his texts and existential tasks: "One's experience . . . seems to lie at the very centre of the world, as the ship which carries one always remains the centre figure of the round horizon" (C, 300). However, "the perfect circle of the horizon" (N, 203), beyond mastery and measurement, is merely the model for the smaller, vacillating circles that signal the relative situational limitations of conceptualization, of which Conrad himself becomes particularly aware during those times when, in mental isolation and perhaps "writing it in water" indeed (UWE, 263), he surrenders to cosmic wave-forms as he tries to create coherent fictions: "Moving in that perfect circle . . . of which I am always the center, I follow the undulant line of the swell—the only motion I am sure of. . . ." [12] Although these circles can intersect, implying the parcelling out of perceptual areas according to a multiplicity of circumscriptions, most commonly the journey a character makes from one circlet to another seems to be linear, if only because it represents an imperceptibly small arc of the Great Circle route of one's life course, "each day [of which] seems to close a circle within the wide ring of the sea horizon" (MS, 7). And this route can never be circumnavigated, "for neither years nor voyages can go on forever" (MS, 22).

Such a trope directly invokes as a possible multiplicative inverse a traditionally significant configuration commonly used by Sir Thomas Browne, with whose works Conrad was familiar (see, e.g., the epigraph to Chance). Browne figures forth Man's life course in a postlapsarian world as a linear scission of an ideal circularity, a "mortall right-lined circle," with the "circle declaring the motion of the indivisible soul . . . according to the divinity of its nature . . . [and] the right lines respecting the motion pertaining unto sense, and vegetation . . ." (I, 166, 220).[13] Since the "mortall right-lined circle must conclude and shut up all," Browne's metaphor fittingly invokes the Greek letter theta, Θ, denoting death, $\Theta\text{ANATO}\Sigma$, while divinity is located at the central point of "mystical decussation" where the "indivisible or divine" and the "divisible and corporeal" (I, 220) are conjoined harmoniously. But in Conrad's fiction there is no such redemptive metaphysical duality. All men are destined to enact a futile attempt at transnavigating the ever-fluctuating circles that denote the limits of their respective subjectivities.

Conrad's motile horizons involve his characters in a devastating parody of Browne's primal Hermetic circle, "allegorical description of Hermes," the familiar *"sphaera cuius centrum ubique, circumferentia nullibi"* (I, 19), for they must remain at the center no matter how much they struggle in linear impercipience. Hence, in steam and stupidity MacWhirr crosses the circular typhoon and Mitchell the Golfo Placido, inscribing huge thetas upon indifferent waters, all the while absurdly imprisoned within their respective ubiquitous centrality. Yet, these are the lucky ones. Their centers remain in horizontal motion due to their obsessions with strict scheduling. Compulsive maintenance of human temporal and semiotic conventions permits no umbral contractures, no "mystical decussation." These points threaten only when simple linearity grows complex enough to require a self-annihilating linguistic structure in order to name it. The Congo river engenders such points. For example, Marlow's painful effort to describe with linear syntax his discovery of something that can only be invoked peripherally, surrounded by the frustrated linearity of only a partial circle of stakes and severed heads,[14] parallels his devious linear penetration by river of an area the human mind can only denote by means of a paradoxical emptiness amidst its energetic cartographical assaults, a place "filled . . . with rivers and lakes and names" but still "a place of darkness," though it was once white (*HD*, 52). Claude Lévi-Strauss defines language as an "unreflecting totalization [of] . . . human reason which has its reason and of which man knows nothing."[15] Marlow's verbose Occidental rationality necessarily derives largely from Aristotle and depends heavily upon the principles of opposition and contradiction. These principles Marlow cannot directly transcend, try as he may "to understand the pauses between the words" (*LJ*, 77). His only means of suggesting even the possibility of such transcendence is through the injection of radical indeterminacy into his discourse, whereby language is shown to be in effect "that which conceals, and at the same time that which reveals itself as that which conceals."[16]

Marlow retains clear moral distinctions when talking of his own voice as a manifestation of "good or evil," although he is unsure that either side of this opposition can be divorced successfully from the other. But when shortly thereafter he speaks in this polarized voice about still another voice, that of Kurtz, complexities escalate: Kurtz's "gift of expression . . . [is] the bewildering, the illuminating, the most exalted and the most contemptible, the pulsating stream of light, or the deceitful flow from the heart of an impenetrable darkness" (*HD*, 113–14). This statement exhibits the form of a definition. It purports to reveal an essence by means of the verb *to be*. But this familiar form is fractured by its content, which collapses the mutually exclusive categories of "bewildering" and "illuminating," "exalted" and "contemptible," and forces the resultant conceptual morass absurdly to represent that part of the form of a definition where intellectual tension normally is relaxed as an explanatory statement of equality is completed. But there is more. What begins as a sequence of opposing concepts nonsensically forced together by means of the coordinate conjunction *and* culminates in a similar pair of antithetical ideas that are juxtaposed syntactically but that are sundered quite logically by the presence of the word *or:* "the pulsating stream of light, or the deceitful flow from the heart of an impenetrable darkness." If this phrase stood alone, the utilization of Aristotelian logic and Western metaphysics during an interpretive response would be appropriate. However, since this phrase, containing the two logically differentiated ideas, is only a part of a larger unit in which two phrases are present that incomprehensibly unite opposed concepts, the seemingly redemptive "or" is annulled both grammatically and by weight of numbers. The phrase containing the rational differentiation stands in opposition to, and serves as an explanatory elaboration of, two phrases that it resembles neither grammatically nor conceptually. Small wonder that Marlow's auditors at this juncture "sigh in a beastly way" (*HD*, 114) to signal their impatience with such absurdity. And although Marlow protests "Absurd be—exploded" (*HD*, 114), he cannot explain himself further. He can only attack his shipmates for not having undergone the experiences that he is trying to articulate.

Of course, Marlow can scarcely be blamed. He is trying to render an awareness that transcends the possibilities of his language. Although philosophers like F. H. Bradley, a contemporary of Conrad, can state the issue abstractly—'The principle of contradiction . . . can not and must not attempt to account for the existence of opposites"[17]—it is extremely difficult to employ this sensibility in an utterance containing specific concepts such as those established by means of nominalization. As J. Hillis Miller puts it, "When one *logos* become two, the circle an ellipse, all the gatherings or bindings of Western logocentrism are untied or cut."[18] In a passage such as the one just analyzed, words that normally function to provide ordination for nouns, and thus preserve the Logos by maintaining proper hierarchy, are drained of significance. The nouns are isolated, bereft of relationships predicated upon tradition or value judgments, and narrative coherence is shown to depend fundamentally upon "unwarranted substitutions leading to ontological claims based on misinterpreted systems of relationship."[19] Moments of heterogenesis loom with respective integrity intact, as language is forced to subvert itself, a process Roland Barthes describes nicely: 'The Word shines forth above a line of relationships emptied of their content; grammar is bereft of its purpose. . . . Connections are not properly speaking abolished, they are merely reserved areas, a parody of themselves, and this void is necessary for the density of the Word to rise out of [the] vacuum. . . ."[20] Thus, Marlow ostensibly intends to describe Kurtz's "ability to talk" (HD, 113), but as the description gets under way in all its conflation of antitheses Marlow is clearly able to describe nothing according to traditional forms of definition. He must invalidate the very act of defining in order to demonstrate through his own linguistic activity the supposed qualities of Kurtz's speech. However, these qualities are inseparable from the characteristics of Marlow's own speech, and all he can accomplish during his statement about polarities is a revelation of the uselessness of ordinate relationships and conjunctions. Instead of the promised description of someone's "ability to talk, his words," the Word itself appears, muttering in effect "I am that I am" in such an ungodly way as to make the constitutive pronouns in this phrase seem antithetical in spite of their common referent.

In such passages Conrad's texts demonstrate their modernity. As James Guetti suggests, in recent fiction emphasis is placed

> not upon some ultimate idea of truth or reality, or even upon some standard ideological dichotomy or paradox, but upon the unreality of imaginative structure of any sort and upon the radical linguistic nature—as opposed to the ideological nature—of the problem of order.
>
> [Sustaining such emphasis] necessitates narrative techniques that are antithetical not only to the traditional means and ends of the novel but also to any sort of intelligibility or coherency.[21]

Yet, if for Conrad "the consistent denial of the possibility of order prepares for the general disintegration of imaginative capacity,"[22] such a disintegration is typically signaled by a veritable explosion of signifiers that disperse noisomely into ontically empty mere "degrees of difference . . . which are not opposites, but points on the same scale, distinctions of the same energy. . . ."[23] Capitulatory silence is loudly announced, and stands in marked contrast to the Augustinian silence that comes from God and is not a matter of sublunary verbalization because it is profoundly communicative and is to be detected exclusively "with the mind instead of with the body."[24] As Stanley Fish notes, this silence is present in the poetry of Milton at those points where Milton most directly specifies the proper relationship between man and God:

> the definition of that relationship . . . is a refining or purging process, which because its direction is away from everything we naturally value, including the value of our thoughts and their expression, is linguistically self-destructive. . . . [Thus,] On the verbal level there is a progressive diminishing, first of the complexity of language and then of its volubility, until finally, as the relationship between the self and God is specified, there is only silence.[25]

More commonly, however, when present in Milton's works semiotic indeterminacy functions restrainedly to figure forth the Divine. When in Paradise

Lost Raphael tries to render Heaven, "what surmounts the reach / Of human sense," as a specific place, he must resort to logically inconsistent modes of description because he is trying to delineate something that lies outside space and time by using analogies bearing spatial and temporal qualities, "By lik'ning spiritual to corporal forms" (V, 571–73). Milton's narrative voice must do the same. Thus, for instance, the jasper in front of the divine throne is at once a static "bright / Pavement" and a dynamic substance that flows by Jacob's Ladder, and that can also alter its very essence: "a bright Sea flow'd / Of Jasper, or of liquid Pearle" (III, 362–63, 518–19).

Elusive fluids in Milton's heaven bear a radically different denotation from the aqueous qualities lurking in Conrad's phenomenal world. Although in supernal contexts it is not possible to determine precisely when Milton's speakers are distorting literal truth by means of corporal tropology, the inseparability of tenor and vehicle is no defect. If Milton's Heaven contains areas that elude conceptualization, such perforations are not definitive flaws, but rather *januae coeli* that exist only to let the substance of God shine through with even greater brilliance.[26] Indeed, Milton is deeply concerned with maintaining the viability of both his language and his nation, for he has "never heard that any empire, any state, did not flourish moderately at least as long as liking and care for its language lasted."[27] As used by Raphael, therefore, paradox reveals the superior authenticity of God, the ground of all being, by intimating the inadequacy of earthbound ideation, within a philosophical context that offers redemption from such debilitating inadequacies. That is, such rhetorical devices are part of an orthodox tradition that validates each localized image and therefore prevents the annulment that would be initiated should one image join fruitlessly with its opposite. But when the narrator of *The Nigger of the "Narcissus"* tries to describe the potent principle of negation upon which he relies when measuring the authenticity of an experience, he employs a significantly different narrative device, combining the ideas of Christian God and heartless ocean in such a way as to rob both of traditional and logical viability:

> On men reprieved by its disdainful mercy, the immortal sea confers in its justice the full privilege of desired unrest. Through the perfect wisdom of its grace they are not permitted to meditate at ease upon the complicated and acrid savour of existence. They must without pause justify their life to the eternal pity that commands toil to be hard and unceasing, from sunrise to sunset, from sunset to sunrise till the weary succession of nights and days tainted by the obstinate clamour of sages, demanding bliss and an empty heaven, is redeemed at last by the vast silence of pain and labour, by the dumb fear and the dumb courage of men obscure, forgetful, and enduring.
>
> (*NN*, 90)

It is not possible to talk about the void, *"la splendeur de l'Inconnu,"* [28] without talking about all sorts of other things as well, whereupon the void is rapidly filled with debris. Nothing always "is" something. Marlow fills the neutral jungle with admirable and despicable devils and the amorality of language with the "exalted" and the "contemptible." And in a parallel manner, the speaker in this passage is not simply suggesting an equation. Little could be further from the traditional Christian God than the narrator's idea of the sea. What the two concepts do have in common is the fact that to each of the respective groups which revere these concepts, God and the sea are each a means of injecting value into human experience. However, the narrator regards the transcendental way to value as detrimental, and therefore eliminates it as a valid alternative by making the sea alone the measure of value precisely because it is harsh and godless. This new definition works against the traditional idea of a benevolent deity, who will ultimately solve all problems and wipe away all tears, and initiates a similar revaluation of the concepts that are usually associated with this idea of God. The "mercy," "pity," and "perfect wisdom" of the sea can "reprieve" men by forcing them to work almost endlessly, thus never giving them a chance to develop any elaborate sense of self-consciousness. Life is hard, but it is only this fact that makes life bearable. Those "sages" who would seek a paradise after death taint human existence. Their heaven is indeed "empty" if all it can boast is bliss and ease, for it lacks the distractions of excruciating labor, the sole means of redeeming the "weary succession of nights and days."

This process of negative redefinition of inherited, traditionally charged vocabulary is definitive of the narrator's perception. As a result, in contrast to the "chosen band" that rescues and deifies James Wait stands a second group, the members of which have been "chosen" in a significantly different way: the narrator sees the crew as "men enough to scorn in their hearts the sentimental voices that bewailed the hardness of their fate. It was a fate unique and their own; the capacity to bear it appeared to them the privilege of the chosen" (NN, 25). In contrast to the egoistic pity that the mariners direct at Wait and ultimately at themselves stands the pitiless "pity" of the sea: while the Narcissus is paralyzed by the deadly calm and the men are tortured, the narrator fancies he can hear "the ripple of a beshrouded ocean whisper its compassion afar—in a voice mournful, immense, and faint . . ." (NN, 104). After the demise of both James Wait and the unifying "sentimental lie" (NN, 155), the crew is "disintegrated by a touch of grace" (NN, 156). This is the grace that is dispensed by a terrible and inscrutable universe, and which in this situation results directly from the frightening demise of a fellow mortal. Sentimental values are warped in the presence of "l'Inconnu," in this case the unfathomable sea, "a sheet of darkling glass crowded with upside-down reflections" (C, 273). Yet to distort values in this way is not merely to substitute alternative definitions for the original concepts. To reflect inversely the very idea of value is to abolish value. Although the narrator of The Nigger of the "Narcissus" still may seem to be communicating as he discusses an "eternal pity" that decrees "unceasing . . . pain and labor," in fact he has created an intellectual impasse closely resembling the one Marlow invented during his efforts to describe Kurtz's speech in *Heart of Darkness*.

So far we have examined only examples in which characters survive the dissolution of their respective lexicons. Now let us consider a similar, but fatal, instance in order to demonstrate the nature and consequences of complete linguistic betrayal. In *Nostromo* Decoud, abandoned in solitude on an island in the Golfo Placido, approaches suicide. Just as he has physically attained a static point in the midst of one of Conrad's mystic circles, so he has to his detriment transcended his linguistic system. To Decoud the solitude seems "a great void," the silence "a tense, thin cord to which he hung suspended by both hands . . . without any sort of emotion whatever. Only toward evening . . . he began to wish the cord would snap" (*N*, 498; cf. *Res*, 274). It is intellectually paralyzing to be told that silence is like a taut cord. Silence is only an absence. There is essentially no tenor from which to generate any kind of meaningful correspondence between stillness (intangible auditory deprivation) and the concept of "a tense, thin cord" (physically immediate fact). A grammatical structure remains, but content has dissolved into an infinitude of stillborn possibilities.

The appropriateness of such dissolution resulting from Decoud's use of the figure of a taut cord can be understood once the situational origin of this figure is discovered. Much earlier in the novel Decoud converses earnestly with Antonia Avellanos about the way she places patriotism above humane commitment. He acccuses Antonia of taking advantage of his affection for her by forcing him to carry out meaningless exercises in journalistic propaganda. The perversions of language that he is compelled to undertake Decoud condemns as "deadly nonsense," an activity causing him an "intellectual death" (*N*, 180). He resists the use of language to create and peddle illusory moral absolutisms, and he dramatizes his own delusion of neutral perspective by roaring at the patriots gathered in Gould's drawing room the words *gran bestia* (*N*, 191), precisely the metaphor he is supposed to reserve exclusively for the enemy. Decoud ultimately defines his situation as official linguistic butcher for the Blanco party as "my life hang[ing] on a thread" (*N*, 180), the very figure of speech to which he will return when contemplating annihilation within the absolute silence of the Golfo Placido. The reason for this return is plain. Decoud originally conceives of the metaphor of the thread as a means of defining for himself his tenuous experience of the world at a time when he is consciously working to destroy the coherence of his language. This work he finds is "Deadly to me!" (*N*, 180), for it leads him to conclude, "in a moment of sudden and complete oblivion . . . as if struck by a bullet,": "I . . . don't really know whether to count myself with the living or with the dead" (*N*, 249). Later, alone in the Golfo Placido, bereft of his mistress, devoid of an object upon which his sustaining irony can operate, convinced that the Blanco forces have been defeated and that consequently he can only escape the island to be murdered on the mainland, and without even a meaningful linguistic structure remaining, Decoud verbally approximates the nothingness of death by generating an incomprehensible metaphor founded upon the vacancy of silence as tenor.

As Charles Sanders Peirce suggests, "The word or sign which man uses *is* the man himself. For, as the fact that every thought is a sign, taken in conjunction with the fact that life is a train of thought, proves that man is a sign; so, that every thought is an external sign. . . . Thus, my language is the sum total of myself; for man is the thought."[29] Fittingly, even Decoud's conception of the moment of death is fraught with metaphoric paralysis. He imagines death as a negation of life, properly enough, but is trapped into absurdity by already having identified life with tense silence. Thus, he can only go on to conceive of death, the release of tension, in terms of a violation of silence. Annihilation for Decoud can only by noisy. The moment when the thread breaks, when he in fact is "struck by a bullet," when the tense silence of life paradoxically becomes the open-ended silence of death with a "sharp, full crack" (N, 499) and he drops beneath the surfaces of both his words and his world, is the moment when Decoud passes beyond the merely inexpressible to merge finally with the Golfo Placido, sign of the ineffable. Indeed, in proximity to death language reveals "the sovereign moment at the farthest point of being where it can no longer act as currency. In the end the articulate man confesses his own impotence."[30]

In order to provide an abstract model that can be used to understand those instances in which Conrad teases the linguistic medium into self-betrayal, it is useful to invoke the concept of syntagmatic and paradigmatic relations among signs that was developed by Ferdinand de Saussure. The following summary is provided by Robert Scholes:

> In a given sentence . . . the meaning of a single word is determined partly by its position in the sentence and its relation to the other words and grammatical units of that sentence. This is the word's syntagmatic (linear, diachronic) aspect, often conceptualized as a horizontal axis along which the sentence is spread out in its necessary order. The meaning of a single word in a sentence is also determined by its relation to some groups of words *not* in the actual sentence but present in a paradigmatic (or "vertical," synchronic) relationship to the actual word. A word is thus defined partly by all the words which might have filled its place but have been displaced by it.[31]

When Conrad wishes in a text to intimate vacancy, he typically does so by depriving the syntagmatic axis of its power to impose orderly arrangement upon the various units in a sentence, while at the same time, through a fusion of antithetical ideas, he inflates the paradigmatic axis, the stockpile of interchangeable meanings, until the exercise of Aristotelian logic is no longer possible. Every *and* has become also an *or*, coordinate relationships have become also adversative relationships, and riddles are no longer excluded but rather assert priority.

Conrad's vast pleasure upon the terminal immersion of his characters in abysmal linguistic riddles is apparent in both the form and thematic content of much of his work. So far this argument has been illustrated largely through analyses of excerpts. However, now that basic concepts are established, a more sustained confirmatory example seems desirable. A useful work to examine at some length according to the present conceptual context is an excellent though neglected short story, "The Tale."[32] Appropriately, the initial problem to overcome in responding to "The Tale" is the misleading title of the work. The fact is that there exist four concentric tales, each of which involves its own narrative perspective, auditor, sphere of experience, and rhetorical logic. The nonhuman narrative voice of the story presents the entire aesthetic fabrication to the reader; the commanding officer presents his confessional tale to his mistress; the Northman recounts his misadventures to the commanding officer; and, while listening to the Northman, the commanding officer listens simultaneously to a "grave murmur in the depth of his very own self, telling another tale" (TH, 73). This story is an excellent example of how in Conrad's work the "inner continuity of each tale . . . derives from the utterance's sense of its own difference [from] conflicting or complementary utterances,"[33] how Conrad insistently substitutes an indeterminate discourse for the referent.

But recognition of the concentric narrative relationships established by the story is not enough. A logical means of connecting these reverberations must be found in order to determine the point at which critical faculties should first properly be engaged with the work. That is, it must be decided which of the four tales takes hermeneutic precedence. Insofar as the "present" of "The Tale" can be identified with the commander's efforts to communicate with his mistress, this work fits Edward W. Said's category of stories in which "the present . . . is . . . one of calm, of critical delay," an extended moment in which "Conrad attempts to achieve a causal relationship between the past and the present."[34] In Conrad's fiction such causal relationships are typically indicated by "a fabric of language generating meaning from the reference of words to other, anterior words,"[35] a kind of palimpsest produced by a single narrator in which the deepest layer of script necessarily takes interpretational priority; as Paul de Man remarks, the "self which was at first the center of the language as its empirical referent now becomes the language of the center as fiction, as metaphor of the self. What was originally a simply referential text now becomes the text of a text, the figure of a figure."[36] In "The Tale" the primary origins of linguistic causation are the irrational absolutist prejudices of the commanding officer, for these prejudices generate the tale arising "in the depth of his very own self" (TH, 73) that justifies (and thereby originates) his disastrous attempt to achieve a decisive, unambiguous act.

The commander cannot accept an epistemologically flawed world. He insists that "everything should be open . . . as the day" (*TH*, 67), and when he realizes that experience is recalcitrant to his demands for clarity he takes psychic refuge in an imagined realm defined by void uniformity, a nocturnal locale "somewhere where there [is] no choice but between truth and death" (*TH*, 64). Although the commander pretends to his mistress to have no knowledge of any place other than the phenomenal world and sarcastically suggests that if she would learn of "the better world" she must "evoke . . . those who have already gone there" (*TH*, 60–61), he conceals the fact that he is a regular sojourner in precisely such territory, where he stalks in amniotic darkness that "truth" which Conrad elsewhere derides as an "elusive and useless loafer."[37] Indeed, the commander's mental state corresponds strikingly with neurosis as defined abstractly by Jacques Lacan: "A failure to accept the primal lack . . . at the center of life itself . . . a vain and impossible nostalgia for that first essential plenitude. . . ."[38] The "depth" from which the lethal tale arises is identical to the subliminal realm where the commander goes in order to evade existential contingencies. That is, manifestations of his neurosis are primarily linguistic. Appropriately, the commander is never able to exercise decisive conscious control over the intellectual constructs that he manipulates as he seeks that precision of expression in which he assumes truth lurks. Indeed, by telling the story of his murder of an entire ship's crew he proceeds immediately to do that which he has just refused to do: "evoke" the dead. And in the course of this evocation the commander reveals his primal script. It is composed of words to which he responds in a compulsively negative manner due to the potential of these words to signify ambiguity, either figuratively or literally. Although he never overcomes this neurosis, the commanding officer does manage to create within a fogbound cove (a predictably circinate enclosure) a situation that satisfyingly responds to his psychic needs, as physical appearance and linguistic compulsions merge congruently to make absolute solutions seem possible, and a deadly semiotic plenum temporarily appears.

As a figurative means of discussing experience in an implicitly moralistic manner, the commander insistently uses a vocabulary derived from exercise of the visual sense. He is obsessed with fabricating a world in which "there's no perhaps" (*TH*, 77), no "murderous complicity" like "fog" (*TH*, 79), no "Mist [which] is deceitful" (*TH*, 64), no need to try to locate or define "a cloud . . . impossible to seize" (*TH*, 63). Consequently, he becomes entrapped hopelessly within his own lexicon while patrolling an area of ocean in which enemy submarines are supposedly being refueled by devious neutrals, an area that is the antipode of his ideal mental territory, "where there [is] no choice but between truth and death" (*TH*, 64). Specifically, when a politically neutral Northman is accidentally encountered within a dense mist in this hazardous area of ocean, an irrational causation is activated within the commander's semiotic matrix that dooms the Northman at once. The commanding officer need only investigate the morally inscrutable situation and impose the worst possible interpretations upon even unimpeachable facts in order to arouse himself to commit the sort of treacherous aggression for which he hates the enemy submarines: causing men "to die from something [they] have not seen" (*TH*, 64). No better dramatization exists in Conrad's works of the perceptual trap initiated by "the intellectual organization of the world according to an idea," which leads to "the expedient of devotion to the idea, which in turn breeds conquest according to the idea." [39]

The commander ignores the sane and accurate advice of his second-in-command and resists the redemptive clarity within the report of his boarding officer: "Papers and everything in perfect order. Nothing suspicious to be detected anywhere" (*TH*, 70–71). The commander prefers to nurse "such suspicions as . . . are not defended easily" (*TH*, 70), encouraged by the metaphoric impact of the fact of foggy weather upon his propensity to categorize morally the phenomenal world. He decides to board the neutral vessel himself, eager to reify his "invincible suspicions" (*TH*, 72). However, in order to achieve such a reification he must discover a signal that bypasses the visual concepts that up to now he has regarded as externalizations of certitude. The "deceitful" mist and the Northman's neutrality have compromised the "telescopes," "sharp eyes," and sunlit illumination "open as the day" (*TH*, 63, 64, 67) from which the commander derives his positive moral analogues. He must now seek out an "atmosphere" that he can only evaluate by means other than sight: he hopes for "some mysterious communication" that he might "sniff" or "taste" (*TH*, 72). The commander's willingness to do violence to his own system of moral analogues is an index of his epistemological desperation. Rather than accept pervasive ambiguity, he ransacks his semiotic matrix until he finds tropes that permit him to discover "a certitude strong enough to provoke action" (*TH*, 72). While in the embrace of a most nonneutral succubus, his military vessel, "a pretty woman who had . . . stuck revolvers in her belt" (*TH*, 63), the commanding officer, unlike Decoud or Marlow, never consciously encounters any lexical dead ends resulting from a fatal overloading of the paradigmatic axis of his language, the stock of interchangeable meanings. His Machiavellian manipulations of metaphoric discontinuities remain invisible to him, enshrouded as they are by an adamantine ontology and consequent unimpeachable moral rectitude. The fluid abyss just beneath his certitudes is as yet no threat to the commander. Triumphantly purging his mind and his world, he sets ambiguity and its emissaries, the sea and the Northman, along with his crew and vessel, upon one another in annihilatory conflict while he remains among seemingly redemptive straight lines and rocks.

Morally sniffing and tasting on board the alien vessel, the commander is in the presence of a man who is able to confront and articulate the fact of uncertainty. The Northman, refusing to shake hands, will not commit himself even to a social gesture. Moreover, he can stare "vaguely into the fog-filled space" (*TH*, 72) outside the chart-room even after having battled the mist and defective engines for days, whereas the commanding officer is annoyed "at being called out again to face the wearisome fog" (*TH*, 68) after an exposure lasting only a few hours. Perhaps worst of all, the Northman states candidly, "I don't know where I am" (*TH*, 73), has blue eyes, and smiles (see *TH*, 74, 77), thus unwittingly reinforcing verbally and physically the rest of the commander's analogues for deceit. In this achromatic story dominated by twilight, shadows, mist, and a landscape "like an India-ink drawing on gray paper" (*TH*, 65), there exist only two sources of color: both the Northman's eyes and the ocean are blue (see *TH*, 63, 74). The commanding officer has long despised the "hypocrisy" (*TH*, 64) of the ambiguous cobalt sea, which is "neither . . . friendly nor . . . hostile" (*TH*, 63). Moreover, he does not like smiles, either, for they connote gloating, invincible treachery: his second-in-command suggests that duplicitous neutrals are "probably chuckling" (*TH*, 66) as they escape, and aboard the Northman's ship the commander feels "himself with astonishing conviction faced by an enormous lie, solid like a wall," which prevents him from gaining the "ugly murderous face" of truth that peeps at him "with a cynical grin" (*TH*, 76).

By sheer accident the commander encounters in the fogbound cove a physical configuration that reflects his own linguistic prejudices with sufficient congruence to allow an illusion of "certitude . . . strong within" (*TH*, 79). The commander's figures of speech engage with the external situation in the cove to provide the commander temporarily with that impalpable point of "uncomplicated coincidence between intention, work, and deed [where] the ghost of a fact . . . can be put to rest."[40] Determined to take advantage of such epistemological luxury, the commanding officer decides that the Northman has been drinking alcoholic beverages (see *TH*, 75), in spite of the fact that he has obviously only been having coffee or tea from the "empty cup . . . on a saucer half-full of some spilt dark liquid"[41] with his "slightly nibbled biscuit" (*TH*, 72). The commander needs to think the Northman is partly intoxicated (see *TH*, 77) in order to convince himself that the neutral confesses to a misdeed when he declares that if he were to deal clandestinely with the Germans he "would . . . take to drink" (*TH*, 79). Even more blatant is the commander's reaction to the Northman's assertion "You can't suspect me of anything," an assertion made in response to the commander's suggestion that the logbook has been faked. Ignoring the context of the Northman's statement in order to make the neutral seem even more underhand, the commander treats the claim of innocence as if it were a suspiciously compulsive *non sequitur* and thinks, "Why should he say this?" (*TH*, 75).

The fateful conversation between the commander and the Northman occurs in the chart-room, a location that makes available comforting depictions that reduce the complexities of the phenomenal world to a symmetrical grid. This setting emphasizes the differing perceptions of the two speakers, for it is a chart-room penetrated by mist (*TH*, 72). One can either admit the fact of incertitude, like the lost Northman; or one can attempt to battle the pervasive fog, like the commander, whose pathological fixation causes him to employ gross military power to try to force the world into sharp definition. The commanding officer is unable to endure the "open-textured" discourse which he encounters in the presence of the neutral, a case "for which [there exist] no rules to determine the applicability of a concept."[42] As a result, having tasted and sniffed enough to achieve a murderous certitude, the commander restores to the conversation those figures of speech he had abandoned earlier when his hazy world no longer responded to tropes derived from the category of visual acuity. He tells the amazed Northman "I am going to clear all you fellows off this coast at once," provides a lethal heading which he says will "be clear," and with no awareness of his self-incriminating diction asserts that the "weather will clear up before very long" (*TH*, 79). The commander now hopes to eliminate moral uncertainty by means of a bearing on a map, a mode of signification that in its structural rigidity transcends discourse, since "numerals are . . . on the border line between grammar and vocabulary." [43] He learns too late that he has made the tragic mistake of confusing potential resolutions inherent both in his lexicon and in numerical grids with the elusive phenomena that the language and grids try to describe. Coasts, courses, and weather can never be as clear as he would like, for they are all neutrals too.

But "The Tale" is a love story, and an adequate reading of the work must ultimately provide an elucidation that allows the commanding officer's military experiences to comment significantly upon his erotic encounter. The commander's platitude "Everything should be open in love and war" (*TH*, 67) suggests that he feels the two areas of experience parallel one another. His remark is a moralistic revision of the well-known line "All's fair in love and war." The nature of the revision indicates that the commander still has not overcome his "temperamental" need for certitude (*TH*, 75), in spite of his recently gained intellectual awareness that his past efforts to transcend ambiguity only intensified it and made a murderer of him. Yet, if the desire for certitude remains, the raw military force with which the commander tried to achieve it is not accessible to him in the parlor, a circle in which he is denied the lethal semiotic luxuries he once found in the cove. Moreover, he can no longer take eidetic refuge in the dark as he once habitually did aboard ship when "at night [he] let his thoughts get away [to a place] where there was no choice but between truth and death" (*TH*, 64) and he could evade the outrageous "hypocrisy" (*TH*, 64) of the ocean. Night and the sea have become one in the sitting room, as the aqueous metaphor decisively imposed by the omniscient narrative voice indicates: "It was a long room. The irresistible tide of the night ran into the most distant part of it . . ." (*TH*, 59). Clarity and solidity are absent.

On his knees in passionate supplication, the commanding officer tries to elicit definitive commitment from still another "neutral" (*TH*, 62), in a situation that parallels directly the fatally fogbound cove in its frustration of visual acuity. At first the "shadowy couch" holds only "the shadowy suggestion of a reclining woman" (*TH*, 59); but as light fades, all physical appearances are negated, and the mistress vanishes into an exclusively auditory dimension, becoming only "the voice from the couch" (*TH*, 63). Devoid of telescopes, logbooks, maps, guns, and even a visual impression of his listener, the commander's entire world is reduced to an immediate verbal performance. In order to coax from his mistress the luxury of decisive action he must through conscious summary confront the linguistic compulsions that were operant but concealed during his conversation with the Northman. Since a strategic shifting of metaphoric ground and a selective neglect of fact characterized the commander's earlier deceitful exchanges with his quarry, it is appropriate that he now encounters only a refractory ricochet of indefinite articles and pronouns as he tries to recount his quest for redemptive certitude. This the commander cannot cope with. His "immobility" (*TH*, 59; cf. "immobility," 67; and motionless," 77) is psychologically definitive, and contrasts decisively with the "feminine mobility" of his noncommital lady that reminds him "of a butterfly's flight" (*TH*, 60). Indeed, he is one of Conrad's lepidopterists, like the narrator of "An Anarchist" and Stein, people who cannot sustain themselves amidst invincible ambiguity, and who in their eagerness to transfix an elusive cosmos can only sink themselves and others. (*Stein* means "stone," of course; Jim becomes at last "a stone figure" on Patusan [*LJ*, 409]).[44] Just as "the whisper of [Stein's] conviction" signifies to Marlow only "a vast and uncertain expanse," dim with the "crepuscular" light of "dawn—or was it . . . the coming of the night?" (*LJ*, 215), so the commander's verbal certitudes falter amidst "the crepuscular light" (*TH*, 59) that the omniscient narrative voice establishes within the parlor, where in this case night is indeed falling.

In the course of his narrative the commander tries repeatedly to employ the sort of paradox of which Marlow is a master (e.g., "dawn—or . . . night"). He now apparently senses the existential necessity for qualifying Aristotle's Law of the Excluded Middle and makes a valiant effort to connect opposites meaningfully. The Northman's lips "twitched. Did they twitch?" He "produced a fatuous smile. Or at least so it appeared to the commanding officer." He is a dissembler "pretending to be drunk, or only trying to appear sober," a moral enigma who "was—or was not—guilty" (*TH*, 77). However, just as the absolutist "depth of his very own self" (*TH*, 73) annulled for the commander both the facts found on board the Northman's ship and the Northman's story, so the commander still remains emotionally unable to take paradoxical dualities seriously as a means of dealing with human experience. As a result, he despairingly negates the profundity of his tale by ironically presenting it in the form of a popular nursery rhyme, "The Bear Went over the Mountain," in which the bear futilely crosses the mountain "to see what he could see. / And all that he could see / Was the other side of the mountain . . ." (cf. *TH*, 63, 65). This is obviously an absurd demeaning of his previous figurative representations of moral propriety in terms of successfully employed visual acuity.

The epistemological problem presented in "The Tale" takes the form of an erotic conflict because Conrad's male protagonists consistently resort to female analogues when struggling to orient themselves toward the dark, elusive otherness that is their experience of the phenomenal world.[45] Thus, personal limitations in or near the bedroom become indices of the various directions taken by flawed ontologies. Conrad's epistemic questers typically are not good lovers. The commander fails to accept a fluid lexicon like that generated by the omniscient narrative voice when it describes, for instance, the woman's reaction as "relief—or . . . disappointment" (*TH*, 62). Although he can play linguistic games over the physical appearance and moral integrity of the Northman, these perceptual complexities receive no validating emotive response from "the depth of his . . . self" (*TH*, 73). A configuration of unified opposites remains for him an impossibility, a negation, rather than a useful perceptual alternative. Consequently, his narrative is pervaded by the word *nothing* (it occurs seventeen times), his only conceptual and verbal correlate for a juncture of polarities. This is precisely why he cannot accept his lady's gesture of sympathetic commitment at the end of the story. Having been a critical neutral for the entire evening, she suddenly embraces him warmly, thus confronting him with still another apparent contradiction.

The fact that he can only be a sorry parody of the very neutrality that has driven him to distraction is significant. The parlor is described by the omniscient narrative voice in a manner that directly parallels the earlier appearance of the cove to the commander. The cove is characterized by "a gloomy hue from the dark cliffs which had no form, no outline, but asserted themselves as a curtain of shadows all round . . . , except in one bright spot, which was the entrance from the open sea" (*TH*, 69). The parlor, where the "irresistible tide of the night" runs, contains a "large single window," the only source of light, "framed rigidly in the gathering shades" (*TH*, 59). Once more the commander has found "the other side of the mountain" and cannot cope with what he fails to see. He can only flee melodramatically into the night, physically if not mentally "disengaged" (*TH*, 81). At the end of the story, that is, the commander is driven from the protective enclosure of the sitting room, just as he had driven the Northman from the cove. But his compulsive physical action is a poor complement to his psychic immobility, and a lethal obstruction in the form of vacancy is probably incorporated somewhere within the heading that he has at last so fittingly provided for himself.

As we have seen, when Conrad's characters approach conceptual breakdown their dependence upon linguistic complexity is radically increased, and this psychic event is typically correlated with the presence of the respective characters within some sort of circular and (usually) watery physical boundary that threatens to convert the life-preserving simplicity of horizontal linear action into a final vertical plunge through the surfaces of both words and world, as language fatally turns upon itself and an inverse transcendence occurs. Whether or not such a breakdown takes place is determined in part by the characters' respective levels of mental sophistication before encountering a potential semiotic vortex. Decoud, highly complex and skeptical, suicidally vanishes into the fluid emptiness beneath after having largely abolished language and being from his perceptions. Marlow, equally complex and skeptical, eludes terminal descendence and thus continues to communicate and sail about; and the commanding officer apparently departs from his tale at a point of hasty transition into one of these two alternatives. But there are other possibilities. In *The Nigger of the "Narcissus,"* for example, Conrad explores the linguistic consequences of the exposure of a group of comparatively simple, barely literate mariners (intellectual antipodes of Decoud and Marlow) to narcissistic seduction as they eagerly pursue flattering verbal reflections of themselves while their ship repeatedly hovers at the brink of a concomitant final inundation. That this very peculiar Narcissus (an asexual vessel with a masculine name is personified as feminine) uniquely does not sink implies that the fictional structure sustaining it dramatizes certain ways in which language, and the threat of the discontinuously fluxile world it creates, can be survived. Let us now examine them.

It is quite significant that Conrad's works contain both a Narcissus and a mirror: the former, of course, is the ship in the novel *The Nigger of the "Narcissus,"* and the latter a metaphoric definition of the sea which is frequently reiterated in an autobiographic book entitled *The Mirror of the Sea.* But there are no literal visual encounters or reflections, for Conrad's Narcissus is not human. The purposefully bewildering transposition of a renowned proper name onto an inanimate structure deprives the reader of all immediately intelligible grounds for understanding the category of "ship" in terms of the category "Narcissus." A process of redefinition is taking place that insists upon the primacy of figurative language. For Conrad words are the source of a distorting self-consciousness that reduces the world to "a convex or a concave mirror," ensuring thereby that awareness never goes beyond "a vain and *floating* appearance,"[46] a watery hallucination. The mirror is generated primarily by a state of mind that Conrad terms "conceit": if "half the words we use have no meaning whatever," one can salvage those which remain only by "understand[ing] each word after the fashion of his own folly and conceit."[47] Such a mental state is especially likely to flourish in situations in which verbal constructs go unchallenged and are perpetuated through flattering ricochets off other human fabrications. The most debilitating sort of verbal constructs are those invented in an effort to convince the inventors of their unique beauty and adequacy.

In marked contrast, men are most effective in dealing with the physical "hazard of life" (*MS*, 28), which commands they "do well, or perish utterly" (*NLL*, 182), when they lack the opportunity or verbal skill necessary to create elaborate and fatuous self-images; when all they have for a linguistic base is an algorithmic technical language that has evolved for centuries in a situation in which it is constantly tested against nonhuman forces like the sea. Conrad defines "technical language" as the "clearness, precision, and beauty of perfected speech," "an instrument wrought into perfection by ages of experience" (*MS*, 13), and even goes so far as to praise mathematics as "the only manner of thinking which approaches the Divine" (*NLL*, 230). This corrective "manner of thinking," however, is only a remote, human approximation of the redemptively autonomous divine "voice" that energetically intervenes as Eve, solitary and immobile, naively admires her own barren "watery image" in the dangerously distracting mock transcendence of a "smooth lake, that to [her] seemed another sky" (see *Paradise Lost*, IV, 455–80). Of course, Conrad's world has no such voice. Hence, opportunities are rare for any salvation from crippling distortions of language resulting from almost inevitable human conceit. Excruciating experience battling the elements as a member of the crew of a sailing ship provides such an opportunity; and in this respect Conrad stands opposed to Freud, who asserts that during experience of pain (as well as during sleep) the self most purely evinces a state of total narcissism.[48] In Conrad, only those capable of an unselfconscious mental state that may even border on the illiterate can develop a relationship with the vessel that permits subsistence at a point where speech is unnecessary and conceit becomes irrelevant, where syntactic structures dissolve into separate categories owing to the cessation of concern with subjective relationships and perception approaches mathematical simplicity. This state ultimately is defined by and maintained tenuously within the ship named the *Narcissus*.

These erotic antitheses (the dilation of self due to seductive "conceit" and the abolition of self) are appropriately both included as lexical potentialities in the ambiguous epigraph to *The Nigger of the "Narcissus,"* which was taken from a passage in the opening volume of Samuel Pepys's *Diary* that deals with the return to England of Charles II from exile: "My Lord in his discourse discovered a great deal of love to this ship." Yet, such complex human problems are qualified by the urgently inhuman presence of the vessel itself. Unlike the mythic youth, Conrad's *Narcissus* cannot share human vulnerability to the echolalia of flattering reflections or verbal constructs. As Conrad observes, "Ships have no ears, and thus they cannot be deceived" (*MS*, 29). By making great and fatal demands they can penetrate human character definitively: "Of all the living creatures upon land and sea, it is ships alone that cannot be taken by barren pretences . . ." (MS, 35). In order to be secure from conceit one must love a ship with a "disinterested sentiment" (MS, 137) "untainted by the pride of possession" (MS, 136): 'The only way for a seaman to the faithful discharge of his trust" (sic) is to "forget one's self, to surrender all personal feeling . . ." (MS, 30). It seems the *Narcissus* is intended to be the repository of the narcissistic urges of its crew, who are safe from confusion so long as they remain "voiceless men . . . inarticulate," who have "no desire" (NN, 25), and who are capable of "forgetting their toil [and] forgetting themselves" (NN, 32). That is, Conrad implies a necessary connection between a freedom from intense self-concern and a lack of linguistic sophistication.

Detrimental ability to manipulate words in an effort to arrive at a comforting and flattering conception of a stable self is derived primarily from an absorption in exclusively human concerns. This ability stands opposed to commitment to a structure like a ship, which is indeed created by men but ultimately not human and beyond complete control, thus forcing its crew to confront a risk of personal annihilation should they permit a distracting sense of self to be detached from the collective repository, the vessel. The presence on board the *Narcissus* of James Wait occasions precisely such a dangerous obsession with that which is exclusively human. Unlike the sea as interpreted by the illiterate (NN, 169) and inarticulate (NN, 26) Singleton, which causes men to "look out for [them]selves" (NN, 57) by looking out for the ship, Wait uses the harassment of speech to urge the crew to look out only for egoistic individuality, only for him. His self-delusive egocentricity tempts the men to generate parallel verbal constructs about themselves, and they are rapidly seduced into a (for them) relatively high level of linguistic complexity while their individual narcissism grows. As the narrator realizes, Wait makes himself "master of every moment of our existence" (NN, 37), causing "undreamt-of subtleties [in] our hearts" (NN, 41): 'Through him we were becoming highly humanized, tender, complex . . ." (NN, 139). The men consequently learn to use language as a means of psychic evasion. They grow sufficiently complex to invent elaborate falsehood, plunging thereby to a dangerously subjective extreme: in emulation of Wait's "obstinate nonrecognition of the only certitude . . ." (NN, 139), death itself, "we lied . . . with gravity, with emotion, with unction . . ." (NN, 139). Linguistically victimized, the men fall prey to conceit before the seductive human mirror of James Wait.

The most excessive victim of such conceit is Podmore, the cook. Appropriately, his verbalizing takes the form of religious proselytizing, for Conrad perceives the use of words to invent an abstract, metaphysical froth such as Christianity as about the most radically invalid distortion of language conceivable. Fatuously grounding his personality upon absolutist moralistic verbiage, Podmore presumes to save souls in the (ironically) "infernal fog of his supreme conceit" (NN, 116), just as the crew members naively presume to validate a flattering revaluation of themselves through delusive contemplation of their own extreme adequacy: "And we were conceited! We boasted of our pluck, of our capacity for work, of our energy" (*NN*, 100). This state of mind is furthered by the avian verbosity of Donkin, the "poll-parrot" who "chatter[s] . . . like a . . . cockatoo" (*NN*, 110), the other member of the crew besides Podmore and James Wait who never succeeds in suppressing his elaborate sense of personal merit, who never can forget himself and love the ship unawares. Donkin's "filthy loquacity" (*NN*, 101) stimulates in the petulant crew "an interminable and conscientious analysis of their unappreciated worth" (*NN*, 103), as he dramatizes Conrad's contention that "capacity for valid language . . . seems joined naturally to . . . shadiness of moral character . . ." (*MS*, 102).

Such human mirrors are porous. Like the surface of the fountain of the mythic Narcissus, they are receptive to a fatal plunge. The crew members, entrapped within "a stormy chaos of speech" (*NN*, 128), are approaching a nearly lethal conceptual breakdown that results in a gradual abandonment of the *Narcissus* to the violent caprice of the elements. Both events threaten a terminal collapse into the nothingness beyond the "mirror of the sea" (see *MS*, 25, 42, 82, 135–36), "the irreconcilable enemy of ships and men" (*MS*, 137), as the *Narcissus* is swamped by an enormous wave that, significantly, is reflective, "like a wall of green glass" (*NN*, 57). These verbose moments are dangerous because of the human compulsion to generate flattering definitions of self, apparent reifications of personality that demand uncritical reverence. As Roland Barthes suggests, "What we say is only a mythic elaboration to satisfy our need for surface."[49] Edward W. Said's general summary is a useful model: as conceit increases, "it becomes impossible to avoid the inception of thought: the thoughtless repetition of a . . . sentiment inspires . . . some *idea of himself* in the mind of the person who has the sentiment. Now thought, under the sway of the ego, systematizes truth simply into an image of the Self in possession of truth."[50] The peril is rather simple: as content grows ever more fatuous, ever more eidetic (as it must), meaning evaporates, leaving only an illusion of intelligibility that is sustained by the fact of grammatical structure alone. The self then restfully contemplates a seemingly firm surface assembled from lies, tropes, and subjective verb forms. Such repose is potentially fatal to persons lacking proper humility, persons like the crew of the *Narcissus*, for temptation to ground one's being upon the specter of a grammatically reified selfhood, mere noises accompanied by a hallucination of formal relationship, is almost irresistible; and once established, the illusion is difficult to dispell. Frequently, only a lethal assault by wind and wave is sufficient, violently agitating, and thus destroying, the reflective surface, which then rises up to consume its creator. As Conrad observes, "After all, every sort of shouting is a transitory thing. It is the grim silence of facts that remains" (*NLL*, 206).

The potentially deadly nature of language is dramatized in *The Nigger of the "Narcissus"* by the manner in which no rhetorical distinctions are maintained between the sounds of the storm and the recalcitrant babble of the men, both of which signify the siren call of the unfathomable that haunts the fringes of all human fabrications, be they ships or sentences. As the men experience a frustrating inability to cope with James Wait, with the flatulent concepts of self that they discover in him, and with the resultant disorder aboard the ship, their speech transgresses the limitations necessary for intelligibility and approximates elemental chaos, becoming "an impassioned screeching babble where words patterned like hail," "moanings, low mutters, a few sobs" (*NN*, 117); a "tumult" replete with "growls and screeches" (*NN*, 121); a "murmur of voices" that, like the tossing waters falling on the ship, "seemed to pile itself higher and higher as if unable to run out quick enough through the narrow doors" (*NN*, 128), and which at last passes "like a broken wave" (*NN*, 129; cf. the primal sounds of the storm [54–55]). Sanity and life are preserved only by the intervention of Captain Allistoun (the name means "temple stone" and defines a locus of veneration opposing the shrine of Wait's cabin), who demands that the men articulate their wishes, the reasons for the mutinous discontent. When they cannot reply to his demand the mariners are forced to confront the fact that, under the influence of James Wait, they have been living in tenuous disorder at the frontiers of human conceptualization. They are humiliated, the fatuous reflections they have generated are negated, and they once again are reduced to the level of "voiceless . . . children" forgetful of themselves (*NN*, 25), which they occupied at the outset. At Allistoun's challenge "Jimmy was forgotten; no one thought of him, alone forward in his cabin . . . clinging to brazen lies . . . transparent deceptions . . . ; he was more forgotten than if he had been dead" (*NN*, 134).

No conceptual breakdown amidst a welter of "transparent" and perforate semiotic patterns can occur on the *Narcissus*. Yet, this is not to say that the crew members' impercipience is contemptible. If the men are undisturbed by the problem of verbalizing the ineffable, the very example of their indifferent placidity is perhaps as accurate an approximation of "the immense indifference of things" (*N*, 501) as any of Decoud's or Marlow's linguistic struggles. When at the moment of Decoud's death the linear figure of the taut cord vanishes, human fictions such as language and courses of action sink along with the corpse into the circinate gulf, into whatever exists beyond human comprehension in the semiotic plenum of silence unperceived. In marked contrast, the crewmen of the *Narcissus*, like MacWhirr crossing his typhoon, remain committed to simple horizontal linearity; and in preserving life and a dull sanity they fittingly transnavigate the "dead calm" off the island of Flores (*NN*, 146) just as they survive the verbose circles (see, e.g., *NN*, 34) in which they gather to sustain alluring and seditious conceptions of self that disappear vertically, along with Wait, into "the faint circle of a vanishing ripple" (*NN*, 160). In both cases metaphoric structures are annulled, either by inflation to the point of chaos or by a failure properly to be comprehended and sustained. The radical price exacted by the former is a loss of sanity and life; that demanded by the latter, the degree of perceptual acuity through which one becomes fully human.

Conrad therefore clearly indicates the dissolution of self is necessary for the survival of an extreme situation, be it a violent physical assault due to an upheaval of the elements or linguistic aggression arising from a seductive conception of a transcendently adequate individual character. Marlow's emphatic assertion in *Heart of Darkness* of the value of hard labor as a means of preventing a destructive verbal obsession is, of course, well known. And disaster threatens aboard the *Narcissus* when the ship is paralyzed by headwinds and the men have leisure time to talk and nurture conceit (*NN*, 125–132). But if such dissolution is desirable in order to maintain the rudiments of humility and sanity, this end can be approximated only through the preservation of perhaps the greatest of illusions: the possibility of accomplishing meaningful individual or collective action in time. In marked contrast to the triumphant selflessness of the crew of the *Narcissus*, Decoud, completely isolated on a small island that lacks even the flutter of a bird's activity, finds his personality begins to dissolve; and very soon he has psychically "merged into the world of cloud and water, of natural forces and forms of nature" (*N*, 497). Decoud undergoes this experience because his languange, the ground of the self, has failed the test of his "intellectual audacity" (*N*, 501). As a result, his perception after this failure is unstructured, devoid of both nominalization and syntax: "The universe [seems] a succession of incomprehensible images" vibrating "with senseless phrases, always the same but utterly incomprehensible . . . mingled into an ironical and senseless buzzing" (*N*, 498, 499). He has entered a limbo of primal noise from which the possibility of temporal development, indeed, linearity itself, has vanished. Without semiotic and grammatical differentiations there can be only the "buzzing," a monotone that is perhaps the closest approximation within time of an experience of time's final absence.

Proper humility, and therefore a measure of security, is possessed only by a person like Conrad, who recognizes the perilous tendency of all lexicons to evaporate even as he writes his novels and sustains thereby an illusion of the possibility of meaningful action in defiance of the fact that "no word is adequate."[51] Likewise, the narrator of *The Nigger of the "Narcissus"* has both survived the mirror of James Wait and preserved his linguistic sophistication, not having been driven back into voicelessness by Allistoun's humiliating criticisms. His personality is most visible in the conceptually vacant tropes he uses in an effort to talk about his experiences during the voyage, tropes that consistently attract attention to the illusory nature of the self. For instance, stars are no sooner personified through a contrary-to-fact grammatical construction that the human basis for the trope (the tenor of the hidden metaphor) is itself exploded as being beyond comprehension: "A multitude of stars . . . peopled the . . . sky. They glittered as if alive . . . as inscrutable as the souls of men" (NN, 29); "they glittered hard and cold . . . as unapproachable as the hearts of men" (NN, 77). A statement that the heavens are inhabited by lifelike stars that are as inexplicable as human souls and hearts simply draws attention to a radical indeterminacy. The concept of a soul or a heart is itself here a trope that remains open-ended. This is precisely the sort of exasperating device that Conrad himself uses constantly in The Mirror of the Sea, a book in which he demonstrates directly the sort of survival techniques he indirectly explores in The Nigger of the "Narcissus" by means of the orientational struggles of the narrator. By continually exploiting the sort of lingual chaos that almost ruins the unaware crew members of the Narcissus, Conrad flaunts his ability to gaze directly into the "mirror of the sea" and balance delicately between a vulnerable, verbalizing, human self and the invulnerable, alinguistic nothingness of the sea, which is "open to all and faithful to none . . . for the undoing of the best" (MS, 148), "uncertain, arbitrary, featureless, and violent . . . endless, boundless, persistent, and futile" (NLL, 184). As Morton Dauwen Zabel observes, Conrad's briny deep "woos man into its mindlessness. . . . The sea is thus a cognate of the East. It is a realm of elemental nature in which the conscious personality and egotism of man dissolve on encountering a force unbroken to the reason and assertive will of civilized life."[52] At sea all human forms are threatened with negation. Even the uproar of a gale, "the thing of mighty sound, is inarticulate," language is thus rendered impotent, and the most "noisy and distracting" storm is recalled elusively and redundantly as "a very quiet silence" (MS, 77–78). Conrad, unlike Decoud, can, through the act of creating fictions, survive the transcendent oxymoron, the primeval buzz.

As he toys with the "mirror of the sea" that threatens to engulf him, the linguistic tricks Conrad performs with unfathomable tropes operate in a manner parallel to the function of the ship in The Nigger of the "Narcissus." For the unintelligent crew of the Narcissus, who are at the mercy of great conceit should a rudimentary selfhood develop, the ship functions as an inhuman Narcissus, a repository of the potentially seductive and discordant selves of its crew. The ship is a human fabrication that stands beyond language and forces the mariners into a situation of extreme tension with their environment where egoistic self-consciousness is irrelevant. It redeems the men from immersion in human reflections like James Wait, from a conceited verbosity that tends toward a lethal plunge into the oceanic, "stormy chaos of speech" (NN, 128). Conrad, in marked contrast, dramatizes the unstable linguistic essence of the self by generating a flurry of signs which suggest the existence of a selfhood as source, but which, due to his insistent revelation of their ultimately nonsensical nature, are not permitted to coagulate into an enduring model. That is, by betraying the communicative function of language through subversion of logic and clarity, Conrad reveals the potential within language for effecting its own betrayal of simple selves that are uncritically founded upon its treacherous surfaces; while at the same time, speaking perpetually *"in articulo mortis"* (*LJ*, 383–84), he demonstrates his own enlightened security from such a betrayal by showing that he can with impunity polish and admire linguistic surfaces that he shatters at the very moment he creates them. For the mariners, a stable but nonhuman figure is offered, the *Narcissus*, with which they can identify only in an unselfconscious way. For Conrad, no such redemptively distracting surrogate is needed, for in his humility he is not in danger of going proudly through the looking glass due to a naive faith in language.

Abbreviations

Volumes in the Dent *Collected Edition of the Works of Joseph Conrad* (London, 1946) are cited according to the following conventions:

AF: *Almayer's Folly—A Story of an Eastern River,* 1895

OI: *An Outcast of the Islands,* 1896

NN: *The Nigger of the "Narcissus,"* 1897

TU: *Tales of Unrest* (contains "Karain, a Memory," "The Idiots," "An Outpost of Progress," "The Return," "The Lagoon"), 1898

LJ: *Lord Jim,* 1900

Y: *"Youth"*

HD: *Heart of Darkness*

ET: *The End of the Tether* ("Youth," *Heart of Darkness,* and *The End of the Tether* are all contained in the *Youth—A Narrative; and Two Other Stories* volume), 1902

T: *Typhoon, and Other Stories* (contains *Typhoon,* "Amy Foster," *Falk,* "To-morrow"), 1903

Rom: *Romance—A Novel* (in collaboration with Ford Madox Ford), 1903

N: *Nostromo—A Tale of the Seaboard,* 1904

MS: *The Mirror of the Sea—Memories and Impressions,* 1906

SA: *The Secret Agent—A Simple Tale,* 1907

SS: *A Set of Six* (contains "Gaspar Ruiz," "The Informer," "The Brute," "An Anarchist," "The Duel," "Il Conde"), 1908

UWE: *Under Western Eyes,* 1911

PR: *A Personal Record,* 1912

TLS: *'Twixt Land and Sea—Tales* (contains "A Smile of Fortune," "The Secret Sharer," "Freya of the Seven Isles"), 1912

C: *Chance—A Tale in Two Parts,* 1913

V: *Victory—An Island Tale,* 1915

WT: *Within the Tides—Tales* (contains "The Planter of Malata," "The Partner," "The Inn of the Two Witches," "Because of the Dollars"), 1915

SL: *The Shadow-Line—A Confession,* 1917

AG: *The Arrow of Gold—A Story between Two Notes,* 1919

Res: *The Rescue—A Romance of the Shallows,* 1920

NLL: *Notes on Life and Letters,* 1921

Rov: *The Rover,* 1923

S: *Suspense—A Napoleonic Novel,* 1925

TH: *Tales of Hearsay* (contains "The Warrior's Soul," "Prince Roman," "The Tale," "The Black Mate"), 1925

LE: *Last Essays,* 1926

Notes

Preface

1. John Feaster, "Conrad and Ford: Criticism at the End of the Tether," *Journal of Modern Literature* 2 (1972): 417–21; Frederick R. Karl, "Conrad Studies," *Studies in the Novel* 9 (1977): 326.

2. Cary Nelson, "Reading Criticism," *PMLA* 91 (1976): 813, 802–3.

Chapter 1

1. Bruce Johnson in *Conrad's Models of Mind* (Minneapolis: Univ. of Minnesota Press, 1971) explores somewhat Conrad's relationship with Schopenhauer but largely ignores Far Eastern philosophy.

2. M. C. Bradbrook, *Joseph Conrad: Poland's English Genius* (Cambridge: Cambridge Univ. Press, 1941) and Thomas Moser, *Joseph Conrad: Achievement and Decline* (Cambridge, Mass.: Harvard Univ. Press, 1957) are two extreme examples.

3. Edward W. Said, *Joseph Conrad and the Fiction of Autobiography* (Cambridge, Mass.: Harvard Univ. Press, 1966), p. 11.

4. Georges Jean-Aubry, *Joseph Conrad: Life and Letters* (Garden City, N.Y.: Doubleday, Page, and Co., 1927), II, 204.

5. A similar approach is used by Edward W. Said in his speculative essay "Conrad and Nietzsche," in *Joseph Conrad: A Commemoration,* ed. Norman Sherry (London: Macmillan, 1976), pp. 65–76.

6. Jean-Aubry, *Life and Letters,* I, 283.

7. Ibid., II, 89; *Letters of Joseph Conrad to Marguerite Poradowska, 1890–1920,* ed. John A. Gee and Paul J. Sturm, (New Haven: Yale Univ. Press, 1940), pp. 45–46; Edward Garnett, *Letters from Joseph Conrad, 1895–1924* (Indianapolis: Bobbs-Merrill, 1928), pp. 44, 46.

8. Bradbrook, *Poland's English Genius,* p. 67; Moser, *Achievement and Deline,* p. 14.

9. J. Hillis Miller, *Poets of Reality* (Cambridge, Mass.: Harvard Univ. Press, 1965), p. 35.

10. R. L. Megroz, *A Talk with Joseph Conrad: A Criticism of His Mind and Method* (London: Faber and Faber, 1926), p. 54.

11. J. M. Kertzer, "Conrad's Personal Record," *UTQ* 44 (1975): 291, 293, 294, 300.

12. Garnett, *Letters,* p. 143.

13. Jean-Aubry, *Life and Letters,* I, 222–23, 280.

14. Ian Watt, "Story and Idea in Conrad's *The Shadow-Line,*" in *Modern British Fiction,* ed. Mark Schorer (New York: Oxford Univ. Press, 1961), p. 120.

15. E. M. Forster, "Joseph Conrad: A Note," in *Abinger Harvest* (London: Edward Arnold, 1936), pp. 134–35.

16. Moser, *Achievement and Decline,* p. 14.

17. Garnett, *Letters,* p. 143.

18. Cedric Watts, "Notes on Conrad's Janiformity," *Journal of the Joseph Conrad Society* (U.K.) 3 (1977): 10–11.

19. See, e.g., R. W. Stallman, "Conrad and 'The Secret Sharer,'" *Accent* 9 (1949): 131–43;

and Edward W. Said, *Fiction of Autobiography*, and "Conrad: The Presentation of Narrative," *Novel*, 7 (1974): 116–32.

20. E. V. Lucas, quoted in Arthur Mizener, *The Saddest Story: A Biography of Ford Madox Ford* (New York: World, 1971), p. 44.

21. Ibid., p. 44.

22. Richard Crashaw, "In the glorious Epiphanie of Our Lord God, a Hymn sung as by the three Kings," in *Poems*, ed. L. C. Martin (Oxford, 1927), p. 255.

23. All quotations from Schopenhauer are taken from *The World as Will and Idea*, trans. R. B. Haldane and J. Kemp, 3 vols. (London, 1883). Volume and page numbers are cited in the text with an abbreviation of the title.

24. William Bysshe Stein, "The Lotos Posture and *The Heart of Darkness*," *MFS* 2 (1956–57): 236, 235. For the iconography of the lotus see W. F. Ward, "The Lotos Symbol: Its Meaning in Buddhist Art and Philosophy," *JAAC* 11 (1952): 135–46.

25. William Bysshe Stein, "*The Heart of Darkness*: A Bodhisattva Scenario," *Conradiana* 2 (1969–70): 39–52; H. C. Brashers, "Conrad, Marlow, and Gautama Buddha," *Conradiana* 1 (1969): 63–71; Francois Lombard, "Conrad and Buddhism," in *Studies in Joseph Conrad, Cahiers d'etudes et de recherches victoriennes et edouardiennes* (Universite Paul Valery, Montpellier, 1975), II, 103–12.

26. Jean-Aubry, *Life and Letters*, II, 121.

27. Robert O. Evans, "A Further Comment on *Heart of Darkness*," *MFS* 3 (1957–58): 358–60.

28. John Galsworthy, *Reminiscences of Conrad* (privately printed, Freelands, 1930), p. 52. An interesting example of the depth of influence Schopenhauer's *The World as Will and Idea* possibly had on Conrad is indicated by the fact that certain rhetorical patterns in Conrad seem to derive from Schopenhauer's writings: for example, the fond use of the word *kernel* (see, e.g., *HD*, 48; *T*, 29; cf. *WWI*, III, 253, 276, 290, 298, 303, 308); the utilization of the word *idea* to indicate the threat of illusion (see e.g., *LJ*, 13, 17, 44, 60, 63, 92, 131, 142, 160, 182, 187, 189, 196, 209, 300).

29. *Joseph Conrad: Letters to William Blackwood and David S. Meldrum*, ed. William Blackburn (Durham, N.C.: Duke Univ. Press, 1958), p. 34. See Norman Sherry, *Conrad's Eastern World* (Cambridge: Cambridge Univ. Press, 1966), pp. 139–70, for specifics of travel books, and Florence Clemens, "Conrad's Favorite Bedside Book: Wallace's *Malay Archipelago*," *South Atlantic Quarterly* 38 (1939): 305–15. See also Jean-Aubry, *Life and Letters*, I, 280, for a letter by Conrad criticizing Hugh Clifford's *In a Corner of Asia* (1899), and *NLL*, 58–60. Cf. *LJ*, 157.

30. Schopenhauer notes his many sources throughout *The World as Will and Idea*. See, e.g., I, 491, 497, 501n.

31. In the Orient violent self-consumption is a definitive attribute of the phenomenal world. See, e.g., the creature of Shiva described by Heinrich Zimmer in *Myths and Symbols in Indian Art and Civilization* (Princeton, N.J.: Princeton Univ. Press, 1946): ". . . having devoured not only its feet and hands, but its arms and legs as well, it was still unable to stop. The teeth went on through its own belly and chest and neck, until only the face remained" (p. 181). Schopenhauer's favorite analogue is "the bulldog ant of Australia . . . , for if it is cut in two, a battle begins between the head and the tail. The head seizes the tail with its teeth, and the tail defends itself bravely by stinging the head" (*WWI*, I, 192). Cf. *Res*, 372.

32. William Bysshe Stein, "Conrad's East: Time, History, Action, and *Maya*," *TSLL* 7 (1965): 274.

33. Dietrich Seckel, *The Art of Buddhism*, trans. Ann E. Keep (Baden-Baden, Germany, 1963; New York: Crown, 1964), p. 155; cf. Miller, *Poets of Reality*, p. 19.

34. Bruce Johnson, "*Heart of Darkness* and the Problem of Emptiness," *SSF* 9 (1972): 391.

35. Hugh Clifford, "The Genius of Mr. Joseph Conrad," *North American Review* 178 (June 1904): 842–52.

36. C. G. Jung, "Commentary on 'The Secret of the Golden Flower,'" in *Alchemical Studies*, trans. R. F. C. Hull (Princeton, N.J.: Bollingen Series XX, 1967), p. 18.

37. Stein, "Conrad's East: Time, History, Action, and *Maya*," p. 265.

38. William Bysshe Stein, "*Almayer's Folly:* The Terrors of Time," *Conradiana* 1 (1968): 31.

39. Ibid., 28.

40. Edward W. Said, "Orientalism," *Georgia Review* 31 (1977): 170.

41. Jean-Aubry, *Life and Letters*, I, 301.

42. Garnett, *Letters*, p. 46.

43. Ibid.

44. L. L. Whyte, *The Next Development in Man* (New York: Holt, 1948), p. 67.

45. Richard de Martino, "The Human Situation and Zen Buddhism," in *Zen Buddhism and Psychoanalysis*, ed. Erich Fromm (New York: Harper, 1960), p. 143.

46. Garnett, *Letters*, p. 59.

47. Ibid., p. 144.

48. Joseph Campbell, *The Masks of God: Oriental Mythology* (New York: Viking Press, 1962), p. 189.

49. See Zimmer, *Indian Art and Civilization*, p. 154, for analysis of the significance of *Om*.

50. Deirdre David, "Selfhood and Language in 'The Return' and 'Falk,'" *Conradiana* 7 (1976): 143. Joel R. Kehler has written an outstanding essay on *Falk*, with which I am in essential agreement: "The Centrality of the Narrator in Conrad's 'Falk,'" *Conradiana* 6 (1974): 19–30.

51. See Erich Neumann, *The Great Mother*, trans. Ralph Manheim (New York: Bollingen Series XLVII, 1955): the Diana of Ephesus is a type of "the Great Many-Breasted Mother" (p. 126; see plate 35).

52. Seckel, *Art of Buddhism*, pp. 103, 128. Appropriately, even the word *pagoda* is seemingly devoid of etymological sources (p. 111).

53. Jean-Aubry, *Life and Letters*, II, 216.

54. Campbell, *Masks of God*, pp. 338–39.

55. *The Hare Kṛṣṇa Cookbook* (New York: Bhaktivedanta Book Trust, 1973), p. 24. Conrad was quite interested in cooking. See Tony Tanner, "'Gnawed Bones' and 'Artless Tales'—Eating and Narrative in Conrad," in *Joseph Conrad: A Commemoration*, ed. Sherry, pp. 17–36.

56. Elliott B. Gose, Jr., "Pure Exercise of Imagination: Archetypal Symbolism in *Lord Jim*," *PMLA* 79 (1964): 138.

57. Seckel, *Art of Buddhism*, p. 27.

58. Denis de Rougemont, *Passion and Society* (London: Faber and Faber, 1956), p. 70.

59. Stein, "*Almayer's Folly:* The Terrors of Time," p. 29.

60. Lloyd Fernando, "Conrad's Eastern Expatriates: A New Version of His Outcasts," *PMLA* 91 (1976): 85.

61. For a different interpretation of this passage, see Wray C. Herbert, "Conrad's Psychic Landscape: The Mythic Element in 'Karain,'" *Conradiana* 8 (1976): 226.

62. See, e.g., Takaaki Sawa, *Art in Japanese Esoteric Buddhism*, trans. Richard L. Gage (New York: Weatherhill, 1972), pp. 31–50. For detailed pictures of this icon, see *Modern Photography* 41 (1977): 84–93.

63. See, e.g., N. V. M. Gonzalez, "Time as Sovereign: A Reading of Conrad's 'Youth,'" *Literary Apprentice* (U. Philippines, 1954), pp. 106–22; Leo Gurko, *Joseph Conrad: Giant in Exile* (New York: Macmillan, 1962), pp. 80–82; Lawrence Graver, *Conrad's Short Fiction* (Berkeley and Los Angeles: Univ. of California Press, 1969), pp. 70–77; Paul S. Bruss, "Conrad's 'Youth': Problems of Interpretation," *College Literature* 1 (1974): 218–29.

64. See, e.g., Murray Krieger, "Conrad's 'Youth': A Naive Opening to Art and Life," *College English* 20 (1959): 275–80.

65. Bruss, "Conrad's 'Youth,'" p. 219.

66. John Howard Wills, "A Neglected Masterpiece: Conrad's 'Youth,'" *TSLL* 4 (1963): 600.

67. Zimmer, *Indian Art and Civilization*, p. 211.

68. Philip Rawson, *Erotic Art of the East* (New York: Putnam's, 1968), p. 166; for excellent photographs of this icon, see illustrations 44, 100, 105, and especially 111; also Detlef Ingo Lauf, *Tibetan Sacred Art: The Heritage of Tantra*, trans. Ewald Osers (Berkeley, Calif.: Shambhala, 1976), plates 43 and 52.

69. Campbell, *Masks of God*, p. 165.

70. Rawson, *Erotic Art of the East*, p. 165.

71. Said, *Fiction of Autobiography*, pp. 137–38.

72. Gose, "Archetypal Symbolism in *Lord Jim*," p. 144.

73. H. G. Wells, quoted in Mizener, *Saddest Story*, p. 50.

74. Garnett, *Letters*, p. 129.

Chapter 2

1. Ian Watt, "Conrad's Preface to *The Nigger of the 'Narcissus,'*" *Novel* 7 (1974): 101.

2. Leo Gurko, *Joseph Conrad: Giant in Exile* (New York: Macmillan, 1962), pp. 86, 90.

3. Albert Guerard, *Conrad the Novelist* (Cambridge, Mass.: Harvard Univ. Press, 1958), p. 294.

4. Samuel Hynes, "Two Rye Revolutionaries," *Sewanee Review* 73 (1965): 152.

5. Paul L. Wiley, *Conrad's Measure of Man* (Madison: Univ. of Wisconsin Press, 1954); J. Hillis Miller, *Poets of Reality* (Cambridge, Mass.: Harvard Univ. Press, 1965); Edward W. Said, *Joseph Conrad and the Fiction of Autobiography* (Cambridge, Mass.: Harvard Univ. Press, 1966); James Guetti, *The Limits of Metaphor: A Study of Melville, Conrad, and Faulkner* (Ithaca, N.Y.: Cornell Univ. Press, 1967); Royal Roussel, *The Metaphysics of Darkness* (Baltimore: The Johns Hopkins Univ. Press, 1971); Bruce Johnson, *Conrad's Models of Mind* (Minneapolis: Univ. of Minnesota Press, 1971); Camille R. La Bossière, *Joseph Conrad and the Science of Unknowing* (Fredericton, N.B., Canada, 1979).

6. M. C. Bradbrook, *Joseph Conrad: Poland's English Genius* (Cambridge: Cambridge Univ. Press, 1941), p. 67; Thomas Moser, *Joseph Conrad: Achievement and Decline* (Cambridge, Mass.: Harvard Univ. Press, 1957), p. 11.

7. Brief and fragmentary dissent has been voiced in the following studies: Wiley, *Conrad's Measure of Man*, p. 72; William R. M. Hussey, " 'He was spared that annoyance,'" *Conradiana* 3 (1971–72): 17–25; Paul S. Bruss, " 'Typhoon': The Initiation of Jukes," *Conradiana* 5 (1973): 46–55; Dennis M. Walsh, "Conrad's 'Typhoon' and the Book of Genesis," *SSF* 11 (1974): 99–101; Christof Wegelin, "MacWhirr and the Testimony of the Human Voice," *Conradiana* 7 (1975): 45–50.

8. Frederick R. Karl, *A Reader's Guide to Joseph Conrad* (New York: Noonday Press, 1960), p. 141; Guerard, *Conrad the Novelist*, p. 294.

9. J. Hillis Miller, "Narrative and History," *ELH* 41 (1974): 456.

10. Victor Shklovsky, quoted in Ingo Seidler, "The Inconolatric Fallacy: On the Limitations of the Internal Method of Criticism," *JAAC* 26 (1967): 13.

11. David Funt, "Roland Barthes and the *nouvelle critique*," *JAAC* 26 (1968): 329.

12. In his prefatory remarks to *The Shadow-Line* Conrad similarly tempts the reader to identify author with narrator, while ultimately indicating that such a naively conceived union is invalid: "From my statement that I thought of this story for a long time under the title of 'First Command' the reader may guess that it is concerned with my personal experience . . . it *is* personal experience seen in perspective with the eye of the mind and coloured by . . . affection" (*SL*, vii). Temporal remove and subjectivity force any autobiography into the category of aesthetic fabrication, something literally untrue, as Conrad insists in later comments on this same novel: "I call it 'A Confession' on the title page, for, from a certain point of view, it is that—and essentially as sincere as any confession can be. The more perfectly so, perhaps, because its object is not the usual one of self-revelation" (Georges Jean-Aubry, *Joseph Conrad: Life and Letters* [Garden City, N.Y.: Doubleday, Page, and Co., 1927], II, 184).

13. Miller, "Narrative and History," p. 457.

14. Edward Garnett, *Letters from Joseph Conrad, 1895–1924* (Indianapolis: Bobbs-Merrill, 1928), p. 155.

15. Edward W. Said, "Conrad: The Presentation of Narrative," *Novel* 7 (1974): 131.

16. Miller, "Narrative and History," p. 462.

17. Geoffrey H. Hartman, "Monsieur Texte II: Epiphony in Echoland," *Georgia Review* 30 (1976): 196.

18. Moser, *Achievement and Decline*, p. 38.

19. Gerard Genette, "Time and Narrative in *A la recherche du temps perdu*," in *Aspects of Narrative*, ed. J. Hillis Miller (New York: Columbia Univ. Press, 1971), p. 93. This idea is developed at greater length in Genette's 200-page essay, "*Discours du recit*," in *Figures III* (Paris, 1972).

20. "Memorandum: On the Scheme for Fitting Out a Sailing Ship for the Purpose of Perfecting the Training of Merchant Service Officers Belonging to the Port of Liverpool" (*LE*, 66–80).

21. I am indebted to W. Allyn Rickett, Professor of Chinese Studies at the University of Pennsylvania, for this information. The name of MacWhirr's ship, the "southern mountain," connects in still another way the man's uncontrolled irrationality with his meeting with the typhoon and its "mountains of water" (*T*, 64), which his lack of prudence precipitates. See C. G. Jung, *The Archetypes and the Collective Unconscious*, trans. R. F. C. Hull (New York: Bollingen Series XX, 1959), p. 219n.: "The mountain stands for the goal of the pilgrimage and ascent, hence it often has the psychological meaning of the self." That MacWhirr has never had to ascend his "mountain," but rather has driven it placidly around on a peaceful Eastern ocean, reflects his flawless psychic density. Indeed, he "sailed over the surface of oceans as some men go skimming over the years of existence" (*T*, 19), like Captain Hagberd of the *Skimmer of the Seas*, in "To-morrow," "one of those sailors that pursue their calling within sight of land" (*T*, 249), or the pirate Peyrol, who has abandoned his risky calling and now bears the nickname "old skimmer of the seas" (*Rov*, 43).

22. Guerard, *Conrad the Novelist*, p. 299.

23. C. G. Jung, *Symbols of Transformation*, trans. R. F. C. Hull (New York: Bollingen Series XX, 1956), p. 298.

24. *Joseph Conrad: Letters to William Blackwood and David S. Meldrum*, ed. William Blackburn (Durham, N.C.: Duke Univ. Press, 1958), p. 133.

25. Basil Bernstein, "Social Class and Psycho-therapy," *British Journal of Sociology* 15 (1964): 59.

26. Ibid., p. 56. The resemblance of Bernstein's categories to Conrad's "convict or idiot" duality is striking.

27. Wiley, *Conrad's Measure of Man*, p. 72.

28. Roman Jakobson, "Two Aspects of Language and Two Types of Aphasic Disturbances," in Jakobson and Morris Halle, *Fundamentals of Language* (The Hague, 1956), p. 69. Jakobson is quoting Kurt Goldstein, *Language and Language Disturbances* (New York: Grune and Stratton, 1948), p. 270.

29. For a fine discussion of Conrad's emblematic use of doors in another tale, see David Ketterer, "'Beyond the Threshold' in Conrad's *Heart of Darkness*," *TSLL* 11 (1969–70): 1013–22.

30. For a brief study of this aspect of Conrad's fiction see Addison C. Bross, "The Unextinguishable Light of Belief: Conrad's Attitude toward Women," *Conradiana* 2 (1969–70): 39–46. Marlow's analogical perception of the "wild and gorgeous apparition of a woman" as the "soul" of the "immense wilderness" and "mysterious life" (*HD*, 135–36) that he encounters in the midst of deepest Africa is but one of many possible examples. Although Conrad usually avoids detailed revelation of the female psyche, it seems that his women use a masculine analogue as an orientational device. In a passage which directly inverts Marlow's feminine vision of the jungle, Mrs. Travers, gazing in confusion at the "abysmal immobility" surrounding her, perceives the inscrutable forest as a "great erection of enormous solid trunks" (*Res*, 285).

31. As Jung observes in *The Archetypes and the Collective Unconscious*, loss of functional contact with the archetypal feminine means for a man "premature rigidity, crustiness, stereotypy, fanatical one-sidedness, obstinacy, [and] pedantry" (p. 71). By isolating MacWhirr emotionally from his wife and daughter in *Typhoon*, Conrad clearly is consciously altering the experiences he once had with a different "good Captain MacW——," a man so attached to his wife that, upon departure from land, he would "in a spirit of grief and discontent" sequester himself for a lengthy interval, "take a long dive . . . only to emerge a few days afterwards" (*MS*, 5).

32. C. G. Jung, *Aion: Researches into the Phenomenology of the Self*, trans. R. F. C. Hull (New York: Bollingen Series XX, 1959), p. 71; see also Jung, *The Archetypes and the Collective Unconscious*, p. 164.

33. Gurko, *Giant in Exile*, p. 90.

34. Ibid.

35. John Palmer, *Joseph Conrad's Fiction* (Ithaca, N.Y.: Cornell Univ. Press, 1968), p. 81.

36. Jean-Aubry, *Life and Letters*, I, 222.

37. Palmer, *Joseph Conrad's Fiction*, p. 82.

38. The minor debate as to who changes in the course of the story is summarized by Bruss, "'Typhoon': The Initiation of Jukes," p. 48, who then concludes interestingly that "it is Mac-Whirr . . . who does not change." To the contrary, it seems just about every character is changed as a result of the experience within the tempest, each in his own way, briefly or permanently.

39. Said, "Conrad: The Presentation of Narrative," p. 122.

40. Bruce Johnson, "Names, Naming, and the 'Inscrutable' in Conrad's *Heart of Darkness*," *TSLL* 12 (1971): 681.

41. Ibid.

42. Maurice Merleau-Ponty, "The Prose of the World," trans. John O'Neill, *TriQuarterly* 20 (1971): 20.

43. Maurice Merleau-Ponty, *Phenomenology of Perception*, trans. Colin Smith (New York: Humanities Press, 1962), p. 179.

44. William Bysshe Stein, "Conrad's East: Time, History, Action, and *Maya*," *TSLL* 7 (1965): 281.

45. Ibid., p. 267.

46. Conrad's familiarity with ancient myth has been demonstrated, in another context, by Robert G. Jacobs in "*Gilgamesh*: The Sumerian Epic That Helped *Lord Jim* to Stand Alone," *Conradiana* 4 (1972): 23–32. The relevance of archetypal methodology to literary studies need scarcely be demonstrated. Some of the more successful applications of this mode of criticism to Conrad scholarship are: Robert O. Evans, "Conrad's Underworld," *MFS* 2 (1956): 56–62; Jerome Thale, "Marlow's Quest," *UTQ* 24 (1955): 351–58; Lilian Feder, "Marlow's Descent into Hell," *NCF* 9 (1955): 280–92; Guerard, *Conrad the Novelist*, pp. 1–59; Elliott B. Gose, Jr., "Pure Exercise of Imagination: Archetypal Symbolism in *Lord Jim*" *PMLA* 79 (1964); Dale Kramer, "Marlow, Myth, and Structure in *Lord Jim*," *Criticism* 8 (1966): 263–79; Claire Rosenfield, *Paradise of Snakes: An Archetypal Analysis of Conrad's Political Novels* (Chicago: Univ. of Chicago Press, 1967); Richard E. Butler, "Jungian and Oriental Symbolism in Joseph Conrad's *Victory*," *Conradiana* 3 (1971–72): 36–54.

47. Wiley, *Conrad's Measure of Man*, p. 74.

48. Jean-Aubry, *Life and Letters*, I, 213.

49. Stein, "Conrad's East: Time, History, Action, and *Maya*," p. 266.

50. Wiley, *Conrad's Measure of Man*, p. 70.

51. Jung, *The Archetypes and the Collective Unconscious*, pp. 18, 379, 258–59.

52. M. Esther Harding, *Psychic Energy: Its Source and Its Transformation* (New York: Bollingen Series X, 1947), p. 310.

53. Ibid., p. 322.

54. Jung, *Symbols of Transformation*, pp. 250–51.

55. *Compact Edition, Oxford English Dictionary* (Oxford: Oxford Univ. Press, 1971), II, 3455.

56. See, e.g., Jung, *Symbols of Transformation*, p. 251; *Aion*, pp. 122, 215. The *Nan-Shan* is threatened in the dark, at midnight, in another story: see *TLS*, 169.

57. See, e.g., *The Faerie Queene*, III, iv, 43; IV, xi, 6.

58. Erich Neumann, *The Origins and History of Consciousness*, trans. R. F. C. Hull (New York: Bollingen Series XLII, 1954), p. 141.

59. Robert Graves, *The Greek Myths* (New York: Braziller, 1959), p. 130; cf. *The Faerie Queene*, VI, i, 8 and vi, 9–11.

60. Stein, "Conrad's East: Time, History, Action, and *Maya*," p. 278.

61. Said, "Conrad: The Presentation of Narrative," p. 120.

62. See Jung, *The Archetypes of the Collective Unconscious*, p. 369: "The centre is often characterized as the 'treasure hard to attain.'" Conrad parodies this mythic paradigm by causing the mariners to struggle with the shining silver during the lull within the hurricane's eye, and he indicates thereby the immaculately pedestrian quality of all their minds, for, in marked contrast to almost all the characters in *Nostromo* and their mystic attitudes toward the San Tomé mine, to Axel Heyst and his hoard of bliss on Samburan, to Jim and his "jewel" at the heart of Patusan, or to Lingard and his secret source of wealth upriver, MacWhirr and his men never conceive of the idea of value in a metaphoric manner. Coins are always just money, in spite of distinct alternate possibilities. The bestial boatswain, for example, having just emerged from the complete blackness of the coal bunker, sees "a silver dollar" as "a bright white disc" (*T*, 58), as Conrad tempts both crew member and reader to perceive a solar analogue of vanished celestial light; but the opportunity for heightened awareness in this instance eludes the boatswain, at least.

63. Jung, *The Archetypes and the Collective Unconscious*, p. 320. MacWhirr's nocturnal voyage through the center of the whirling circle of wind and water, occurring devoid of literal or figurative illumination, contrasts directly with the sort of experience described by Poe in "A Descent into the Maelström," where the narrator escapes death by use of his wits, thereby rising to a higher level of consciousness, as he combats by moonlight the, significantly, rightward-spinning vortex (the ship drops into the whirlpool on its starboard side). As Jung observes: "The difference between the 'natural' individuation process, which runs its course unconsciously, and the one which is consciously realized, is tremendous. In the first case consciousness nowhere intervenes; the end remains as dark as the beginning. In the second case so much darkness comes to light that the personality is permeated with light, and consciousness necessarily gains in scope and insight" (*Psychology and Religion: West and East*, trans. R. F. C. Hull [New York: Bollingen Series XX, 1958], p. 468).

Chapter 3

1. Gillian Beer, *The Romance* (London: Methuen, 1970), p. 4. See also Paul Strohm, "The Origin and Meaning of Middle English *Romaunce*," *Genre* 10 (1977): 1–28.

2. Henry Knight Miller, "The 'Digressive' Tales in Fielding's *Tom Jones* and the Perspective of Romance," *PQ* 54 (1975): 270.

3. Northrop Frye, *Anatomy of Criticism* (Princeton, N.J.: Princeton Univ. Press, 1957), pp. 187–88.

4. Earl Wasserman, *The Subtler Language* (Baltimore: The Johns Hopkins Univ. Press, 1959), pp. 10–11.

5. Henry Knight Miller, *Henry Fielding's "Tom Jones" and the Romance Tradition* (Victoria, B.C., Canada: English Literary Studies, 1976), p. 15.

6. Robert Kiely, *The Romantic Novel in England* (Cambridge, Mass.: Harvard Univ. Press, 1972), p. 2.

7. For an interpretation of the novel from this perspective see Eric Rothstein, "Allusion and Analogy in the Romance of *Caleb Williams*," *UTQ* 37 (1967): 18–30. Also useful is C. R. Knopf, "*Caleb Williams* and the Attack on Romance," *Studies in Romanticism* 15 (1976): 81–87.

8. Frederic Jameson, "Magical Narratives: Romance as Genre," *NLH* 7 (1975): 141, 142.

Chapter 4

1. Conrad's reading of Dickens's novels is cited by the author himself (*PR,* 71); by Jocelyn Baines in *Joseph Conrad: A Critical Biography* (New York: McGraw-Hill, 1960), pp. 19, 143; and by Morton Dauwen Zabel in his Introduction to *The Portable Conrad* (New York: Viking Press, 1947), where he remarks that Conrad was devoted early in his life to "the Dickens of *Bleak House*" (p. 7).

2. Robert Kiely, *Robert Louis Stevenson and the Fiction of Adventure* (Princeton, N.J.: Princeton Univ. Press, 1966), p. 20.

3. Georges Jean-Aubry, *Joseph Conrad: Life and Letters* (Garden City, N.Y.: Doubleday, Page, and Co., 1927), II, 147.

4. H. G. Wells, in *Saturday Review* (London) 81 (1896): 510.

5. See E. T. Schell, "*Youth* and *Hyckescorner:* Which Came First?" *PQ* 45 (1966): 468–74.

6. Morse Peckham, *Beyond the Tragic Vision* (New York: Braziller, 1962), pp. 17, 43–44.

7. J. Hillis Miller, *Poets of Reality* (Cambridge, Mass.: Harvard Univ. Press, 1965), pp. 53, 35. Conrad remarks, "I never could invent an effective lie—a lie that would sell, and last, and be admirable" (*Joseph Conrad's Letters to R. B. Cunninghame Graham*, ed. C. T. Watts [London: Cambridge Univ. Press, 1969], p. 85).

8. Morse Peckham, *Man's Rage for Chaos: Biology, Behavior, and the Arts* (Philadelphia: Chilton, 1965), p. 11.

9. Here (and elsewhere) my reading of this story differs in several significant ways from the excellent interpretation published by Joel R. Kehler, "'The Planter of Malata': Renouard's Sinking Star of Knowledge," *Conradiana* 7 (1976): 148–62.

10. Robert Graves, *The Greek Myths* (New York: Braziller, 1959), pp. 49–50.

11. C. G. Jung, *The Archetypes and the Collective Unconscious*, trans. R. F. C. Hull (New York: Bollingen Series XX, 1959), p. 327. For additional elucidation of this character type see Jerome J. McGann, "The Beauty of the Medusa: A Study in Romantic Literary Iconology," *Studies in Romanticism* 11 (1972): 3–25.

12. Francis Quarles, quoted in Gretchen L. Finney, "Music: A Book of Knowledge in Renaissance England," *Studies in the Renaissance* 6 (1959): 40. My application of the concept of an "emblem" to Conrad's works takes into account Elizabeth K. Hill's recent objection to "the widespread modern practice of using the term *emblem* to indicate both a rhetorical trope and a genre," and is meant to adhere to what Ms. Hill suggests is the traditional denotation of this concept, "a moral sign and not a poetic figure": "What Is an Emblem," *JAAC* 29 (1970): 261.

13. St. Augustine, *De Musica*, trans. R. C. Taliaferro (Annapolis, 1939), p. 148.

14. Gillian Beer, *The Romance* (London: Methuen, 1970), pp. 9–10.

15. John Stevens, *Medieval Romance* (New York, 1973), p. 24. A far more useful abstract framework with regard to Conradian romance is provided by Laurence A. Michel in the chapter entitled "Conrad: Romance and Tragedy" in his *The Thing Contained: Theory of the Tragic* (Bloomington: Indiana Univ. Press, 1970): "What makes the dialectic fruitful is that the pairings can, and do, shift: truth, we say, is autonomous and must therefore be good; man's moral integrity is destroyed by a lie. But when we approach truth or reality it turns out to be inhuman, appalling, transcendent or destructive to all lesser goods and hence, in ordinary humanistic terms, evil. Illusion is to be fought and condemned, because it informs those patently evil and unhuman activities which Conrad constantly castigates as folly, delusion, lugubrious drollery, imbecility, farce, insanity; it is the worst of evils, the consort of rapacity and pitilessness. Yet

without dreams, idealisms, and those peculiarly Conradian constructions Deliberate Belief and Surface Truth, there can be no beauty in human action . . ." (p. 93).

16. See the collection of James's prefaces, Henry James, *The Art of the Novel,* intro. R. P. Blackmur (New York: C. Scribner's Sons, 1937), p. 320.

17. Tzvetan Todorov, "The Origin of Genres," *NLH* 8 (1976): 160, 159.

18. Tzvetan Todorov, *The Fantastic: A Structural Approach to a Literary Genre* (Ithaca: Cornell Univ. Press, 1975), p. 41.

19. H. G. Wells, *Experiment in Autobiography* (New York: Macmillan, 1934), p. 530.

20. I find it useful to read these two tales as a sequence involving the same narrator (the mate in both stories is Mr. Burns), though this assumption is not indispensible to the subsequent interpretations.

21. Todorov, *Fantastic,* p. 37.

22. William Bysshe Stein, "The Eastern Matrix of Conrad's Art," *Conradiana* 1 (1968): 12.

23. Isabel MacCaffrey, *Spenser's Allegory: The Anatomy of Imagination* (Princeton, N.J.: Princeton Univ. Press, 1976), p. 279.

24. Northrop Frye, *Anatomy of Criticism* (Princeton, N.J.: Princeton Univ. Press, 1957), p. 163.

25. In his famous essay 'The 'Uncanny'" Freud observes, "A study of dreams, phantasies, and myths has taught us that a morbid anxiety connected with the eyes and with going blind is often enough a substitite for the dread of castration. In blinding himself, Oedipus, that mythical law-breaker, was simply carrying out a mitigated form of the punishment of castration" (in *On Creativity and the Unconscious,* trans. Joan Riviere [New York, 1958], p. 137).

26. The German text is taken from the libretto supplied with the London recording of Richard Wagner, *Das Rheingold* (OSA 1309), p. 19.

27. Ibid., pp. 7–8.

28. Ibid., p. 26.

29. Ibid., p. 10.

30. Frye, *Anatomy of Criticism,* pp. 186, 193, 187.

Chapter 5

1. *Theocritus,* ed. and trans. A. F. S. Gow (Cambridge, 1950), I, 65–67; cf. Virgil's *"locos laetos et amoena virecta"* (*Aeneid,* VI, 638).

2. David Evett, " 'Paradice's Only Map': The *Topos* of the *Locus Amoenus* and the Structure of Marvell's *Upon Appleton House,*" *PMLA* 85 (1970): 506.

3. E. R. Curtius, *European Literature and the Latin Middle Ages,* trans. Willard R. Trask (New York: Pantheon, 1953), p. 202.

4. See Peter Demetz, "The Elm and the Vine: Notes toward the History of a Marriage Topos," *PMLA* 73 (1958), 521–32.

5. Robert Graves, *The Greek Myths* (New York: Braziller, 1959), p. 280.

6. Harry Berger, Jr., "Spenser's Gardens of Adonis: Force and Form in the Renaissance Imagination," *UTQ* 30 (1960): 141.

7. Monolithic statements to the contrary, of course, are central to Thomas Moser's *Joseph Conrad: Achievement and Decline* (Cambridge, Mass.: Harvard Univ. Press, 1957) and Bernard C. Meyer's *Joseph Conrad: A Psychoanalytic Biography* (Princeton, N.J.: Princeton Univ. Press, 1967).

8. Addison C. Bross clarifies Conrad's impatience with puritanical extremism by noting the absurd reason for the name Erminia; it "refers ironically to the legend that the ermine may be caught by surrounding its lair with filth, for it will be captured or die rather than stain its coat" ("*A Set of Six:* Variations on a Theme," *Conradiana* 7 [1975]: 31). A likely source for the character of Erminia is Tasso's *Gerusalemme Liberata,* wherein a valiant lady of the same name miraculously comes upon the lacerated and unconscious Tancred, fallen in battle, and saves his

life (see XIX, 102–13). This sequence of events parallels the way in "Gaspar Ruiz" the fallen protagonist, physically mutilated and suffering from the "hallucination . . . of the volleys fired at him within fifteen paces, of his head being cut off at a blow," awakens to a lovely vision of Erminia: "Lying on his back, he stared up at her. Her face was pale and her eyes were very dark; her hair hung down black as ebony against her white cheeks; her lips were full and red" (SS, 21–22). As is frequently the case in Conrad's fiction, extremes of disorientation and physical harm result in a desperate susceptibility to eidetic love. In such a state a character typically exchanges one sort of coma for another as he awakens from a nearly lethal faint to an ultimately lethal woman. Like Gaspar Ruiz opening his eyes to Erminia, the bewildered and starving Yanko Goorall, his romance shattered of a kind "American Kaiser" and a land "where true gold could be picked up on the ground," perceives the stuttering, dim-witted Amy Foster "with the aureole of an angel of light" (T, 116, 124). Events like these are, of course, sepulchral variations of the redemption scenario of traditional romances. Early in the nineteenth century John Keats established the pattern for such variations, which it seems Conrad follows closely: in Lamia the swooning Lycius recovers only "from one trance . . . / Into another" (I, 296–97) as he falls prey to his serpentine lady.

9. Gerald H. Levin, "An Allusion to Tasso in Conrad's Chance," NCF 13 (1958): 149.

10. For excellent discussions of narrative perspective in Chance, see John Palmer, Joseph Conrad's Fiction (Ithaca, N.Y.: Cornell Univ. Press, 1968), pp. 198–220; Robert N. Hudspeth, "Conrad's Use of Time in Chance," NCF 21 (1966): 283–89; and Ian Watt, "Conrad, James, and Chance," in Imagined Worlds: Essays on Some English Novels and Novelists in Honour of John Butt, ed. Maynard Mack and Ian Gregor (London: Methuen, 1968), pp. 301–22. For simpler responses to narrative perspective in this novel, see Graham Hough, "Chance and Joseph Conrad," in Image and Experience: Reflections on a Literary Revolution (Lincoln, Nebr.: Bison Books, 1960), pp. 211–22; and Elsa Nettles, James and Conrad (Athens: Univ. of Georgia Press, 1977), pp. 75–76.

11. Palmer, Joseph Conrad's Fiction, pp. 211–12.

12. All quotations from Tasso's Gerusalemme Liberata are taken from the Capricorn Books reprint of the definitive Edward Fairfax translation of 1600, intro. John Charles Nelson (New York, 1963). References are to canto and stanza.

13. Quoted in Meyer Abrams, Natural Supernaturalism (New York: Norton, 1971), p. 467.

14. Browne means to qualify the potency of chance by invoking the Christian God, of course. Conrad, in marked contrast, entraps his characters in an inflexible psychological determinism that serves only to make them more vulnerable to cosmic accident. For further discussion of this issue see Bruce Harkness, "The Epigraph of Conrad's Chance," NCF 9 (1954): 209–22; and Wolfgang B. Fleischmann, "Conrad's Chance and Bergson's Laughter," Renascence 14 (1961): 66–71.

15. C. G. Jung, Psychology and Religion: West and East, trans. R. F. C. Hull (New York: Bollingen Series XX, 1958), pp. 556, 156.

16. Frederick Jackson Turner, The Frontier in American History (New York, 1950), p. 3.

17. Harold P. Simonson, The Closed Frontier: Studies in American Literary Tragedy (New York, 1970), p. 5.

18. Ibid., pp. 5–6.

19. See, e.g., Emile Male, The Gothic Image, trans. Dora Nussey (New York: Harper Torchbooks, 1958), p. 14.

20. See Eloise Knapp Hay, The Political Novels of Joseph Conrad (Chicago: Univ. of Chicago Press, 1963): "Conrad chose to name it Costaguana after the bird excrement used in explosives" (p. 171). Juliet McLauchlan in her fine monograph Conrad: Nostromo (London: Edward Arnold, 1969) claims Costaguana means "Palm Coast" and opposes Ms. Hay's suggestion: "Two Spanish dictionaries give 'palm' as the first meaning for guano, 'palm leaves' second, and 'bird dung' only third. There is textual evidence for Palm Coast: Costaguana's flag has two

green palm trees . . ." (pp. 10–11). Conrad, of course, is quite aware of the conflicting meanings of *guano*, and of the tendency for *loci amoeni* to assert their excrementitious essences: just as pastoral palms denote dung, so Jim's pursuit of an insular dream threatens to one point to lead him to "a guano island" (*LJ*, 161).

Chapter 6

1. Ian Watt, *The Rise of the Novel* (London: Chatto and Windus, 1957), p. 12.

2. A useful compilation of quotations like these can be found in Ioan Williams, ed., *Novel and Romance 1700–1800: A Documentary Record* (New York: Barnes and Noble, 1970).

3. J. Hillis Miller, *The Disappearance of God* (Cambridge, Mass.: Harvard Univ. Press, 1963), pp. 11–12.

4. Alastair Fowler, "The Life and Death of Literary Forms," *NLH* 2 (1971): 211–13. Also helpful is Evelyn J. Hinz's theoretical article, "Hierogamy versus Wedlock: Types of Marriage Plots and Their Relationship to Genres of Prose Fiction," *PMLA* 91 (1976): 900–913.

5. Edward Garnett, *Letters from Joseph Conrad, 1895–1924* (Indianapolis: Bobbs-Merrill, 1928), p. 80.

6. Ibid., p. 230.

7. Ibid., pp. 110, 120.

8. Harold Bloom, "The Internalization of Quest Romance," reprinted in *The Ringers in the Tower* (Chicago: Univ. of Chicago Press, 1971), p. 16.

9. Garnett, *Letters*, p. 94.

10. Cf. Heinrich Zimmer, *Myths and Symbols in Indian Art and Civilization* (Princeton, N.J.: Princeton Univ. Press, 1946), p. 181, and J. Hillis Miller's excellent discussion of time in *Poets of Reality* (Cambridge, Mass.: Harvard Univ. Press, 1965), pp. 52–53.

11. Cf. Miller, *Poets of Reality:* "The imperfection of the Professor's detonator is a symptom of his inability to reconcile time and eternity" (p. 53).

12. See Edmund Spenser, *The Shepheards Calender*, "July," 19–20.

13. Richard Hinckley Allen remarks in *Star Names: Their Lore and Meaning* (New York: Dover Books, 1963): "The constellation's stormy character appeared in early Hindu, and perhaps even in earlier Euphratean days, and is seen everywhere among classical writers with allusions to his direful influence. Vergil termed it *aquosus, nimbosus,* and *saevus;* Horace, *tristis* and *nautis infestus;* Pliny, *horridus sideribus;* and the Latin sailors had a favorite saying, *Fallit saepissime nautas Orion*" (p. 306).

14. For a fine analysis of symmetry and asymmetry see Martin Gardner, *The Ambidextrous Universe: Left, Right, and the Fall of Parity* (New York: Mentor Books, 1969).

15. The first chapter of *Chance* originally was conceived as part of a tale that Conrad tentatively entitled "Explosives" (see Jocelyn Baines, *Joseph Conrad: A Critical Biography* [New York: McGraw-Hill, 1960], p. 382). The *Ferndale*'s cargo of dynamite, of course, figures forth the psychology of many of the persons on board.

16. Ravi Ravindra, "Time in Christian and Indian Traditions," *Dalhousie Review* 51 (1971): 8–9.

17. See Lynn White, Jr., "Christian Myth and Christian History," *JHI* 3 (1942): 147–58.

18. In *Chance* Franklin, the mate aboard the *Ferndale*, tells a similarly sentimental tale to Young Powell. Moreover, characters in *The Rescue* and "The Franklin's Tale" share a concern both with keeping one's word and with maintaining a good name, as they struggle with triangular love affairs. See also Joel R. Kehler, "A Note on the Epigraph to Conrad's *The Rescue*," *ELN* 12 (1975): 184–87.

19. Edmund Husserl, *The Phenomenology of Internal Time-Consciousness* (Bloomington: Indiana Univ. Press, 1964), p. 63.

20. David Hume, *A Treatise of Human Nature*, ed. L. A. Selby-Bigge (Oxford, 1888), p. 252.

21. Jessie Conrad, *Joseph Conrad As I Knew Him* (London, 1926), p. 144.

22. Georges Jean-Aubry, *Joseph Conrad: Life and Letters* (Garden City, N.Y.: Doubleday, Page, and Co., 1927), I, 227.

23. Paul L. Wiley, *Conrad's Measure of Man* (Madison: Univ. of Wisconsin Press, 1954), p. 174. In order to determine more rigorously what constitutes a romance as well as whether or not *The Rescue*, termed a "romance" by the author himself, is indeed the "most representative" of Conrad's novels, future analyses might apply the criteria developed by Karl Kroeber in *Styles in Fictional Structure* (Princeton, 1971)—see especially the "Novel and Romance" chapter and the appendix of statistical "tabulations"—and by Barron Brainerd in "An Exploratory Study of Pronouns and Articles as Indices of Genre in English," *Language and Style* 5 (1972): 239–59, and "On the Distinction between a Novel and a Romance: A Discriminant Analysis," *Computer and Humanities* 7 (1973): 259–70.

Chapter 7

1. J. Hillis Miller, "The Fiction of Realism: *Sketches by Boz, Oliver Twist,* and Cruikshank's Illustrations," in *Dickens Centennial Essays,* ed. Ada Nisbet and Blake Nevius (Berkeley: Univ. of California Press, 1971), p. 85.

2. See, e.g., Morse Peckham, *Man's Rage for Chaos: Biology, Behavior, and the Arts* (Philadelphia: Chilton, 1965), *Art and Pornography* (New York: Basic Books, 1969), and *The Triumph of Romanticism: Collected Essays by Morse Peckham* (Columbia: Univ. of South Carolina Press, 1970); Morton W. Bloomfield, ed., *The Interpretation of Narrative,* Harvard English Studies, I (Cambridge, Mass.: Harvard Univ. Press, 1970); J. Hillis Miller, ed., *Aspects of Narrative: Selected Papers from the English Institute* (New York: Columbia Univ. Press, 1971); and Frank Kermode, *The Sense of an Ending: Studies in the Theory of Fiction* (Oxford: Oxford Univ. Press, 1966).

3. Mark Schorer, "Notes on the Creative Act and Its Function," in *The World We Imagine: Selected Essays by Mark Schorer* (New York, 1968), p. 395.

4. Schorer, "Technique as Discovery," ibid., p. 10.

5. Walker Gibson, "Authors, Speakers, Readers, and Mock Readers," *College English* 11 (1950): 265–69.

6. Kermode, *Sense of an Ending,* p. 24.

7. Ibid., p. 19.

8. Peckham, *Man's Rage for Chaos,* p. xi.

9. Wayne Booth, *The Rhetoric of Fiction* (Chicago: Univ. of Chicago Press, 1961), p. 153; see also Joseph E. Baker, "Aesthetic Surface in the Novel," *Trollopian* 2 (1947): 91–106; Norman Friedman, "Point of View: The Development of a Critical Concept," *PMLA* 70 (1955): 1160–84; Marvin Mudrick, "Character and Event in Fiction," *Yale Review* 50 (1961): 202–18; Dorritt Cohn, "Narrated Monologue: Definition of a Fictional Style," *Comparative Literature* 18 (1966): 97–112; Lubomir Dolezel, "The Typology of the Narrator: Point of View in Fiction," in *To Honor Roman Jakobson: Essays on the Occasion of His Seventieth Birthday* (The Hague: Mouton, 1967), I, 541–52; Peter L. Irvine, "The 'Witness' Point of View in Fiction," *South Atlantic Quarterly* 69 (1970): 217–25; Robert Weimann, "Point of View in Fiction," in *Preserve and Create: Essays in Marxist Literary Criticism,* ed. Gaylord C. LeRoy and Ursula Beitz (New York, 1973), pp. 54–75.

10. I will continue to use the term "omniscient" for the sake of convenience, although I am aware of the relevant objections to the term that have been raised by some critics of the novel. In *The Nature of Narrative* (New York: Oxford Univ. Press, 1966) Robert Kellogg and Robert Scholes differentiate between the concept of omniscience as it is applied to a deity and to a narrative voice in fiction: "God *knows* everything because He *is* everywhere—simultaneously. But a narrator . . . is imbedded in a time-bound artifact. He does not 'know' simultaneously but consecutively. He is not everywhere at once but now here, now there, now looking into this

mind or that. . . . He is time-bound and space-bound as God is not . . . we can separate the omniscient narrator in fiction into a multifarious element and a monistic element. The multiple perceptions of this kind of narrator coalesce into a single reality, a single truth" (pp. 272–73). Similarly, J. Hillis Miller in *The Form of Victorian Fiction* (Notre Dame, Ind.: Notre Dame Univ. Press, 1968) qualifies the omniscience of a narrative voice by noting that "immanent omniscience is both like and unlike the knowledge traditionally ascribed to God. It is an authentic perfection of knowledge. The omniscient narrator is able to remember perfectly all the past, to foresee the future course of events, and to penetrate with irresistible insight the most secret crevice in the heart of each man. He can know the person better than the person knows himself . . ." (p. 64). However, whereas "God's knowledge is of a world and of human souls which he himself has made . . . omniscient narrators of Victorian novels, on the other hand, have perfect knowledge of a world they have not made [and therefore] talk as if they were confronting directly or in historical retrospect a world independent of their knowledge of it, but a world over which they happen to have extraordinary powers" (p. 65). All these qualifications should be kept in mind when the word "omniscient" appears in this chapter, for I feel that they are applicable to the omniscient narrative voice as Conrad develops it in his novels using the third-person point of view.

11. J. Hillis Miller, *Charles Dickens: The World of his Novels* (Bloomington, Ind.: Midland Books, 1969), p. 178.

12. Georges Jean-Aubry, *Joseph Conrad: Life and Letters* (Garden City, N.Y.: Doubleday, Page, and Co., 1927), II, 338.

13. Ibid., p. 150.

14. John Palmer, *Joseph Conrad's Fiction* (Ithaca, N.Y.: Cornell Univ. Press, 1968), pp. 13, 3.

15. Ibid., pp. 6, 12.

16. Apart from reading these stories as integral units in a significantly ordered series, I fail to see how the presence of the frame of an anonymous persona can be aesthetically justified. Once Marlow's narrative situations in "Youth" and *Heart of Darkness* (and, by extension, *Lord Jim* and *Chance*) are compared, it becomes clear that there exists a negative progression that serves to qualify Marlow's ability to maintain a congenial relationship with his audience, to generate even an illusion of being understood, and to sustain his authority and dominance of the narrative. In "Youth" Marlow discusses with final credibility only his own experiences of his own isolated subjectivity as it learns a universal lesson about inevitable age and death while existing among other men who, along with the physical events of the voyage, amount to little more than objective phenomena to Marlow's youthful ego. Because of the broad nature of its theme, Marlow's tale is readily comprehensible to his substantial and friendly audience, and consequently Marlow need debate with no one; he need only confirm this positive situation by means of frequent rhetorical questions that at once join and pacify him and his auditors. In *Heart of Darkness* (and *Lord Jim*) Marlow's subject matter is quite remote from the experiences of the members of his audience, who sympathize very little with him as he struggles for words and attempts to compensate for his auditors' skepticism by repeatedly urging himself upon them through persistent allusions to a fictive second-person character, a passive and cooperative "you" whose reactions to the tale are orchestrated exlusively by the teller (see Bruce Morrissette, "Narrative 'You' in Contemporary Literature," *Contemporary Literature Studies* 2 [1965]: 1–24). In *Heart of Darkness* (and *Chance*) the nameless narrator grows ever more dominant until he rivals Marlow in narrative duration and intellectual impact; indeed, he even serves effectively to challenge and qualify Marlow in *Chance*, an elusive work in which the anonymous and abrasive persona is all that remains of Marlow's former sociable body of attentive listeners. For further discussion of this issue, see the following fine but neglected essays: William York Tindall, "Apology for Marlow," in *From Jane Austen to Joseph Conrad*, ed. Robert C. Rathburn and Martin Steinmann, Jr. (Minneapolis: Univ. of Minnesota Press, 1958), pp. 274–85; Juliet McLauchlan, "Conrad's 'Three Ages of Man': The 'Youth' Volume," in *Joseph Conrad: Commemorative Essays*, ed. Adam Gillion and Ludwik Krzyzanowski (New York: Astra, 1975), pp.

188–201. Also useful are: Francis Wentworth Cutler, "Why Marlow?" *Sewanee Review* 26 (1918): 29–38; John Oliver Perry, "Action, Vision, or Voice: The Moral Dilemma in Conrad's Tale Telling," *MFS* 10 (1964): 3–15.

17. Seymour Gross, "A Further Note on the Function of the Frame in 'Heart of Darkness,'" *MFS* 3 (1957): 170.

18. Ibid.

19. Although most discussions of the function of point of view in *Lord Jim* center around the character of Marlow, any adequate reading of the novel must weigh heavily the information made available in the opening four chapters, which give the reader, from the third-person omniscient point of view, all the evidence needed to define the character of Jim apart from any of Marlow's enigmatic meditations. Suspecting that Jim is a profound reflection of himself, Marlow develops a defensive strategy of trying to redeem Jim's character in order to evade the frightening implications consequent upon such a recognition. He seeks to achieve an impossibility, to exorcise the "ghost of doubt" (*LJ*, 51) that haunts him after he realizes that his "youth—in its day—had resembled [Jim's] youth" (*LJ*, 51). Indeed, Marlow admits, for instance, that his idea of Jim's submission to the inquiry being a redemptive act is entirely due to an angry reaction to Brierly's adopting a tone toward Marlow that implies Marlow "was no more . . . than an insect" (*LJ*, 68) as Brierly asks Marlow to arrange Jim's escape: "On account of that provocation . . . I became positive in my mind that the inquiry was a severe punishment to that Jim, and that his facing it . . . was a redeeming feature. . . . I hadn't been so sure of it before" (*LJ*, 68–69). The only objectively valid glimpses we get of Jim's character occur in chapters one through four, and they indicate conclusively that, in spite of Marlow's self-protective doubts, Jim is indeed "nothing more rare than brass" (*LJ*, 46). For an excellent discussion of the significance of the details presented about Jim from the third-person omniscient narrative perspective, see Tony Tanner's *Conrad: 'Lord Jim'* (London: Edward Arnold, 1963), pp. 16–23. An interpretation of the function of the omniscient narrator in *Lord Jim* that differs from mine has recently been offered by J. Hillis Miller, who maintains in his essay "The Interpretation of *Lord Jim*" (in Bloomfield, ed., *Interpretation of Narrative*, pp. 211–28) that the third-person narrative voice provides no solution to the novel since "no point of view is entirely trustworthy" (p. 220). Although I agree with Miller's analysis of Marlow's biased story-telling, no textual evidence is presented to support his assertion that the omniscient narrator fails to be "entirely trustworthy"; rather, this aspect of *Lord Jim* is dismissed by means of a subjunctive clause that I feel is not warranted by the text. Although Miller affirms that the third-person narrative voice "has . . . superhuman powers of insight, including direct access to Jim's mind . . .," he feels that the narrative voice "relinquishes that access early in the story . . . as though it could not provide a satisfactory avenue to the truth behind Jim's life" (p. 221).

20. J. Hillis Miller, *Poets of Reality* (Cambridge, Mass.: Harvard Univ. Press, 1965), pp. 18–19.

21. Miller, *Form of Victorian Fiction*, p. 30.

22. Peckham, "Order and Disorder in Fiction," in *Triumph of Romanticism*, pp. 300–301.

23. John Feaster, "Currents in Conrad Criticism: A Symposium," *Conradiana* 4, no. 3 (1971): 5.

24. Miller, *Aspects of Narrative*, p. vii.

25. Feaster, "Currents in Conrad Criticism," p. 5.

26. Bruce Johnson, "Currents in Conrad Criticism: A Symposium," *Conradiana*, 4, no. 3 (1971): 11.

27. J. Hillis Miller, *Thomas Hardy: Distance and Desire* (Oxford: Oxford Univ. Press, 1970), p. vii.

28. See, e.g., Albert Guerard, *Conrad the Novelist* (Cambridge, Mass.: Harvard Univ. Press, 1958), pp. 107, 203–10; Vernon Young, "Trial by Water: Joseph Conrad's *The Nigger of the 'Narcissus,'*" in *The Art of Joseph Conrad: A Critical Symposium*, ed. R. W. Stallman (East Lansing: Michigan State Univ. Press, 1960), p. 119.

29. Miller, *Aspects of Narrative*, p. vii.

30. Peckham, "Discontinuity in Fiction: Persona, Narrator, Scribe," in *Triumph of Romanticism*, p. 327.

31. Peckham, "Order and Disorder in Fiction," p. 311.

32. Peckham, *Art and Pornography*, pp. 105–6.

33. See Guerard, *Conrad the Novelist*, p. 112.

34. Peckham, "Order and Disorder in Fiction," p. 314.

35. Wolfgang Iser, "Indeterminacy and the Reader's Response," in *Aspects of Narrative*, ed. Miller, pp. 10–11.

36. Peckham, "Order and Disorder in Fiction," p. 313.

37. Marion Michael, "Currents in Conrad Criticism: A Symposium," *Conradiana* 5, no. 3 (1971): 14.

38. Peckham, "Discontinuity in Fiction," p. 321.

39. Young, "Trial by Water," p. 119.

40. Guerard, *Conrad the Novelist*, p. 107.

41. Ibid.

42. Martin Price, "Irrelevant Detail and the Emergence of Form," in *Aspects of Narrative*, ed. Miller, p. 89.

43. Miller, *Poets of Reality*, pp. 18–19.

44. Jean-Aubry, *Life and Letters*, I, 222.

45. Iser, "Indeterminacy and the Reader's Response," p. 23. See also Michel Foucault, *The Order of Things* (New York: Vintage, 1973): "At the beginning of the nineteenth century . . . literature becomes progressively more differentiated from the discourse of ideas, and encloses itself within a radical intransitivity; it becomes detached from all the values that were able to keep it in general circulation during the Classical age . . . , and creates within its own space everything that will ensure a ludic denial of them" (p. 300).

46. John Palmer, Introduction to *Twentieth Century Interpretations of "The Nigger of the 'Narcissus'"* (Englewood Cliffs, N.J.: Spectrum Books, 1969), pp. 10–11.

47. John Feaster, "Conrad and Ford: Criticism at the End of the Tether," *Journal of Modern Literature* 2 (1972): 417–21.

48. Miller, "Fiction of Realism," p. 86.

49. See J. L. Austin, *How to Do Things with Words*, ed. J. O. Urmson (Cambridge, Mass.: Harvard Univ. Press, 1962), p. 1.

50. See Harry Berger, Jr., "Archaism, Vision, and Revision: Studies in Virgil, Plato, and Milton," *Centennial Review* 11 (1967): 24–52.

51. Leo Spitzer, "Linguistic Perspectivism in the *Don Quijote*," in *Linguistics and Literary History* (Princeton, N.J.: Princeton Univ. Press, 1948), p. 73.

52. David Lodge, "Conrad's *Victory* and *The Tempest*': An Amplification," *MLR* 59 (1964): 198.

53. Lena's inadequacy is emphasized by the narrative voice when it informs the reader that Lena is incapable of understanding or coping with the situation into which Heyst has led her: "She had no general conception of the conditions of the existence he had offered to her. Drawn into its peculiar stagnation she remained unrelated to it because of her ignorance" (*V*, 247–48).

54. Conrad lavished attention on even the peripheral aspects of his novels. His title pages "always taxed his scruples as severely as any part of his manuscripts . . . and the epigraphs he placed below them . . . were always chosen with extreme care, Conrad taking pains as his wife insists that these 'quotations had always a close and direct relation to the contents of the book itself' and they should express 'the mood in which the work was written'" (Jessie Conrad, quoted in Morton D. Zabel, "Chance and Recognition," in *Modern British Fiction*, ed. Mark Schorer [New York: Oxford Univ. Press, 1969], p. 65). Milton's *Comus* is a work presented according to

the conventions of Christian allegory. Critics commonly conclude, because of this epigraph, that *Victory* is a modern extension of such conventions. Thus, John Palmer in *Joseph Conrad's Fiction* suggests the epigraph is Conrad's way of announcing that the novel is "a secular allegory" with "a consistent overtone of Christian allegory" (pp. 174, 188). Such interpretations naively fail to take into account both the intellectual context of the early twentieth century and Conrad's own radical skepticism. See also, e.g., R. W. Stallman, "The Structure and Symbolism of Conrad's *Victory*," *Western Review* 13 (1949): "*Victory* . . . ends as it began, upon an act of faith and redemption" (p. 149) and "Lena [is] the embodiment of faith" (p. 152); Seymour L. Gross, "The Devil in Samburan: Jones and Ricardo in *Victory*," *NCF* 16 (1961): "On the allegorical level there is a triumphant assertion of life's values . . . a hope of heaven" (p. 84). Sharon Kaehle and Howard German perceptively analyze the characters in *Victory* as nonallegorical dramatizations, in "Conrad's *Victory*: A Reassessment," *MFS* 10 (1964): 55–71. Douglas B. Park also opposes allegorical readings in "Conrad's *Victory*: The Anatomy of a Pose," *NCF* 31 (1976): 150–69.

55. See Eugene Hollahan, "Beguiled into Action: Silence and Sound in *Victory*," *TSLL* 16 (1974): "The word *silence* occurs ninety times, with the related forms *silent, silently* . . . bringing the total to one hundred and seventeen. In addition, the words *sound* and *sounds* occur thirty-six times" (p. 349).

56. Translated by Edward W. Said, and quoted in his *Beginnings* (New York: Basic Books, 1975), p. 231.

57. Jean-Aubry, *Life and Letters*, I, 222.

58. Angus Fletcher, *The Transcendental Masque: An Essay on Milton's "Comus"* (Ithaca, N.Y.: Cornell Univ. Press, 1971), p. 166.

59. See J. A. Mazzeo, "St. Augustine's Rhetoric of Silence: Truth vs. Eloquence and Things vs. Signs," in *Renaissance and Seventeenth-Century Studies* (New York: Columbia Univ. Press, 1964), pp. 1–28.

60. D. W. Robertson, Jr., *A Preface to Chaucer: Studies in Medieval Perspectives* (Princeton, N.Y.: Princeton Univ. Press, 1962), pp. 126–27.

61. For a thorough summary of the specific events, see Fletcher, *Transcendental Masque*, pp. 53–55. For auditory iconography in *Comus*, see John Demaray, *Milton and the Masque Tradition: The Early Poems, "Arcades," and Comus* (Cambridge, Mass.: Harvard Univ. Press, 1958), p. 132. Cf. Conrad's cogent remark, "The power of sound has always been greater than the power of sense" (*PR*, xi).

62. Stanley Fish, *Surprised by Sin: The Reader in "Paradise Lost"* (Berkeley: Univ. of California Press, 1967), p. 220n.

63. *The Shorter Oxford English Dictionary*, I, 113.

64. Fletcher, *Transcendental Masque*, p. 166.

65. Donald A. Dike, "The Tempest of Axel Heyst," *NCF* 18 (1962): 101.

66. Guerard, *Conrad the Novelist*, pp. 273–74, 259.

67. Palmer, *Joseph Conrad's Fiction*, p. 183.

68. Thomas Moser, *Joseph Conrad: Achievement and Decline* (Cambridge, Mass.: Harvard Univ. Press, 1957), p. 108.

69. See F. R. Leavis, *The Great Tradition* (New York, 1948), p. 209.

70. Leo Gurko, *Joseph Conrad: Giant in Exile* (New York: Macmillan, 1962), pp. 214–15.

71. J. Hillis Miller in *Poets of Reality* analyzes in terms of *The Secret Agent* Conrad's use of obese characters to "remind us of the scandal of our incarnation" (p. 50).

72. James Joyce, of course, uses the same device of an official report in "A Painful Case," a story that is concerned with problems similar to those dramatized in *Victory*.

73. Royal Roussel, *The Metaphysics of Darkness* (Baltimore: The Johns Hopkins Univ. Press, 1977), pp. 188–89.

Chapter 8

1. Morse Peckham, "The Infinitude of Pluralism," *Critical Inquiry* 3 (1977): 805, 804, 805, 812.

2. James Guetti, *The Limits of Metaphor: A Study of Melville, Conrad, and Faulkner* (Ithaca, N.Y.: Cornell Univ. Press, 1967), p. 1.

3. F. R. Leavis, *The Great Tradition* (London: Chatto and Windus, 1950), p. 180. In *The Sacred Wood* (London: Methuen, 1920), T. S. Eliot offers a contrasting and even more debatable judgment. While castigating Swinburne for writing poetry in which "the object has ceased to exist, because the meaning is merely the hallucination of meaning," Eliot apparently laments a violation of the potential in language for pure representation; and he goes on, amusingly, to praise Conrad's writing for satisfying the need for concrete referentiality by providing "new objects [and] new groups of objects . . ." (pp. 149–50).

4. Peckham, "Infinitude of Pluralism," p. 810.

5. Ibid., p. 812.

6. Ibid., p. 810. Cynthia Chase cogently observes that "the deconstructive operation, while it consists in pointing out that the concept of causality amounts to an aberrant and arbitrary ordering of rhetorical elements, is itself no more than an equally aberrant reordering of these elements, the performance of another tropological operation. It is for this specific reason that a deconstruction is not a refutation, or that a deconstructive 'refutation' can claim for itself no more authority than the refuted concept" ("The Decomposition of the Elephants: Double-Reading *Daniel Deronda*," *PMLA* 93 [1978]: 220).

7. Kathleen Raine, *Blake and Tradition* (Princeton, N.J.: Princeton Univ. Press, 1968), I, 82. This book contains a fine detailed discussion of the concept. Cf. also *Paradise Lost*, VIII, 619: "the clear hyaline, the glassy sea."

8. Edward Garnett, *Letters from Joseph Conrad, 1895–1924* (Indianapolis: Bobbs-Merrill, 1928), p. 144. Cf. Conrad's remark that "Marconi's electric waves could [not] be made evident without the sending-out and receiving instruments [and] without mankind my art . . . could not exist" (*Conrad to a Friend: 150 Selected Letters from Joseph Conrad to Richard Curle*, ed. Richard Curle [London, 1928], p. 191).

9. Gerald Morgan, "Narcissus Afloat," *Humanities Association of Canada Bulletin* 15 (1964): 54.

10. Edward W. Said, "Conrad: The Presentation of Narrative," *Novel* 7 (1974): 122.

11. Georges Poulet, *The Metamorphoses of the Circle* (Baltimore: The Johns Hopkins Univ. Press, 1966), p. xxvii.

12. *Letters of Joseph Conrad to Marguerite Poradowska, 1890–1920*, ed. John A. Gee and Paul J. Sturm (New Haven: Yale Univ. Press, 1940), p. 52.

13. Volume and page references are to *The Works of Sir Thomas Browne*, ed. Geoffrey Keynes, 4 vols. (Chicago: Univ. of Chicago Press, 1964). For further discussion of Browne's use of tropes see Margaret A. Heideman, "*Hydriotaphia* and *The Garden of Cyrus*: A Paradox and a Cosmic Vision," *UTQ* 19 (1950): 235–46, and Lawrence A. Breiner, "The Generation of Metaphor in Thomas Browne," *MLQ* 38 (1977): 261–75.

14. Conrad's use of this particular circular shape when he wishes to denote "*le neant*" (*NLL*, 94) is repeated in *Lord Jim* when Marlow stumbles upon the grave of Jewel's mother (see *LJ*, 322).

15. Claude Levi-Strauss, *The Savage Mind* (Chicago: Univ. of Chicago Press, 1966), p. 252.

16. Jerry Wasserman, "Narrative Presence: The Illusion of Language in *Heart of Darkness*," *Studies in the Novel* 6 (1974): 337. See also Sanford Pinsker, *The Languages of Joseph Conrad*, *Costerus* 7 (1978); Jeremy Hawthorn, *Joseph Conrad: Language and Fictional Self-Consciousness* (London, 1979).

17. F. H. Bradley, *The Principles of Logic* (Oxford: Oxford Univ. Press, 1922), p. 145.

18. J. Hillis Miller, "Ariachne's Broken Woof," *Georgia Review* 31 (1977): 44.

19. Paul de Man, "Action and Identity in Nietzsche," *Yale French Studies* 52 (1975): 20.

20. Roland Barthes, "Action Sequences," in *Patterns of Literary Style*, ed. Joseph Strelka (University Park: Pennsylvania State Univ. Press, 1971), p. 14.

21. Guetti, *Limits of Metaphor*, pp. 11, 127.

22. Ibid., p. 8.

23. J. Hillis Miller, "Tradition and Difference," *Diacritics* 2 (1972): 12.

24. St. Augustine, *City of God*, XI, 2.

25. Stanley Fish, "Inaction and Silence: The Reader in *Paradise Regained*," in *Calm of Mind: Tercentenary Essays on "Paradise Regained" and "Samson Agonistes*," ed. Joseph Anthony Wittreich, Jr. (Cleveland: Case Western Reserve Univ. Press, 1971), p. 27.

26. See Ananda K. Coomaraswamy, "Traditional Symbolism: The Sundoor and Related Motifs," in *Coomaraswamy*, ed. Roger Lipsey (Princeton, N.J.: Princeton Univ. Press, 1977), I, 415–544. Conrad mercilessly parodies this teleology in *The Rescue*, for example, when the obtuse Lingard, obsessed with his redemptive mission, perceives in the setting sun a straight road to a heavenly door: "The falling sun . . . shot out on the polished dark surface of the sea a track of light, straight and shining, resplendent and direct; a path of gold and crimson and purple, a path that seemed to lead dazzling and terrible from the earth straight into heaven through the portals of a glorious death" (*Res*, 14).

27. *The Familiar Letters of John Milton*, ed. D. L. Clark, trans. David Masson, vol XII of *The Works of John Milton* (New York: Columbia Univ. press, 1931–38), p. 33.

28. Georges Jean-Aubry, *Joseph Conrad: Life and Letters* (Garden City, N.Y.: Doubleday, Page, and Co., 1927), I, 217.

29. Charles Sanders Peirce, *Values in a Universe of Chance* (Stanford, Calif.: Stanford Univ. Press, 1958), p. 71.

30. Georges Bataille, *Death and Sensuality: A Study of Eroticism and the Taboo* (New York: Walker, 1962), p. 276.

31. Robert Scholes, *Structuralism in Literature* (New Haven: Yale Univ. Press, 1974), p. 19.

32. Frederick R. Karl in *A Reader's Guide to Joseph Conrad* (New York: Noonday Press, 1960) judges it a "minor" story that "need engage us but a moment" (p. 297), and Lawrence Graver in *Conrad's Short Fiction* (Berkeley: Univ. of California Press, 1969) concludes after a brief plot summary that Conrad, "through narrative sophistication and insistent symbolism . . . , makes claims for greater suggestiveness" than the story accomplishes (p. 198). See also Walter F. Wright, *Romance and Tragedy in Joseph Conrad* (Lincoln, Nebr., 1949), pp. 95–96; Osborn Andreas, *Joseph Conrad: A Study in Non-Conformity* (New York, 1959), p. 174. Only Porter Williams, Jr., in "Story and Frame in Conrad's 'The Tale,'" *SSF* 5 (1967–68): 179–85, approaches the work with any rigor.

33. Said, "Conrad: The Presentation of Narrative," p. 126.

34. Edward W. Said, *Joseph Conrad and the Fiction of Autobiography* (Cambridge, Mass.: Harvard Univ. Press, 1966), pp. 94–95.

35. J. Hillis Miller, Foreword to *Aspects of Narrative* (New York: Columbia Univ. Press, 1971), p. vii.

36. Paul de Man, "Nietzsche's Theory of Rhetoric," *Symposium* (Spring 1974), p. 40.

37. Jean-Aubry, *Life and Letters*, I, 208.

38. Jacques Lacan, quoted in Frederic Jameson, *The Prison-House of Language* (Princeton, N.J.: Princeton Univ. Press, 1972), p. 172.

39. Said, *Fiction of Autobiography*, p. 138.

40. Said, "Conrad: The Presentation of Narrative," p. 120.

41. This phrase is clearly differentiated from a similar phrase, appearing in *Lord Jim*, that indeed denotes the consumption of an alcoholic beverage: the French Lieutenant sits "drowsily over a tumbler half full of some dark liquid" (*LJ*, 138).

42. Richard J. Scalafani, "'Art,' Wittgenstein, and Open-Textured Concepts," *JAAC* 29 (1971): 336.

43. Alf Sommerfelt, "The Interrelationships between Language and Culture," *TSLL* 1 (1960): 451.

44. For a fine discussion of this problem see Paul S. Bruss, "Marlow's Interview with Stein: The Implications of the Metaphor," *Studies in the Novel* 5 (1973): 491–503.

45. Joyce Carol Oates handles the problem perceptively, albeit tangentially, in "'The Immense Indifference of Things': The Tragedy of Conrad's *Nostromo*," *Novel* 9 (1975): 5–22.

46. Jean-Aubry, *Life and Letters*, I, 216; italics mine.

47. Ibid., p. 222.

48. Sigmund Freud, *The Standard Edition of the Complete Psychological Works*, ed. James Strachey (London: Hogarth Press, 1961), XIV, 73.

49. "Style and Its Image," in *Literary Style: A Symposium*, ed. Seymour Chatman (Oxford: Oxford Univ. Press, 1971), p. 15.

50. Said, *Fiction of Autobiography*, p. 138.

51. Jean-Aubry, *Life and Letters*, I, 280.

52. Morton Dauwen Zabel, *Craft and Character* (New York: Viking, 1957), p. 182.

Index

Acrasia, 92, 137
Aissa, meaning of, 92
Alberich, 85–87
Allistoun, meaning of, 219
Anthony, Captain, 14, 96–107 passim
Aphrodite, 62
Arcturus, 63. *See also* Stars, in Conrad
Ariosto, 53
Aristotle, 7, 201, 207, 213
Armida, gardens of, 96–107 passim
Ashoka, 21
Aufheben, Hegelian concept of, 175
Augustine, 65, 90

Babalatchi, 12, 22
Barthes, Roland, 202–3, 218
Beer, Gillian, 66–67
Benjamin, Walter, 178–79
Berger, Harry, 175
Bernstein, Basil, 37
Bloom, Harold, 126
Booth, Wayne, 152
Bradbrook, M. C., 31
Bradley, F. H., 202
Brahman, 9–10
Brashers, H. C., 8
Browne, Sir Thomas, 105, 200–201
Buddha, tableaux in *Heart of Darkness*, 8–11
Buddhism, 20–21, 24, 28
Burney, Fanny, 125

Calypso, cave of, 89
Cannibalism: in Conrad, 19–21, 127–29; in Schopenhauer and Oriental philosophy, 20
Cerberus, 47
Chaucer, "The Franklin's Tale," 138–39, 142
Circles: in Conrad, 28–29, 37, 49–50, 90, 132–33, 181, 199–201, 214–15; in prior romance tradition, 132
Clifford, Hugh, 11
Coleridge, Samuel Taylor, 11, 126, 196
Comedy, 84–85
Conrad, Joseph, works of: *Almayer's Folly*, 56, 89–96, 129; "Anarchist, An," 63–67; *Arrow of Gold, The*, 16, 96; "Black Mate, The," 5; *Chance*, 26, 96–107, 200, 205; *End of the Tether, The*, 155–57; *Falk*, 19–21, 127; "Freya of the Seven Isles," 77–88, 96, 102; "Gaspar Ruiz," 96; *Heart of Darkness*, 8, 36, 59, 142, 147, 154–55, 201–2; "Informer, The," 96, 126–27; "Karain," 9, 22–24; "Lagoon, The," 26–27; *Last Essays*, 34; *Lord Jim*, 27–30, 96, 108, 129, 145–46, 201, 221, 237 n. 19; *Mirror of the Sea, The*, 6, 33–34, 67–68, 200, 215–17, 221; *Nigger of the "Narcissus," The*, 6, 34–35, 38, 102, 162–75, 204–6, 215–22; *Nostromo*, 66, 102, 109–24, 128–31, 157–60, 198–99, 220; *Notes on Life and Letters*, 18, 21, 34, 36, 141, 216; *Outcast of the Islands, An*, 12, 14, 56, 90–96; *Personal Record, A*, 5–6; "Planter of Malata, The," 59–63, 96, 102; *Rescue, The*, 56, 102, 108, 125–48; "Return, The," 17; *Romance*, 56, 107–9; *Secret Agent, The*, 18, 127; *Shadow-Line, The*, 19,

36–37, 66–67, 69–71, 102; "Smile of Fortune, A," 71–77, 96; "Tale, The," 208–15; *Typhoon*, 31–50; *Under Western Eyes*, 17–18; *Victory*, 18, 147–48, 175–94; "Youth," 24–26, 57–58, 154
Crashaw, Richard, 7
Curtius, E. R., 89

Davidson, 50, 187–88, 192–94
de Man, Paul, 208
de Martino, Richard, 15
de Rougemont, Denis, 22
de Saussure, Ferdinand, 207
Descartes, 125
Dickens, Charles, 56, 152, 160
Discontinuity: in Conrad's metaphors, 25–26, 69–70, 82–83, 168, 195–97, 206–7, 210, 220–22; in Conrad's physical universe, 5–6, 197–99; in Conrad's point of view devices, 151, 162, 170–74, 188, 190, 235–36 n. 10, 236–37 n. 16, 237 n. 19; in Conrad's stated opinions, 4–6, 227 n. 12

Echidna, 47
Edith, meaning of, 147
Eliot, George, 125
Embrace, in Conrad, 94–96, 102
Erminia, meaning of, 232–33 n. 8
Evans, Robert O., 8–9
Explosions, in Conrad, 126–30, 132–33, 138, 206–7

Fish, Stanley, 180–81, 203
Forster, E. M., 6, 50
Fowler, Alastair, 126
Frankenstein, 13
Freia, 85–86
Frontier, in Conrad. *See* Light, in Conrad
Frye, Northrop, 54, 84, 87–88

Garden: in Conrad, 69–70, 73–76, 78, 82–83, 88, 96–107, 111, 124, 145; in prior romance tradition, 89
Genette, Gerard, 32–33, 44
Gibson, Walker, 152
Guerard, Albert, 171, 188
Guetti, James, 203

Heyst, Axel, 18, 57, 176–94 passim
Hydra, 47

Interlude of Youth, The, 57
Inverse, multiplicative, 196
Inversions, in Conrad, 4–5, 7, 196–99
Iser, Wolfgang, 170, 175
Islam, in Conrad, 21

Jacobus, meaning of, 72
Jakobson, Roman, 37
James, Henry, 68
Jameson, Frederic, 55
Jewels, in Conrad, 108–9, 115–16, 132, 230 n. 62
Johnson, Bruce, 11
Joyce, James, 125
Jukes, 33, 39–40, 50
Jung, C. G., 11, 35, 40–41, 45, 49, 109